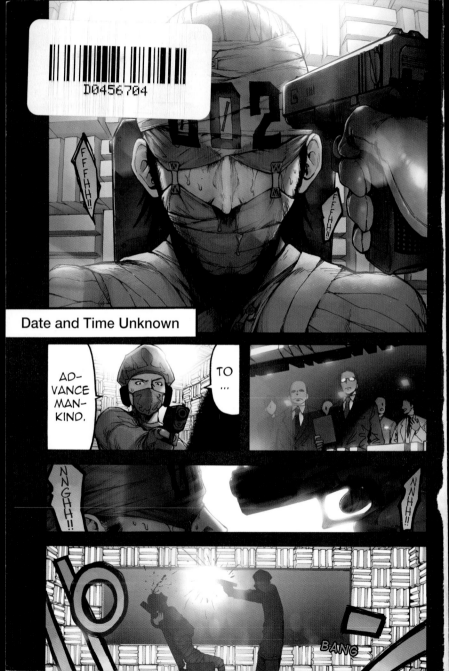

Date and Time Unknown

AD-VANCE MAN-KIND.

TO ...

FFFHH!!

FFFHH!!

NNGHH!!

NNHHH!!

BANG

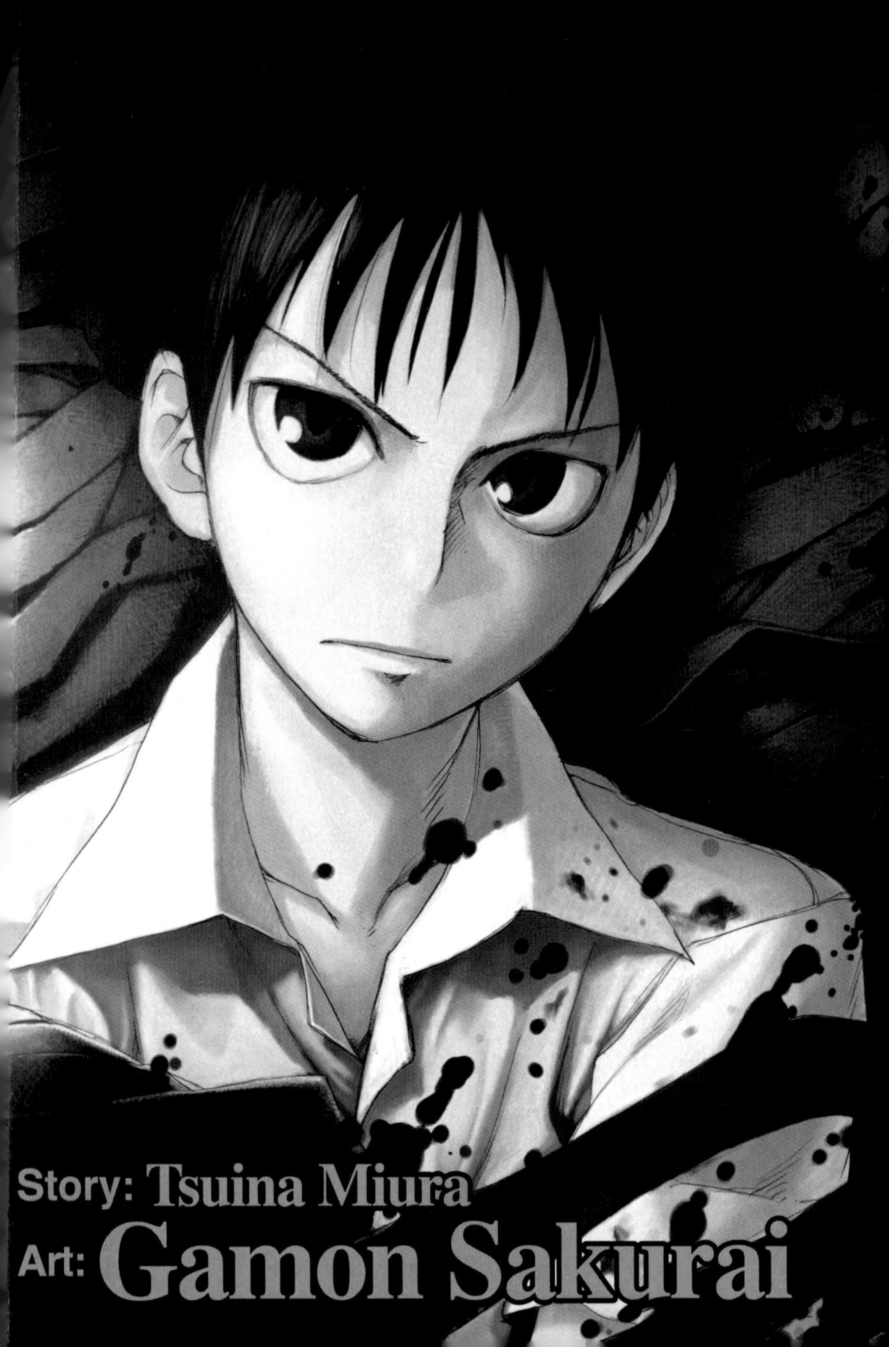

Story: Tsuina Miura
Art: Gamon Sakurai

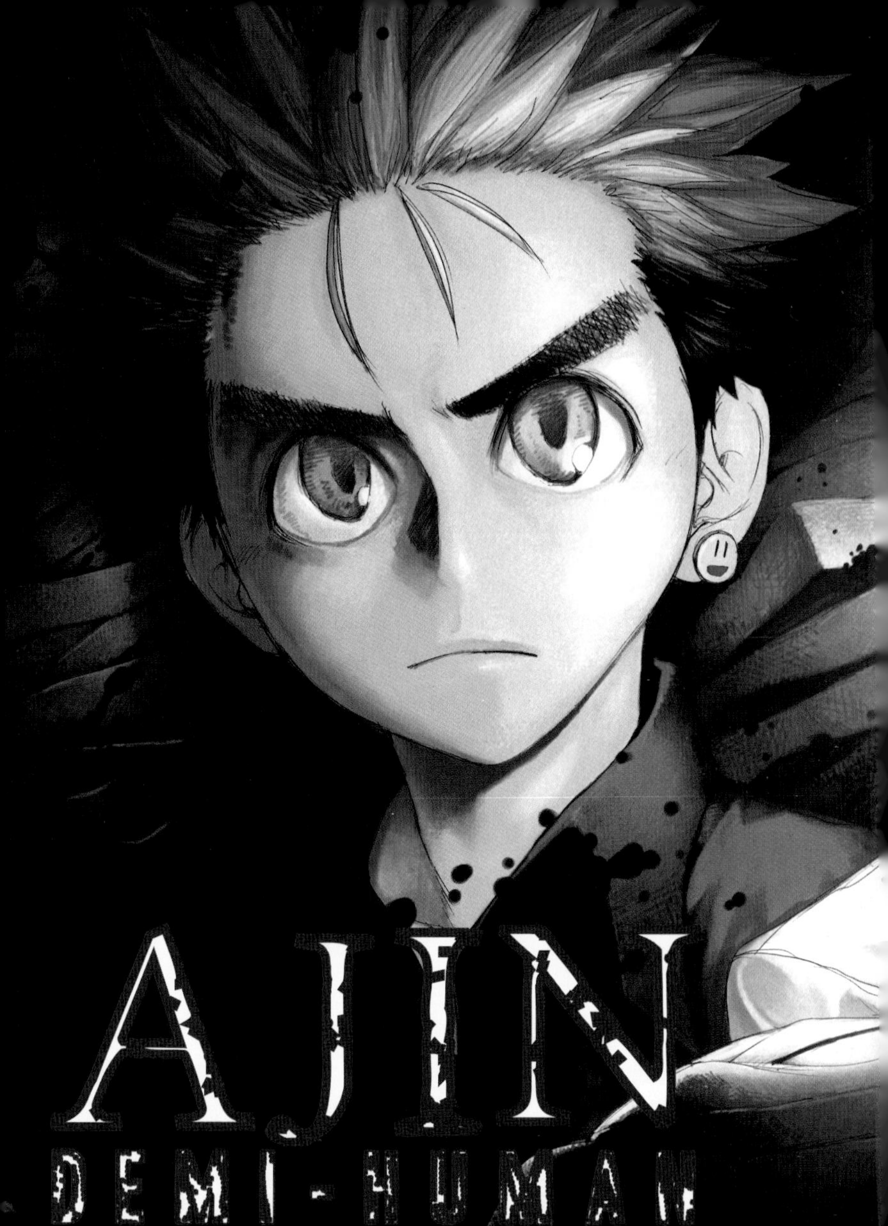
AJIN
DEMI-HUMAN

File 01: Detection and Subsequent Actions

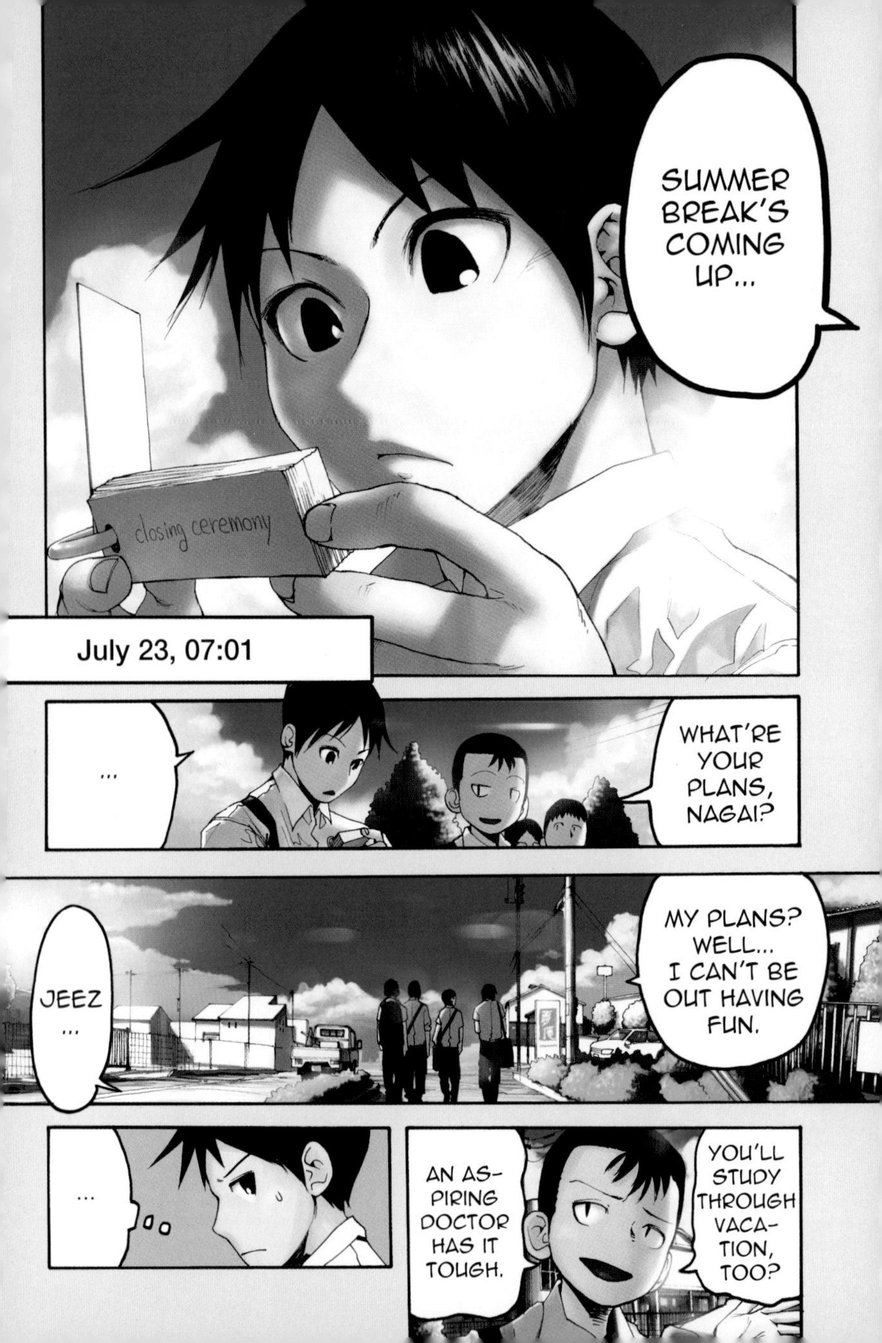
SUMMER BREAK'S COMING UP...
closing ceremony
July 23, 07:01
WHAT'RE YOUR PLANS, NAGAI?
...
MY PLANS? WELL... I CAN'T BE OUT HAVING FUN.
JEEZ ...
YOU'LL STUDY THROUGH VACA-TION, TOO?
AN AS-PIRING DOCTOR HAS IT TOUGH.
...

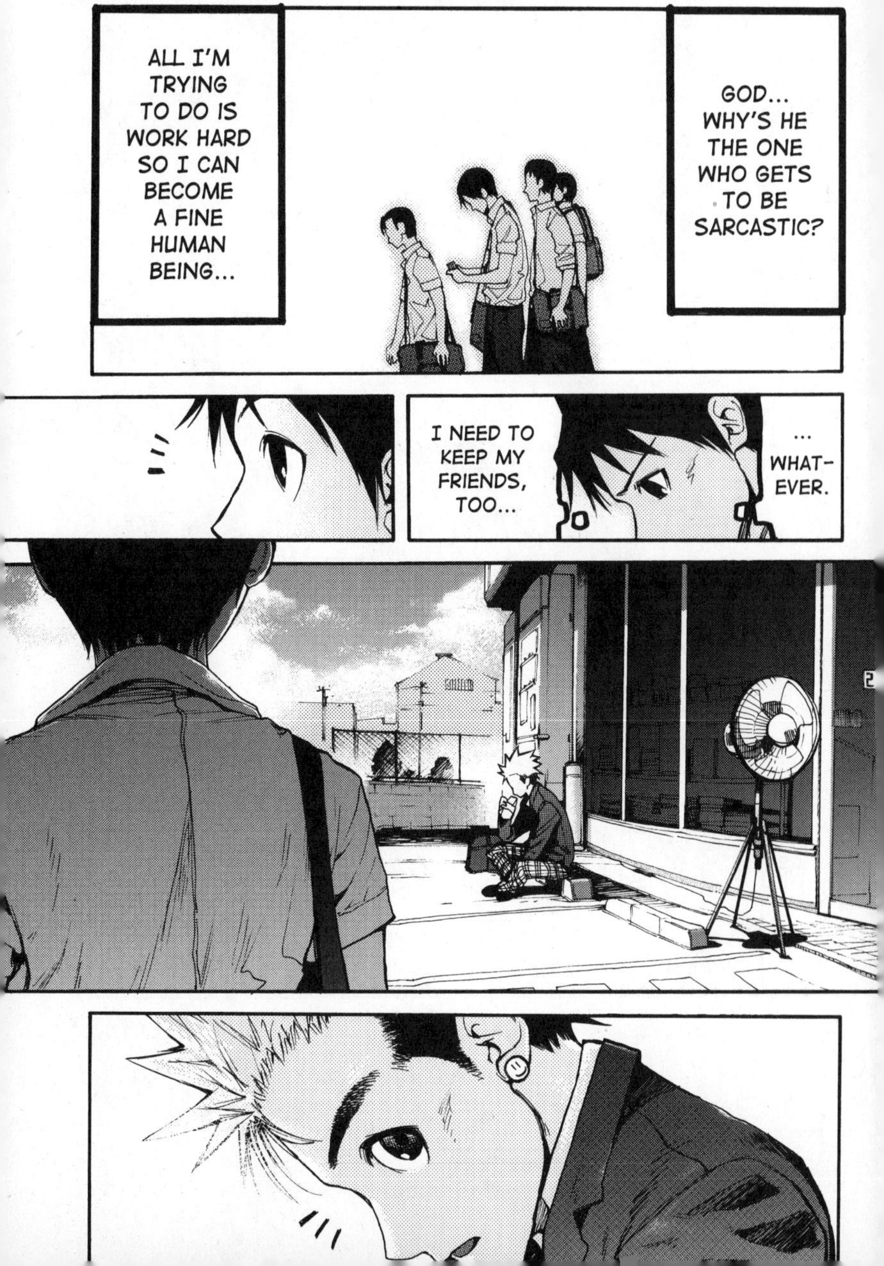
GOD... WHY'S HE THE ONE WHO GETS TO BE SARCASTIC?
ALL I'M TRYING TO DO IS WORK HARD SO I CAN BECOME A FINE HUMAN BEING...
... WHAT-EVER.
I NEED TO KEEP MY FRIENDS, TOO...

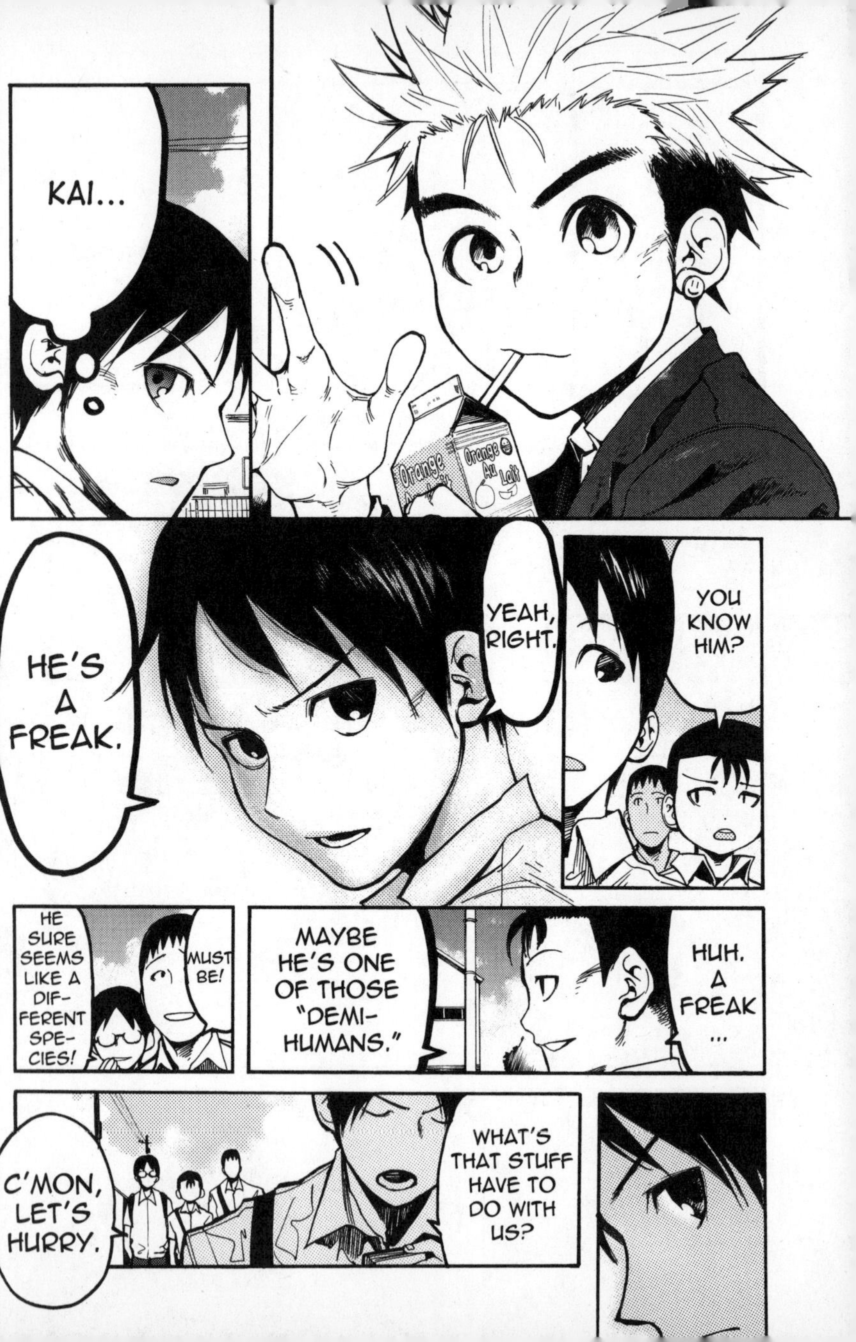
Orange Au Lait
KAI...
YOU KNOW HIM?
YEAH, RIGHT.
HE'S A FREAK.
HUH. A FREAK ...
MAYBE HE'S ONE OF THOSE "DEMI-HUMANS."
MUST BE!
HE SURE SEEMS LIKE A DIFFERENT SPECIES!
WHAT'S THAT STUFF HAVE TO DO WITH US?
C'MON, LET'S HURRY.

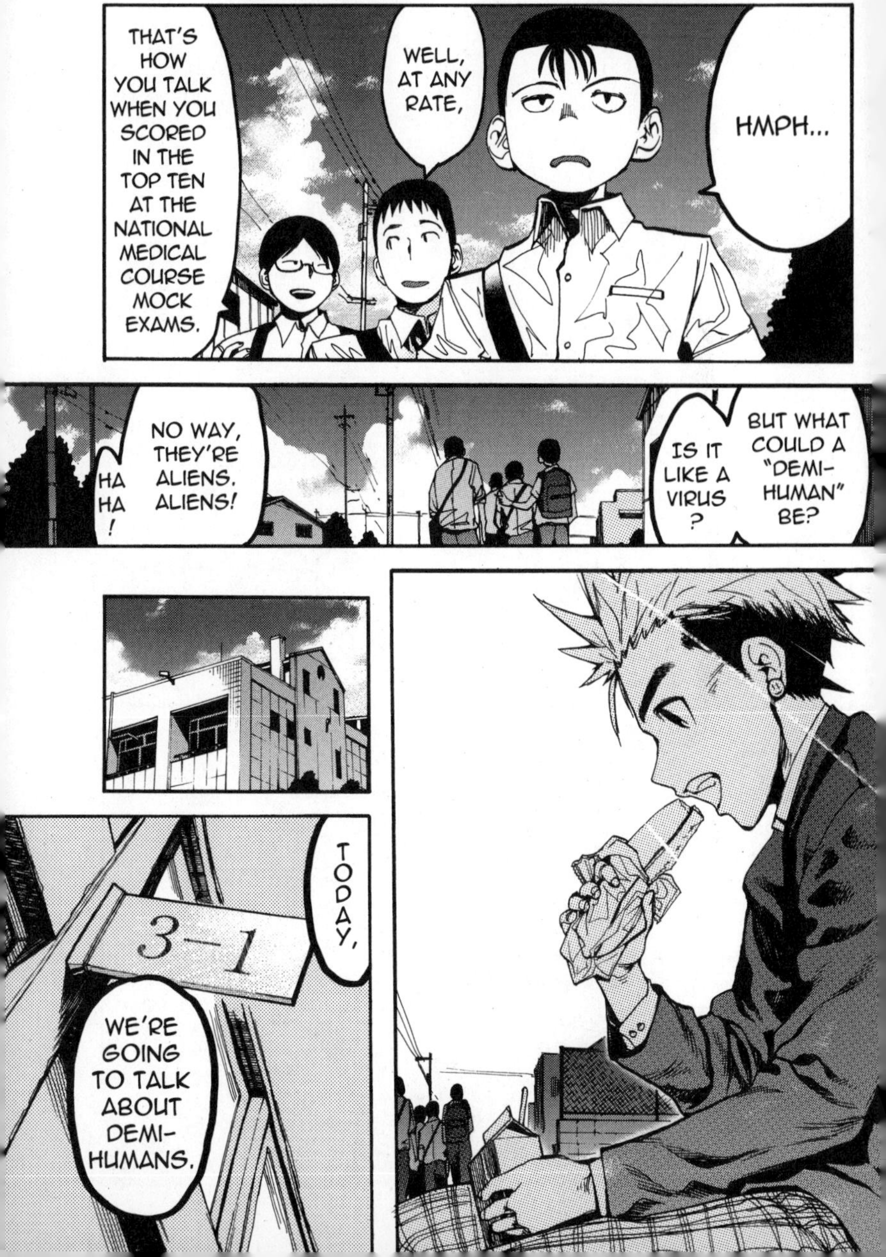
HMPH...
WELL, AT ANY RATE,
THAT'S HOW YOU TALK WHEN YOU SCORED IN THE TOP TEN AT THE NATIONAL MEDICAL COURSE MOCK EXAMS.
BUT WHAT COULD A "DEMI-HUMAN" BE?
IS IT LIKE A VIRUS?
NO WAY, THEY'RE ALIENS. ALIENS!
HA HA!
TODAY,
WE'RE GOING TO TALK ABOUT DEMI-HUMANS.

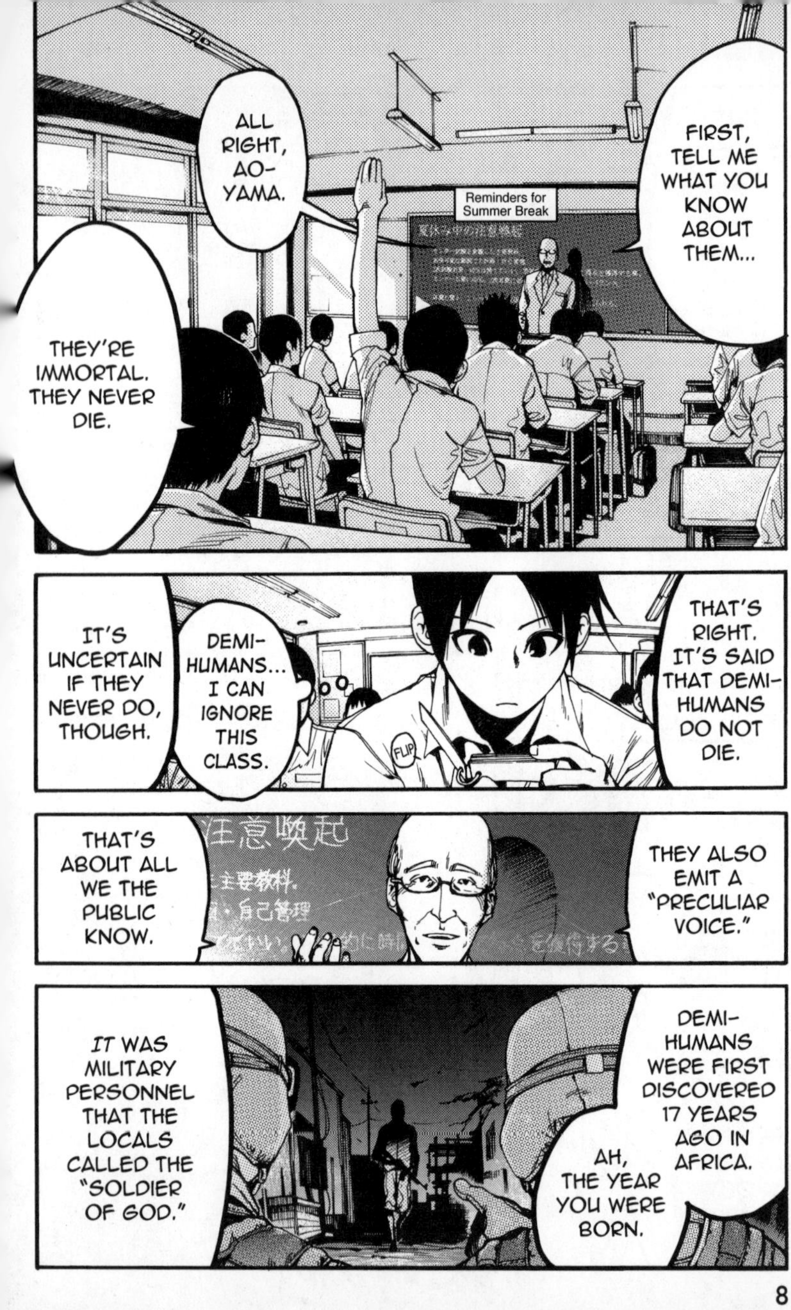
FIRST, TELL ME WHAT YOU KNOW ABOUT THEM...
ALL RIGHT, AO-YAMA.
Reminders for Summer Break
THEY'RE IMMORTAL. THEY NEVER DIE.
THAT'S RIGHT. IT'S SAID THAT DEMI-HUMANS DO NOT DIE.
FLIP
DEMI-HUMANS... I CAN IGNORE THIS CLASS.
IT'S UNCERTAIN IF THEY NEVER DO, THOUGH.
THEY ALSO EMIT A "PRECULIAR VOICE."
THAT'S ABOUT ALL WE THE PUBLIC KNOW.
DEMI-HUMANS WERE FIRST DISCOVERED 17 YEARS AGO IN AFRICA.
AH, THE YEAR YOU WERE BORN.
IT WAS MILITARY PERSONNEL THAT THE LOCALS CALLED THE "SOLDIER OF GOD."

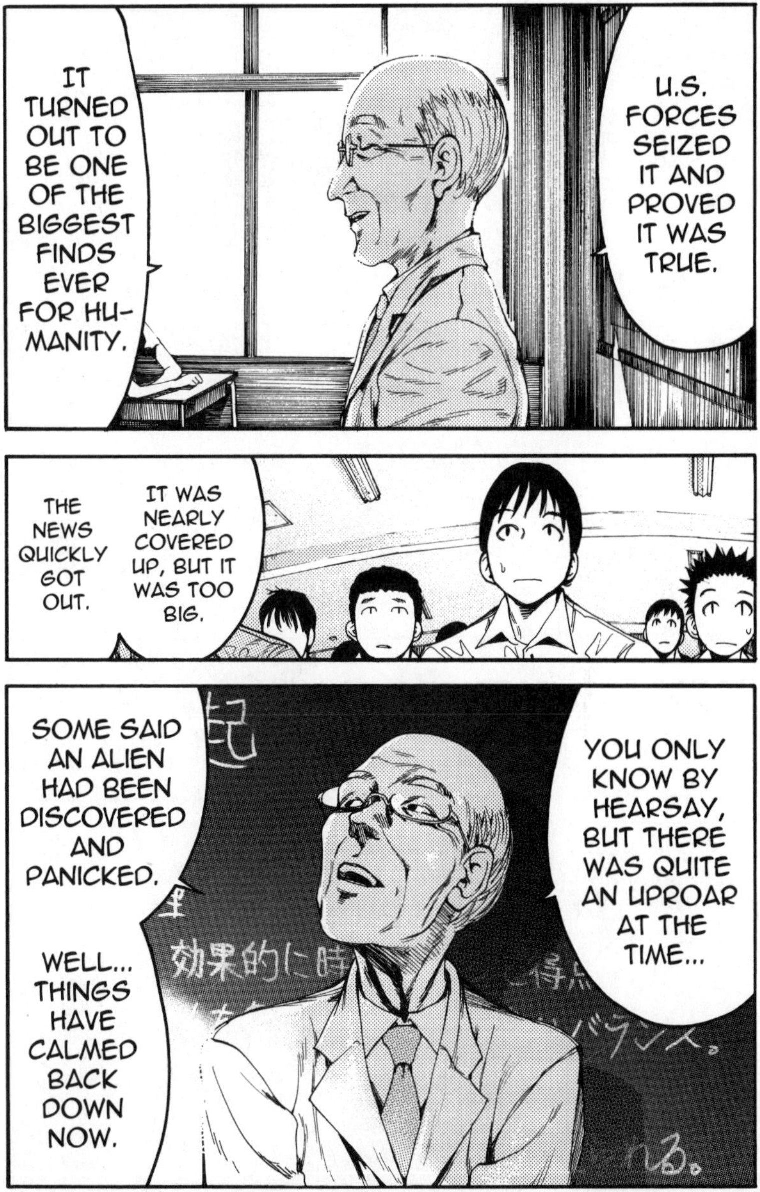
U.S. FORCES SEIZED IT AND PROVED IT WAS TRUE.
IT TURNED OUT TO BE ONE OF THE BIGGEST FINDS EVER FOR HU-MANITY.
IT WAS NEARLY COVERED UP, BUT IT WAS TOO BIG.
THE NEWS QUICKLY GOT OUT.
YOU ONLY KNOW BY HEARSAY, BUT THERE WAS QUITE AN UPROAR AT THE TIME...
SOME SAID AN ALIEN HAD BEEN DISCOVERED AND PANICKED.
WELL... THINGS HAVE CALMED BACK DOWN NOW.

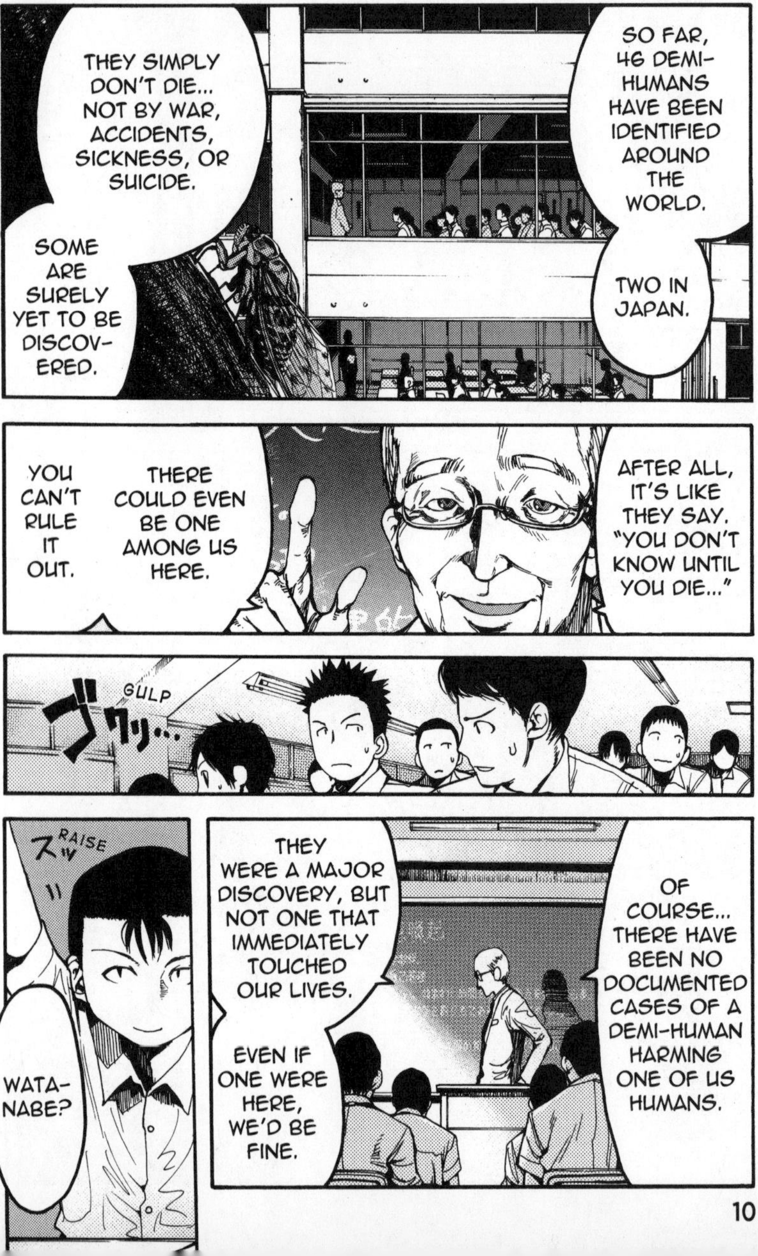
SO FAR, 46 DEMI-HUMANS HAVE BEEN IDENTIFIED AROUND THE WORLD.
TWO IN JAPAN.
THEY SIMPLY DON'T DIE... NOT BY WAR, ACCIDENTS, SICKNESS, OR SUICIDE.
SOME ARE SURELY YET TO BE DISCOV-ERED.
AFTER ALL, IT'S LIKE THEY SAY. "YOU DON'T KNOW UNTIL YOU DIE..."
THERE COULD EVEN BE ONE AMONG US HERE.
YOU CAN'T RULE IT OUT.
ゴクリ…
GULP
OF COURSE... THERE HAVE BEEN NO DOCUMENTED CASES OF A DEMI-HUMAN HARMING ONE OF US HUMANS.
THEY WERE A MAJOR DISCOVERY, BUT NOT ONE THAT IMMEDIATELY TOUCHED OUR LIVES.
EVEN IF ONE WERE HERE, WE'D BE FINE.
スッ
RAISE
WATA-NABE?

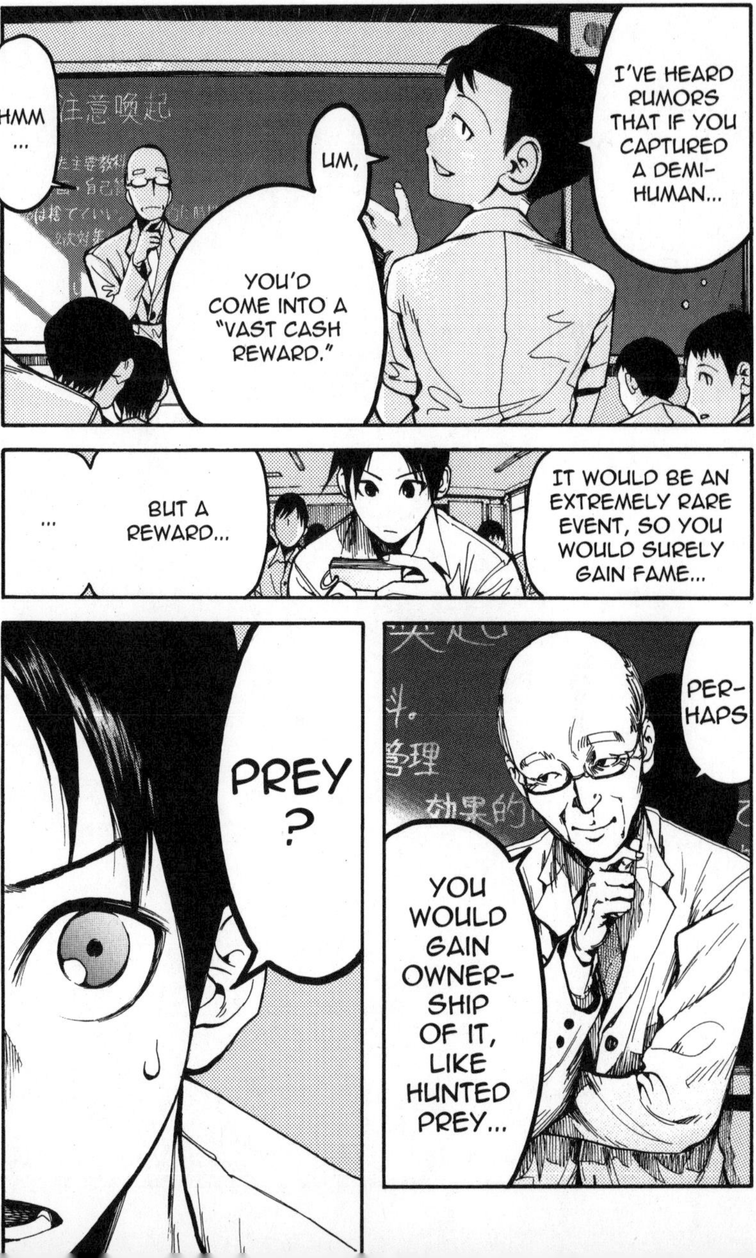
I'VE HEARD RUMORS THAT IF YOU CAPTURED A DEMI-HUMAN...
UM,
YOU'D COME INTO A "VAST CASH REWARD."
HMM ...
IT WOULD BE AN EXTREMELY RARE EVENT, SO YOU WOULD SURELY GAIN FAME...
BUT A REWARD...
...
PERHAPS
YOU WOULD GAIN OWNERSHIP OF IT, LIKE HUNTED PREY...
PREY ?

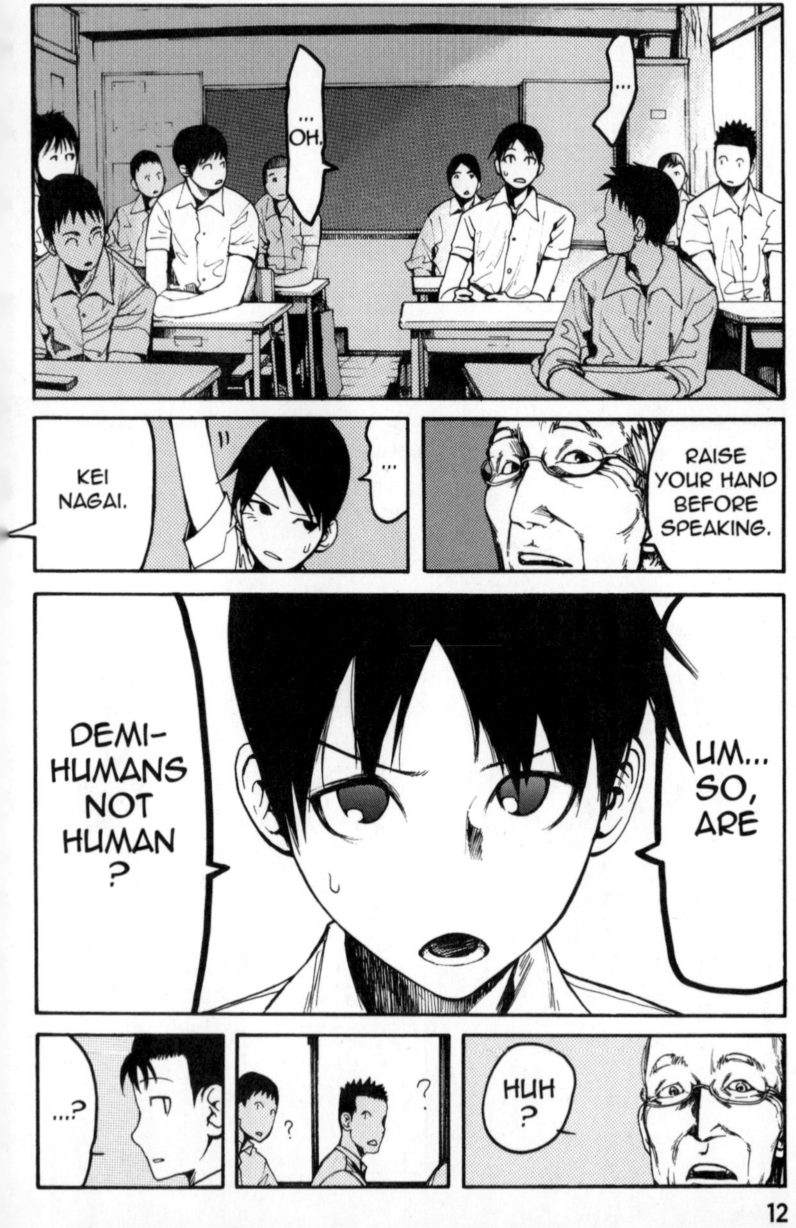
...
... OH.
RAISE YOUR HAND BEFORE SPEAKING.
...
KEI NAGAI.
UM... SO, ARE
DEMI-HUMANS NOT HUMAN?
HUH?
?
?
...?

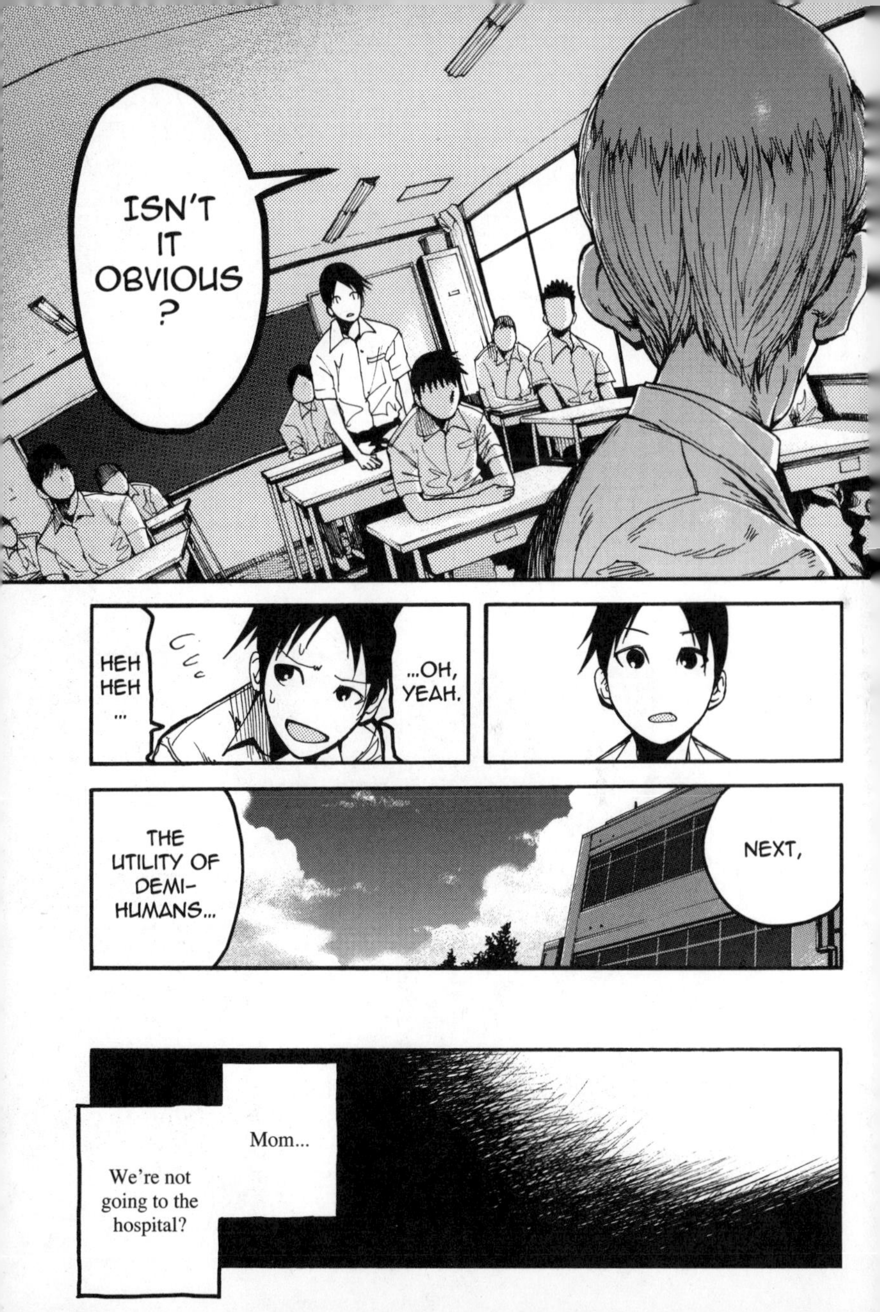
ISN'T IT OBVIOUS?
...OH, YEAH.
HEH HEH ...
NEXT,
THE UTILITY OF DEMI-HUMANS...
Mom...
We're not going to the hospital?

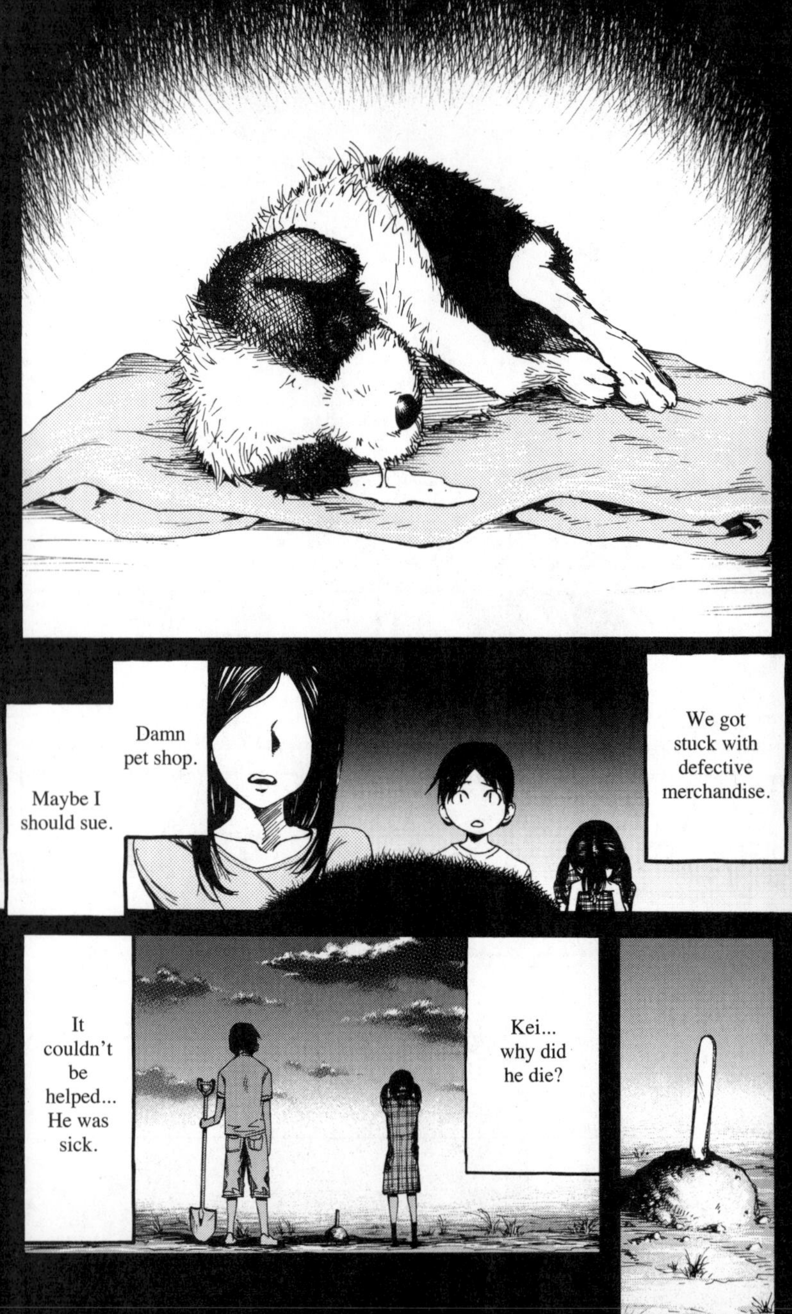
We got stuck with defective merchandise.
Damn pet shop.
Maybe I should sue.
Kei... why did he die?
It couldn't be helped... He was sick.

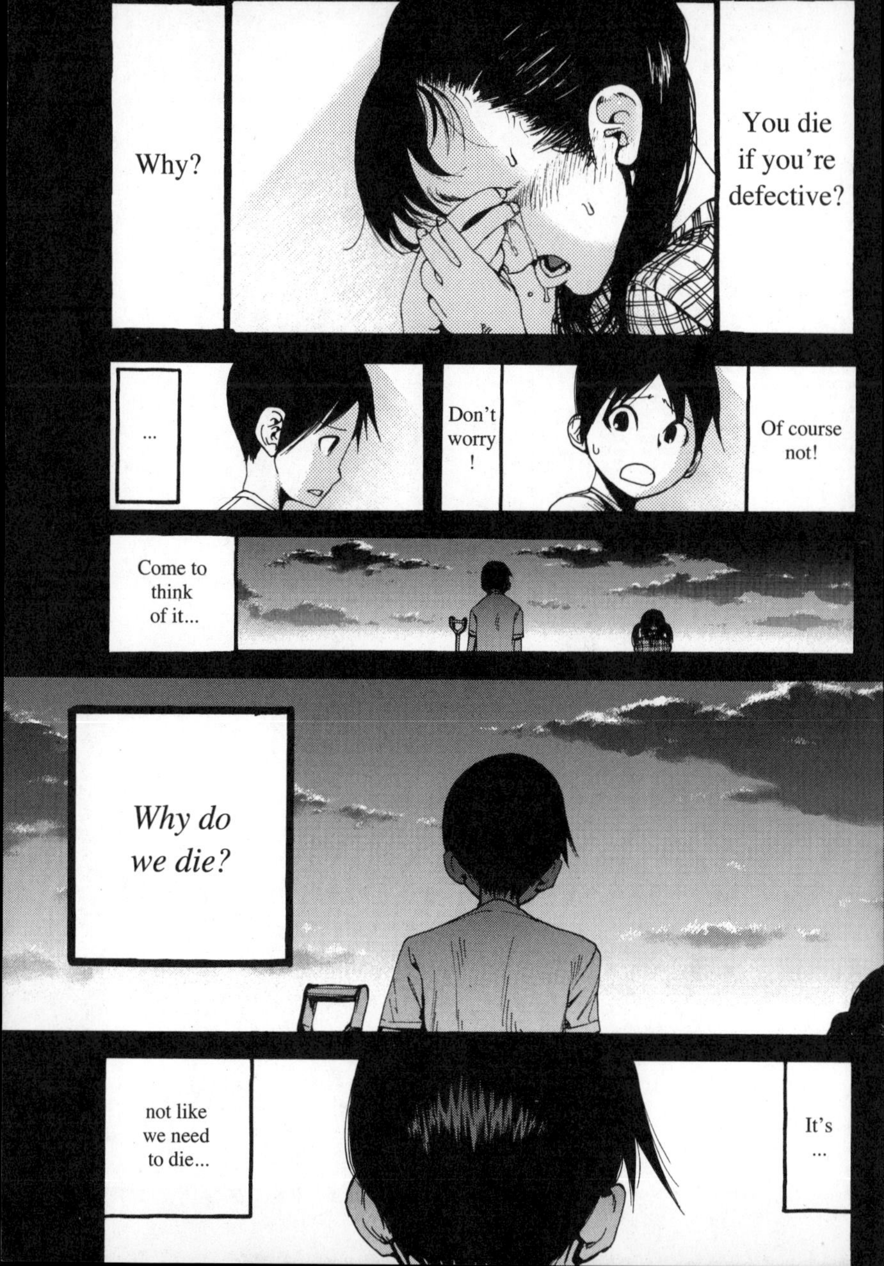
You die if you're defective?
Why?
Of course not!
Don't worry!
...
Come to think of it...
Why do we die?
It's ...
not like we need to die...

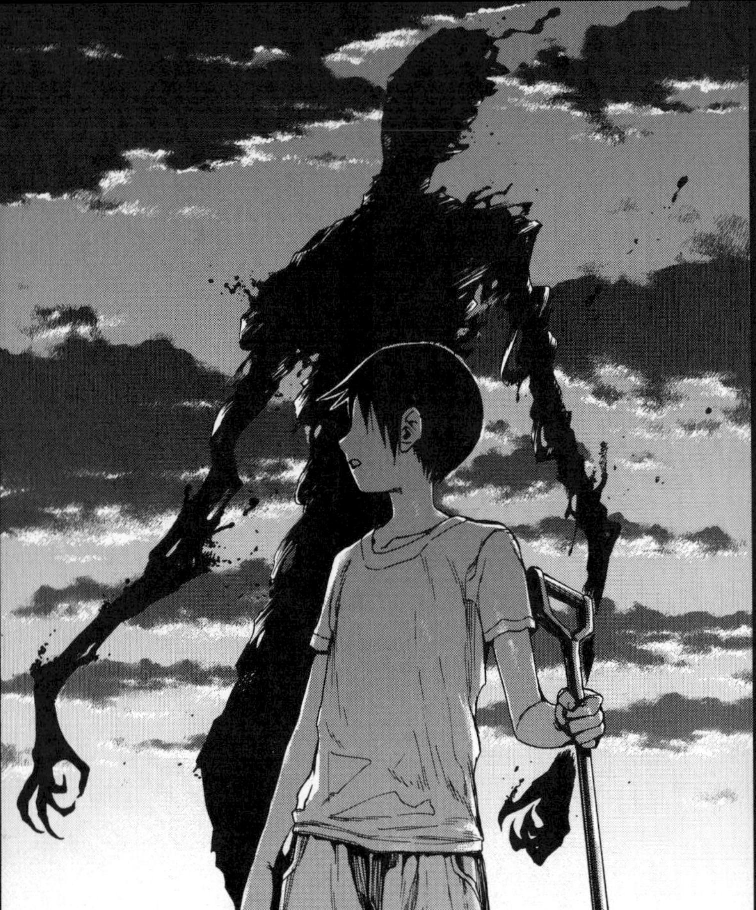

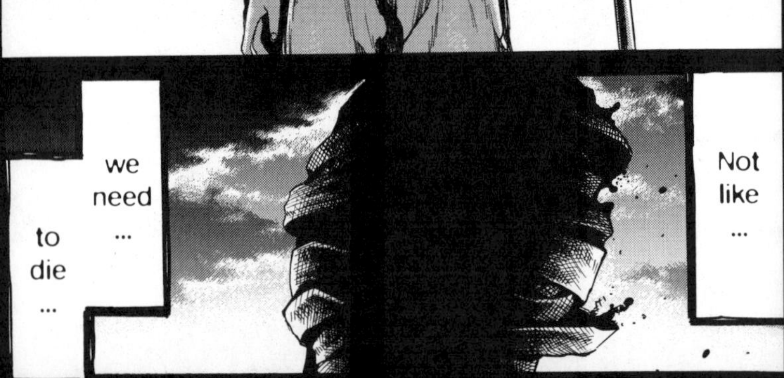

Not like ...
we need ...
to die ...

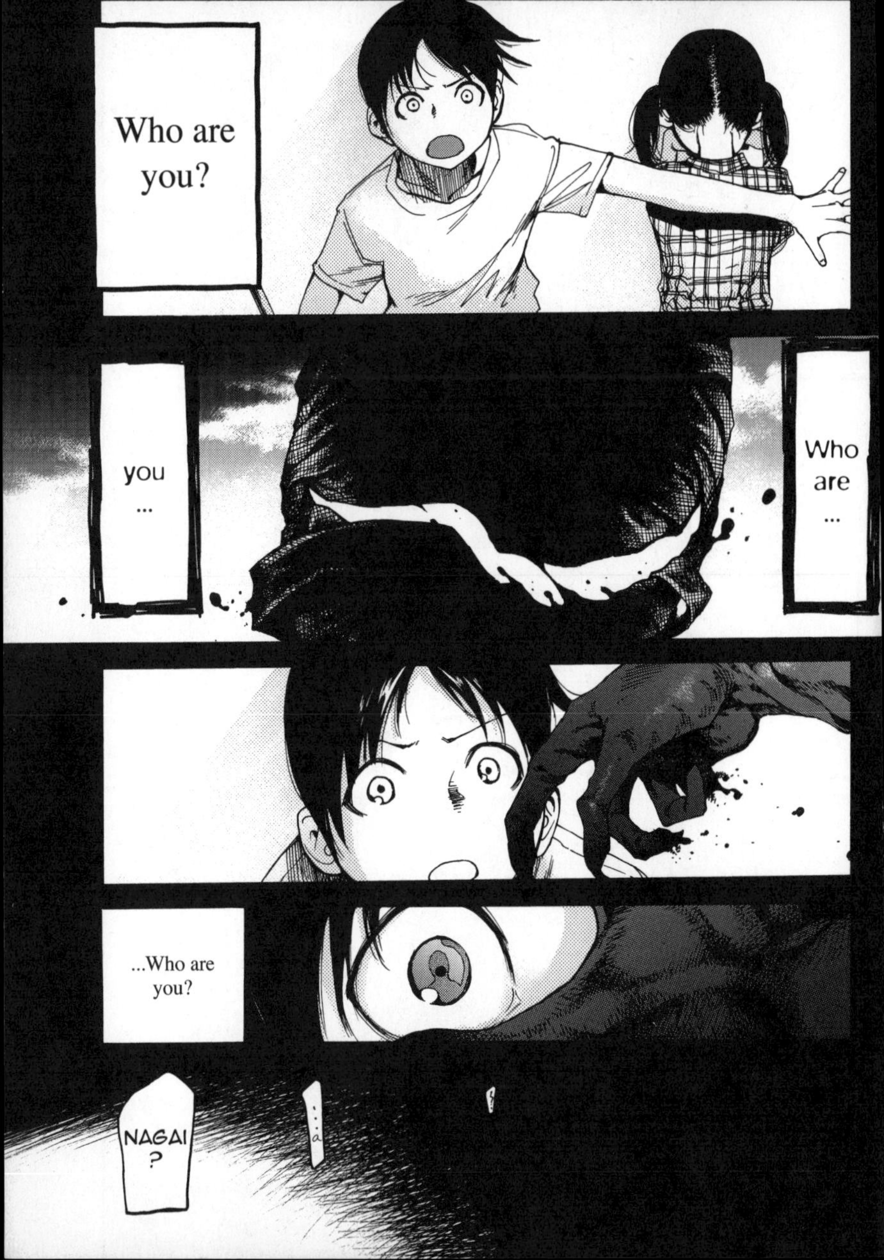
Who are you?
Who are ...
you ...
...Who are you?
!?
...a
NAGAI?

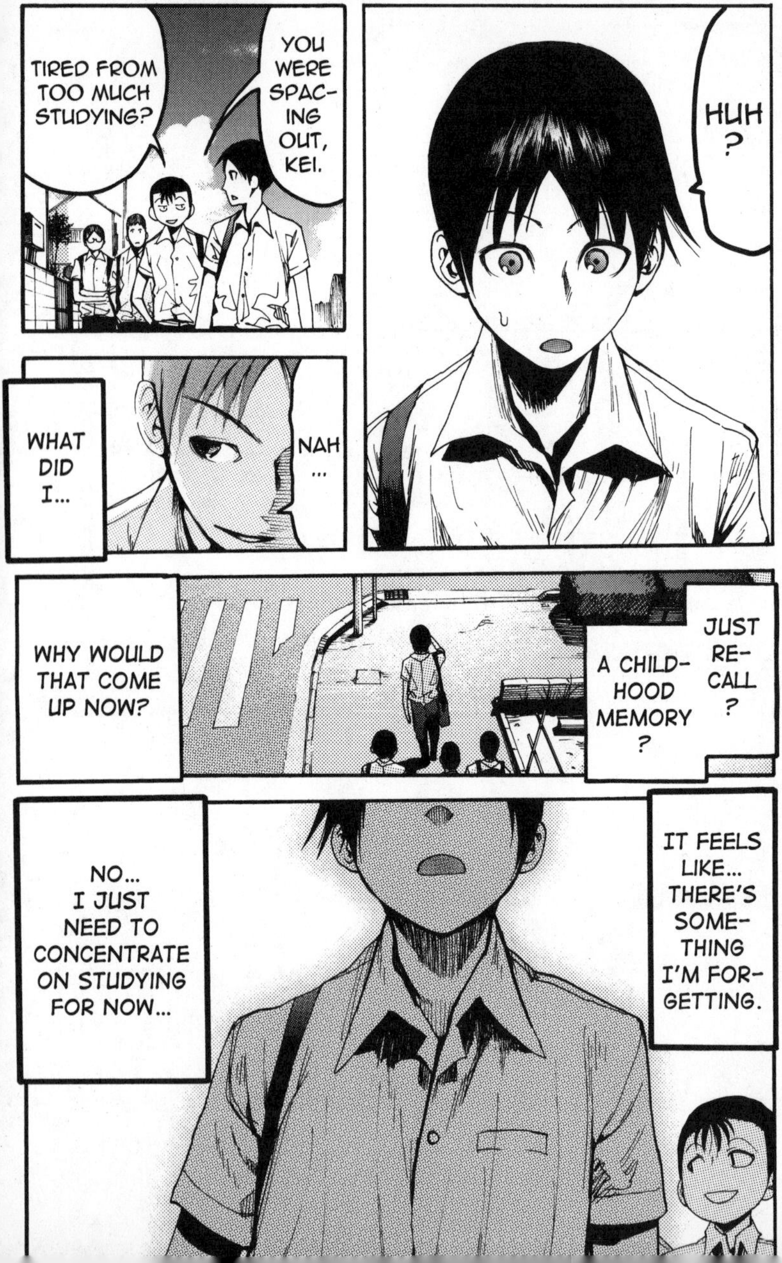
HUH?
YOU WERE SPACING OUT, KEI.
TIRED FROM TOO MUCH STUDYING?
NAH...
WHAT DID I...
JUST RECALL?
A CHILDHOOD MEMORY?
WHY WOULD THAT COME UP NOW?
IT FEELS LIKE... THERE'S SOMETHING I'M FORGETTING.
NO... I JUST NEED TO CONCENTRATE ON STUDYING FOR NOW...

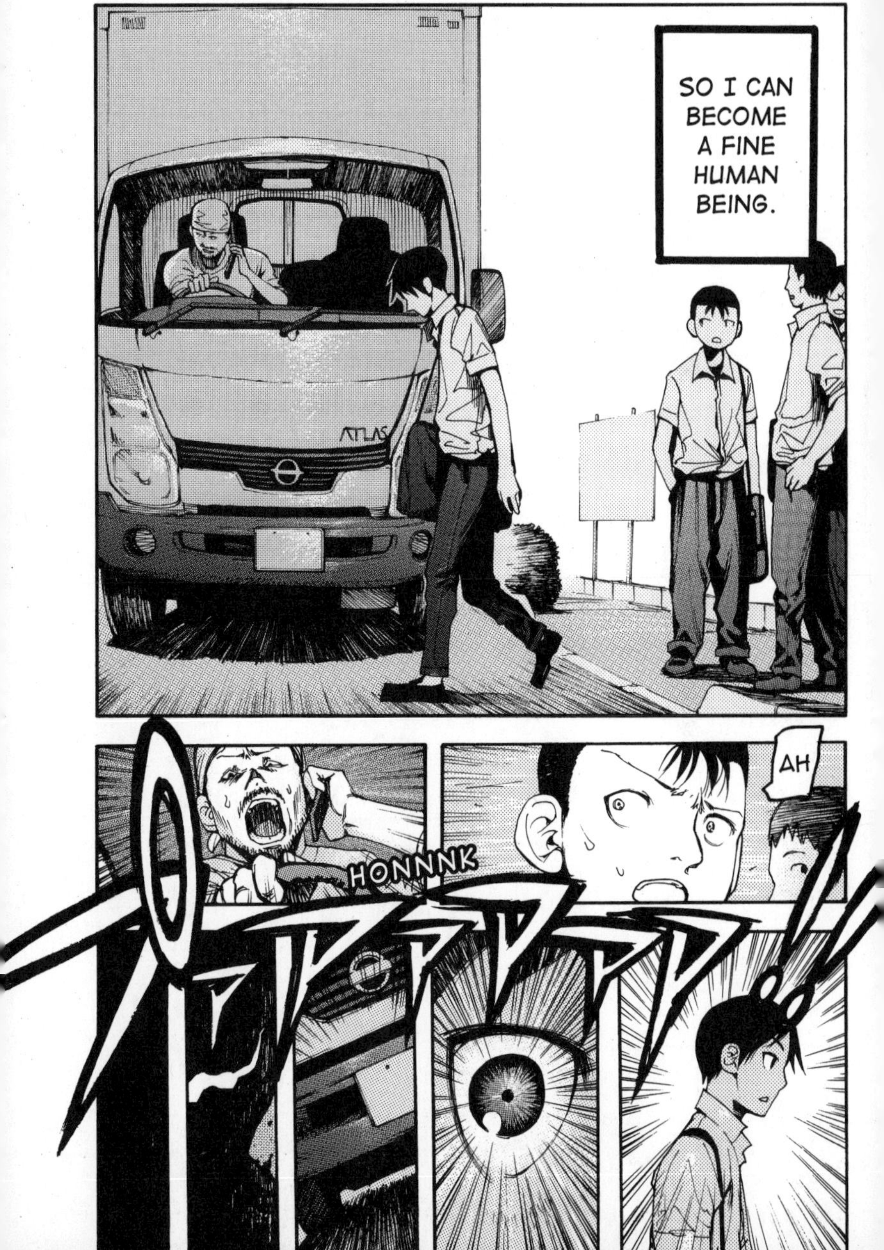
SO I CAN BECOME A FINE HUMAN BEING.
ATLAS
AH
HONNNK

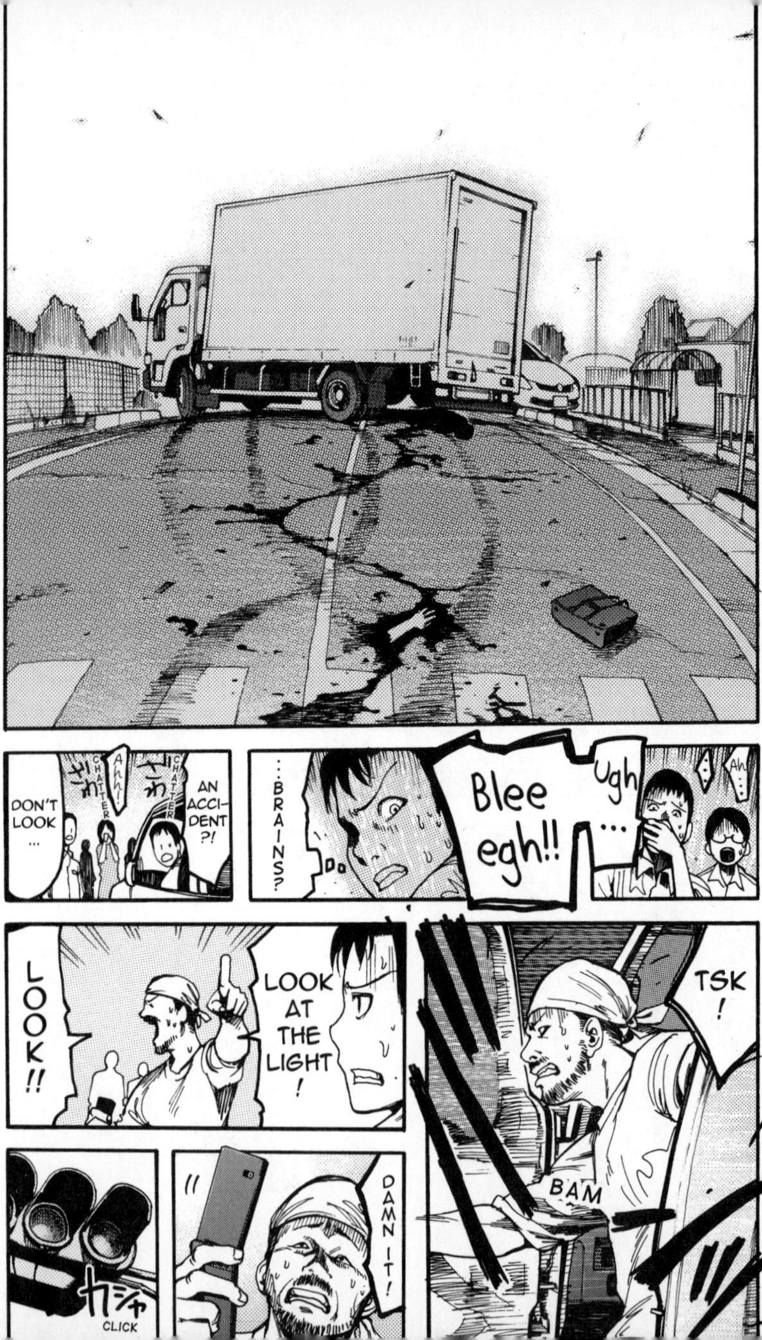
Ah...
Ugh...
Bleeegh!!
...BRAINS?
AN ACCIDENT?!
ざわ
CHATTER
Ahh!
ざわ
CHATTER
DON'T LOOK...
TSK!
BAM
LOOK AT THE LIGHT!
LOOK!!
DAMN IT!
!!
カシャ
CLICK

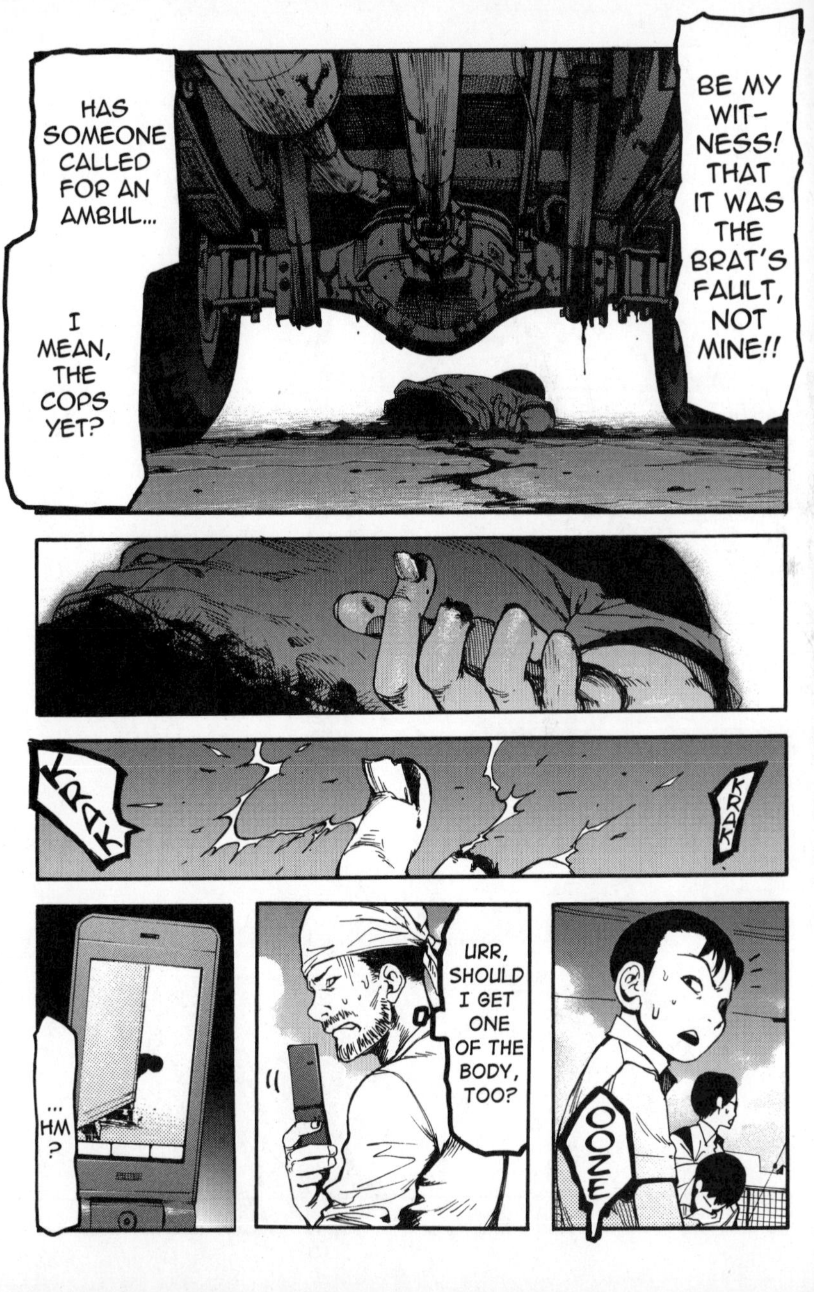
BE MY WIT-NESS! THAT IT WAS THE BRAT'S FAULT, NOT MINE!!
HAS SOMEONE CALLED FOR AN AMBUL...
I MEAN, THE COPS YET?
KRAK
KRAK
OOZE
URR, SHOULD I GET ONE OF THE BODY, TOO?
...HM?

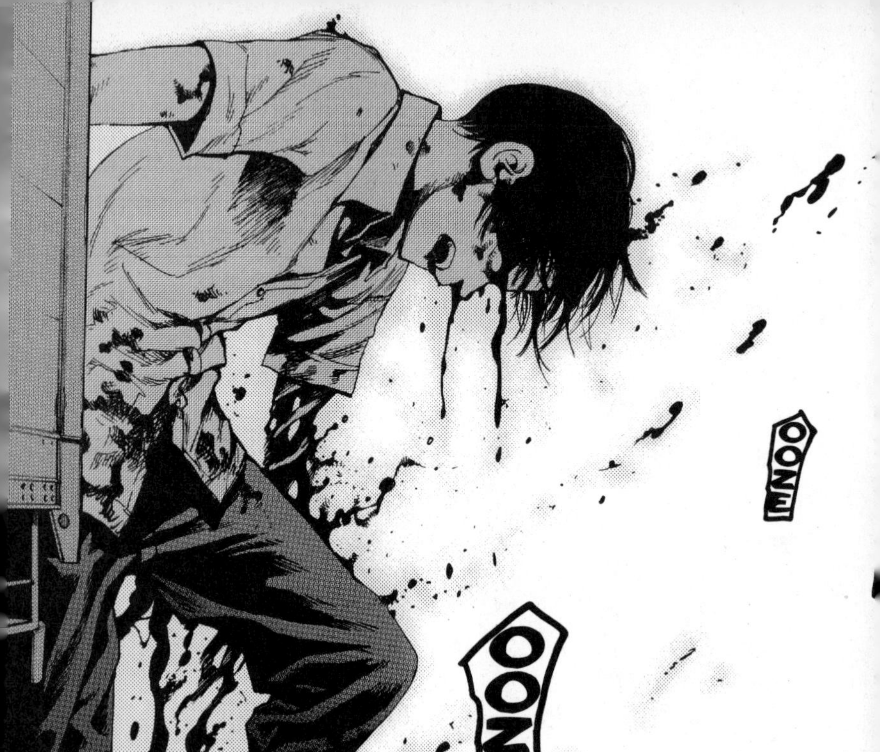
OOZE
OOZE

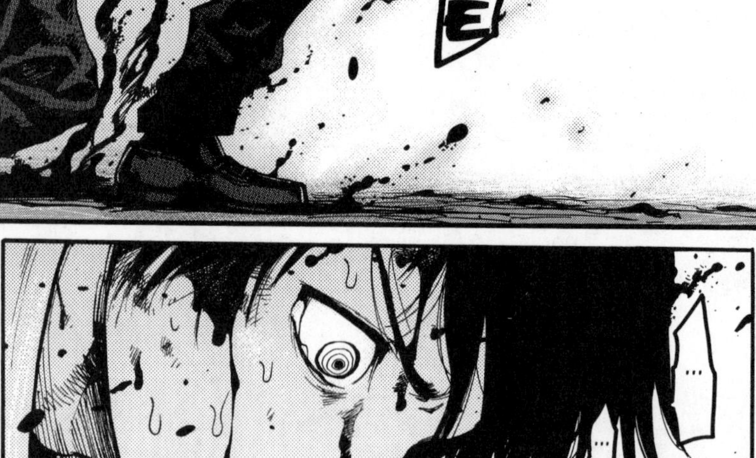
...
...

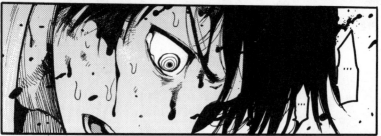

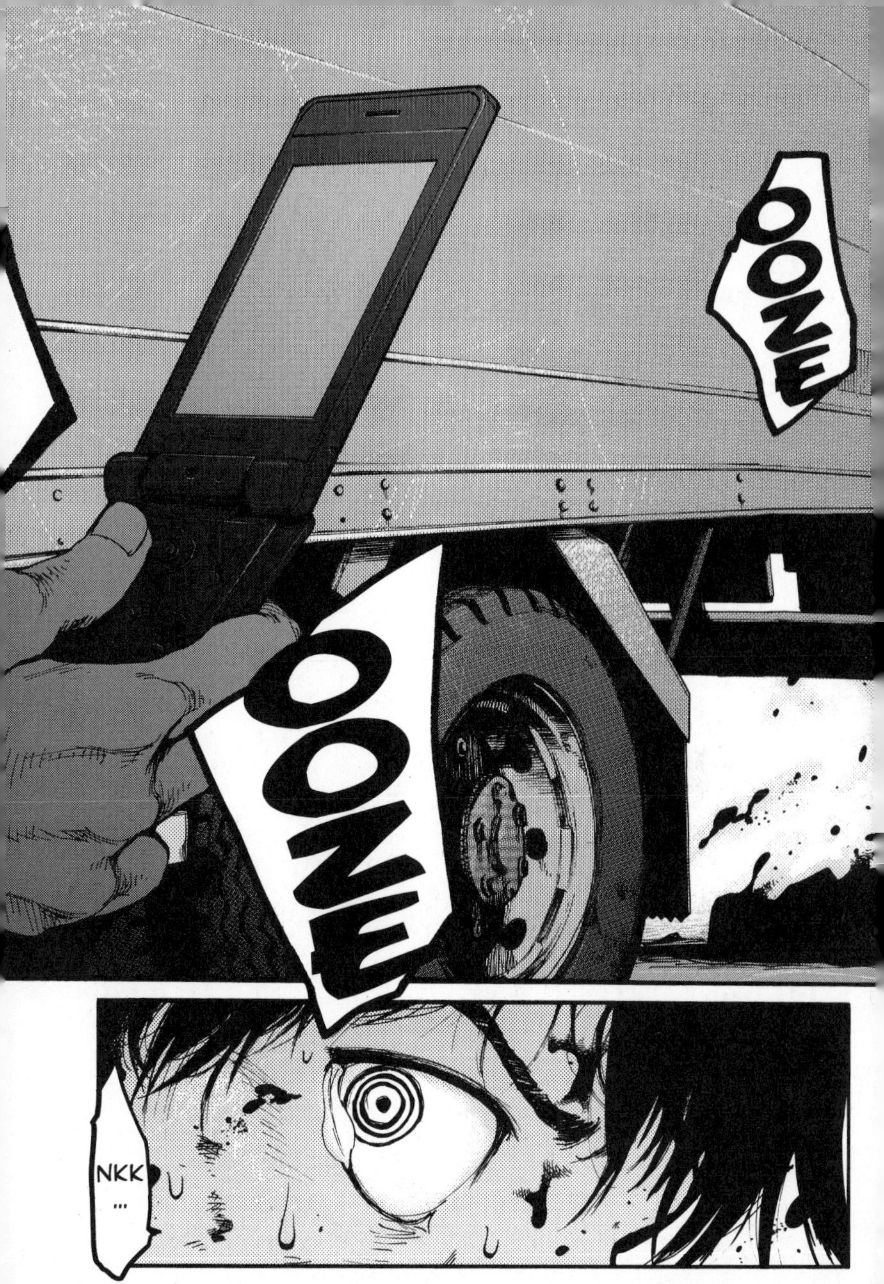
OOZE
OOZE
NKK
...

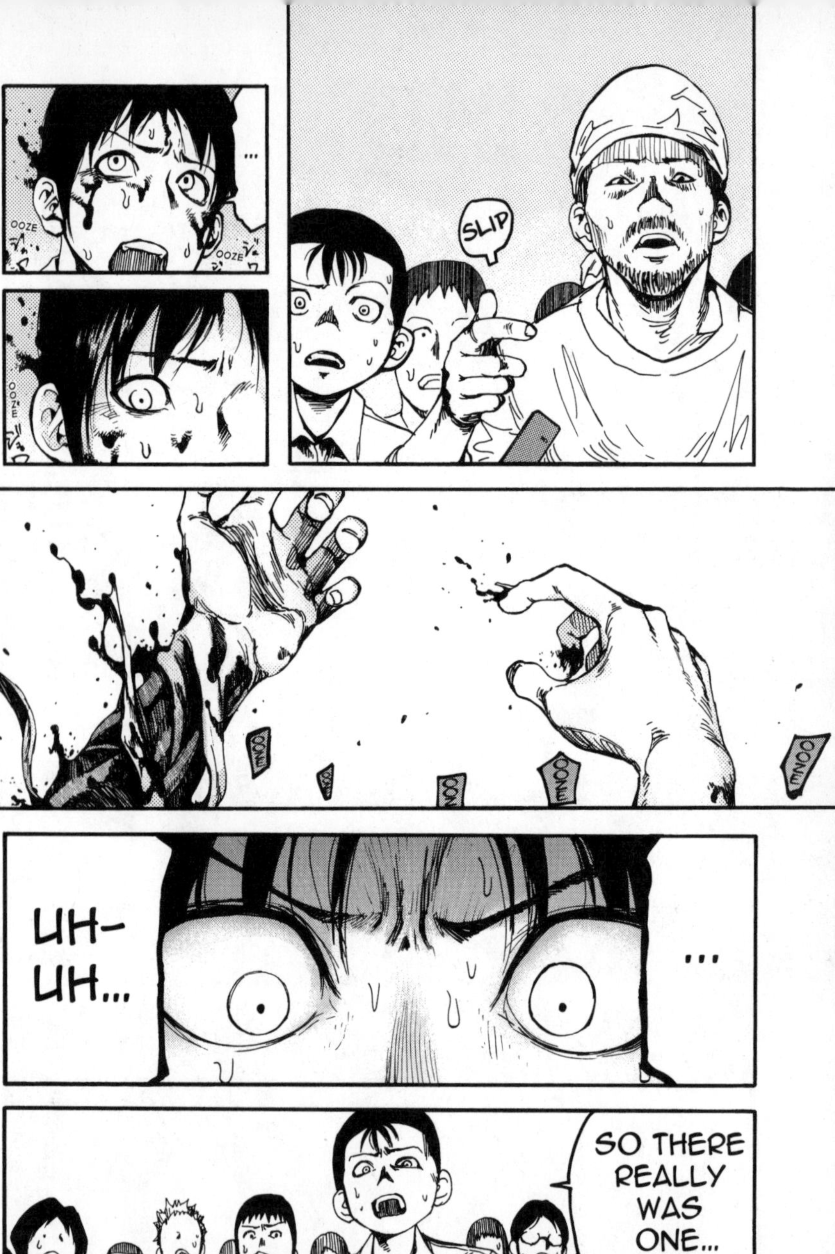
SLIP
...
OOZE
OOZE
OOZE
OOZE
OOZE
OOZE
OOZE
OOZE
...
UH-UH...
SO THERE REALLY WAS ONE...

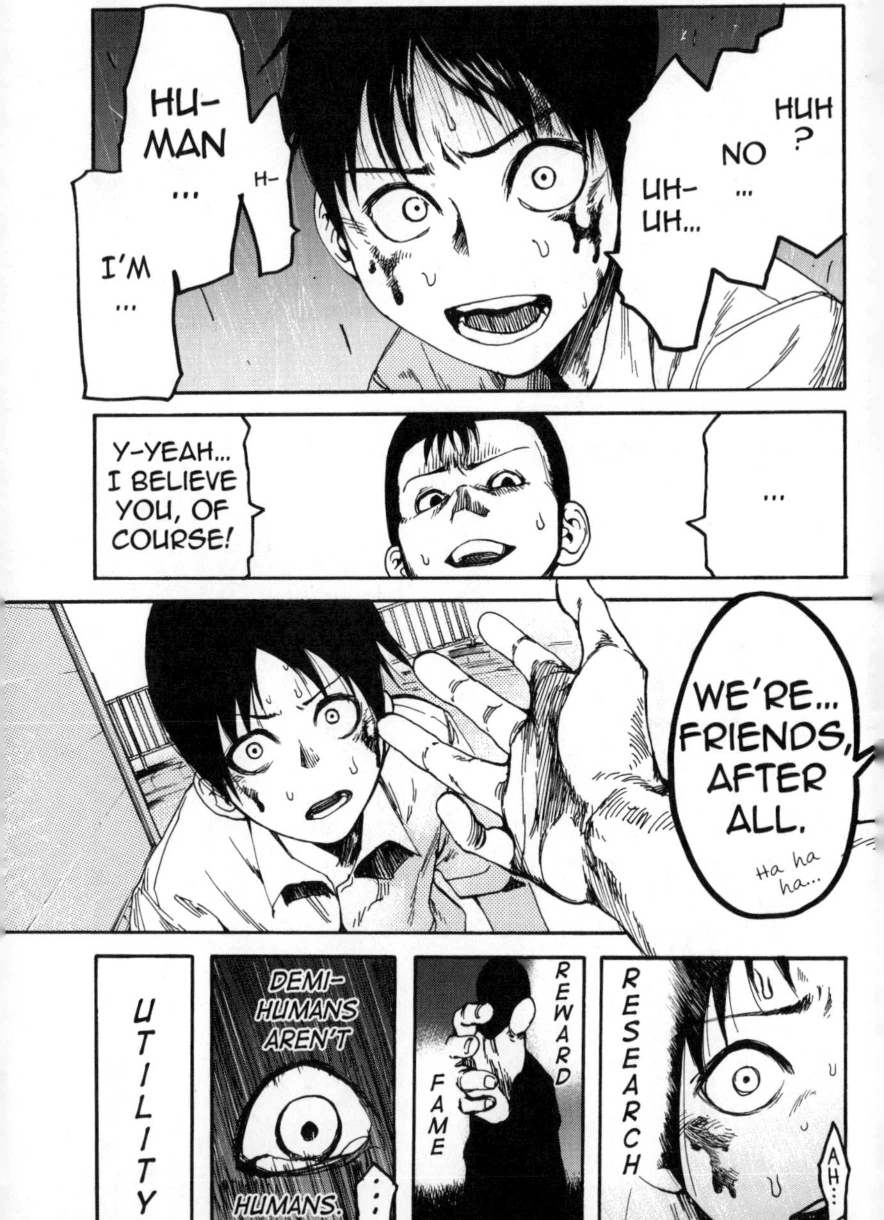
HUH?
NO...
UH-UH...
H-
HU-MAN...
I'M...
...
Y-YEAH... I BELIEVE YOU, OF COURSE!
WE'RE... FRIENDS, AFTER ALL.
Ha ha ha...
AH...
RESEARCH
REWARD
FAME
DEMI-HUMANS AREN'T
...
HUMANS.
UTILITY

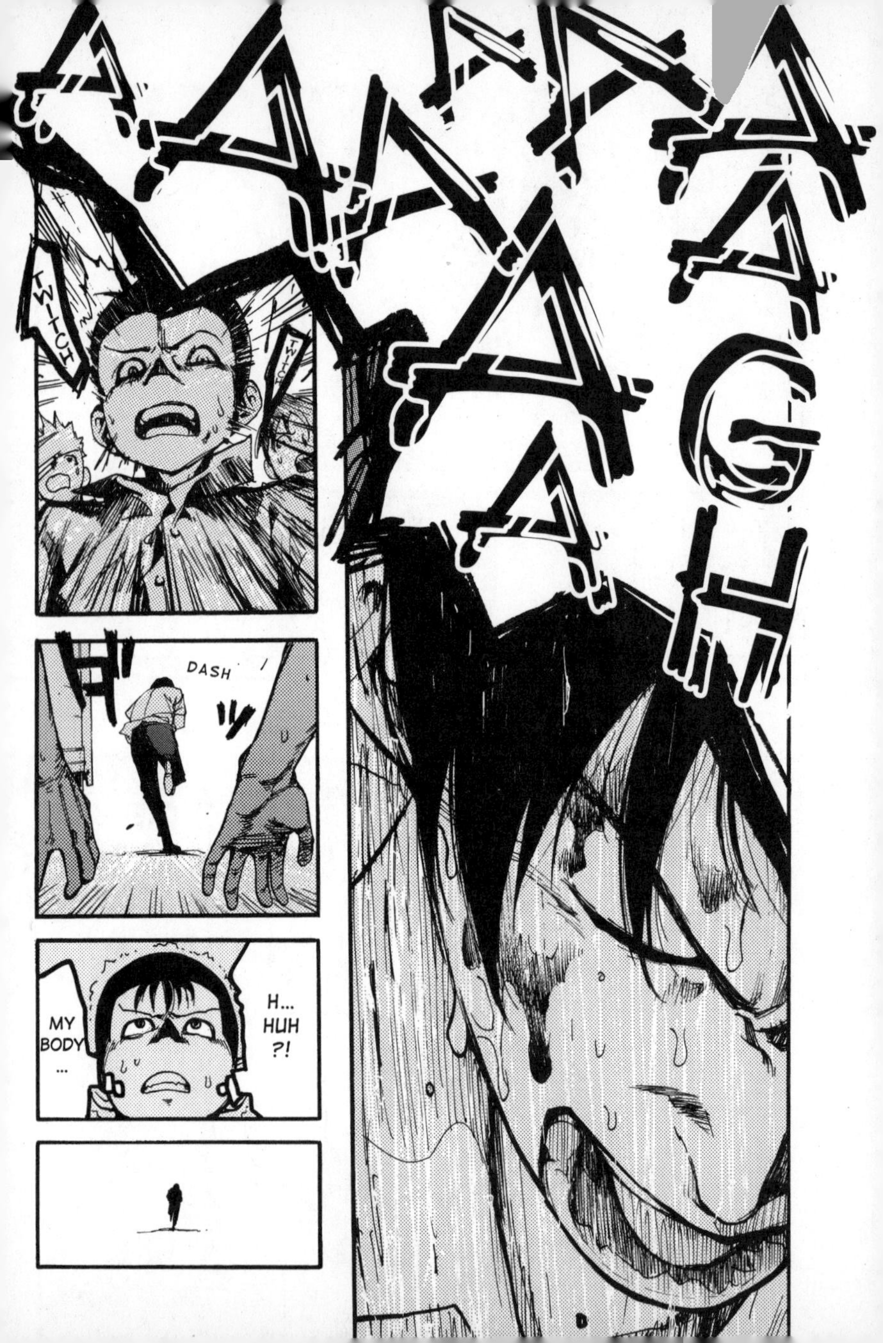
AAAAAAAAAAAAAGH
TWITCH
TWITCH
DASH
H... HUH ?!
MY BODY ...

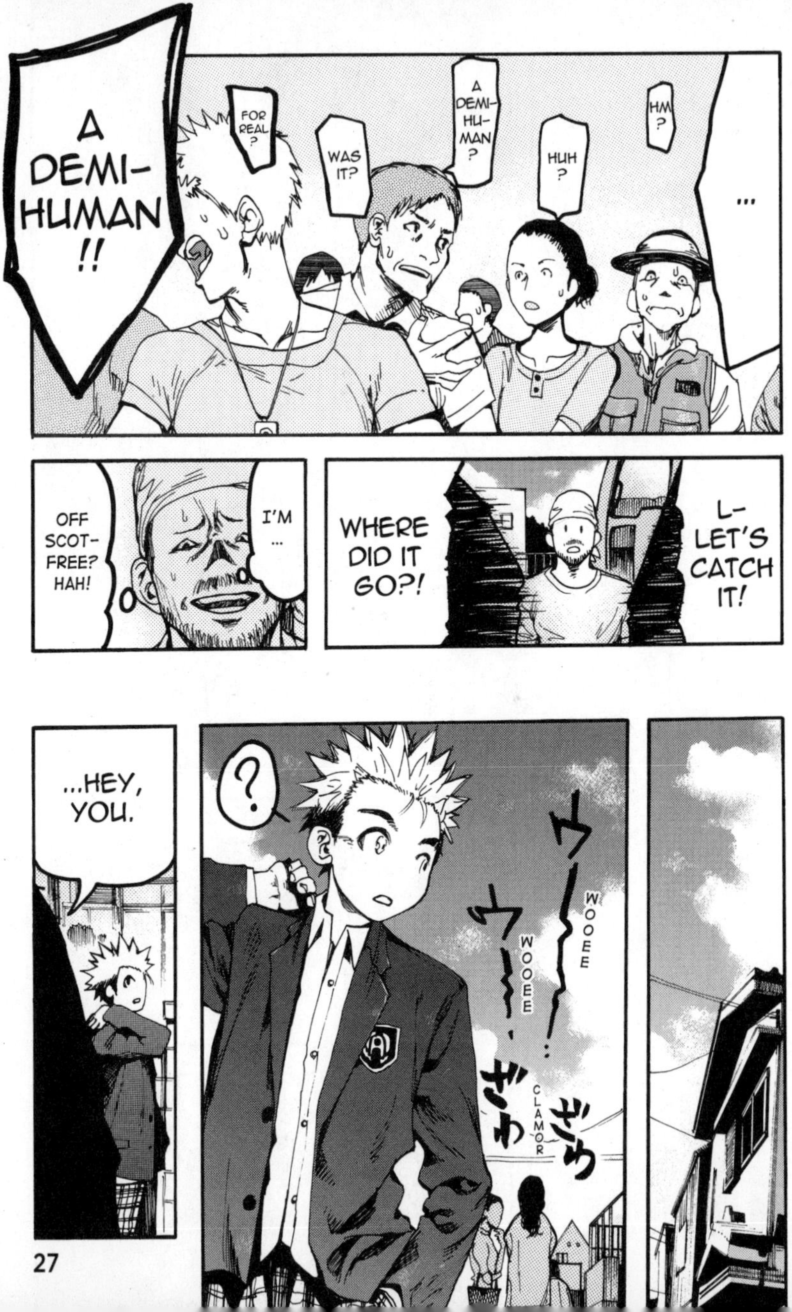
...
HM?
HUH?
A DEMI-HUMAN?
WAS IT?
FOR REAL?
A DEMI-HUMAN!!
L-LET'S CATCH IT!
WHERE DID IT GO?!
I'M ...
OFF SCOT-FREE? HAH!
?
WOOEE
WOOEE
CLAMOR
...HEY, YOU.

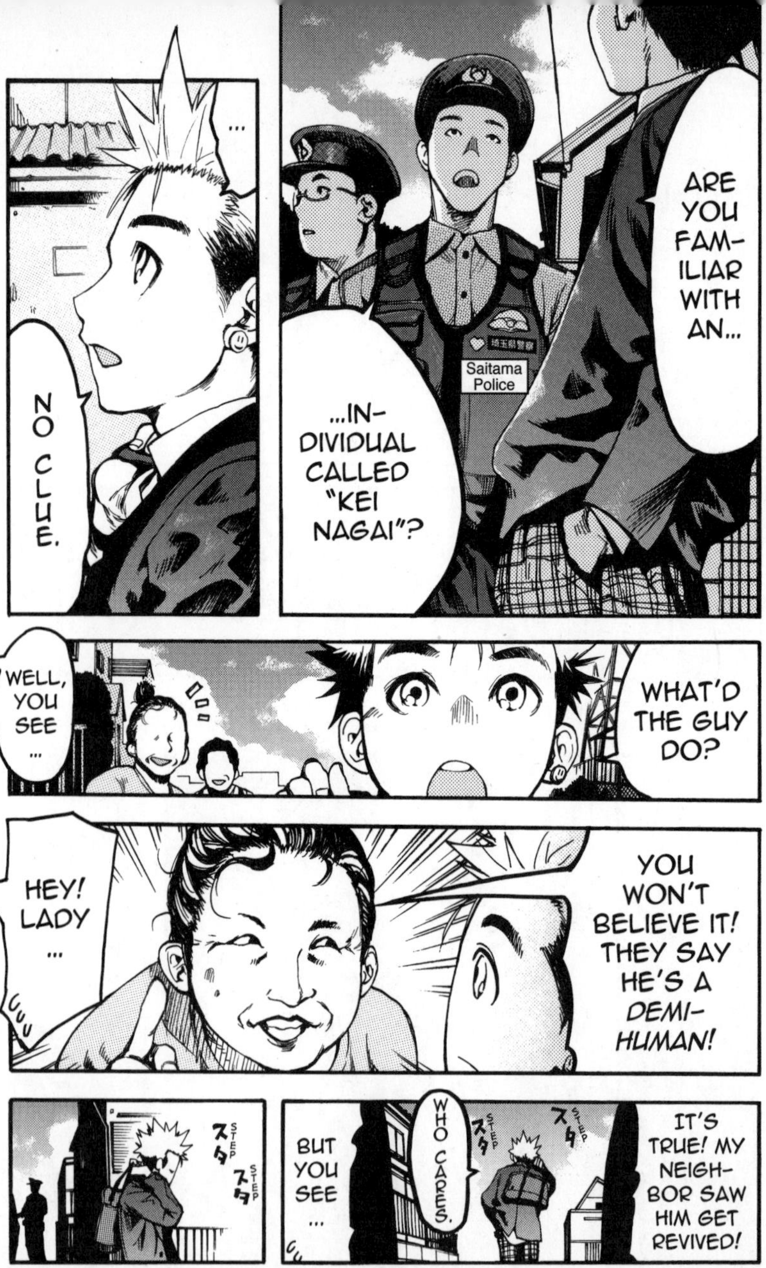
ARE YOU FAMILIAR WITH AN...
Saitama Police
...INDIVIDUAL CALLED "KEI NAGAI"?
...
NO CLUE.
WHAT'D THE GUY DO?
WELL, YOU SEE ...
YOU WON'T BELIEVE IT! THEY SAY HE'S A *DEMI-HUMAN*!
HEY! LADY ...
IT'S TRUE! MY NEIGHBOR SAW HIM GET REVIVED!
スタ STEP
スタ STEP
WHO CARES.
BUT YOU SEE ...
スタ STEP
スタ STEP

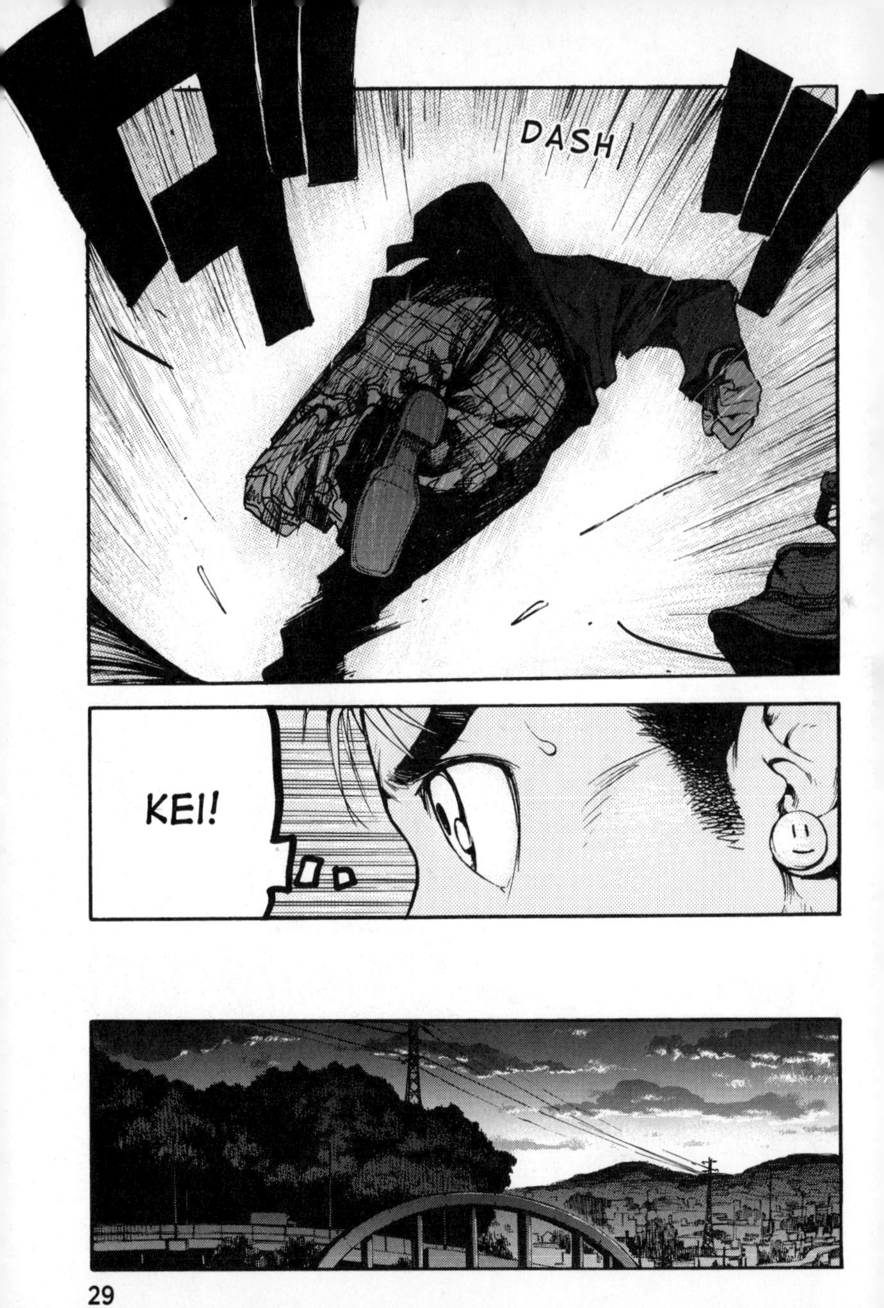
DASH
KEI!

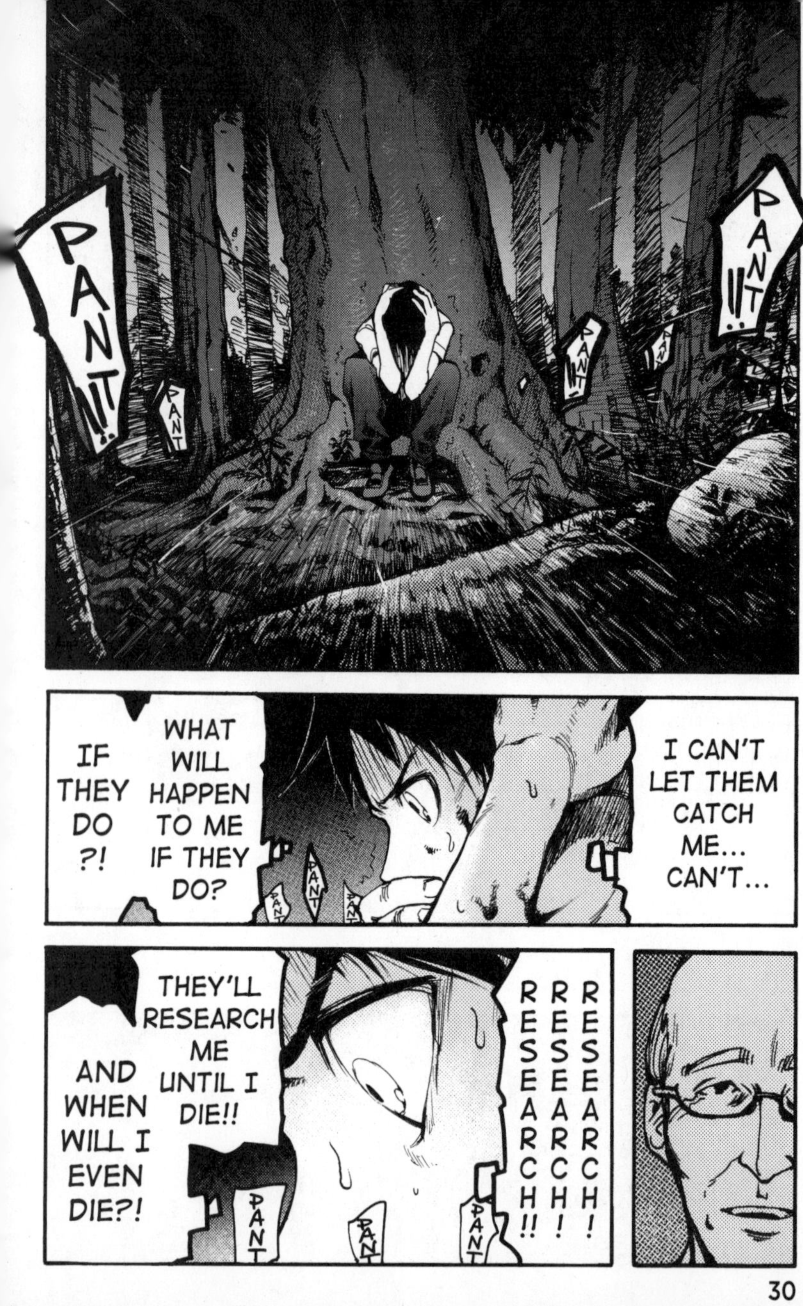
PANT!!
PANT!!
PANT
PANT!!
PANT
I CAN'T LET THEM CATCH ME... CAN'T...
WHAT WILL HAPPEN TO ME IF THEY DO?
IF THEY DO?!
PANT
PANT
PANT
RESEARCH!
RESEARCH!
RESEARCH!!
THEY'LL RESEARCH ME UNTIL I DIE!!
AND WHEN WILL I EVEN DIE?!
PANT
PANT
PANT

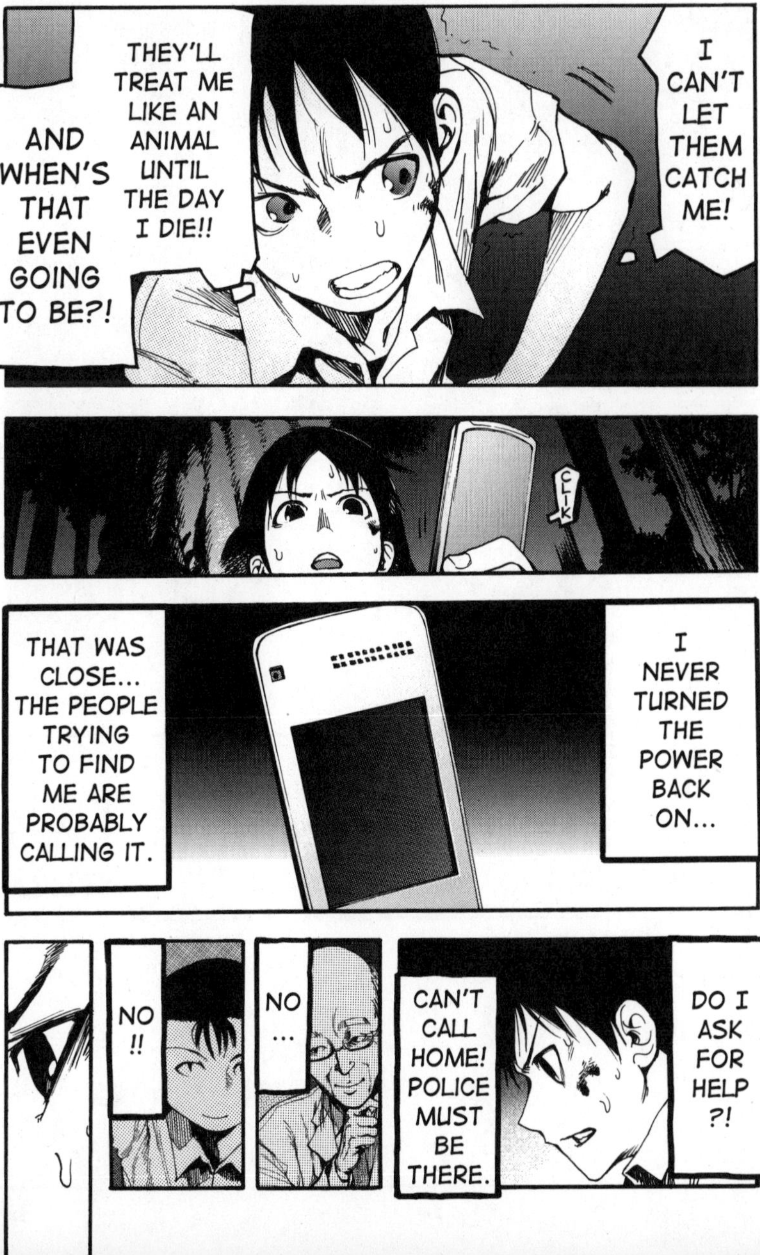
I CAN'T LET THEM CATCH ME!
THEY'LL TREAT ME LIKE AN ANIMAL UNTIL THE DAY I DIE!!
AND WHEN'S THAT EVEN GOING TO BE?!
CLIK
I NEVER TURNED THE POWER BACK ON...
THAT WAS CLOSE... THE PEOPLE TRYING TO FIND ME ARE PROBABLY CALLING IT.
DO I ASK FOR HELP?!
CAN'T CALL HOME! POLICE MUST BE THERE.
NO...
NO!!

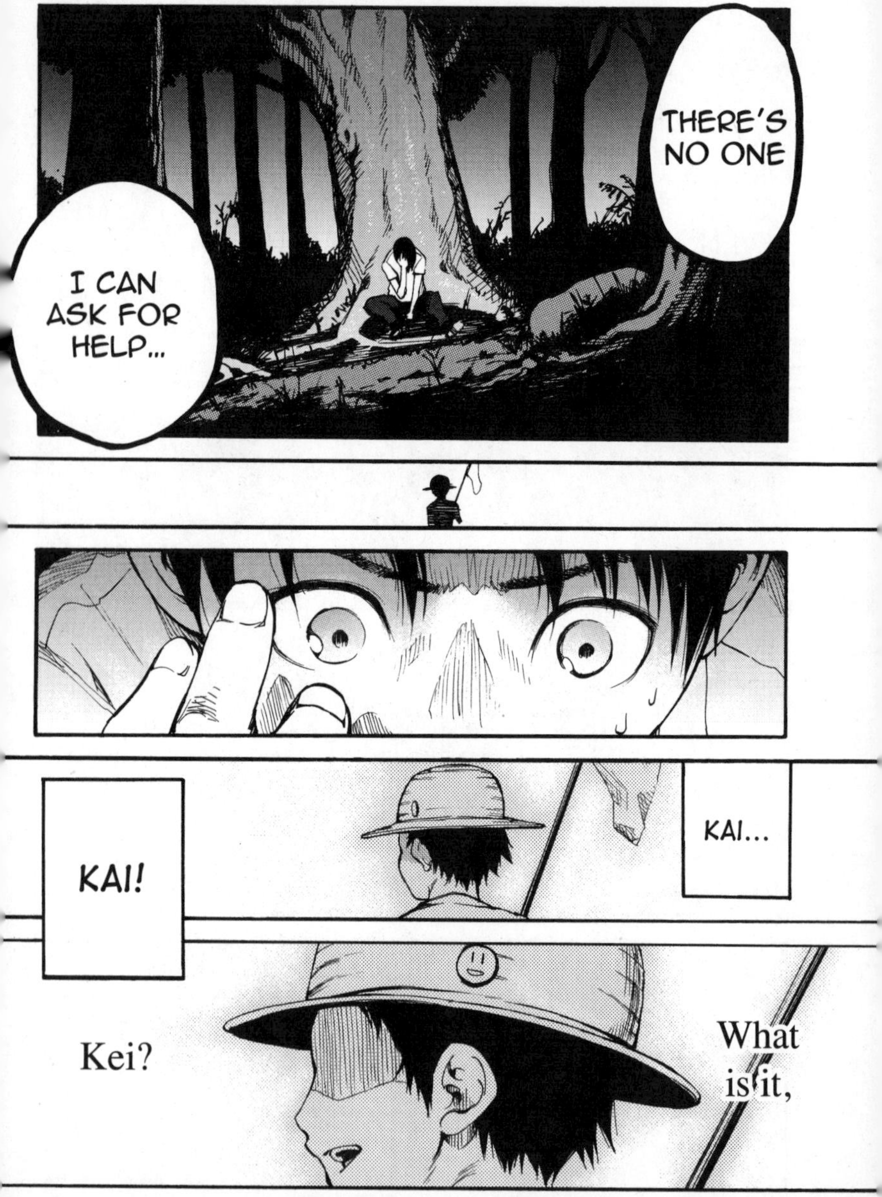
THERE'S NO ONE
I CAN ASK FOR HELP...
KAI...
KAI!
What is it,
Kei?

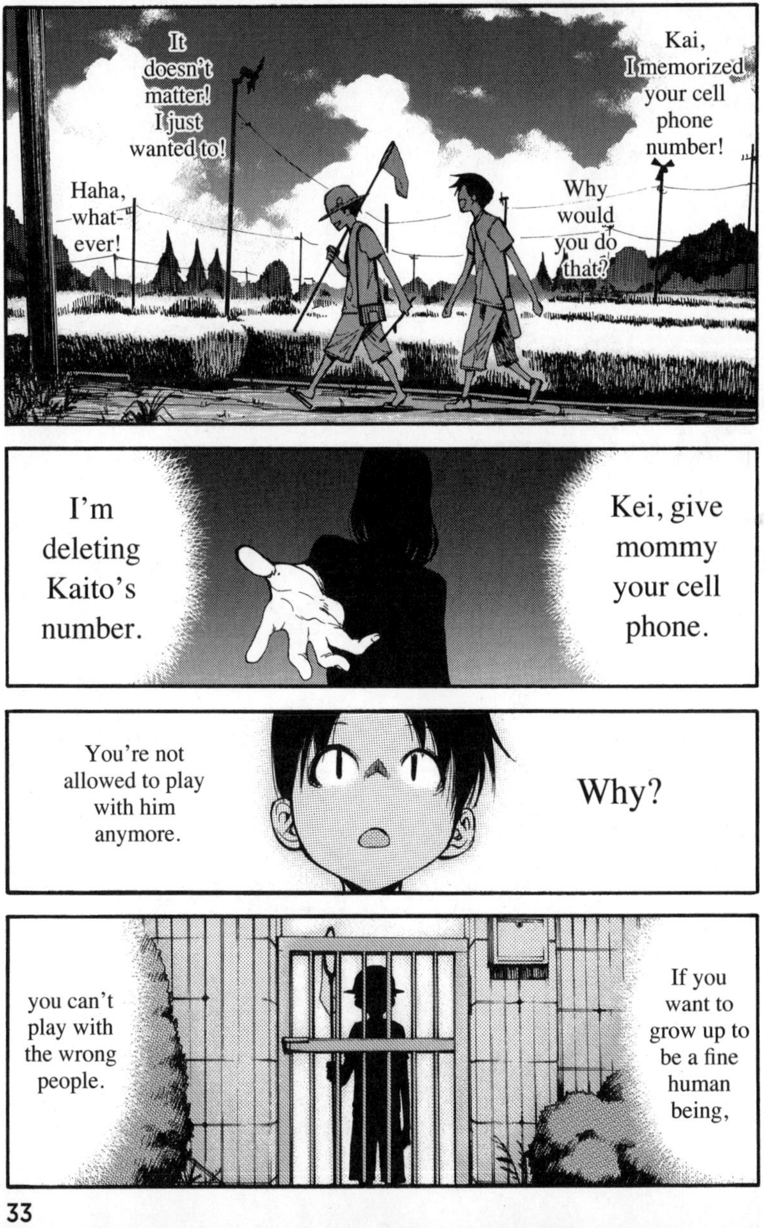
Kai, I memorized your cell phone number!
Why would you do that?
It doesn't matter! I just wanted to!
Haha, whatever!
Kei, give mommy your cell phone.
I'm deleting Kaito's number.
Why?
You're not allowed to play with him anymore.
If you want to grow up to be a fine human being,
you can't play with the wrong people.

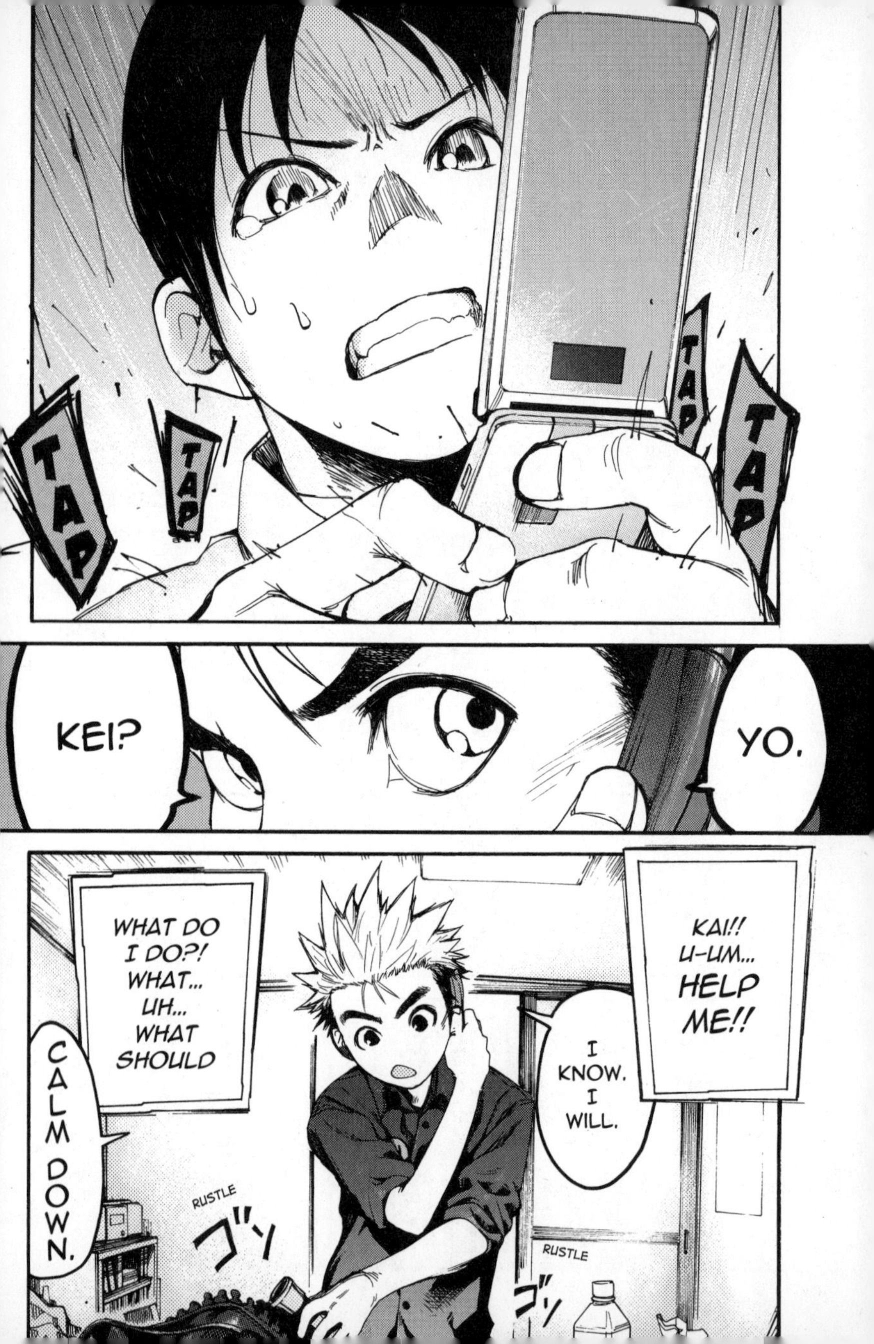
TAP
TAP
TAP
TAP
YO.
KEI?
KAI!! U-UM... HELP ME!!
I KNOW. I WILL.
WHAT DO I DO?! WHAT... UH... WHAT SHOULD
RUSTLE
ゴッ
CALM DOWN.
RUSTLE
ゴッ

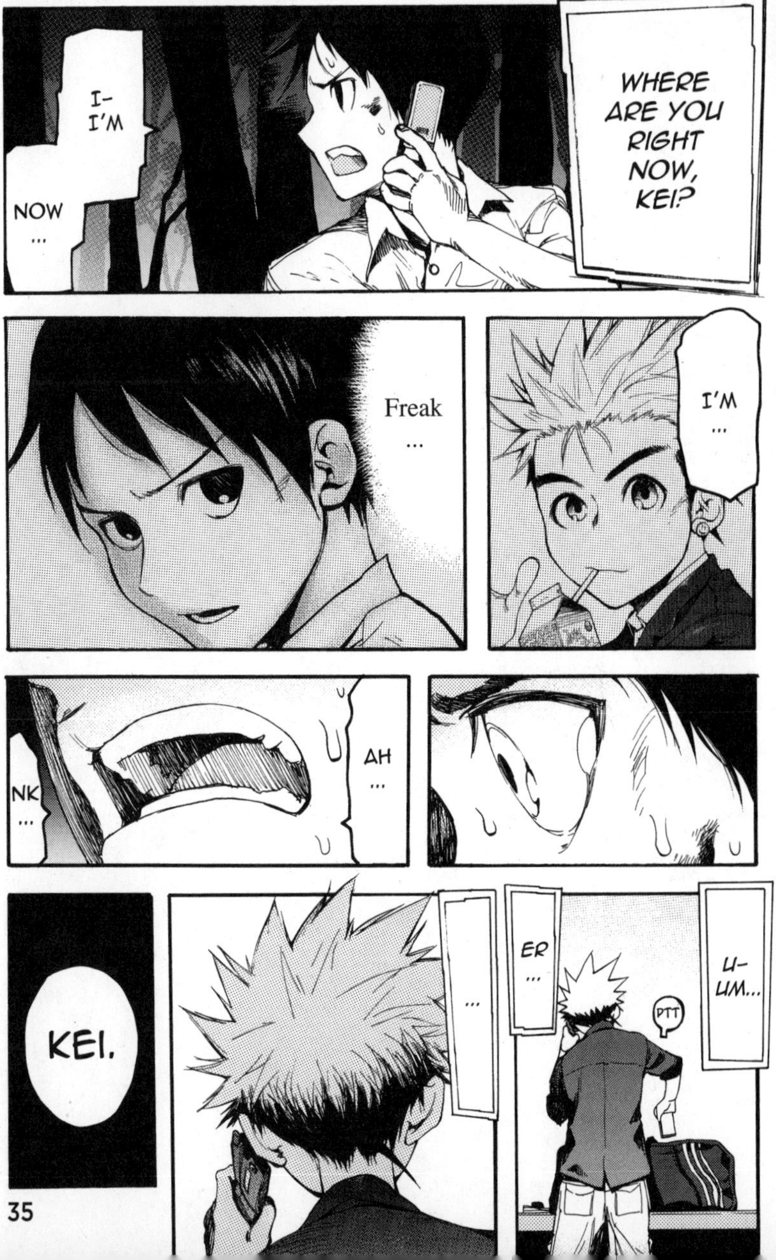
WHERE ARE YOU RIGHT NOW, KEI?
I- I'M
NOW ...
I'M ...
Freak ...
AH ...
NK ...
U- UM...
PTT
ER ...
...
KEI.

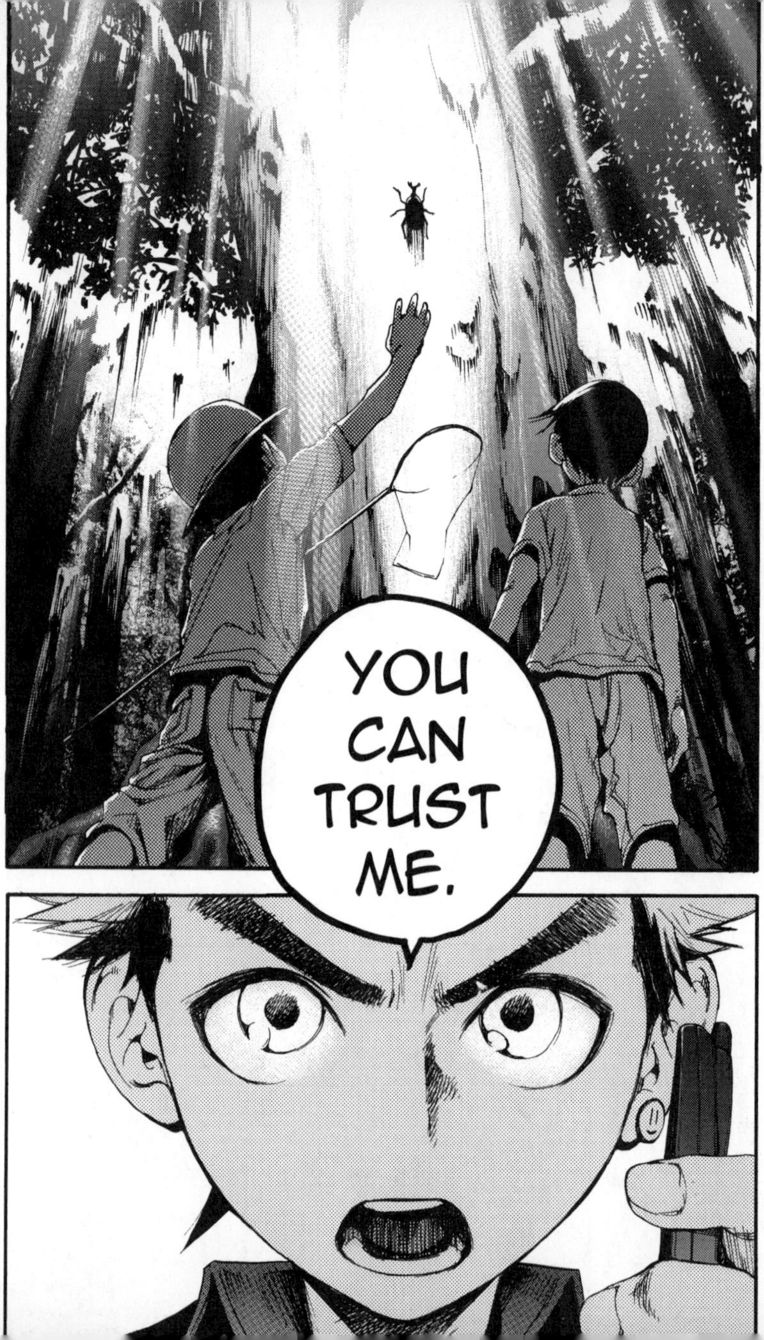
YOU CAN TRUST ME.

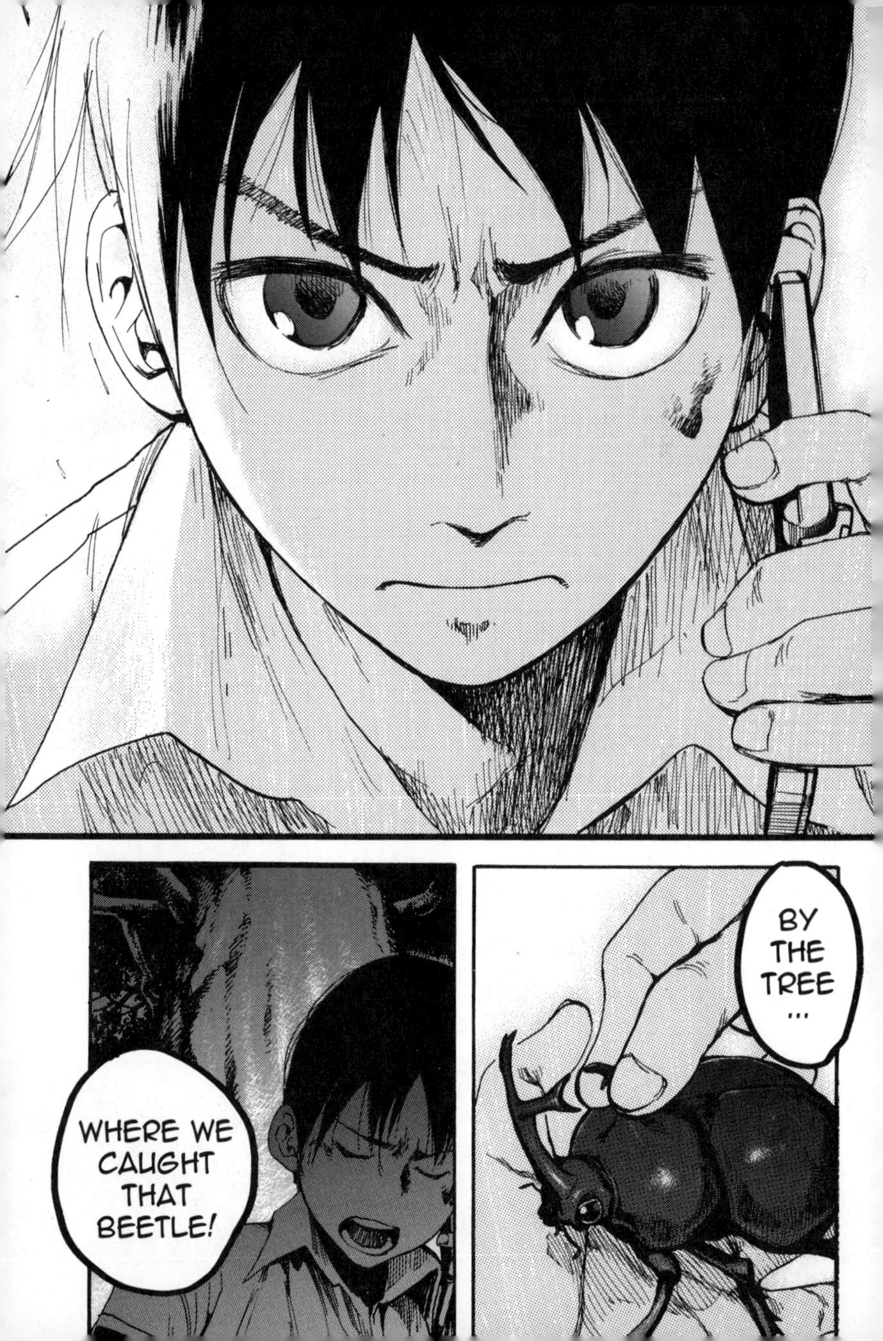
BY THE TREE ...
WHERE WE CAUGHT THAT BEETLE!

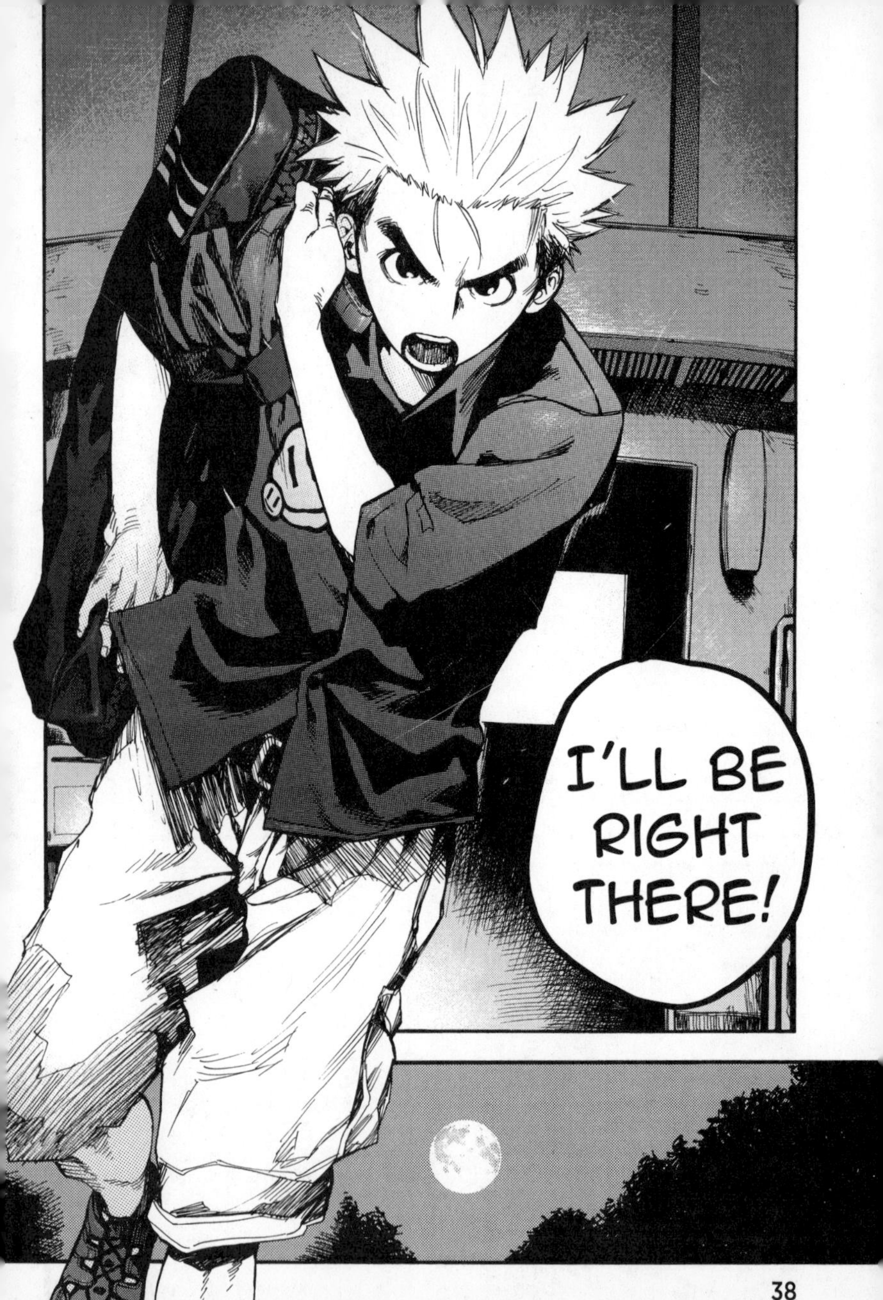
I'LL BE RIGHT THERE!

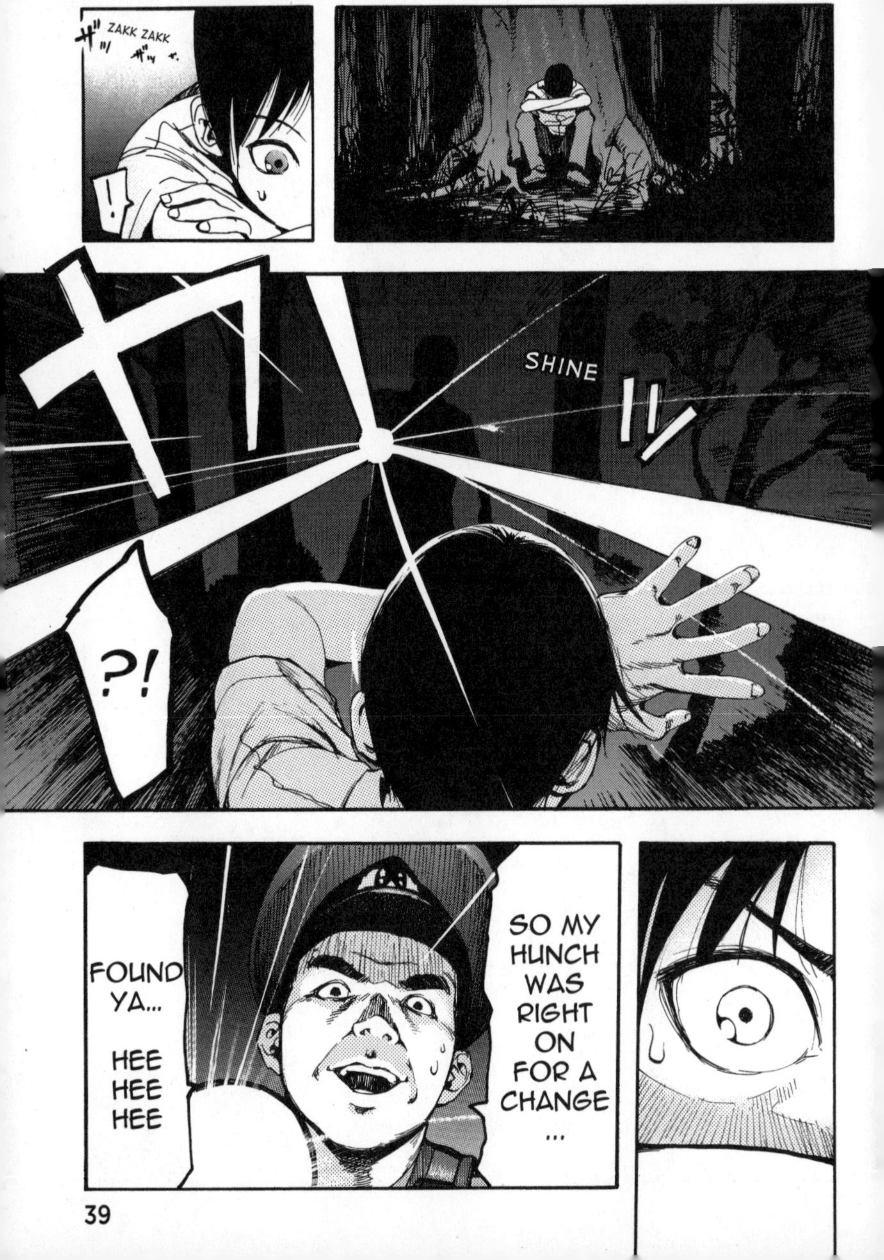
ZAKK ZAKK
!
SHINE
?!
SO MY HUNCH WAS RIGHT ON FOR A CHANGE ...
FOUND YA...
HEE HEE HEE

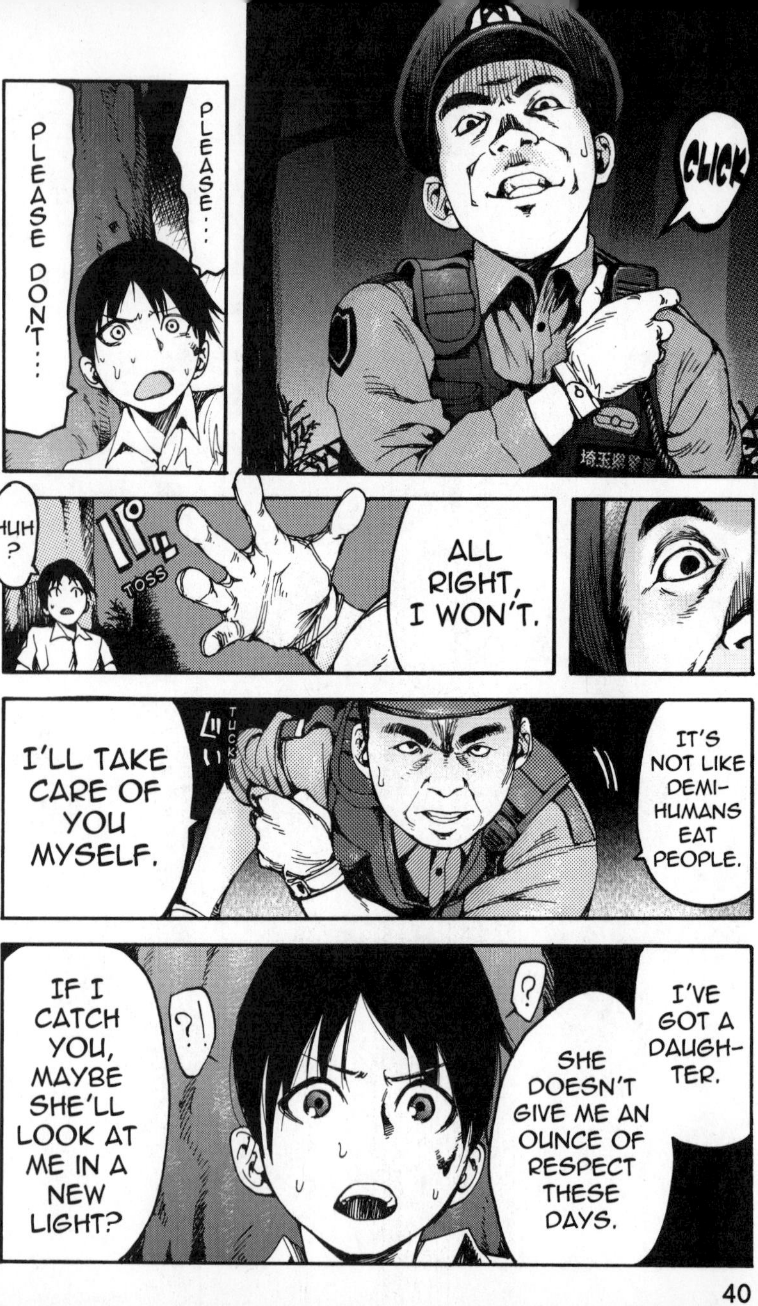
CLICK
PLEASE...
PLEASE DON'T...
ALL RIGHT, I WON'T.
TOSS
HUH?
IT'S NOT LIKE DEMI-HUMANS EAT PEOPLE.
TUCK
I'LL TAKE CARE OF YOU MYSELF.
I'VE GOT A DAUGHTER.
SHE DOESN'T GIVE ME AN OUNCE OF RESPECT THESE DAYS.
?
?!
IF I CATCH YOU, MAYBE SHE'LL LOOK AT ME IN A NEW LIGHT?

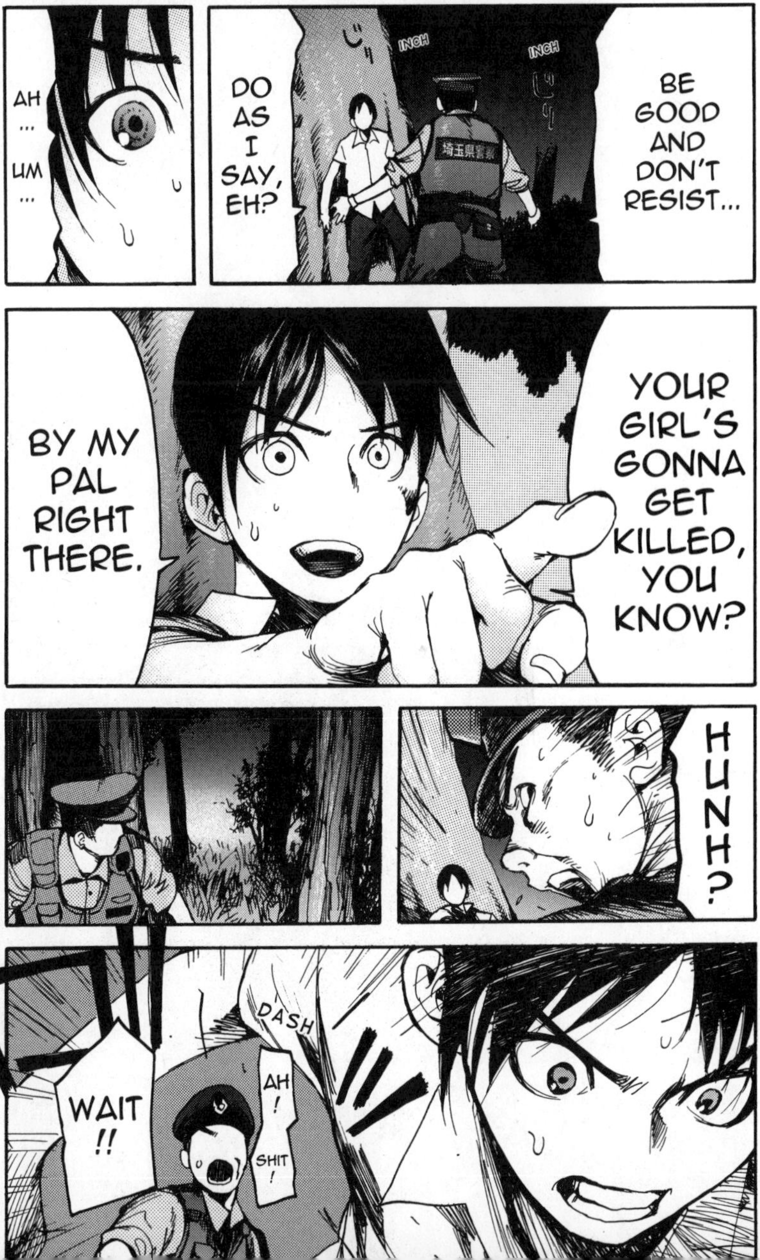
INCH
INCH
BE GOOD AND DON'T RESIST...
DO AS I SAY, EH?
AH... UM...
YOUR GIRL'S GONNA GET KILLED, YOU KNOW?
BY MY PAL RIGHT THERE.
HUNH?
DASH
AH! SHIT!
WAIT!!

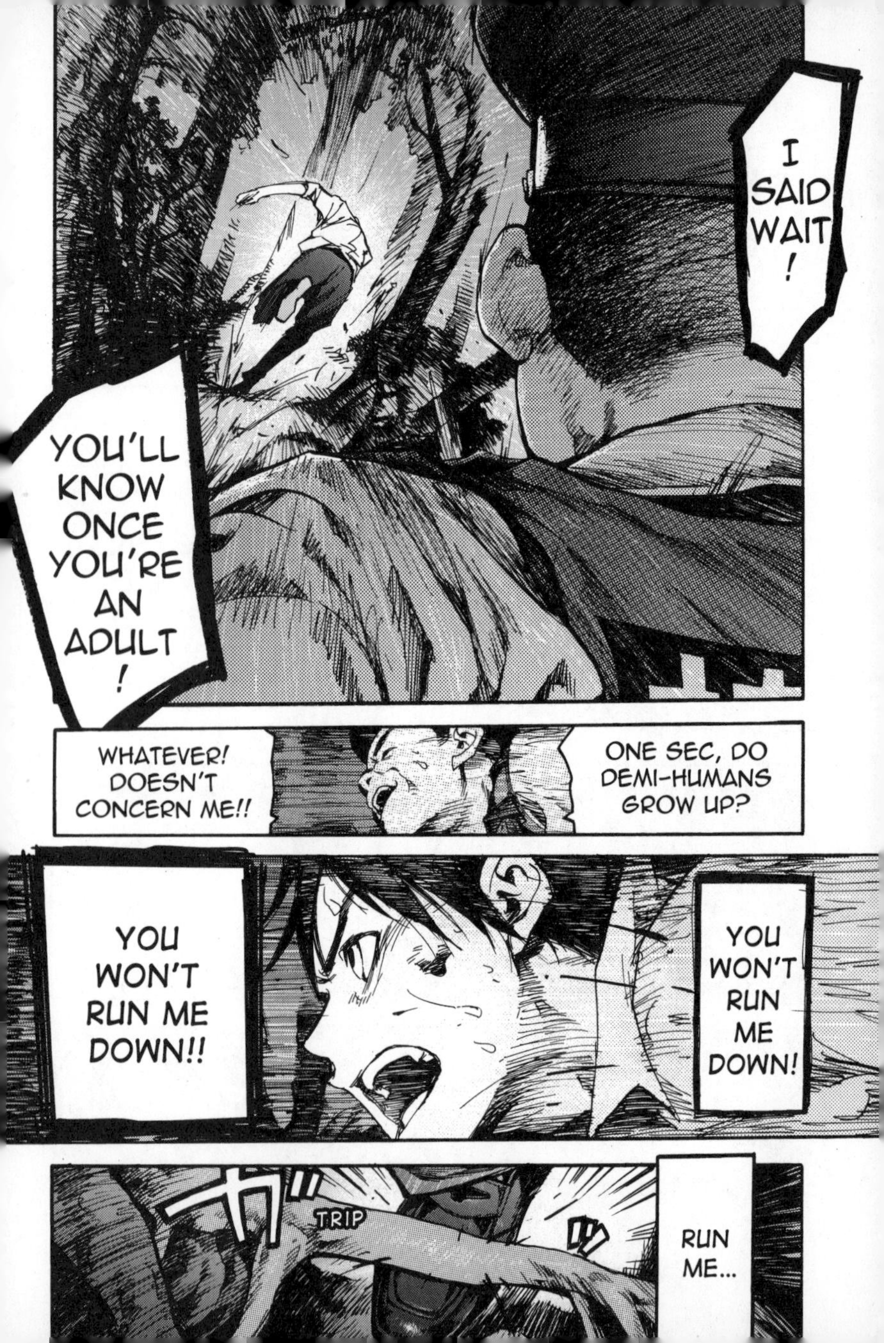
I SAID WAIT!
YOU'LL KNOW ONCE YOU'RE AN ADULT!
ONE SEC, DO DEMI-HUMANS GROW UP?
WHATEVER! DOESN'T CONCERN ME!!
YOU WON'T RUN ME DOWN!
YOU WON'T RUN ME DOWN!!
RUN ME...
TRIP

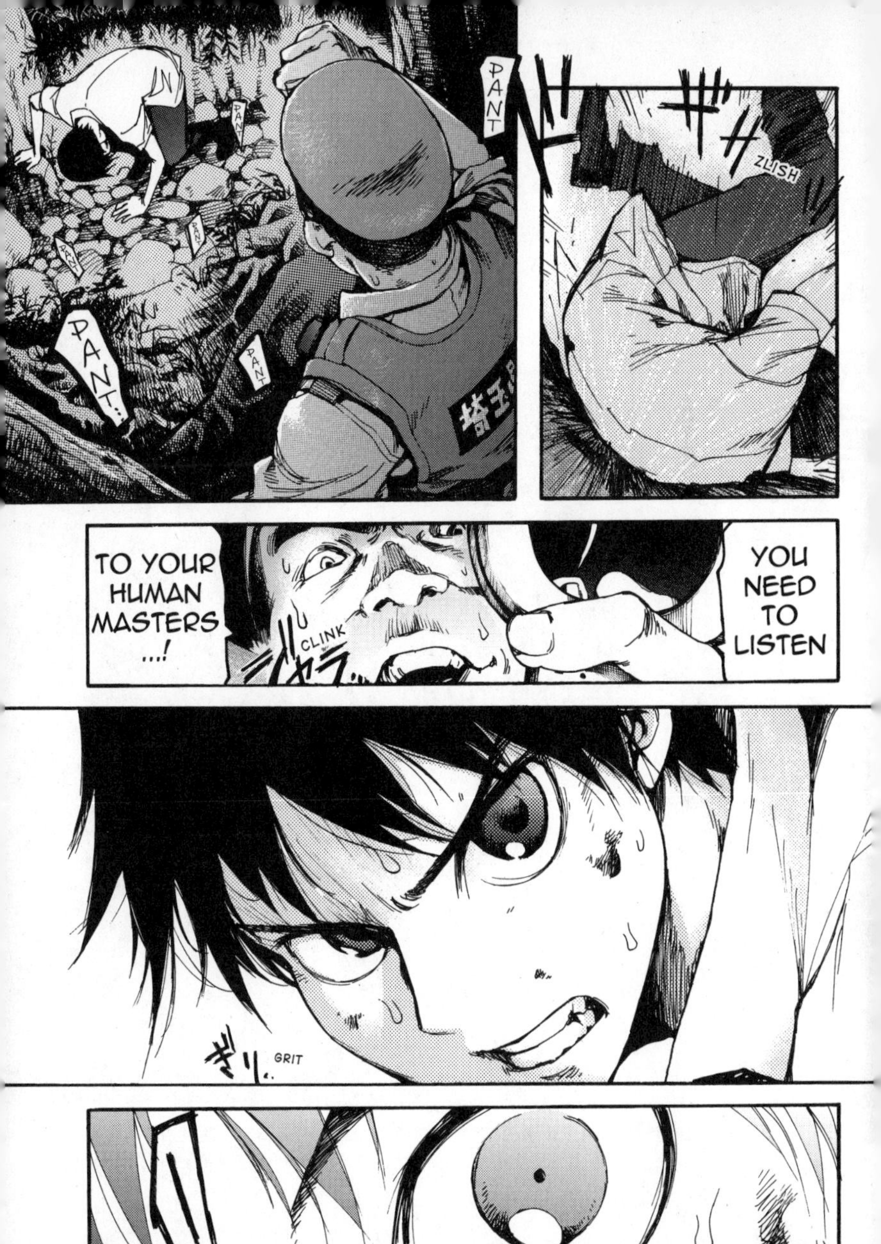
ZLISH
PANT
PANT
PANT
PANT
PANT...
PANT
YOU NEED TO LISTEN
TO YOUR HUMAN MASTERS ...!
CLINK
GRIT
!

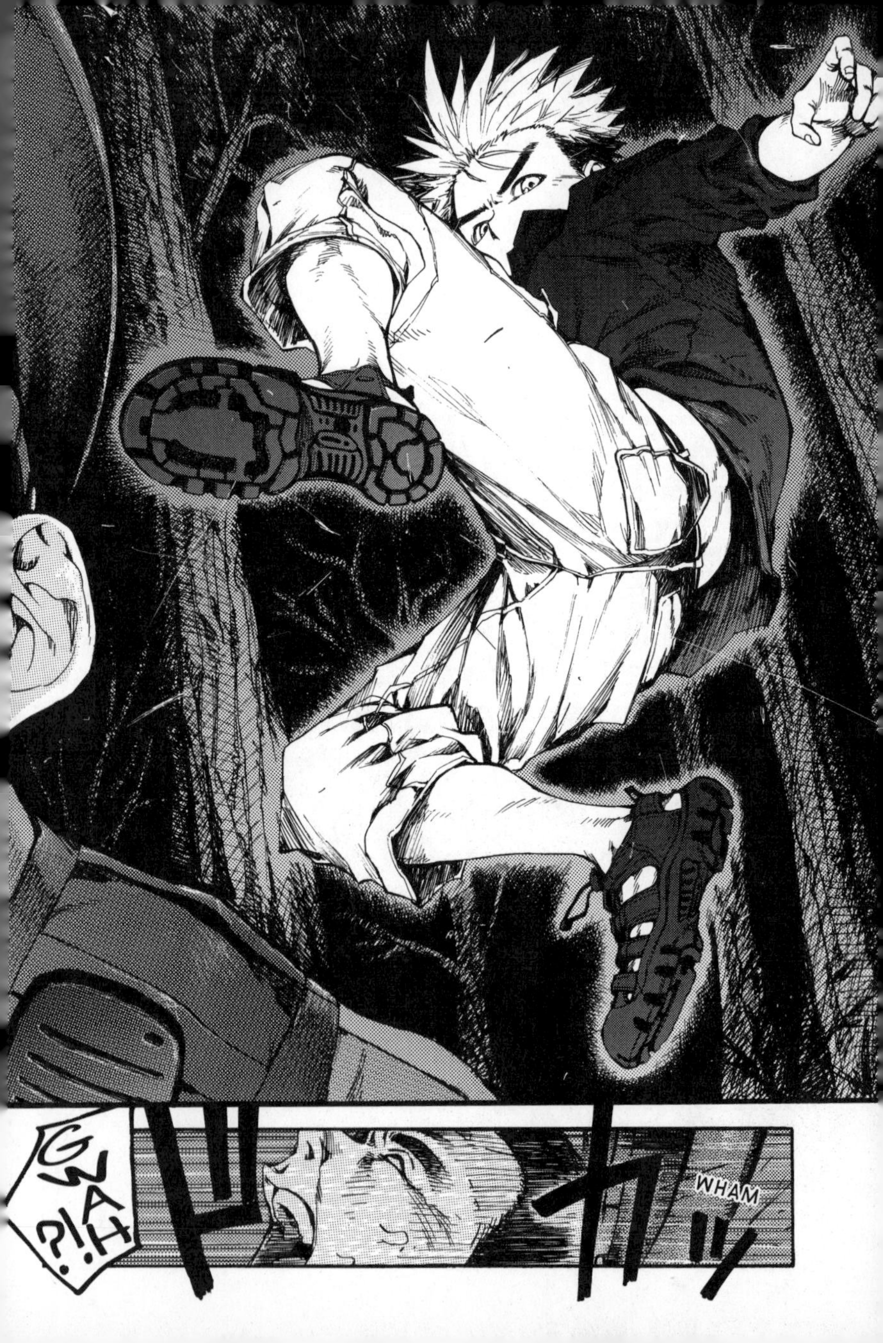
WHAM
GWAH?!

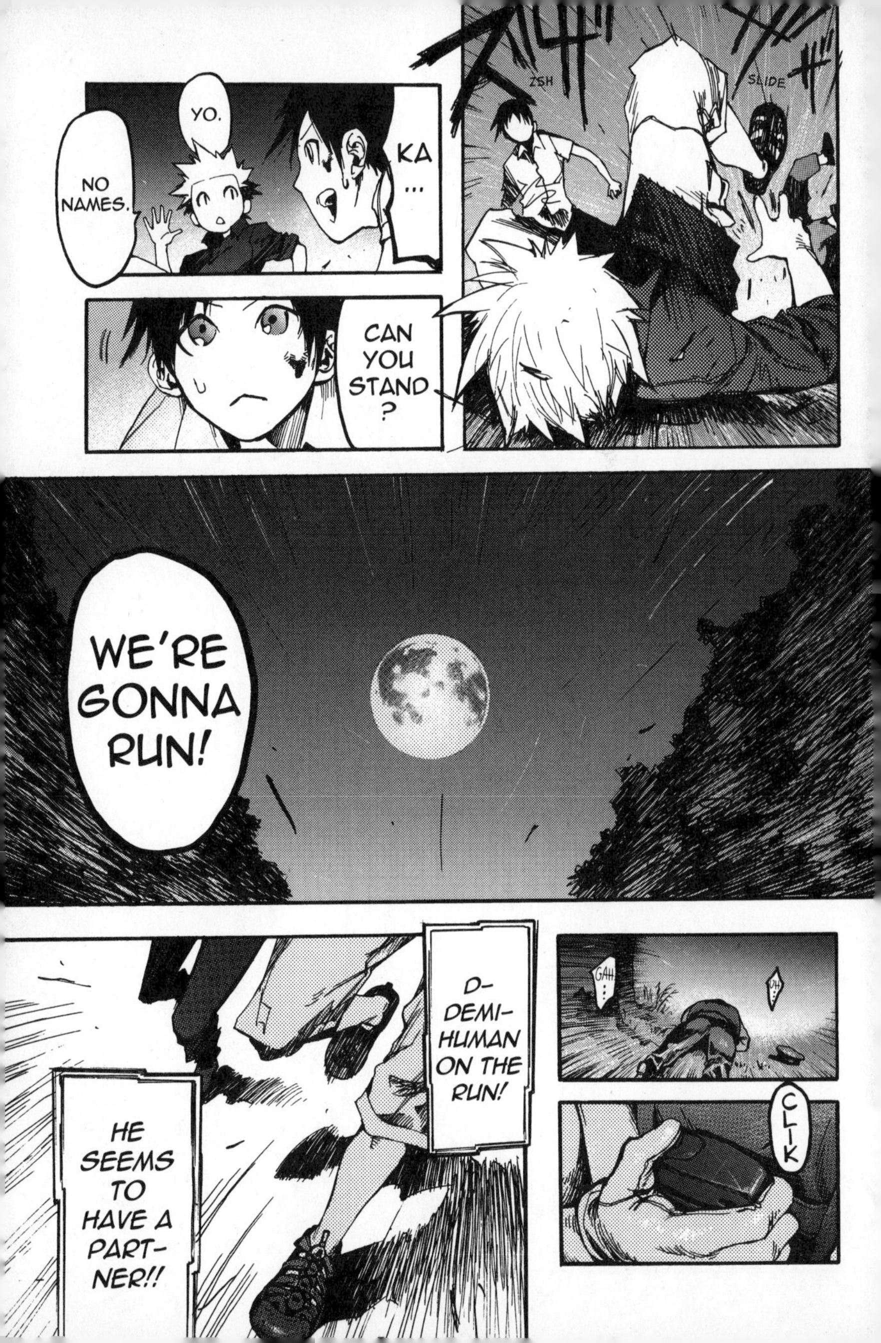
SLIDE
ZSH
KA...
YO.
NO NAMES.
CAN YOU STAND?
WE'RE GONNA RUN!
GAH...
OH
CLIK
D-DEMI-HUMAN ON THE RUN!
HE SEEMS TO HAVE A PARTNER!!

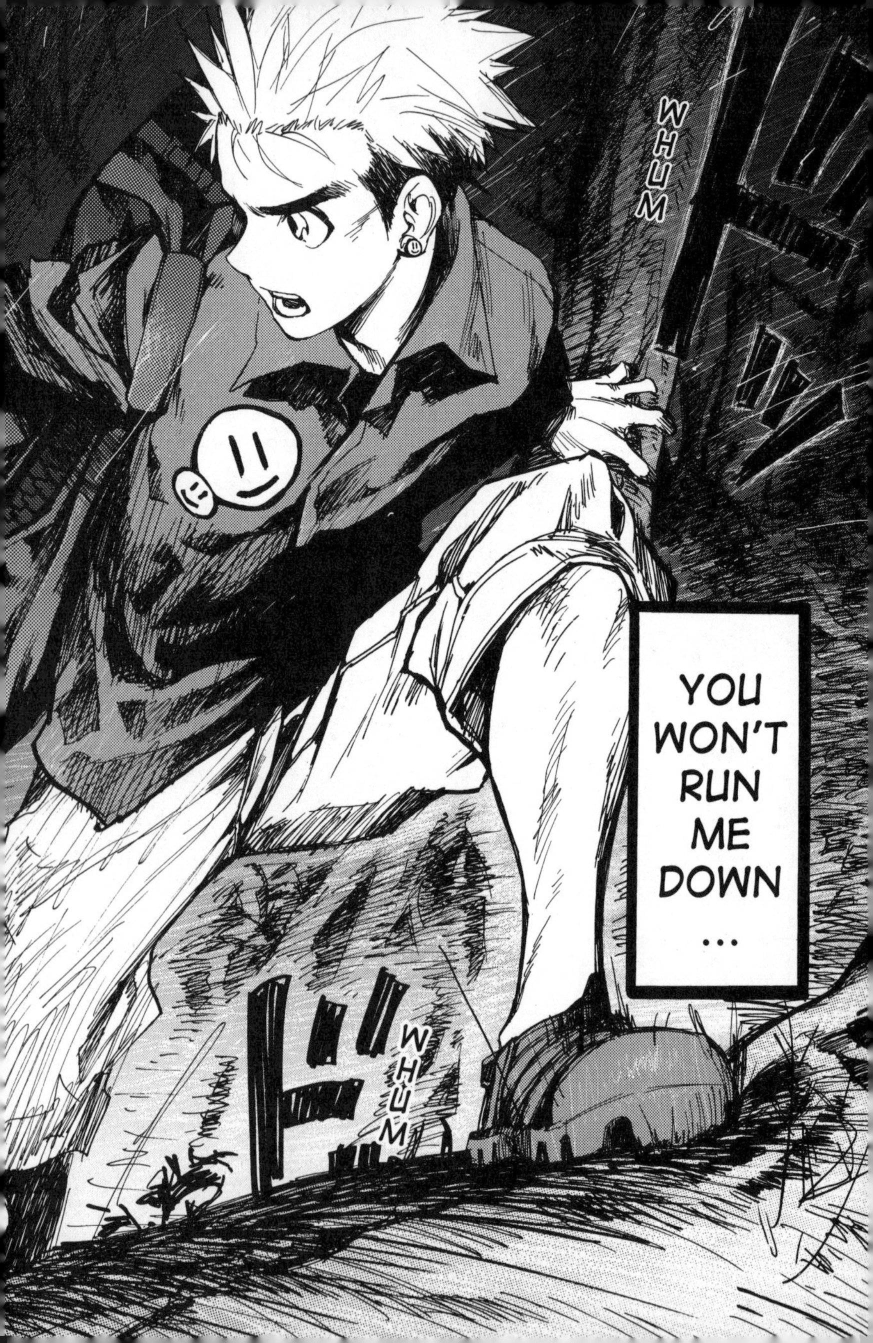
WHUM
YOU WON'T RUN ME DOWN ...
WHUM

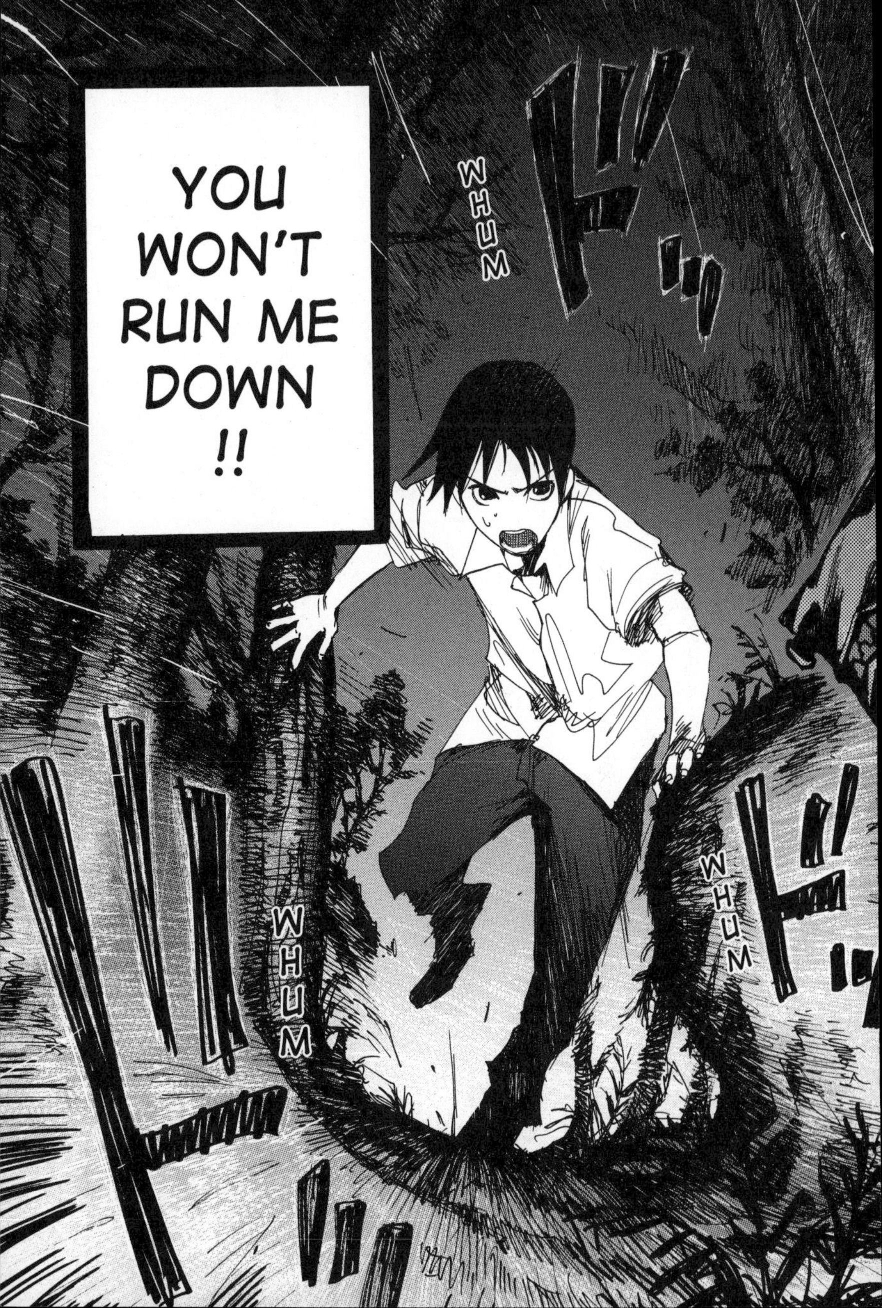
YOU WON'T RUN ME DOWN !!
WHUM
WHUM
WHUM

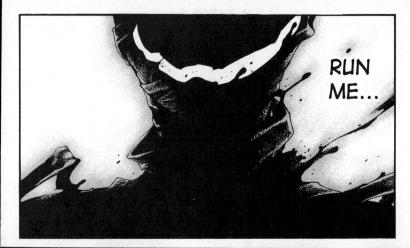

RUN
ME...

BA-
DUMP

Y-
YUP.

KEI!
DON'T
STOP.

WHUM

WHUM

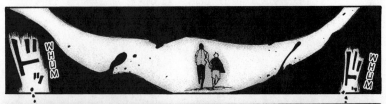

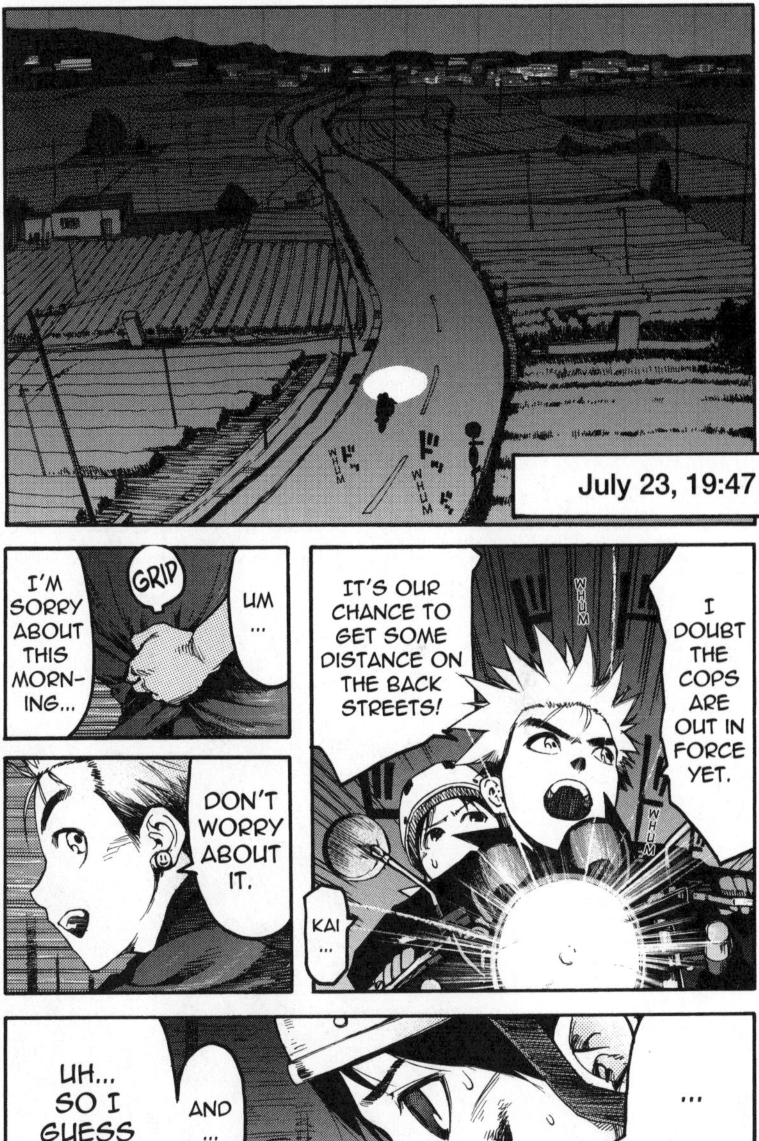
July 23, 19:47
WHUM
WHUM
WHUM
I DOUBT THE COPS ARE OUT IN FORCE YET.
IT'S OUR CHANCE TO GET SOME DISTANCE ON THE BACK STREETS!
KAI ...
UM ...
GRIP
I'M SORRY ABOUT THIS MORNING...
DON'T WORRY ABOUT IT.
...
AND ...
UH... SO I GUESS

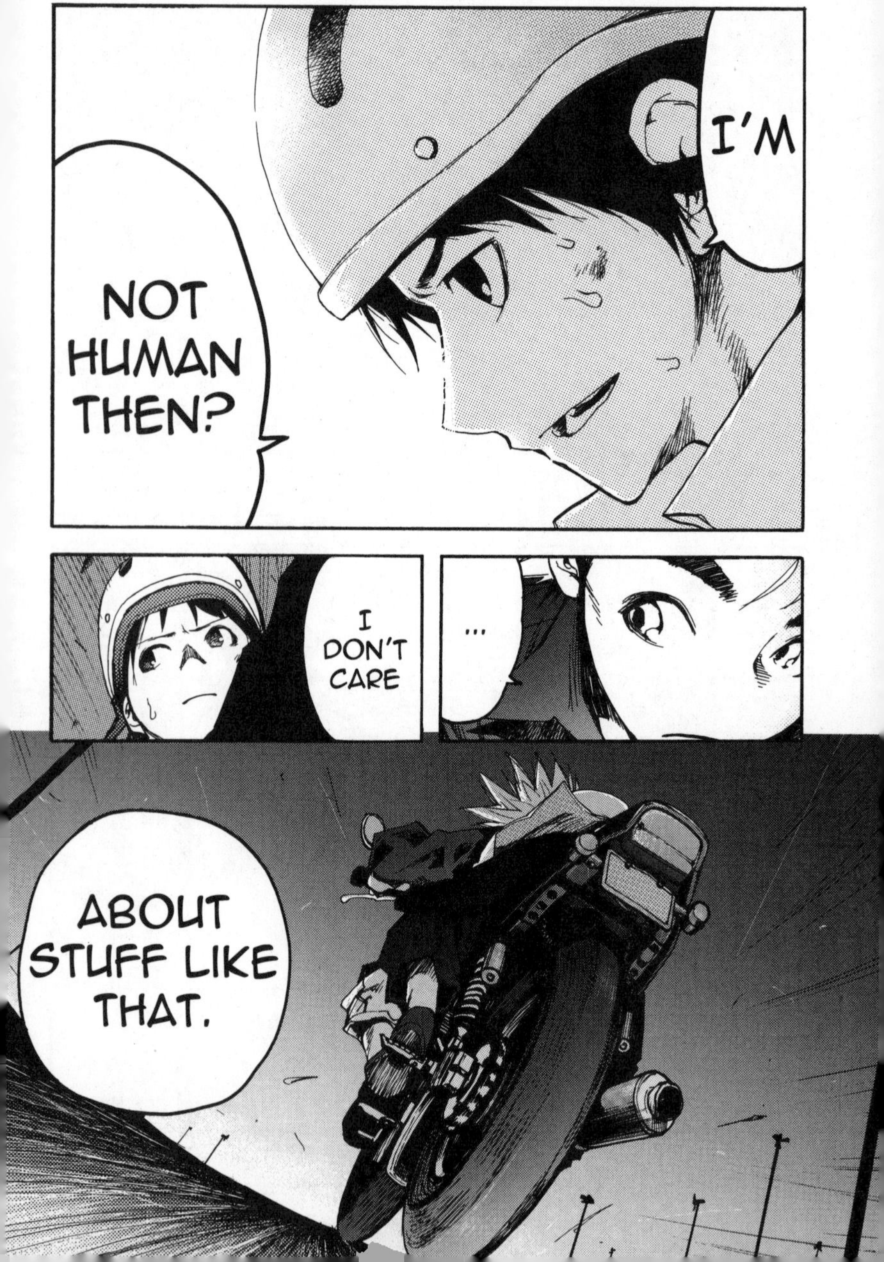
I'M
NOT HUMAN THEN?
...
I DON'T CARE
ABOUT STUFF LIKE THAT.

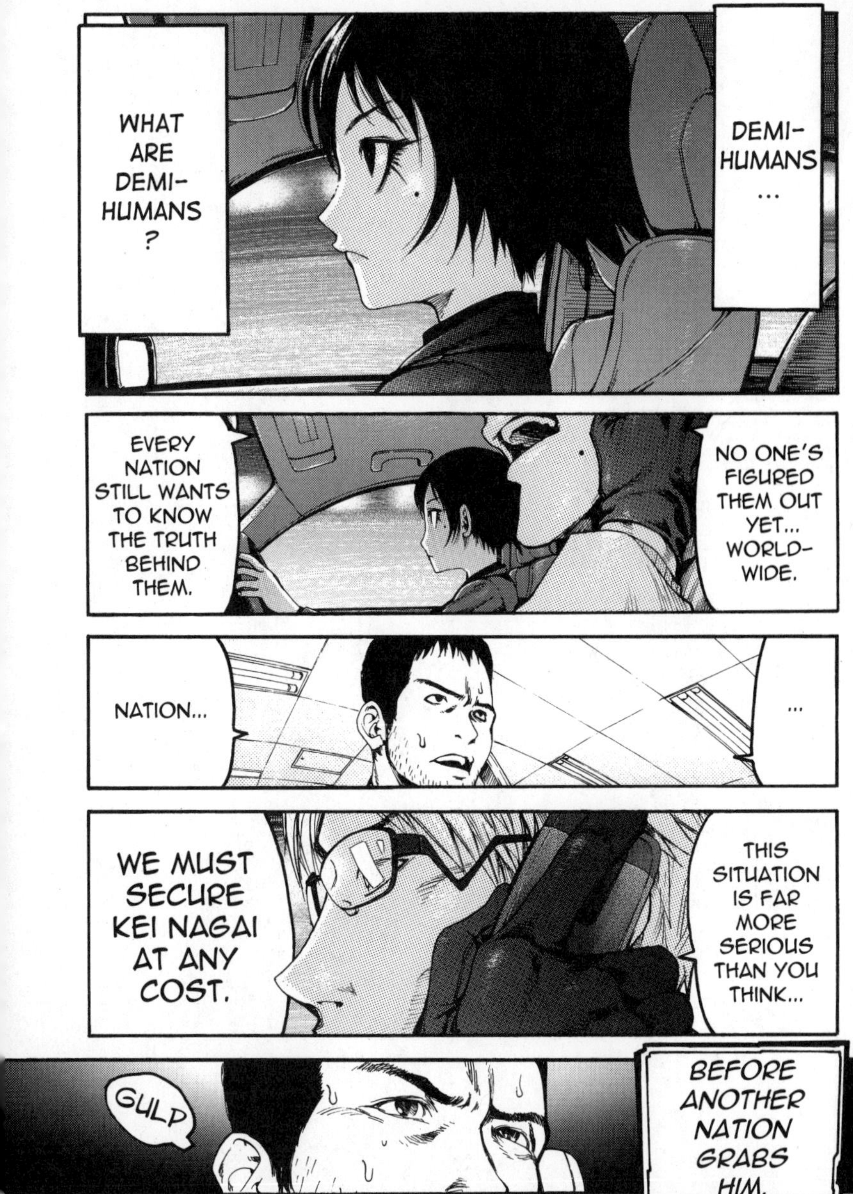
DEMI-HUMANS...
WHAT ARE DEMI-HUMANS?
NO ONE'S FIGURED THEM OUT YET... WORLD-WIDE.
EVERY NATION STILL WANTS TO KNOW THE TRUTH BEHIND THEM.
...
NATION...
THIS SITUATION IS FAR MORE SERIOUS THAN YOU THINK...
WE MUST SECURE KEI NAGAI AT ANY COST.
BEFORE ANOTHER NATION GRABS HIM.
GULP

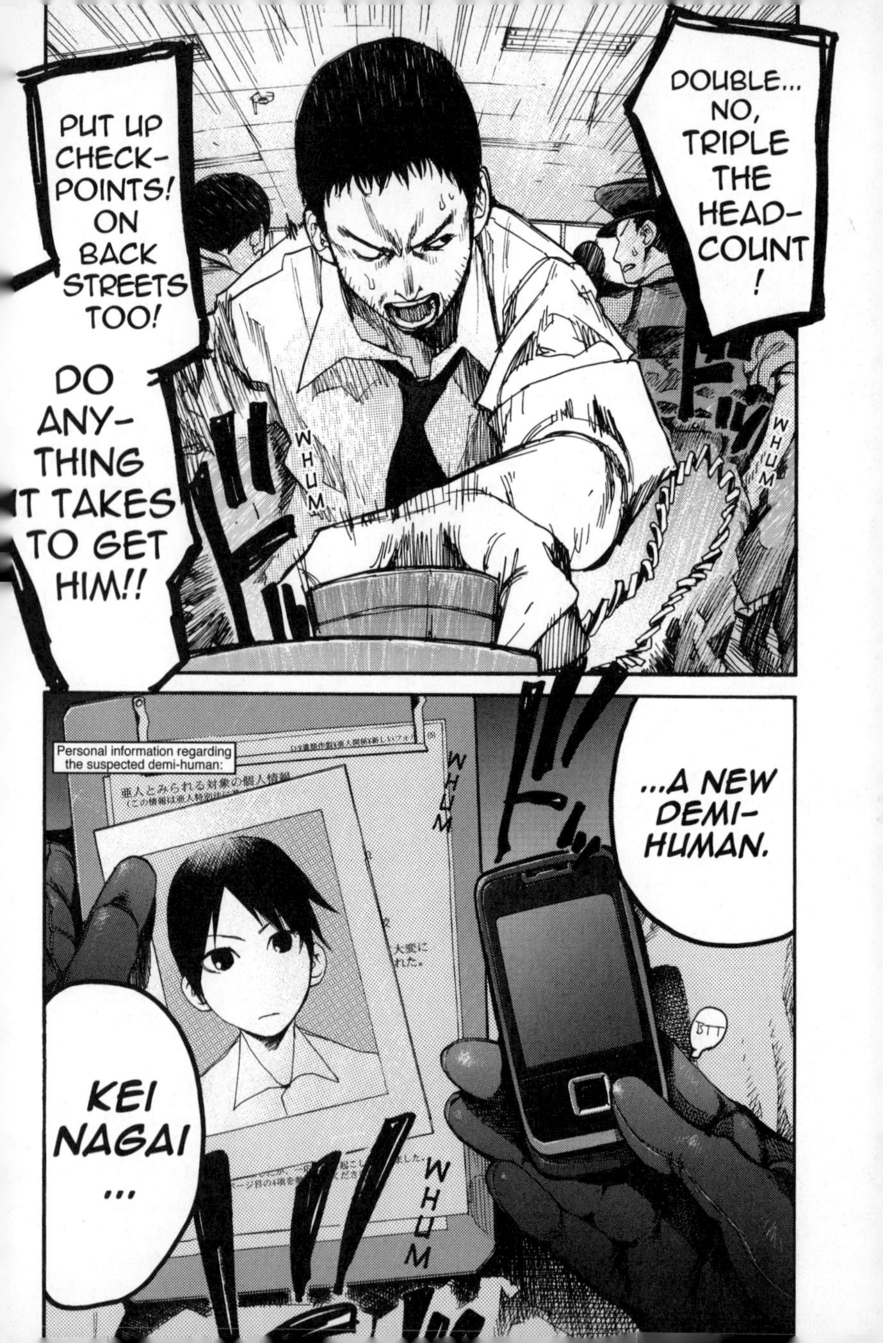
DOUBLE... NO, TRIPLE THE HEAD-COUNT!
PUT UP CHECK-POINTS! ON BACK STREETS TOO!
DO ANY-THING IT TAKES TO GET HIM!!
WHUM
WHUM
...A NEW DEMI-HUMAN.
WHUM
Personal information regarding the suspected demi-human:
BTT
KEI NAGAI...
WHUM

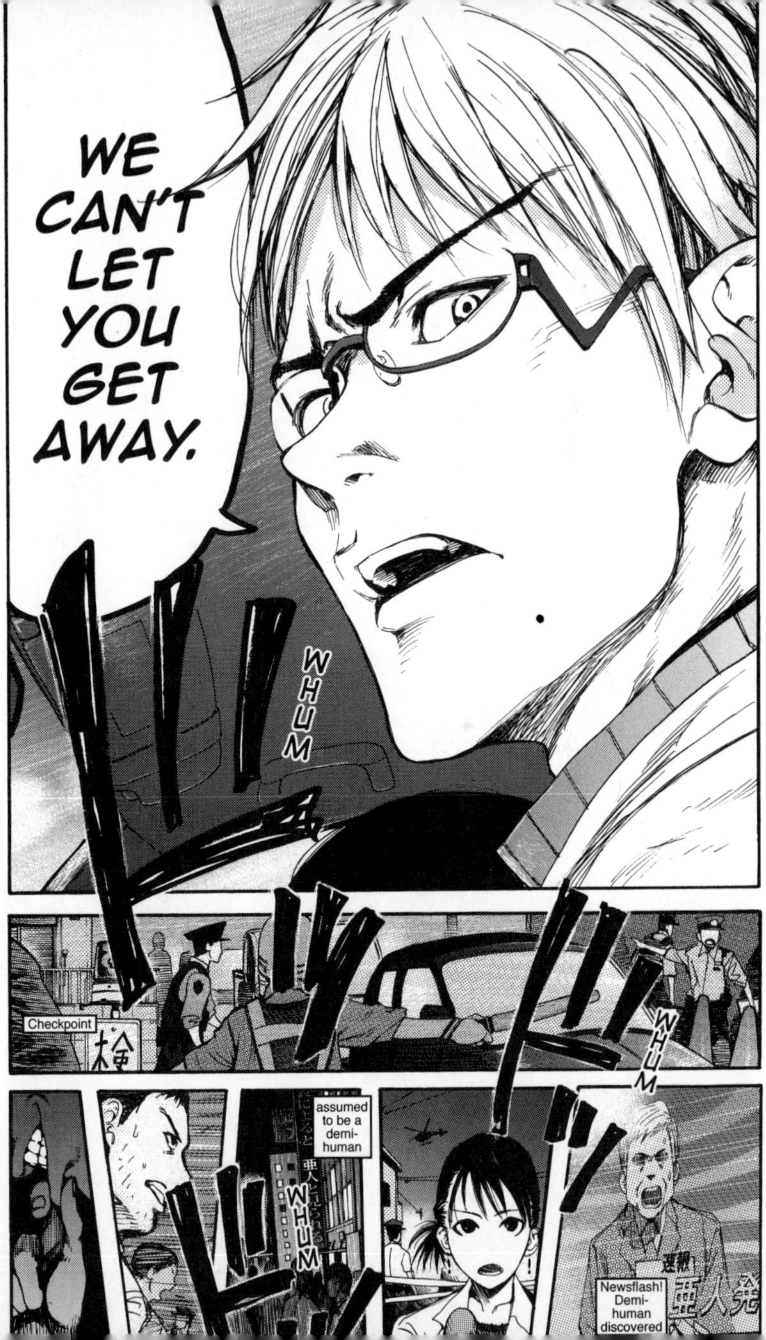
WE CAN'T LET YOU GET AWAY.
WHUM
WHUM
Checkpoint
Newsflash! Demi-human discovered
assumed to be a demi-human
WHUM

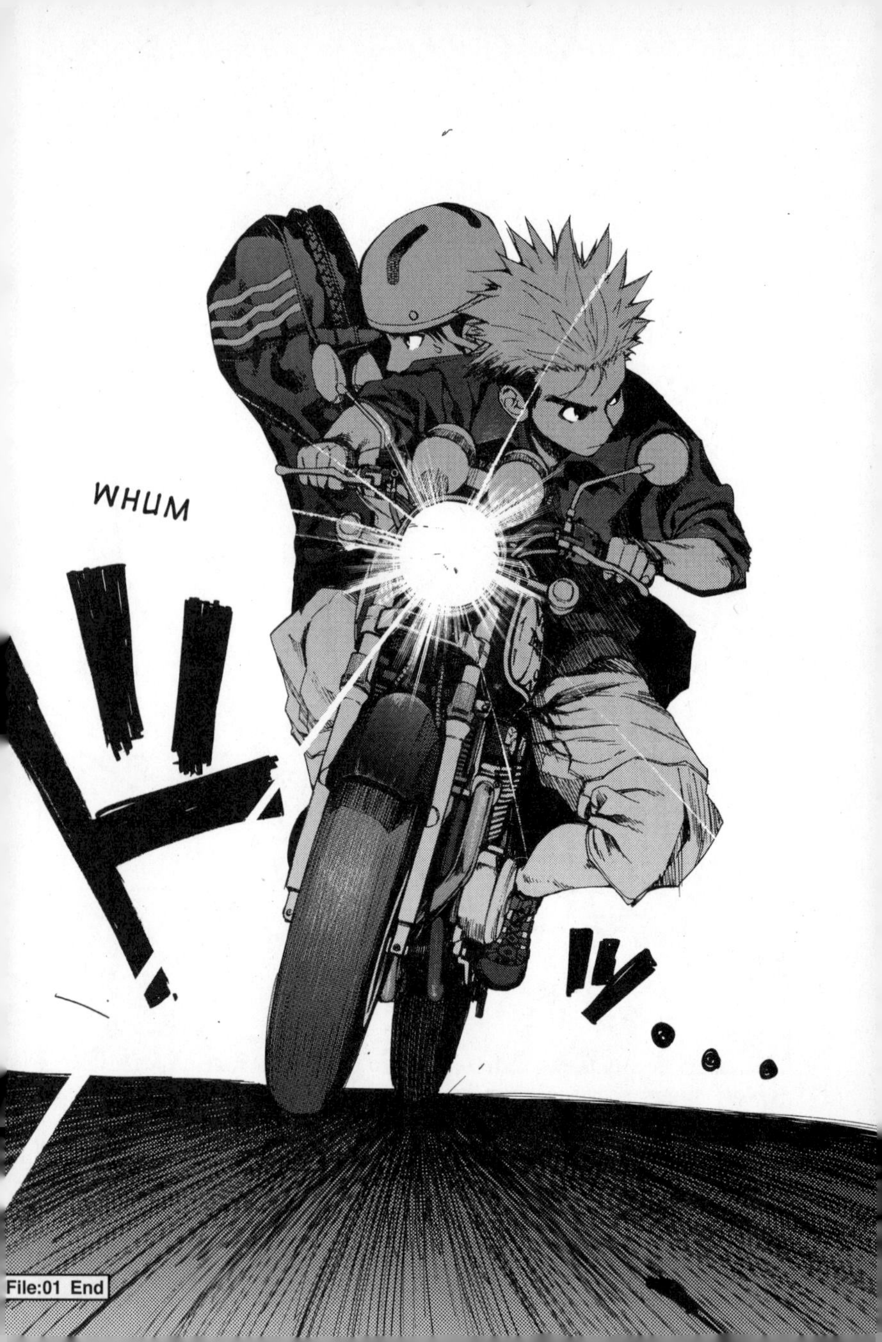
WHUM
File:01 End

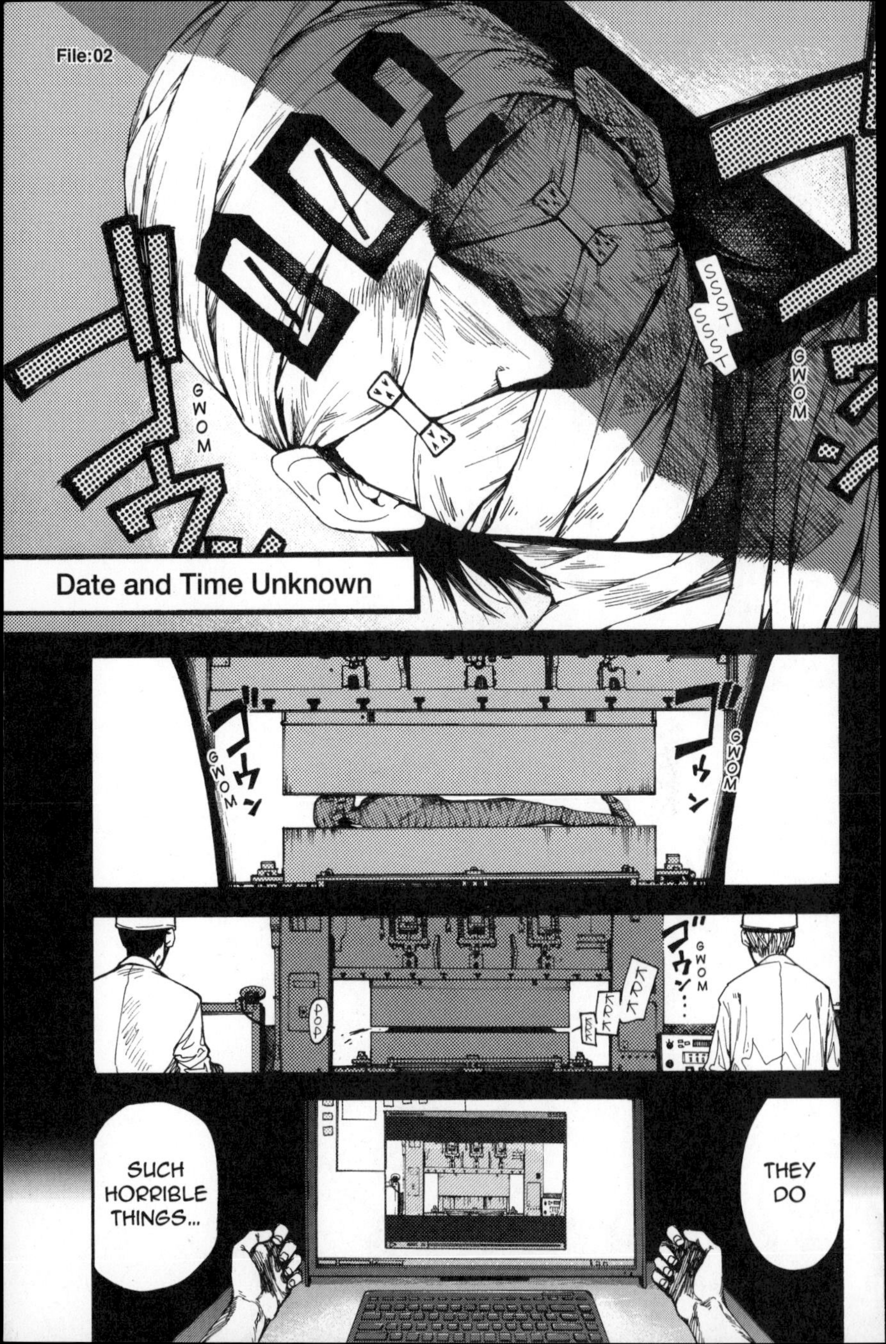
SSST
SSST
GWOM
GWOM
Date and Time Unknown
ゴウン
GWOM
ゴウン
GWOM
ゴウン…
GWOM
KRK
KRK
KRK
POP
THEY DO
SUCH HORRIBLE THINGS...

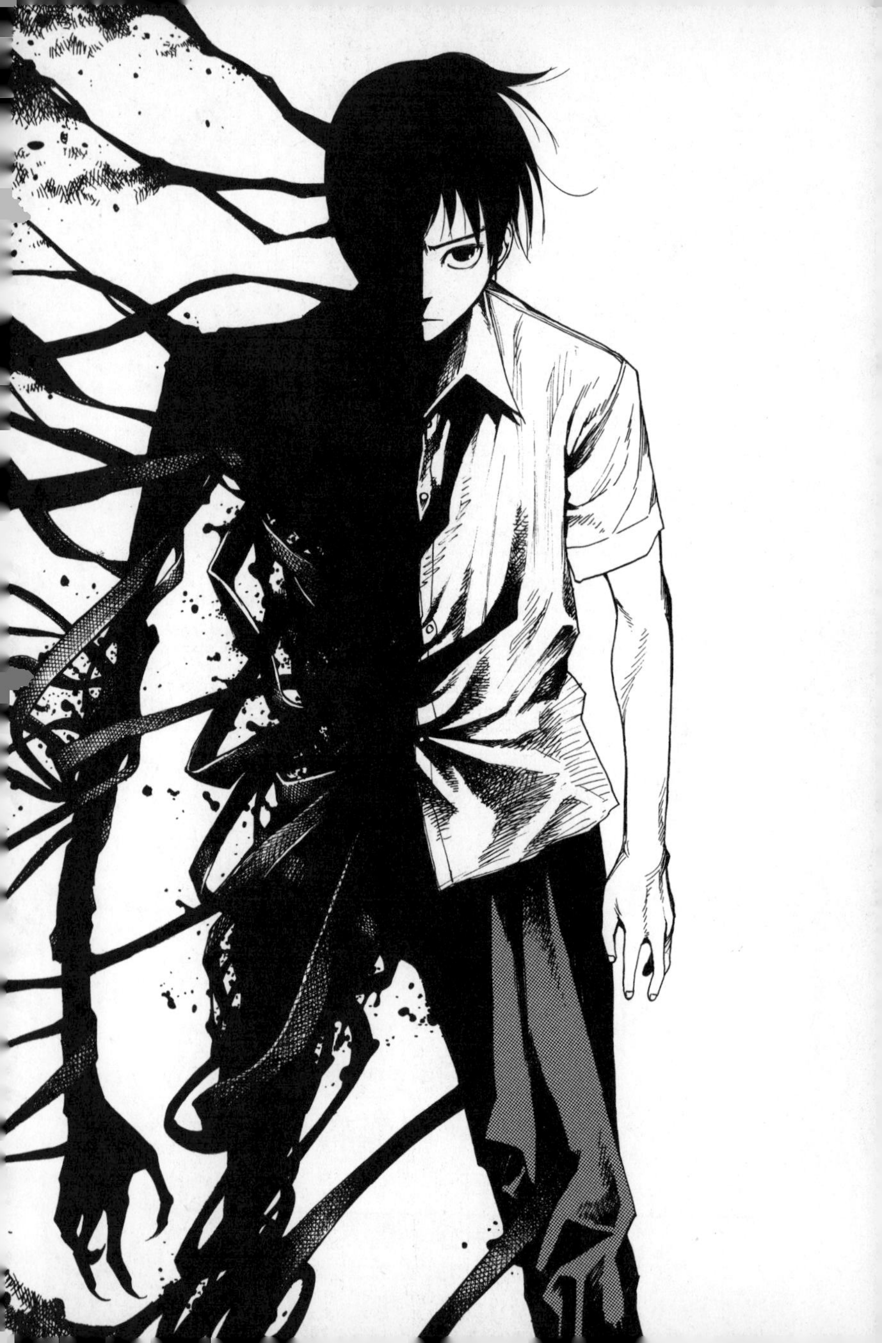

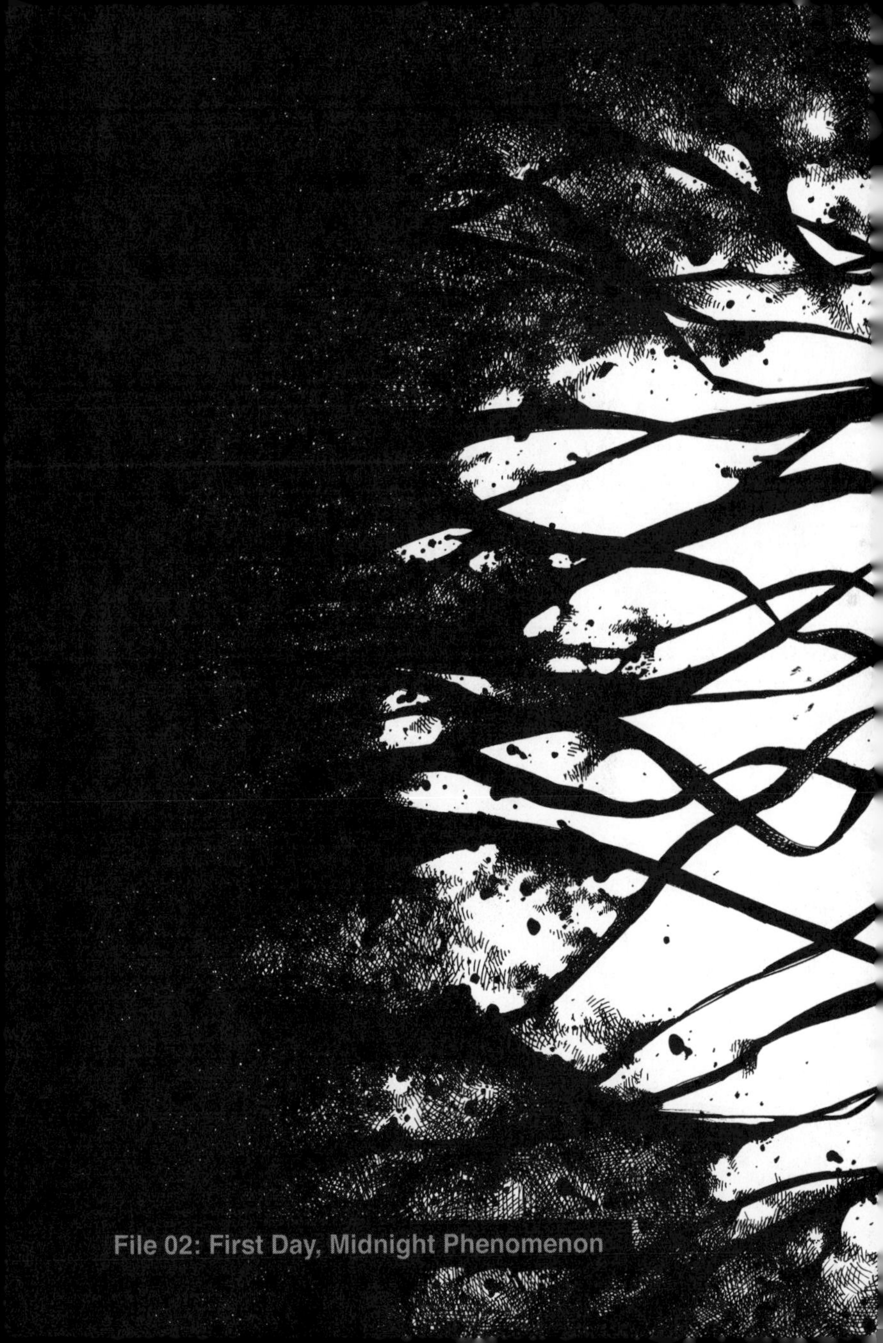

File 02: First Day, Midnight Phenomenon

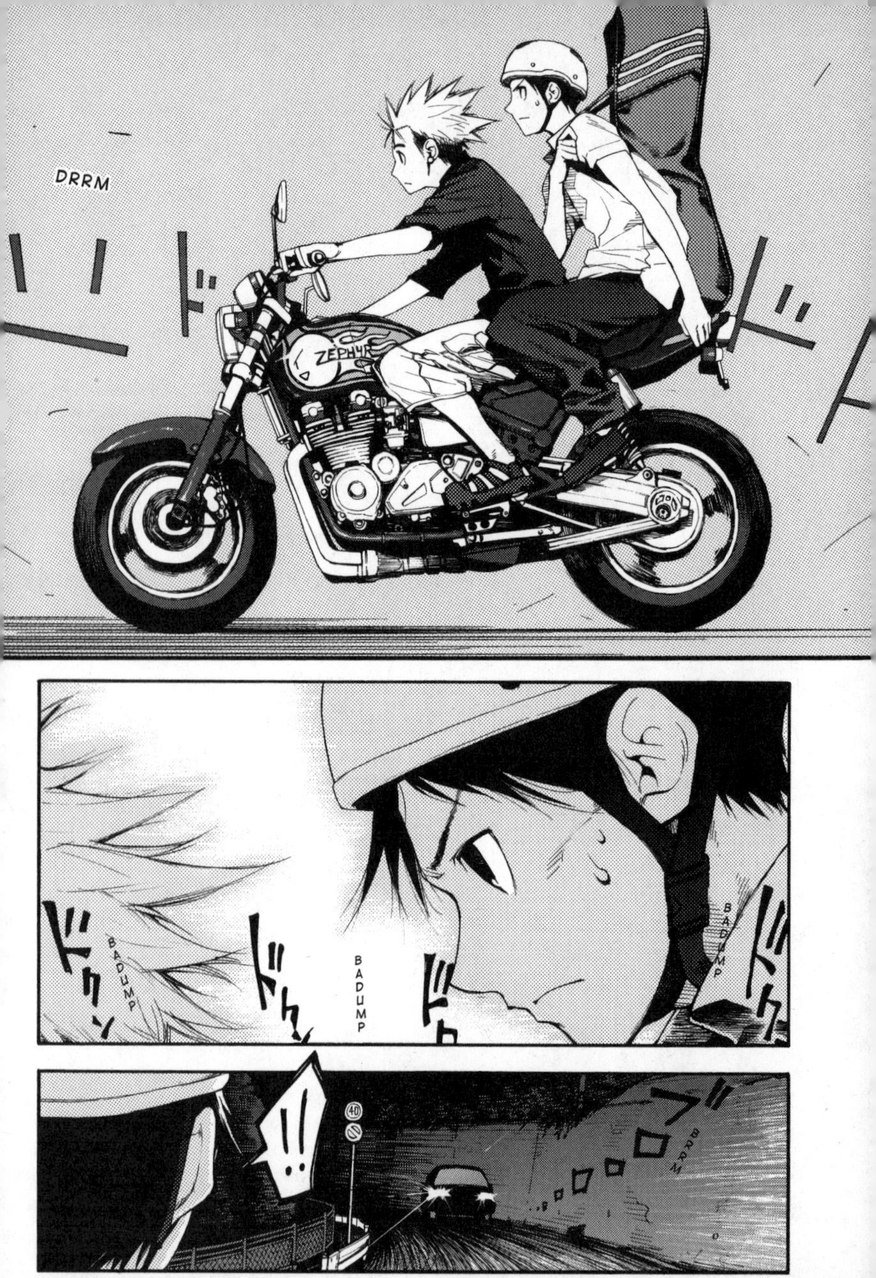
DRRM
ZEPHYR
BADUMP
BADUMP
BADUMP
BRRM
!!

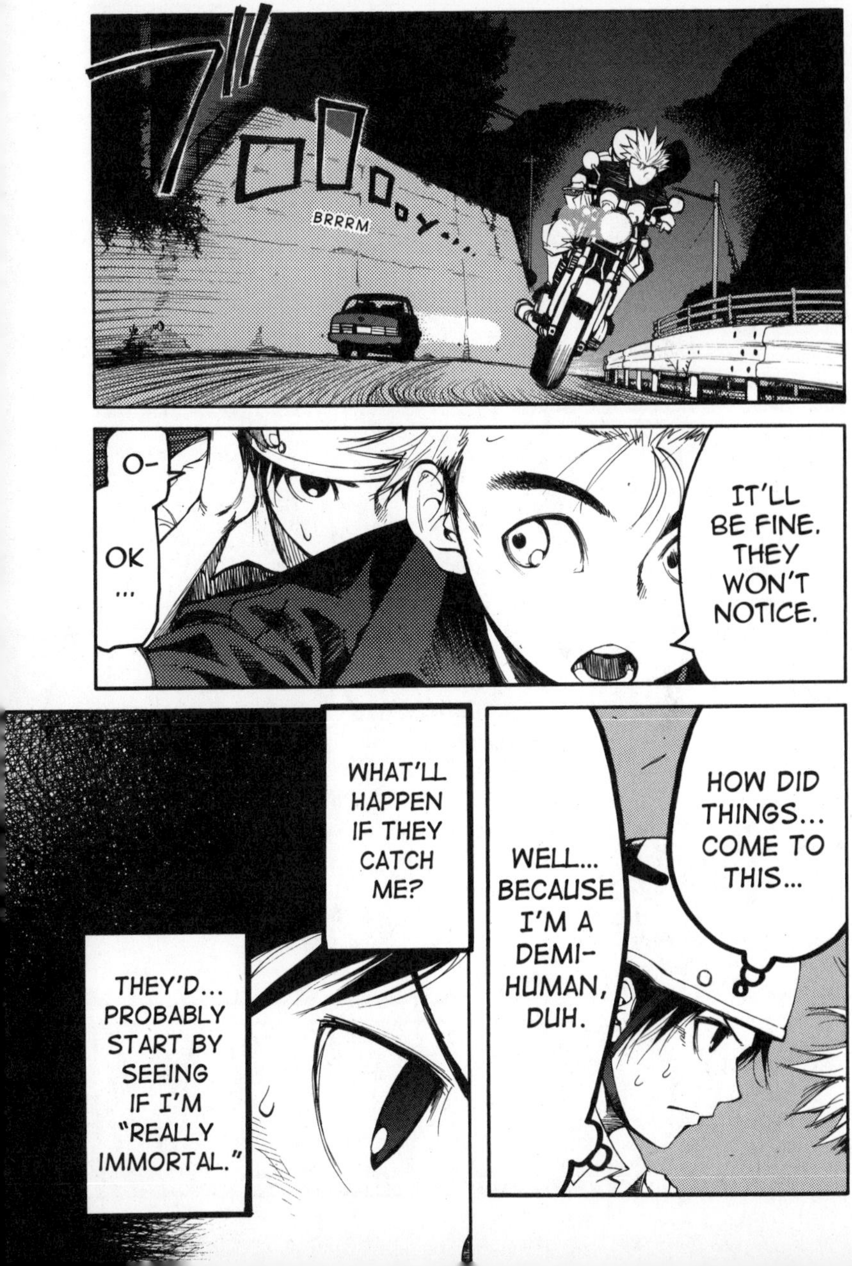
BRRRM
IT'LL BE FINE. THEY WON'T NOTICE.
O- OK ...
HOW DID THINGS... COME TO THIS...
WELL... BECAUSE I'M A DEMI-HUMAN, DUH.
WHAT'LL HAPPEN IF THEY CATCH ME?
THEY'D... PROBABLY START BY SEEING IF I'M "REALLY IMMORTAL."

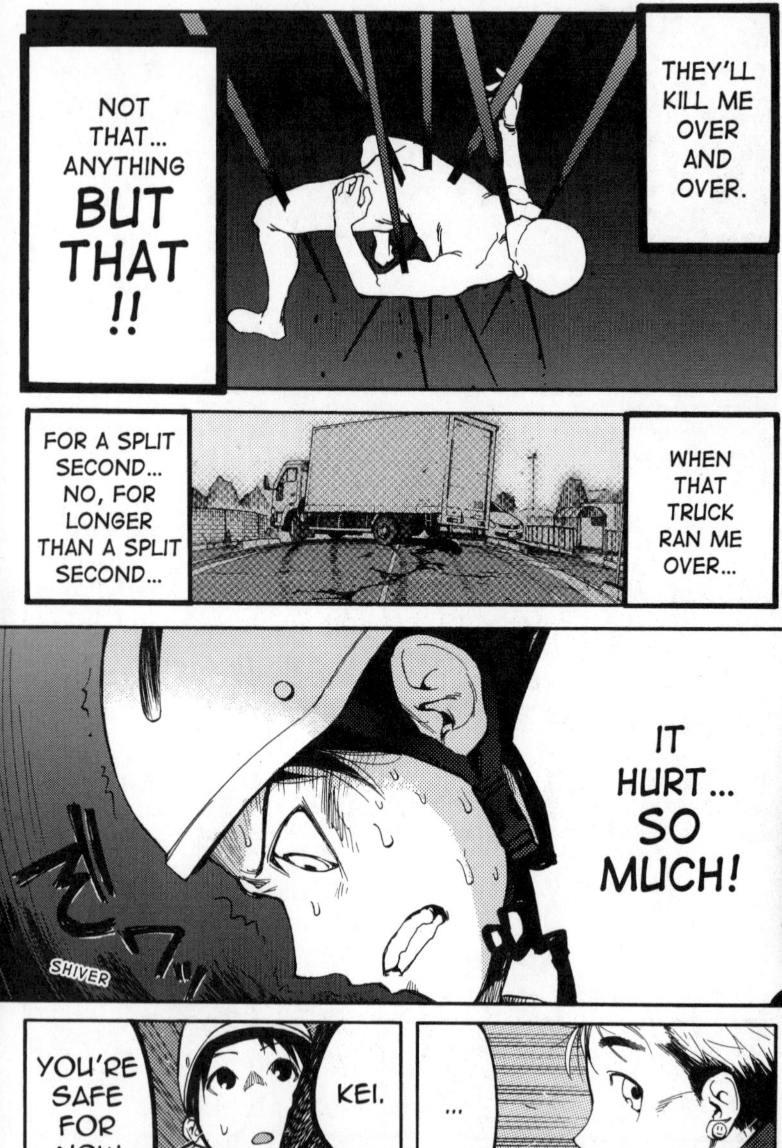

THEY'LL KILL ME OVER AND OVER.
NOT THAT... ANYTHING BUT THAT !!
WHEN THAT TRUCK RAN ME OVER...
FOR A SPLIT SECOND... NO, FOR LONGER THAN A SPLIT SECOND...
IT HURT... SO MUCH!
SHIVER
...
KEI.
YOU'RE SAFE FOR NOW.

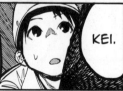

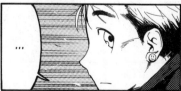

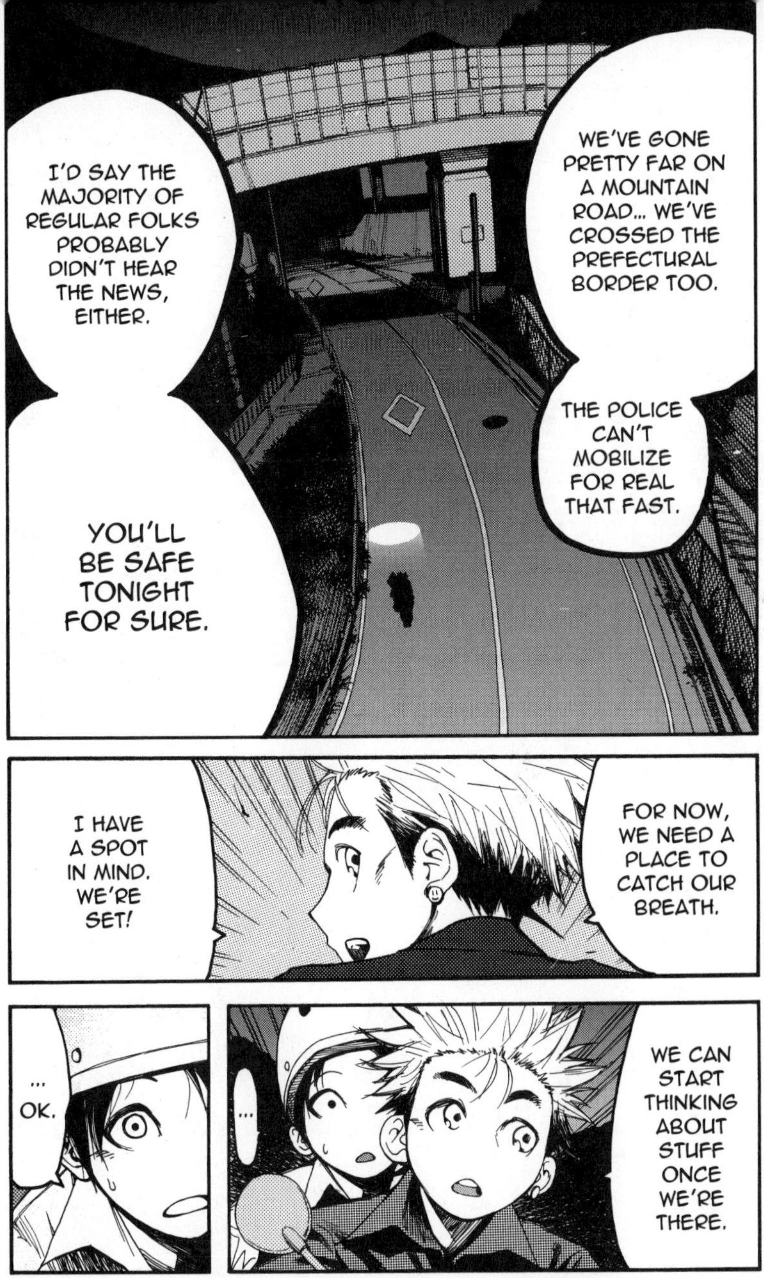
WE'VE GONE PRETTY FAR ON A MOUNTAIN ROAD... WE'VE CROSSED THE PREFECTURAL BORDER TOO.
THE POLICE CAN'T MOBILIZE FOR REAL THAT FAST.
I'D SAY THE MAJORITY OF REGULAR FOLKS PROBABLY DIDN'T HEAR THE NEWS, EITHER.
YOU'LL BE SAFE TONIGHT FOR SURE.
FOR NOW, WE NEED A PLACE TO CATCH OUR BREATH.
I HAVE A SPOT IN MIND. WE'RE SET!
WE CAN START THINKING ABOUT STUFF ONCE WE'RE THERE.
...
... OK.

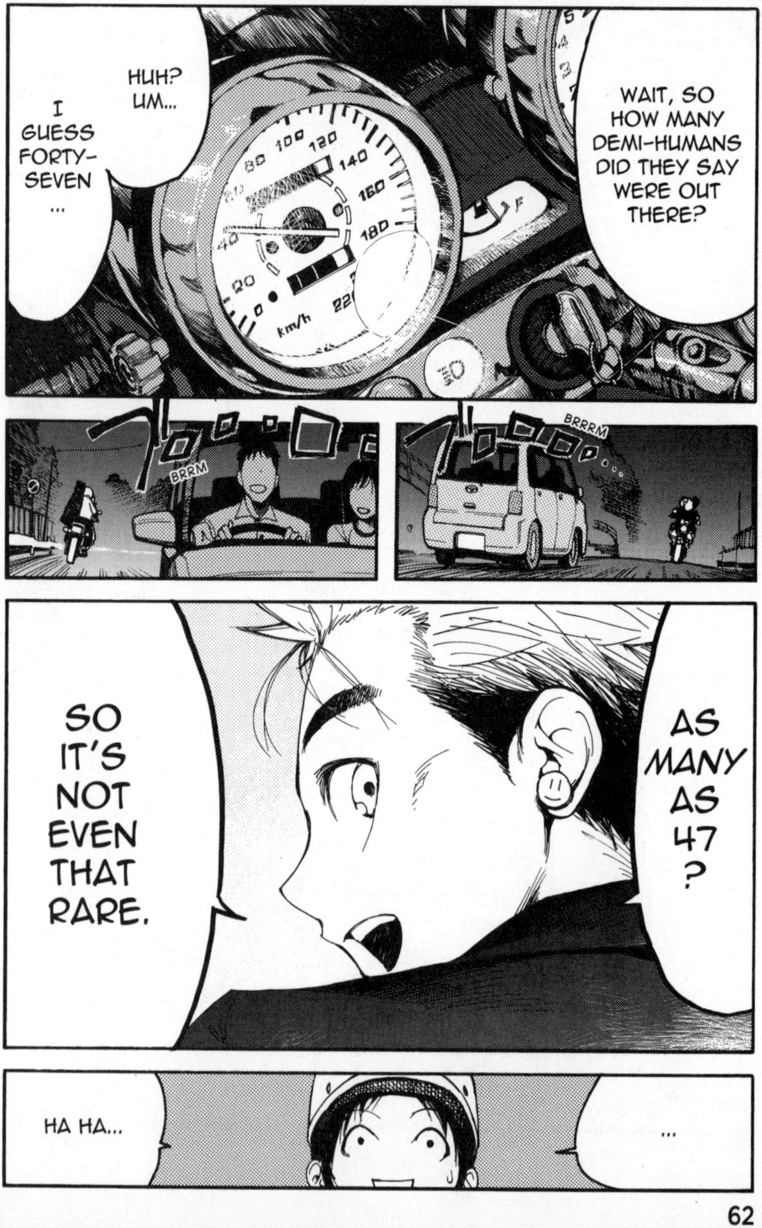
WAIT, SO HOW MANY DEMI-HUMANS DID THEY SAY WERE OUT THERE?
HUH? UM...
I GUESS FORTY-SEVEN ...
BRRRM
BRRM
AS MANY AS 47 ?
SO IT'S NOT EVEN THAT RARE.
...
HA HA...

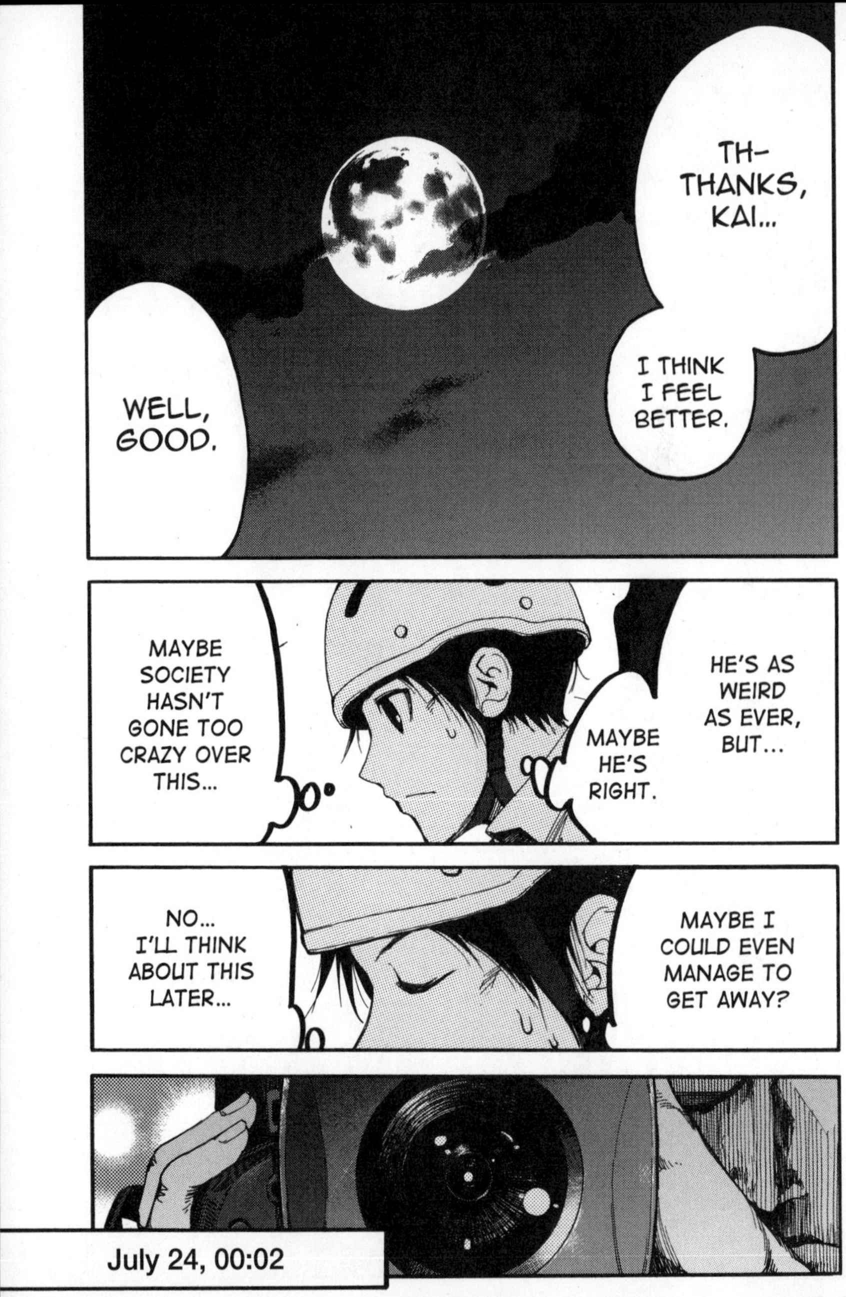
TH- THANKS, KAI...
I THINK I FEEL BETTER.
WELL, GOOD.
HE'S AS WEIRD AS EVER, BUT...
MAYBE HE'S RIGHT.
MAYBE SOCIETY HASN'T GONE TOO CRAZY OVER THIS...
MAYBE I COULD EVEN MANAGE TO GET AWAY?
NO... I'LL THINK ABOUT THIS LATER...
July 24, 00:02

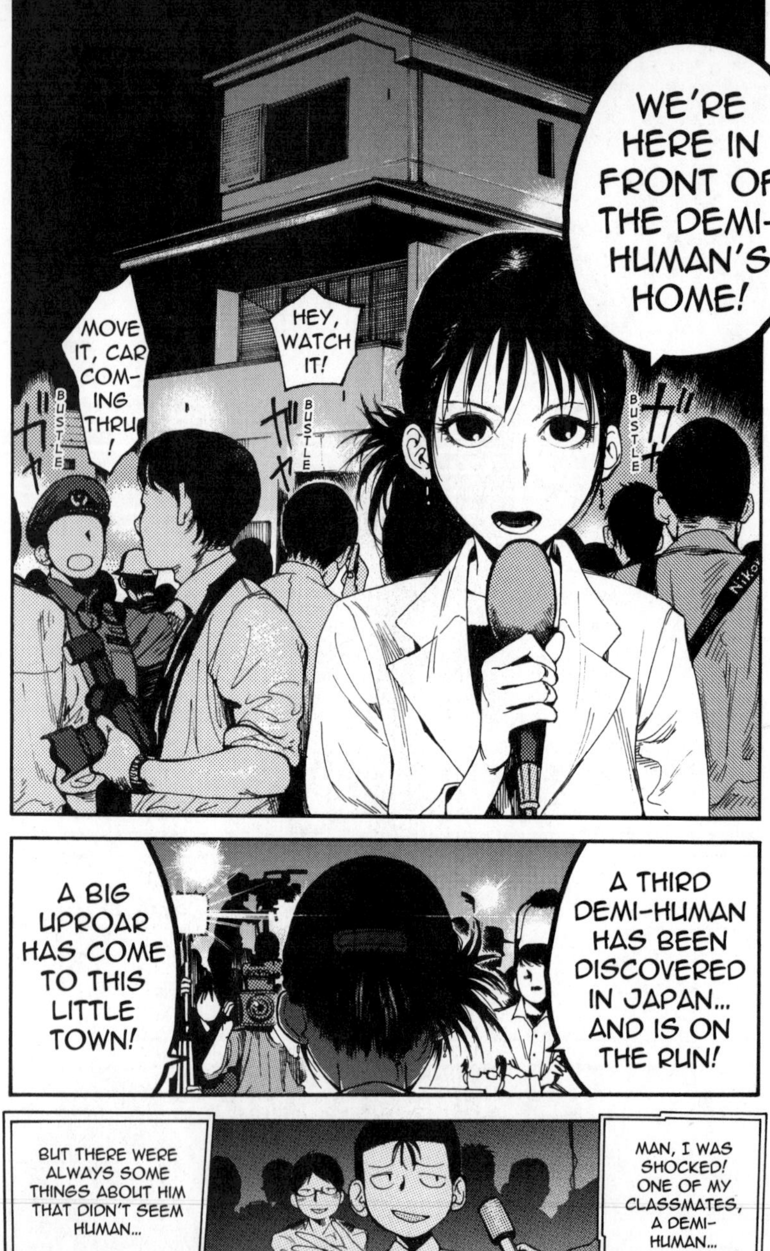
WE'RE HERE IN FRONT OF THE DEMI-HUMAN'S HOME!
BUSTLE
HEY, WATCH IT!
BUSTLE
MOVE IT, CAR COMING THRU!
BUSTLE
A THIRD DEMI-HUMAN HAS BEEN DISCOVERED IN JAPAN... AND IS ON THE RUN!
A BIG UPROAR HAS COME TO THIS LITTLE TOWN!
MAN, I WAS SHOCKED! ONE OF MY CLASSMATES, A DEMI-HUMAN...
BUT THERE WERE ALWAYS SOME THINGS ABOUT HIM THAT DIDN'T SEEM HUMAN...

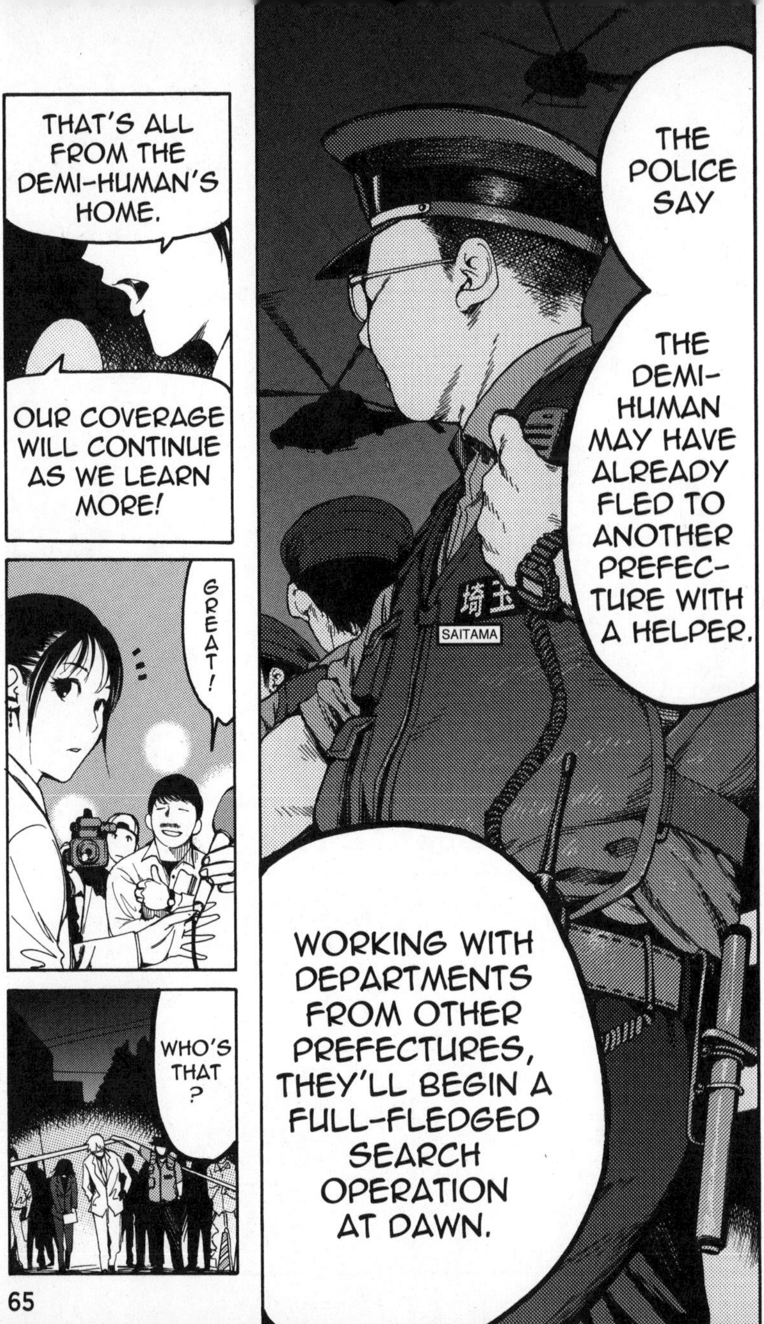
THE POLICE SAY
THE DEMI-HUMAN MAY HAVE ALREADY FLED TO ANOTHER PREFECTURE WITH A HELPER.
SAITAMA
WORKING WITH DEPARTMENTS FROM OTHER PREFECTURES, THEY'LL BEGIN A FULL-FLEDGED SEARCH OPERATION AT DAWN.
THAT'S ALL FROM THE DEMI-HUMAN'S HOME.
OUR COVERAGE WILL CONTINUE AS WE LEARN MORE!
GREAT!
WHO'S THAT?

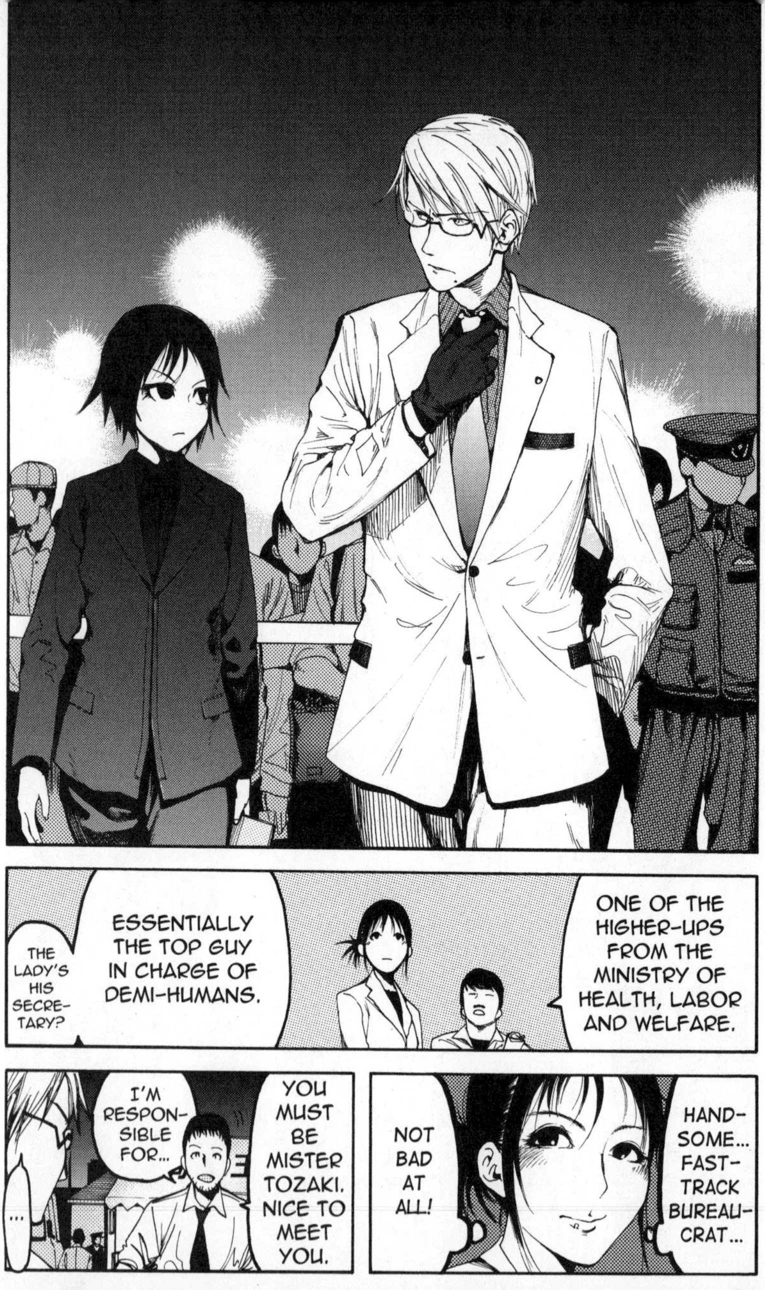
ONE OF THE HIGHER-UPS FROM THE MINISTRY OF HEALTH, LABOR AND WELFARE.
ESSENTIALLY THE TOP GUY IN CHARGE OF DEMI-HUMANS.
THE LADY'S HIS SECRETARY?
HANDSOME... FAST-TRACK BUREAUCRAT...
NOT BAD AT ALL!
YOU MUST BE MISTER TOZAKI. NICE TO MEET YOU.
I'M RESPONSIBLE FOR...
...

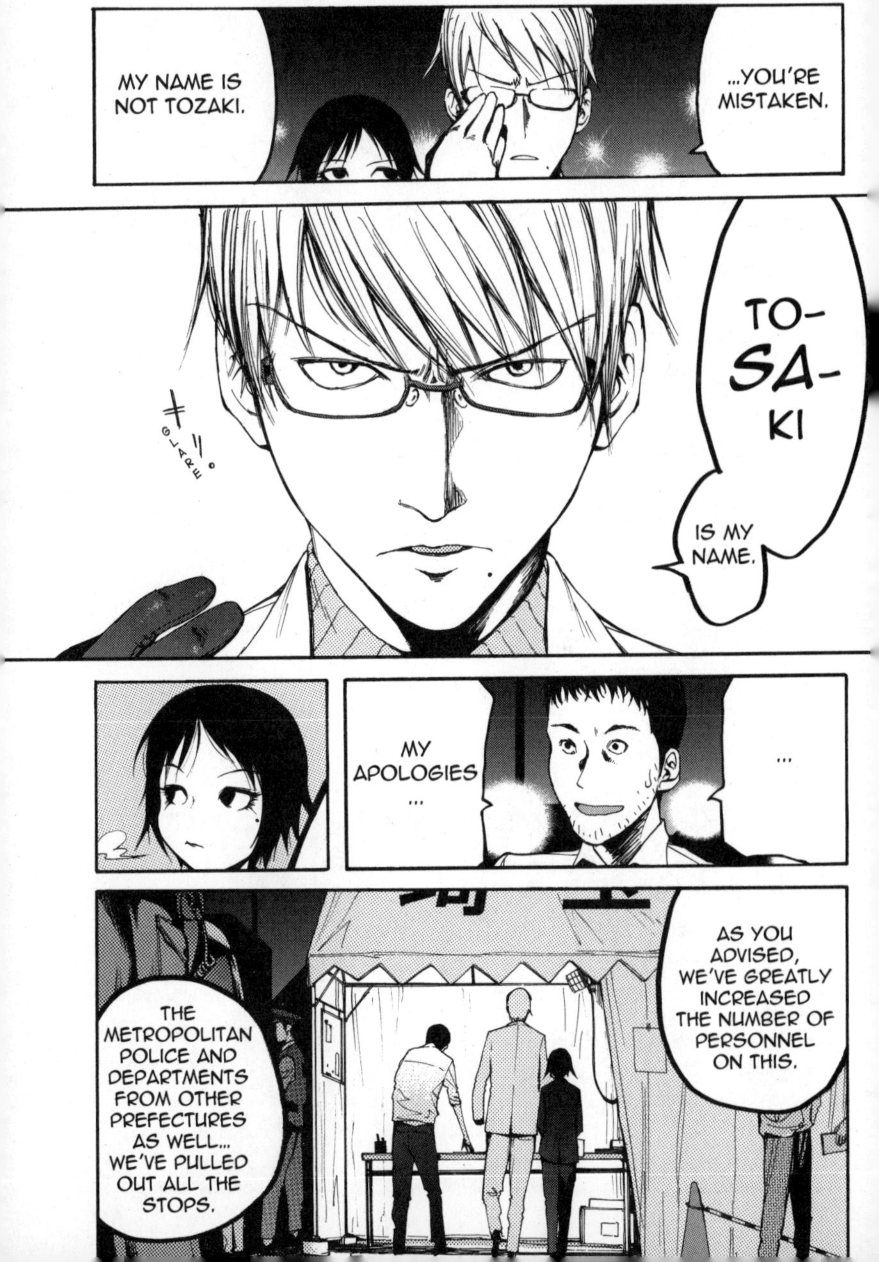
...YOU'RE MISTAKEN.
MY NAME IS NOT TOZAKI.
TO-SA-KI
IS MY NAME.
GLARE
...
MY APOLOGIES ...
AS YOU ADVISED, WE'VE GREATLY INCREASED THE NUMBER OF PERSONNEL ON THIS.
THE METROPOLITAN POLICE AND DEPARTMENTS FROM OTHER PREFECTURES AS WELL... WE'VE PULLED OUT ALL THE STOPS.

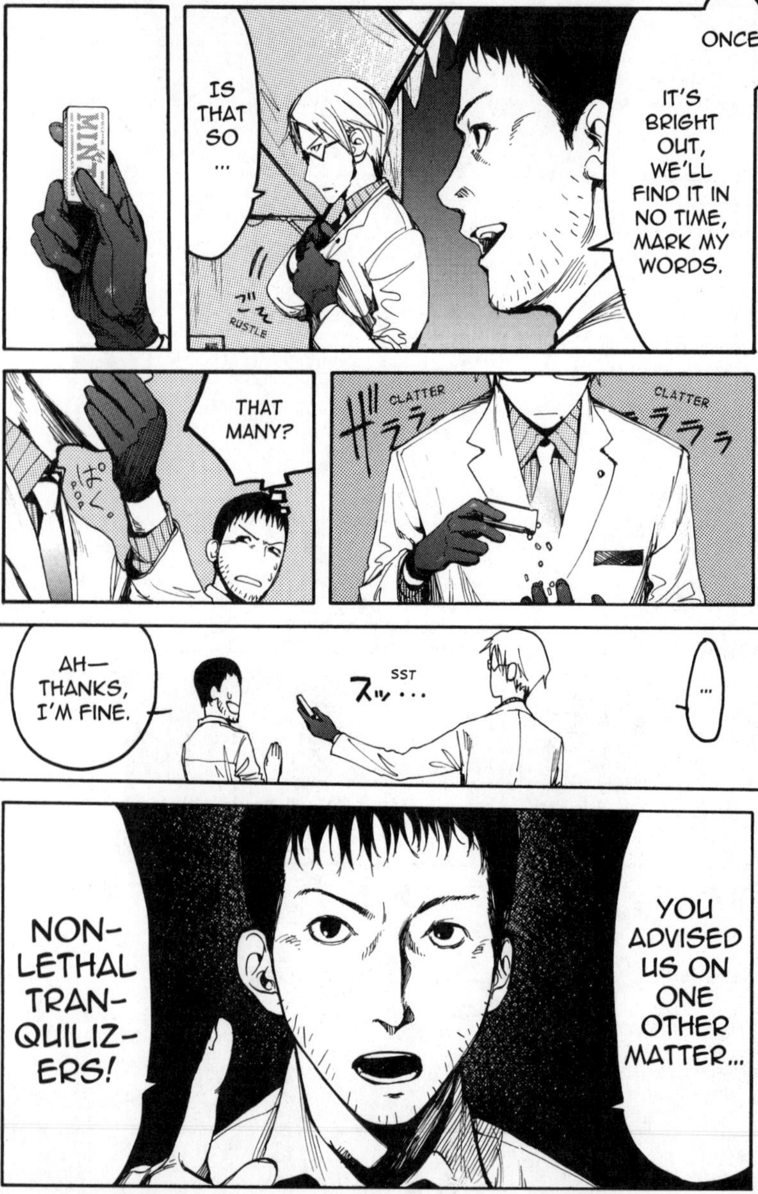
ONCE
IT'S BRIGHT OUT, WE'LL FIND IT IN NO TIME, MARK MY WORDS.
IS THAT SO ...
RUSTLE
MINT
CLATTER
CLATTER
THAT MANY?
POP
...
SST
スッ...
AH— THANKS, I'M FINE.
YOU ADVISED US ON ONE OTHER MATTER...
NON-LETHAL TRAN-QUILIZ-ERS!

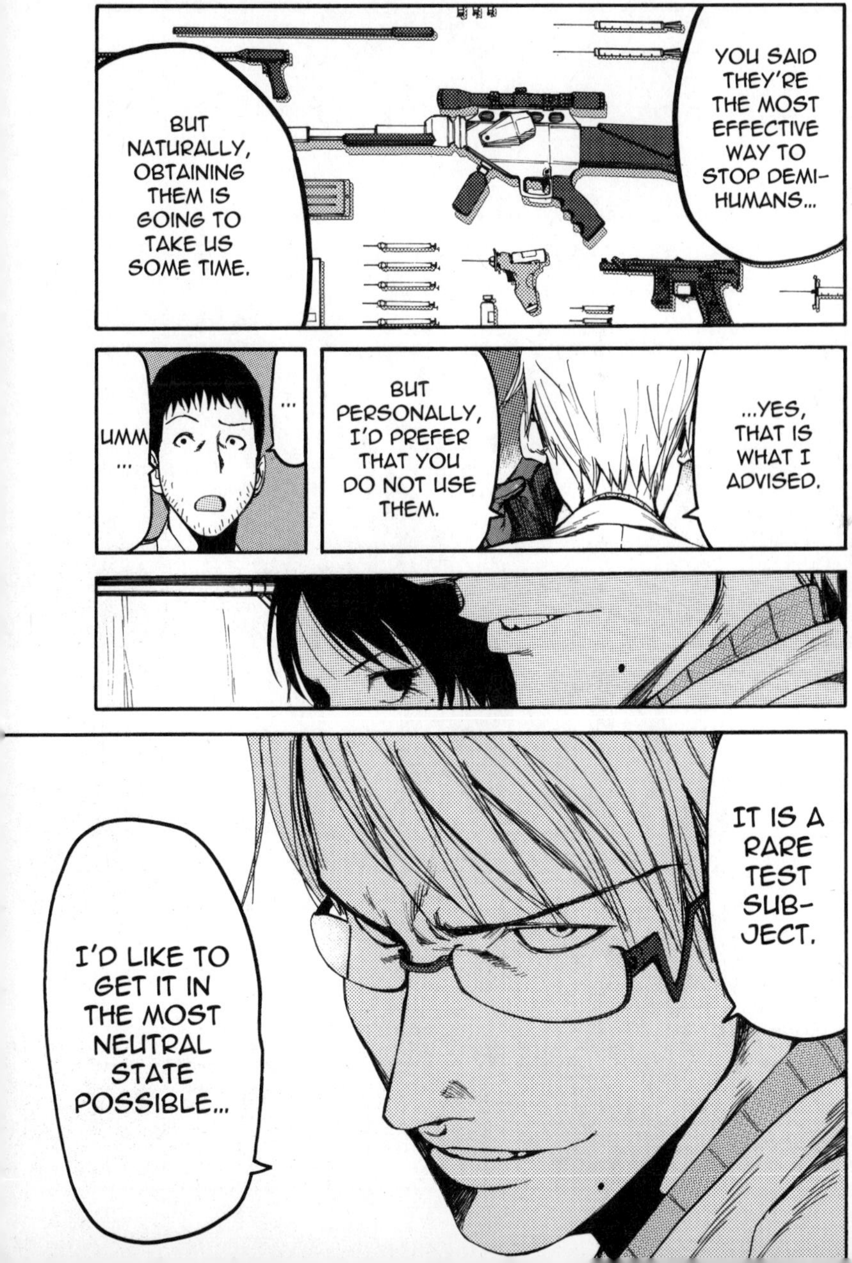
YOU SAID THEY'RE THE MOST EFFECTIVE WAY TO STOP DEMI-HUMANS...
BUT NATURALLY, OBTAINING THEM IS GOING TO TAKE US SOME TIME.
...YES, THAT IS WHAT I ADVISED.
BUT PERSONALLY, I'D PREFER THAT YOU DO NOT USE THEM.
...
UMM ...
IT IS A RARE TEST SUB-JECT.
I'D LIKE TO GET IT IN THE MOST NEUTRAL STATE POSSIBLE...

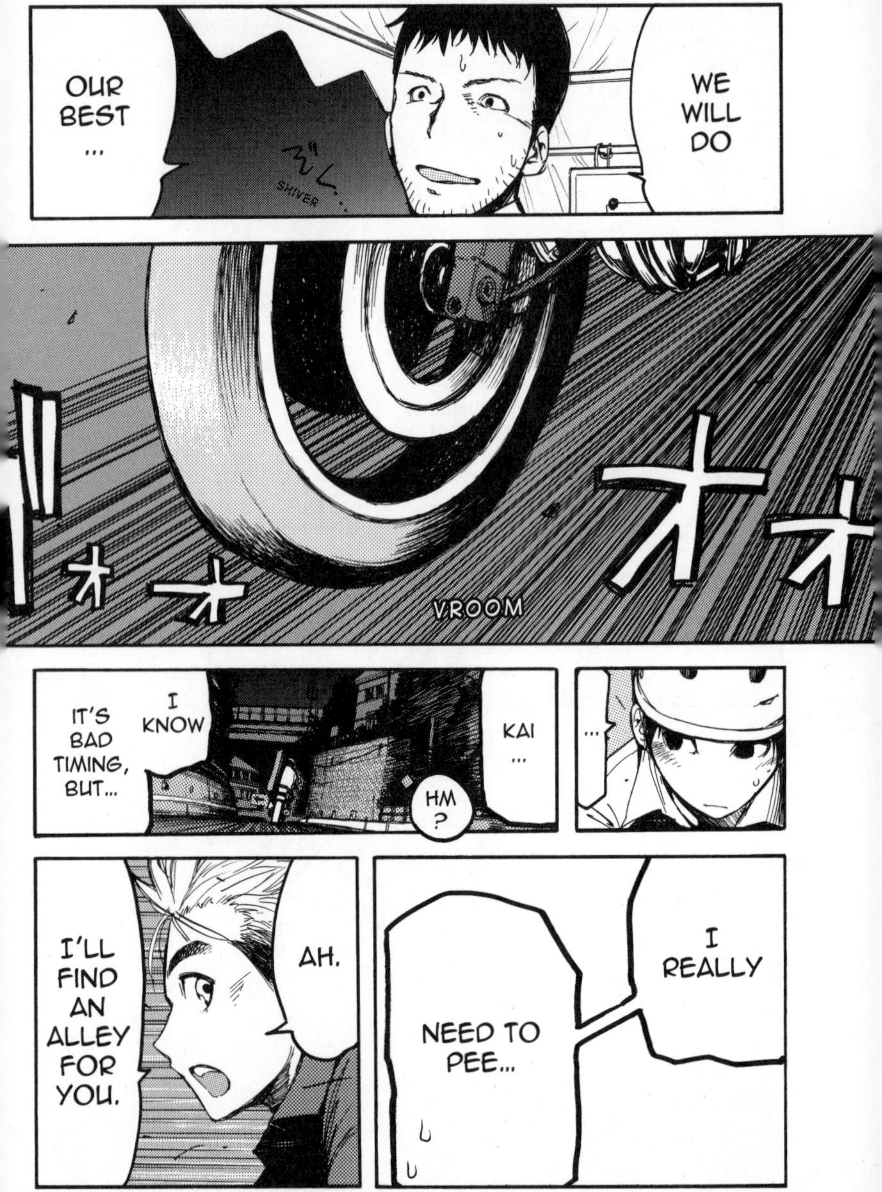
WE WILL DO
OUR BEST ...
SHIVER
VROOM
...
KAI ...
HM ?
I KNOW
IT'S BAD TIMING, BUT...
I REALLY
NEED TO PEE...
AH.
I'LL FIND AN ALLEY FOR YOU.

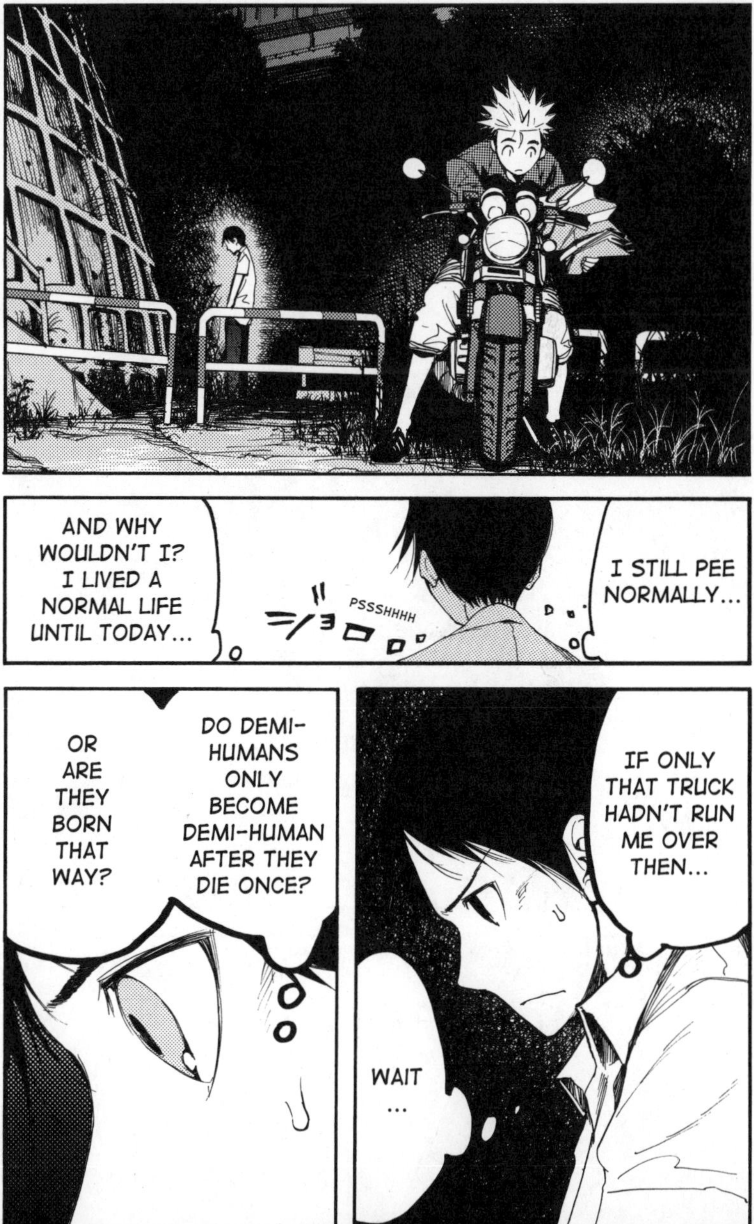
I STILL PEE NORMALLY...
PSSSHHHH
AND WHY WOULDN'T I? I LIVED A NORMAL LIFE UNTIL TODAY...
IF ONLY THAT TRUCK HADN'T RUN ME OVER THEN...
WAIT...
DO DEMI-HUMANS ONLY BECOME DEMI-HUMAN AFTER THEY DIE ONCE?
OR ARE THEY BORN THAT WAY?

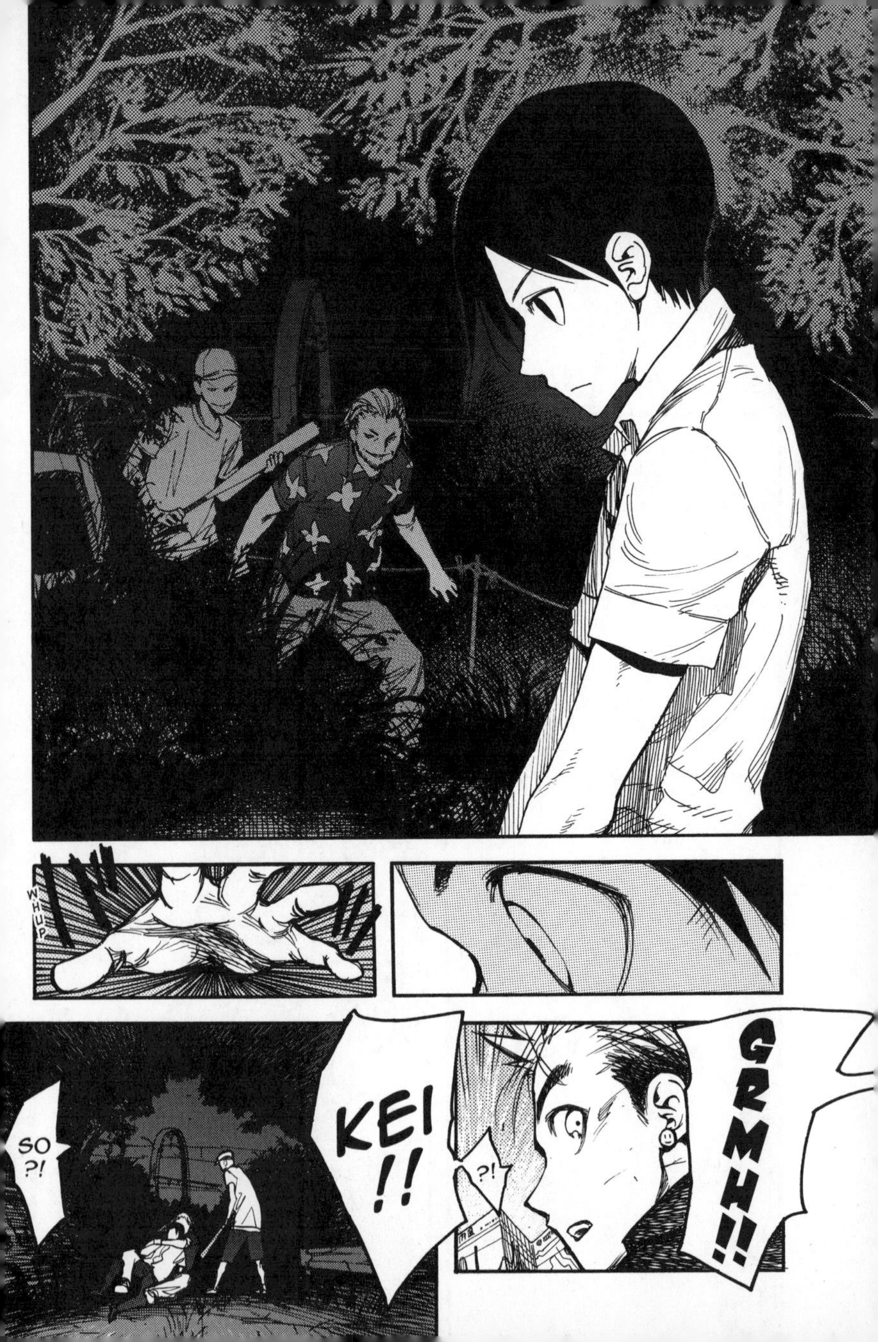
WHUP
GRMH!!
KEI!!
?!
SO ?!

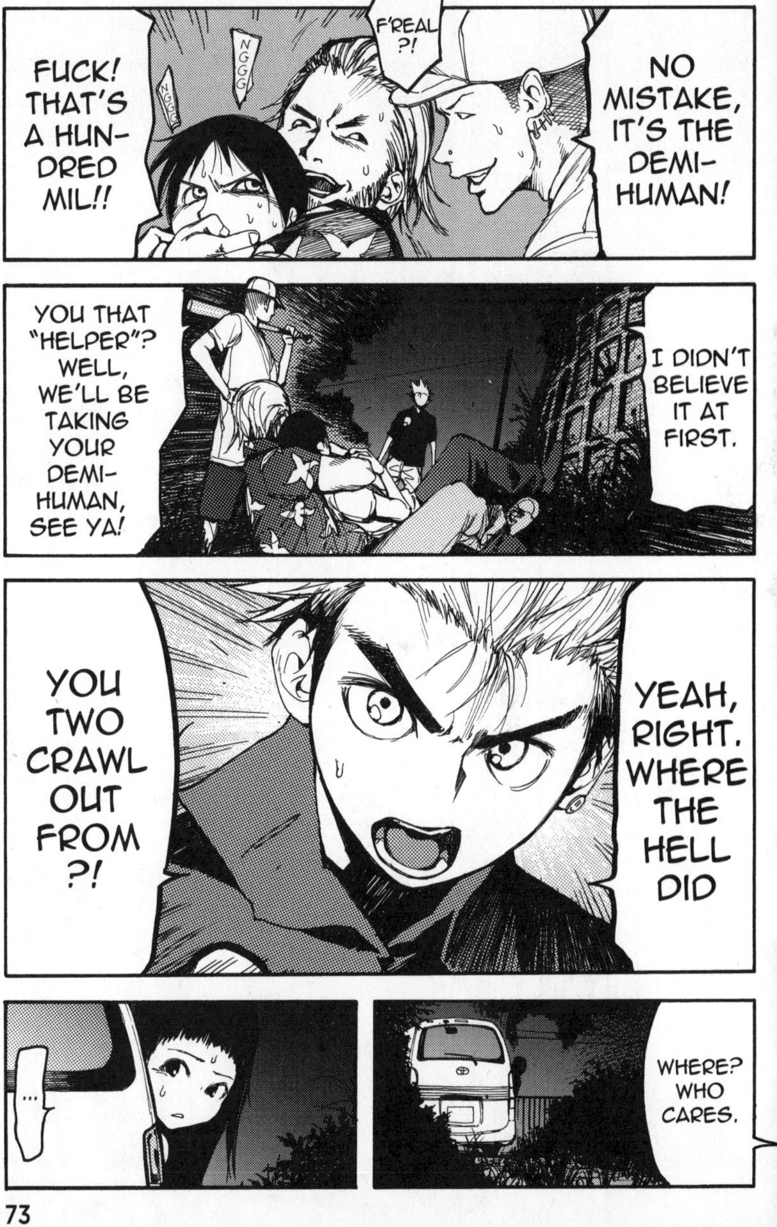
NO MISTAKE, IT'S THE DEMI-HUMAN!
F'REAL?!
NGGG
NGGG
FUCK! THAT'S A HUN-DRED MIL!!
I DIDN'T BELIEVE IT AT FIRST.
YOU THAT "HELPER"? WELL, WE'LL BE TAKING YOUR DEMI-HUMAN, SEE YA!
YEAH, RIGHT. WHERE THE HELL DID
YOU TWO CRAWL OUT FROM?!
WHERE? WHO CARES.
...

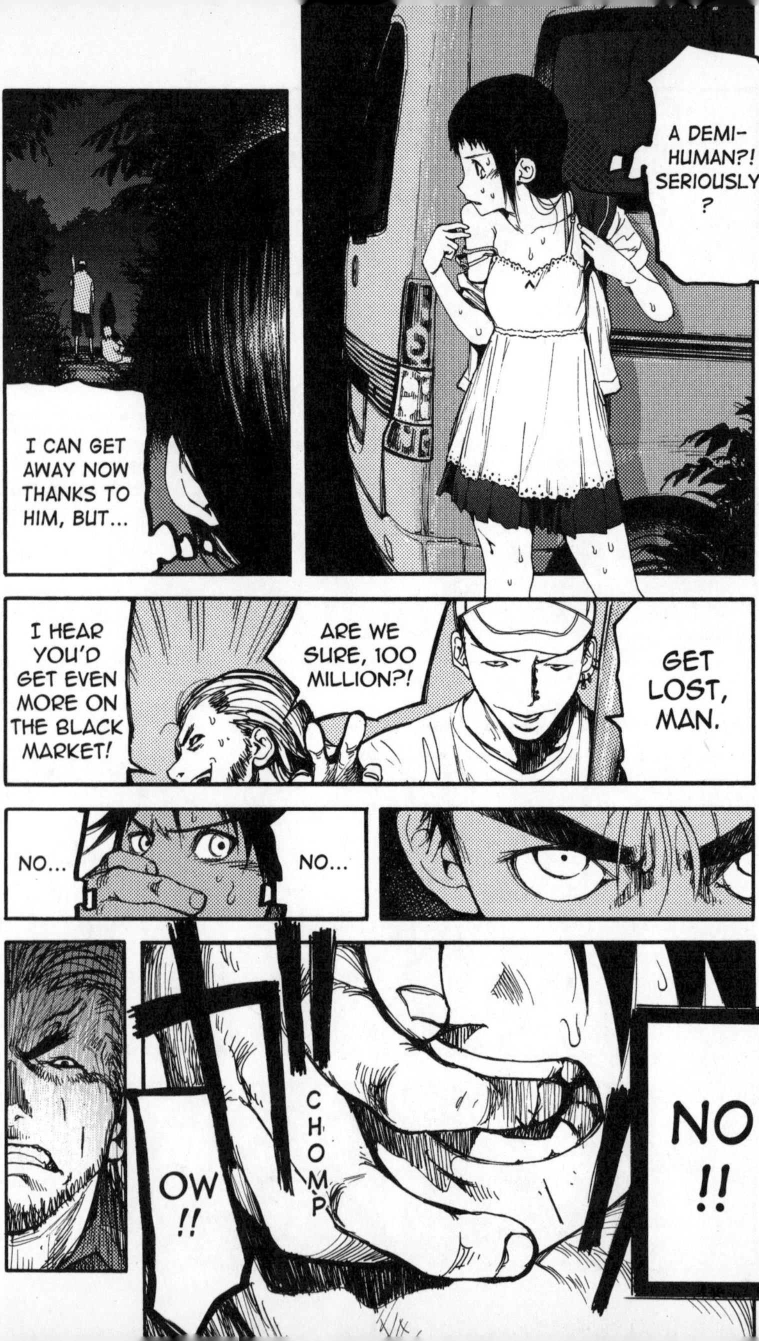
A DEMI-HUMAN?! SERIOUSLY?
I CAN GET AWAY NOW THANKS TO HIM, BUT...
GET LOST, MAN.
ARE WE SURE, 100 MILLION?!
I HEAR YOU'D GET EVEN MORE ON THE BLACK MARKET!
NO...
NO...
NO!!
CHOMP
OW!!

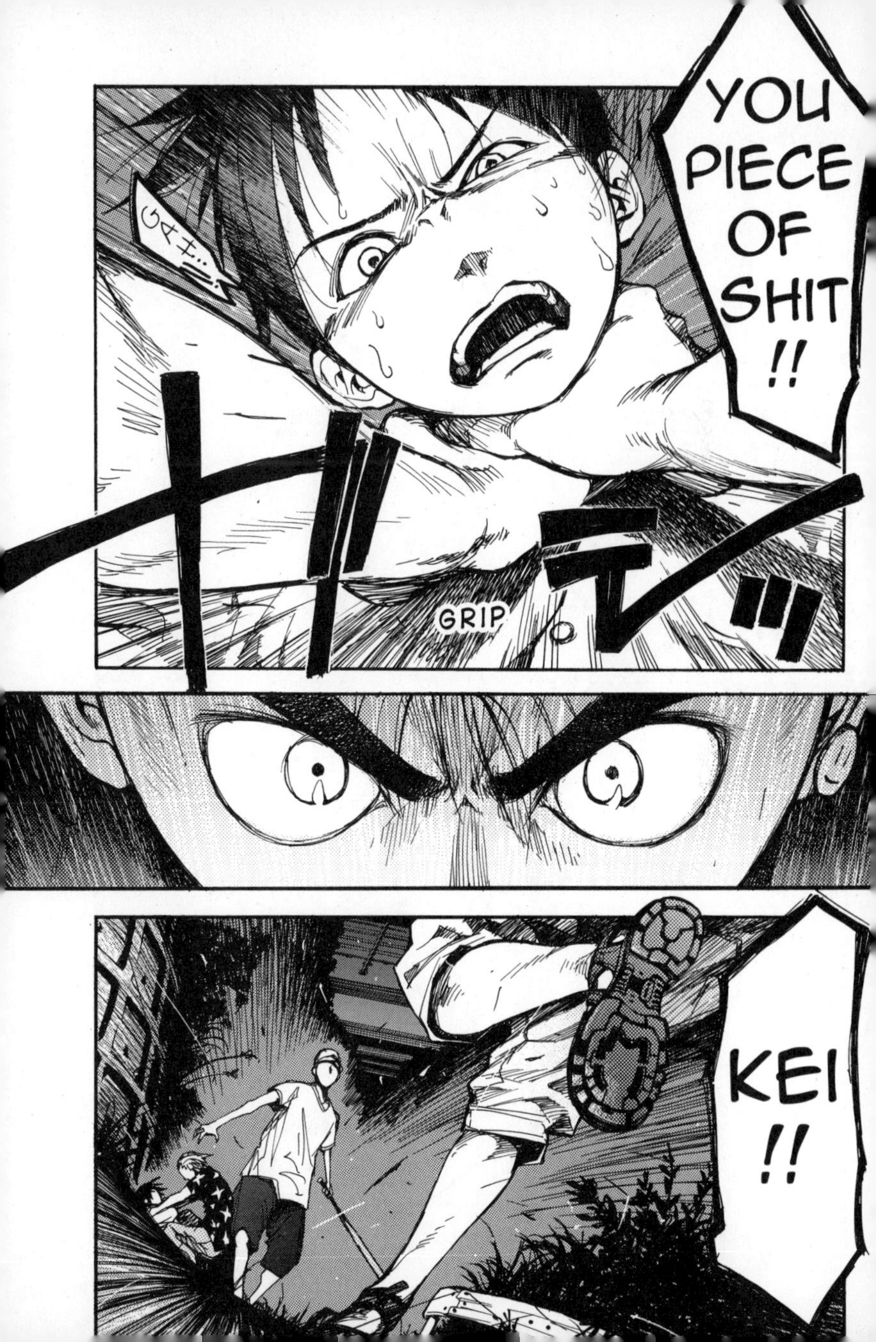
YOU PIECE OF SHIT!!
GRIP
KEI!!

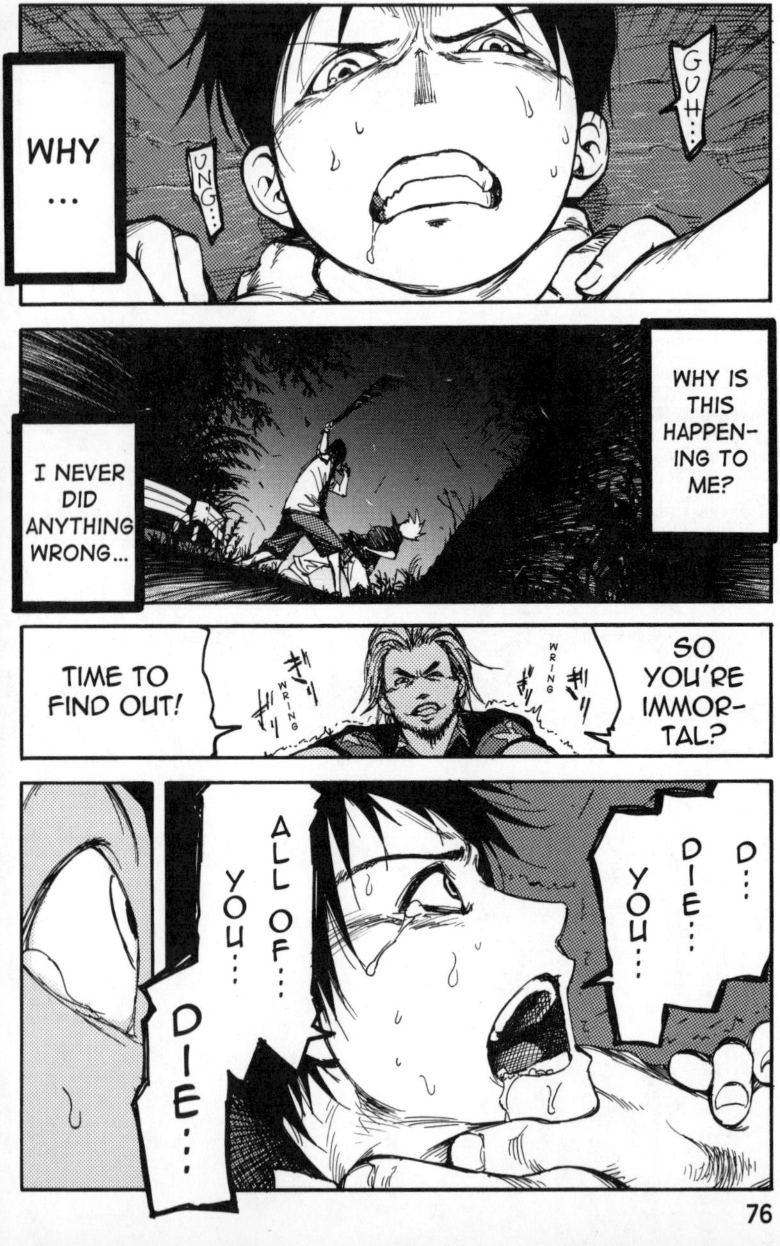
GUH...
UNG...
WHY ...
WHY IS THIS HAPPENING TO ME?
I NEVER DID ANYTHING WRONG...
SO YOU'RE IMMORTAL?
WRING
WRING
TIME TO FIND OUT!
D... DIE... YOU...
ALL OF... YOU...
DIE...

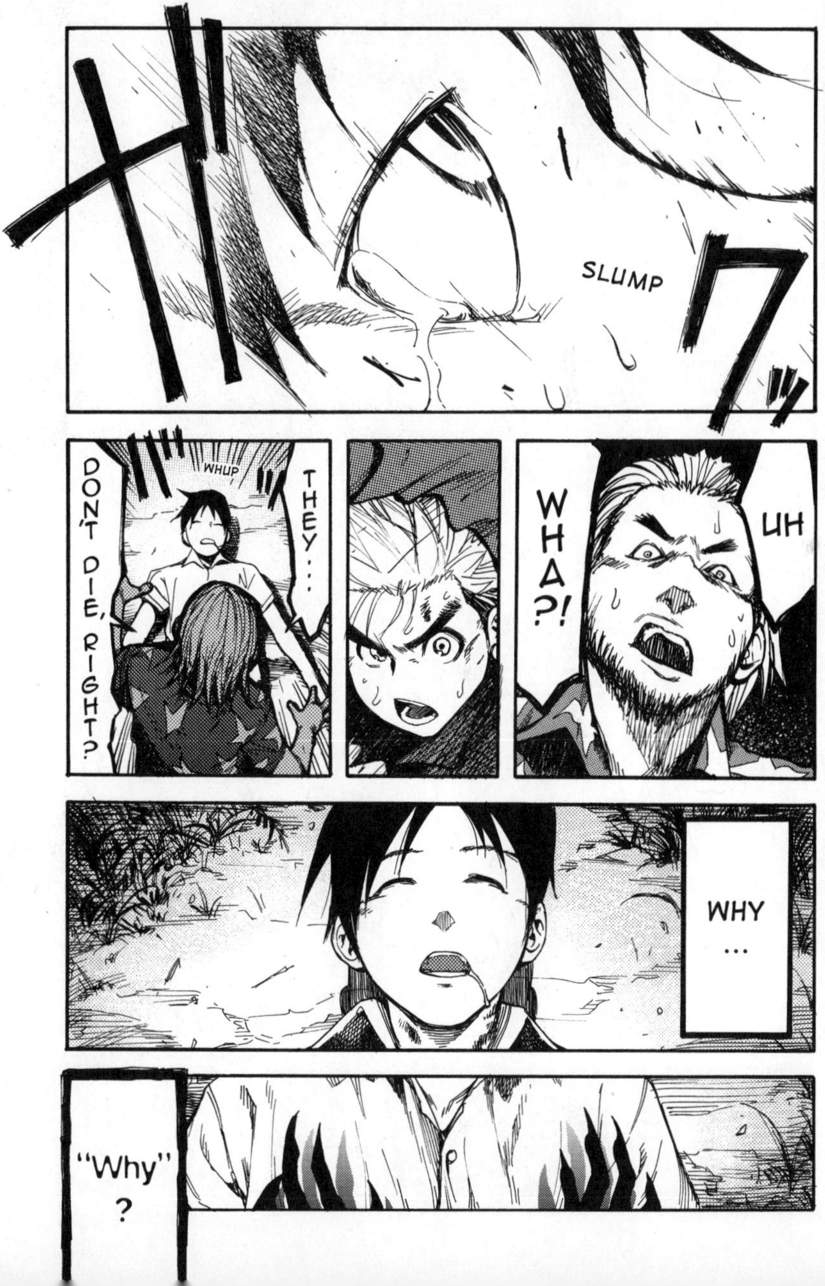
SLUMP
UH
WHA?!
THEY...
WHUP
DON'T DIE, RIGHT?
WHY ...
"Why" ?

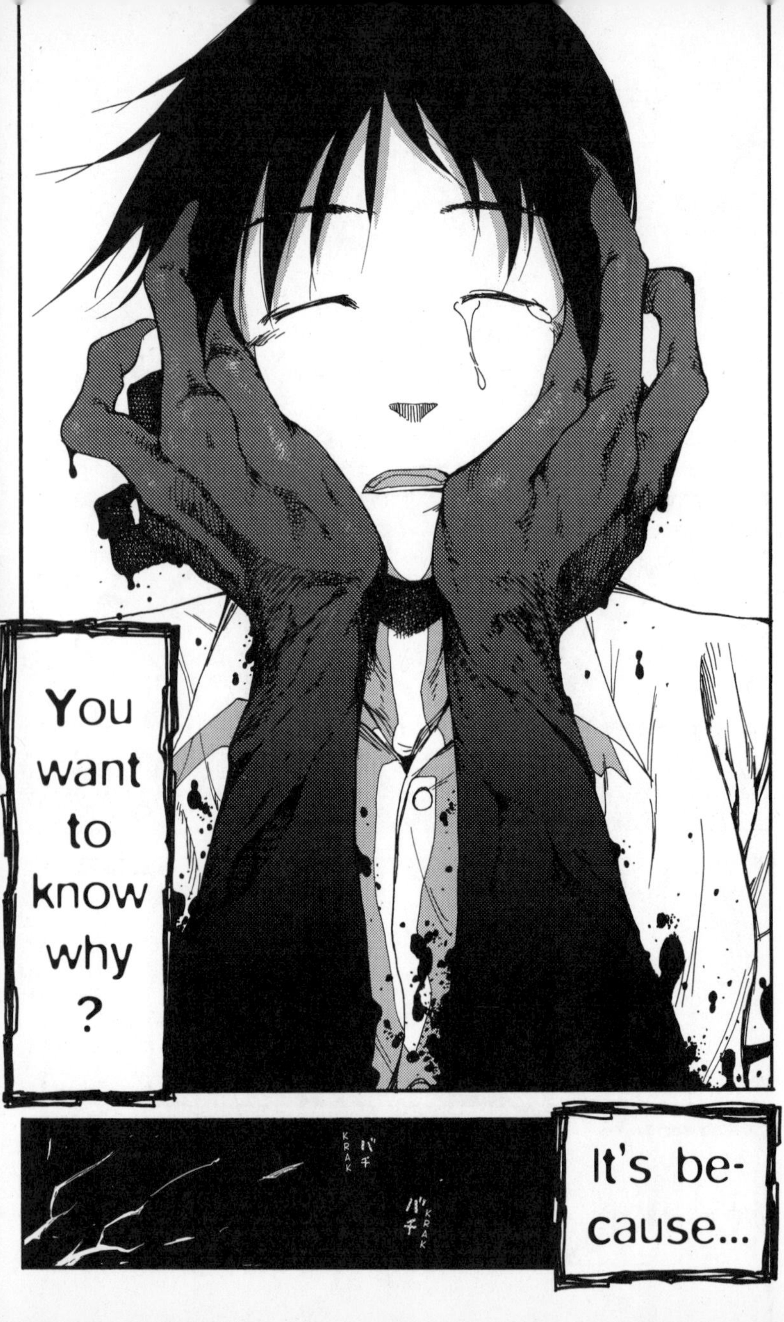
You want to know why?
It's be-cause...
バチ KRAK
バチ KRAK

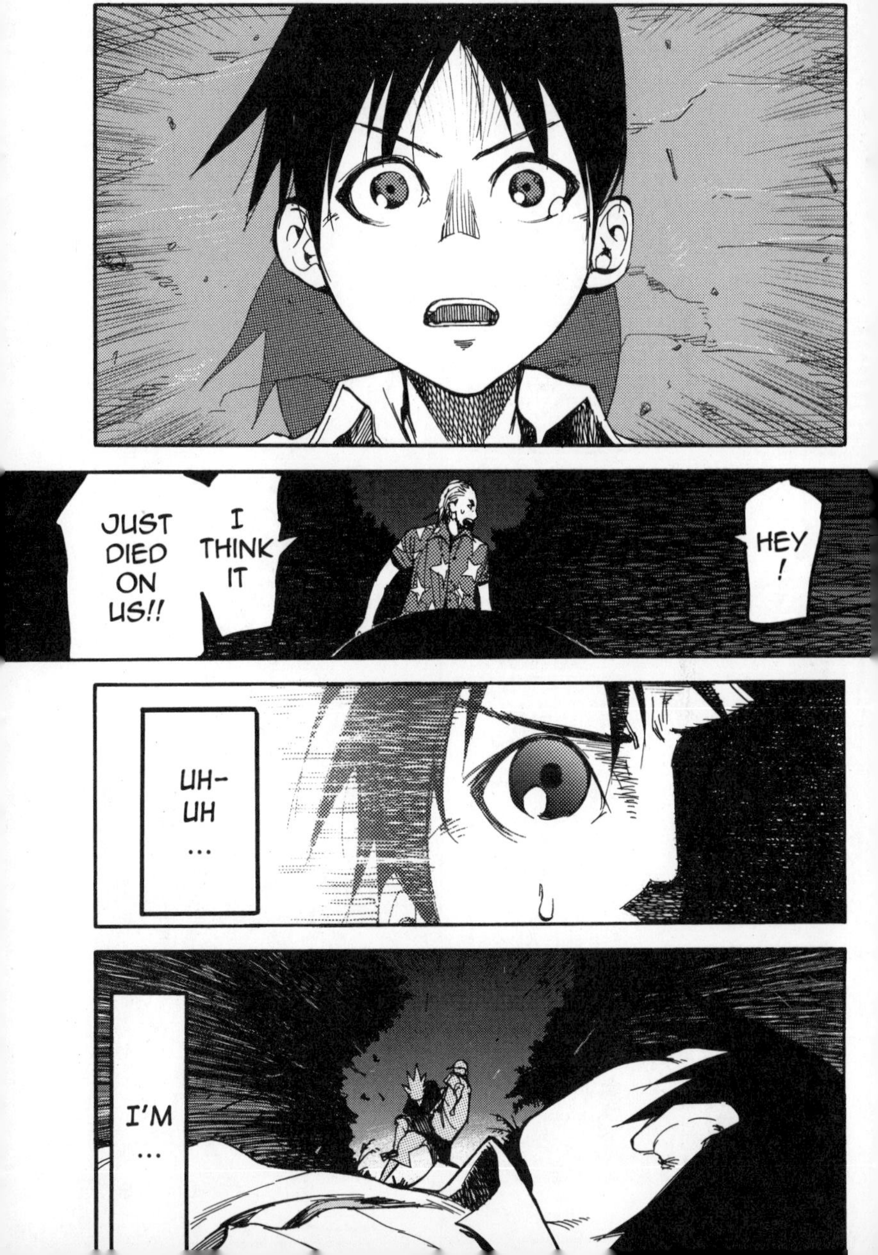
HEY!
I THINK IT
JUST DIED ON US!!
UH-UH...
I'M...

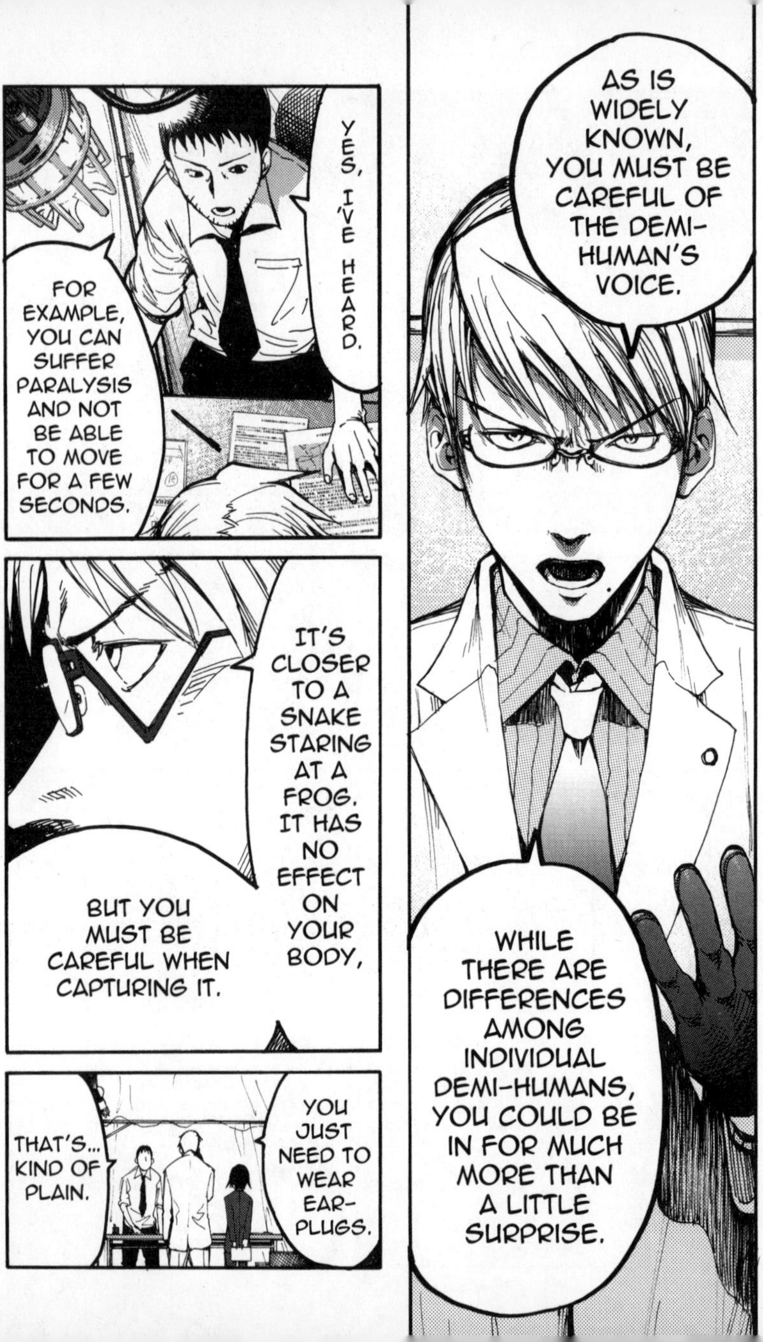
AS IS WIDELY KNOWN, YOU MUST BE CAREFUL OF THE DEMI-HUMAN'S VOICE.
WHILE THERE ARE DIFFERENCES AMONG INDIVIDUAL DEMI-HUMANS, YOU COULD BE IN FOR MUCH MORE THAN A LITTLE SURPRISE.
YES, I'VE HEARD.
FOR EXAMPLE, YOU CAN SUFFER PARALYSIS AND NOT BE ABLE TO MOVE FOR A FEW SECONDS.
IT'S CLOSER TO A SNAKE STARING AT A FROG. IT HAS NO EFFECT ON YOUR BODY,
BUT YOU MUST BE CAREFUL WHEN CAPTURING IT.
YOU JUST NEED TO WEAR EAR-PLUGS.
THAT'S... KIND OF PLAIN.

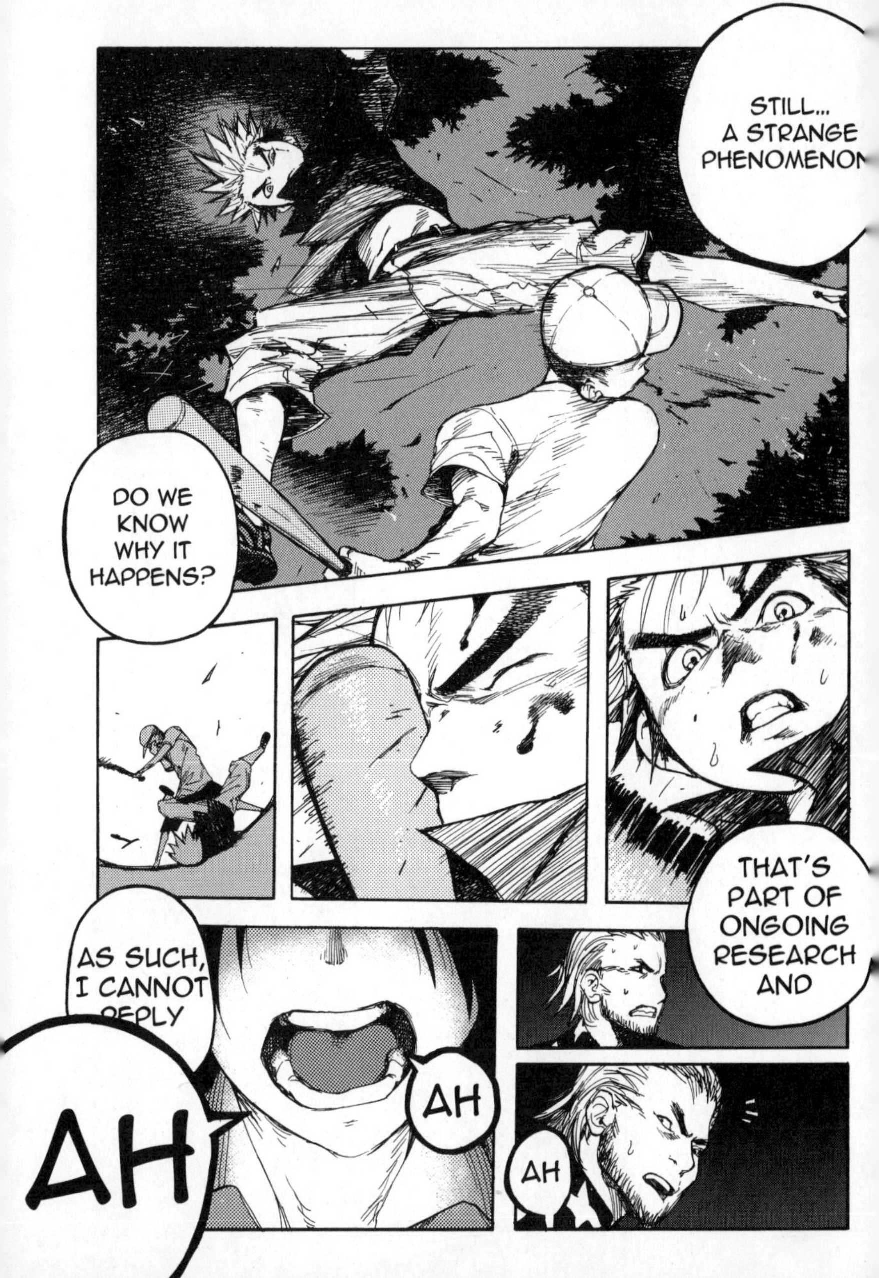
STILL... A STRANGE PHENOMENON
DO WE KNOW WHY IT HAPPENS?
THAT'S PART OF ONGOING RESEARCH AND
AH
AS SUCH, I CANNOT REPLY
AH
AH

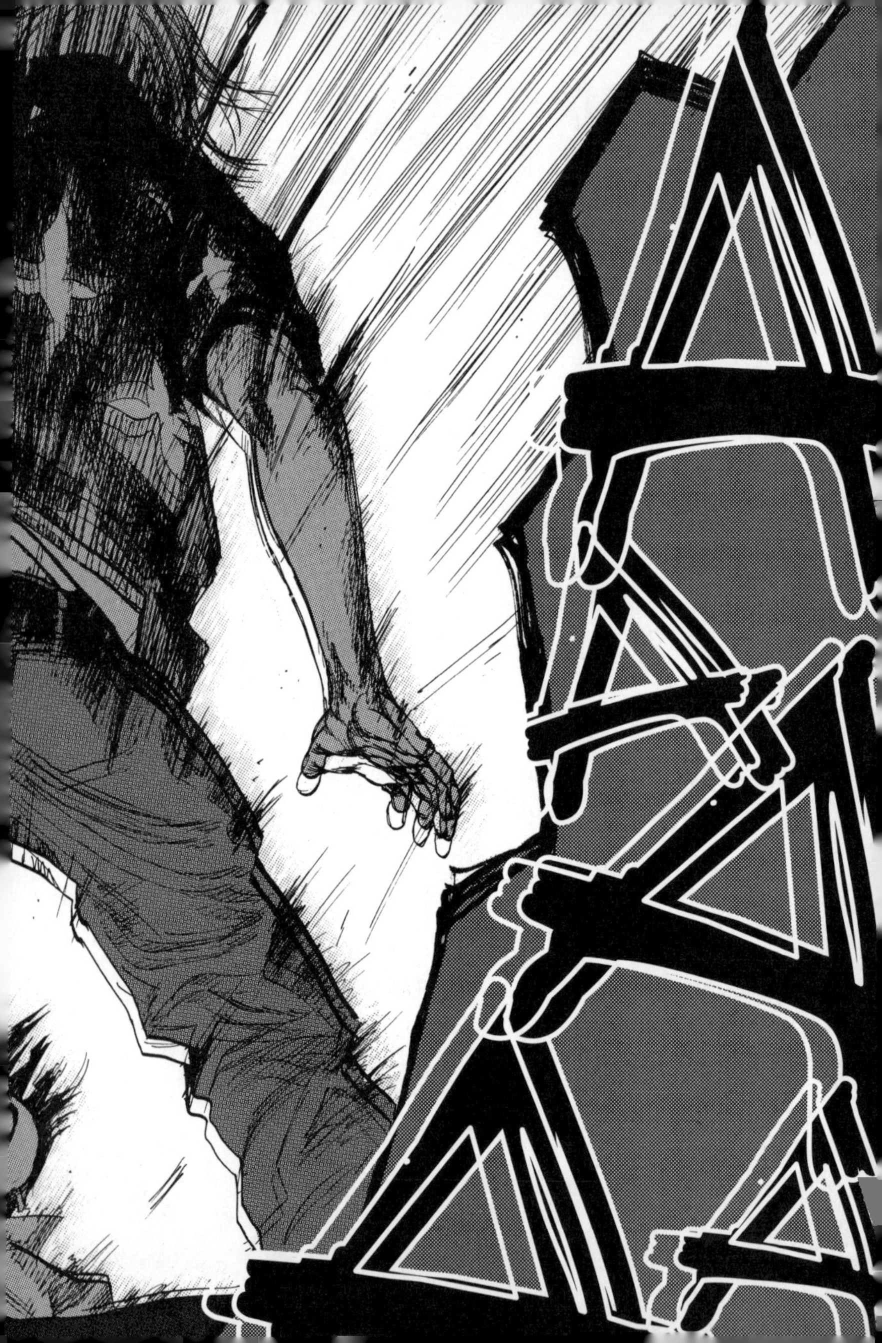

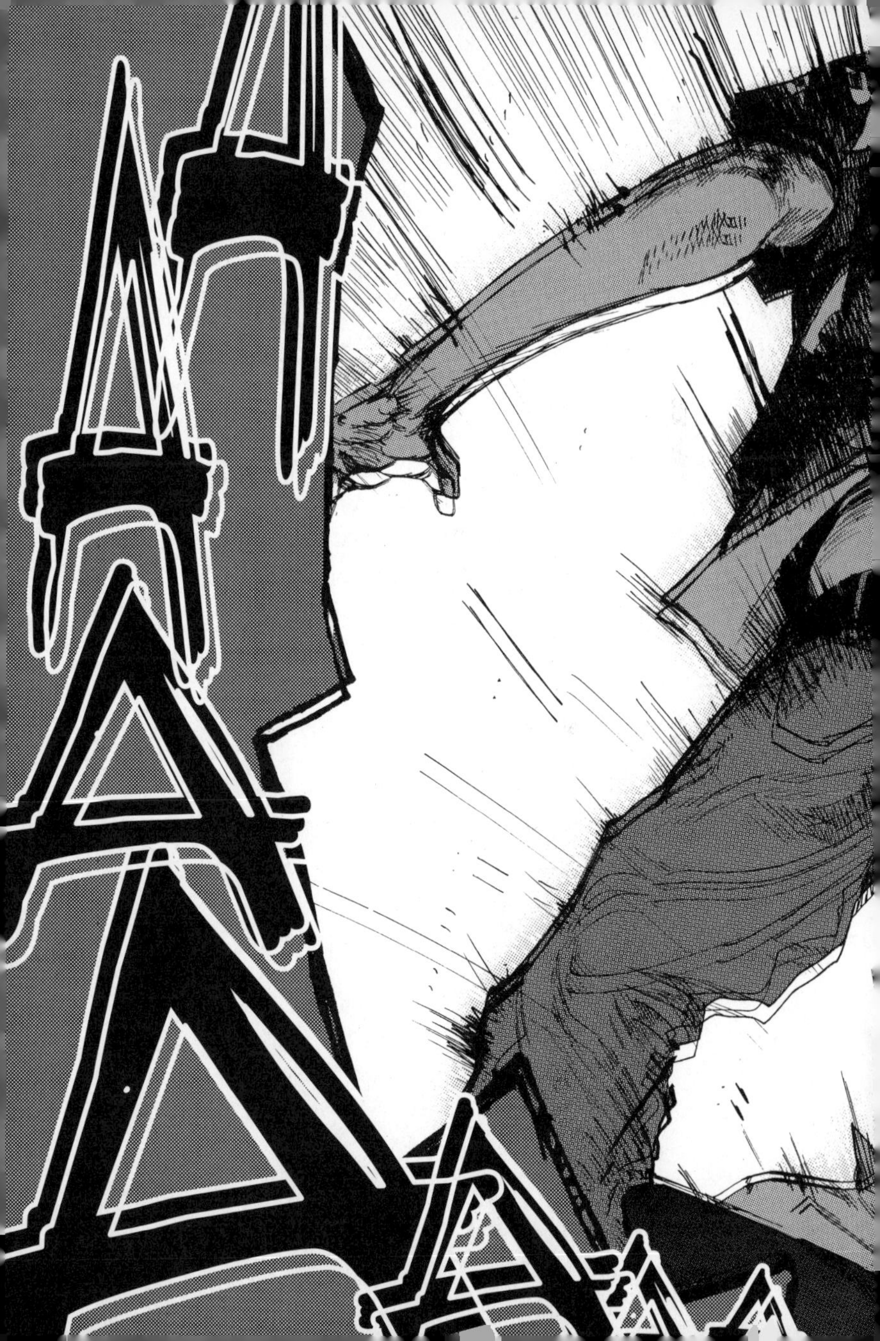

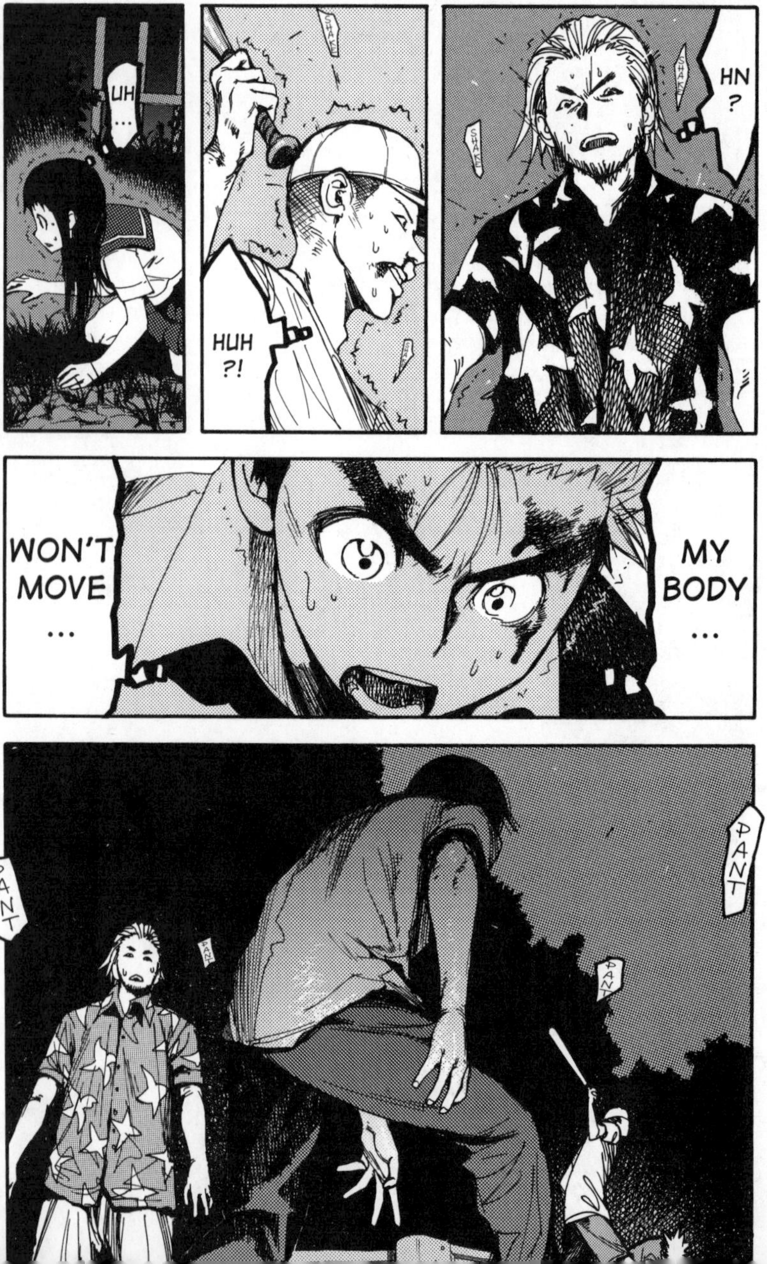

HN?
SHAKE
SHAKE
SHAKE
HUH?!
UH...
MY BODY...
WON'T MOVE...
PANT
PANT
PANT
PANT

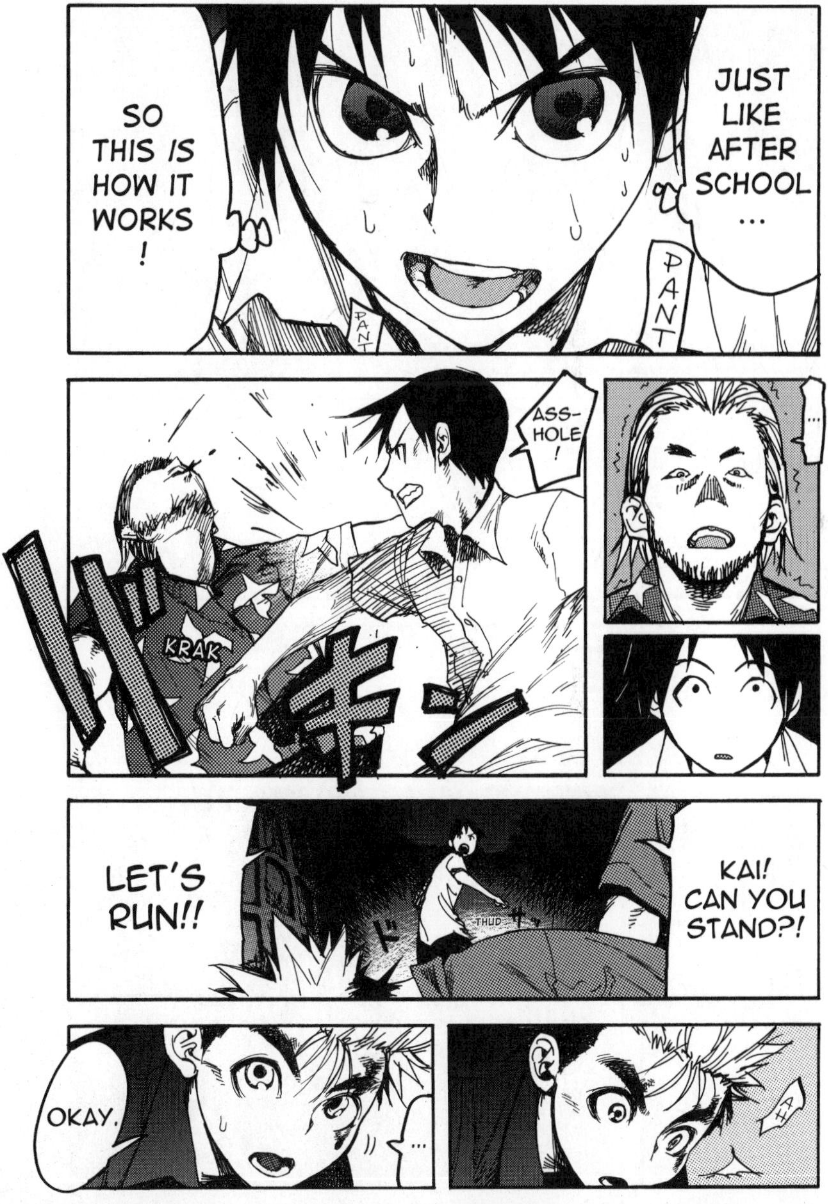
JUST LIKE AFTER SCHOOL ...
PANT
SO THIS IS HOW IT WORKS!
PANT
...
ASS-HOLE!
KRAK
KAI! CAN YOU STAND?!
THUD
LET'S RUN!!
AH
...
OKAY.

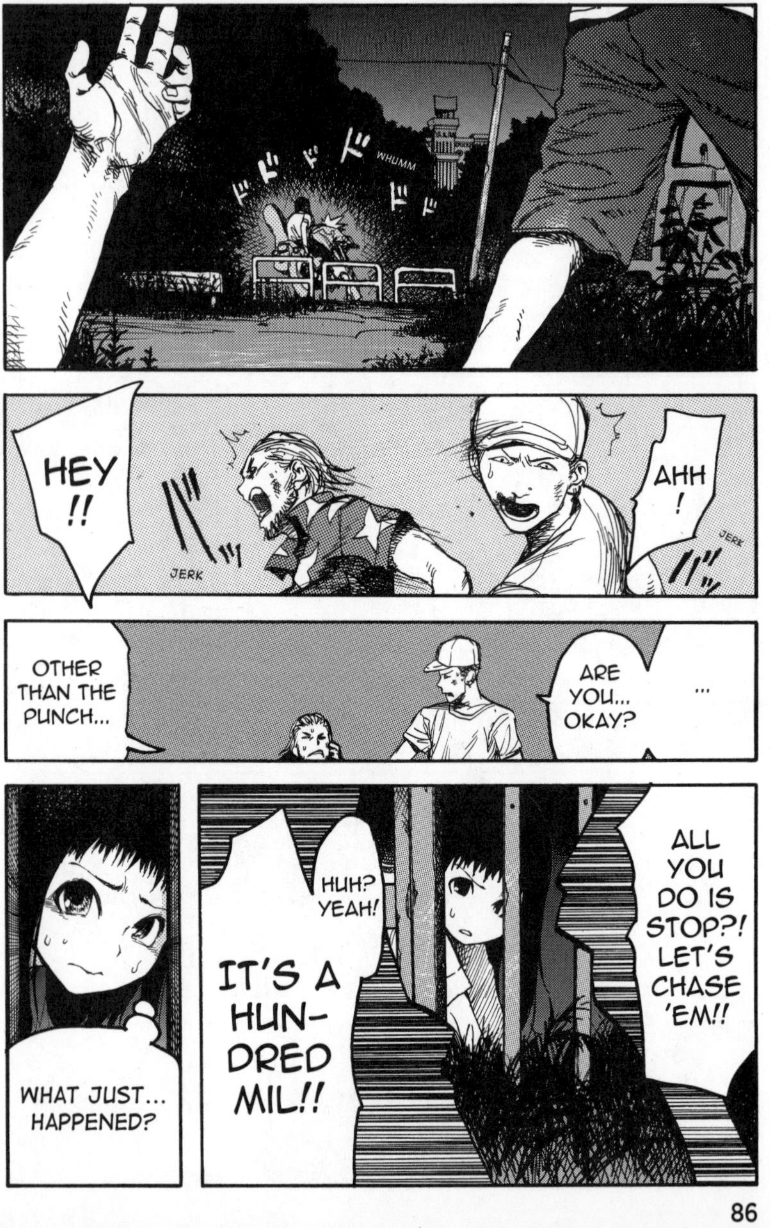
ドドドドドド
WHUMM
AHH !
JERK
HEY !!
JERK
...
ARE YOU... OKAY?
OTHER THAN THE PUNCH...
ALL YOU DO IS STOP?! LET'S CHASE 'EM!!
HUH? YEAH!
IT'S A HUN- DRED MIL!!
WHAT JUST... HAPPENED?

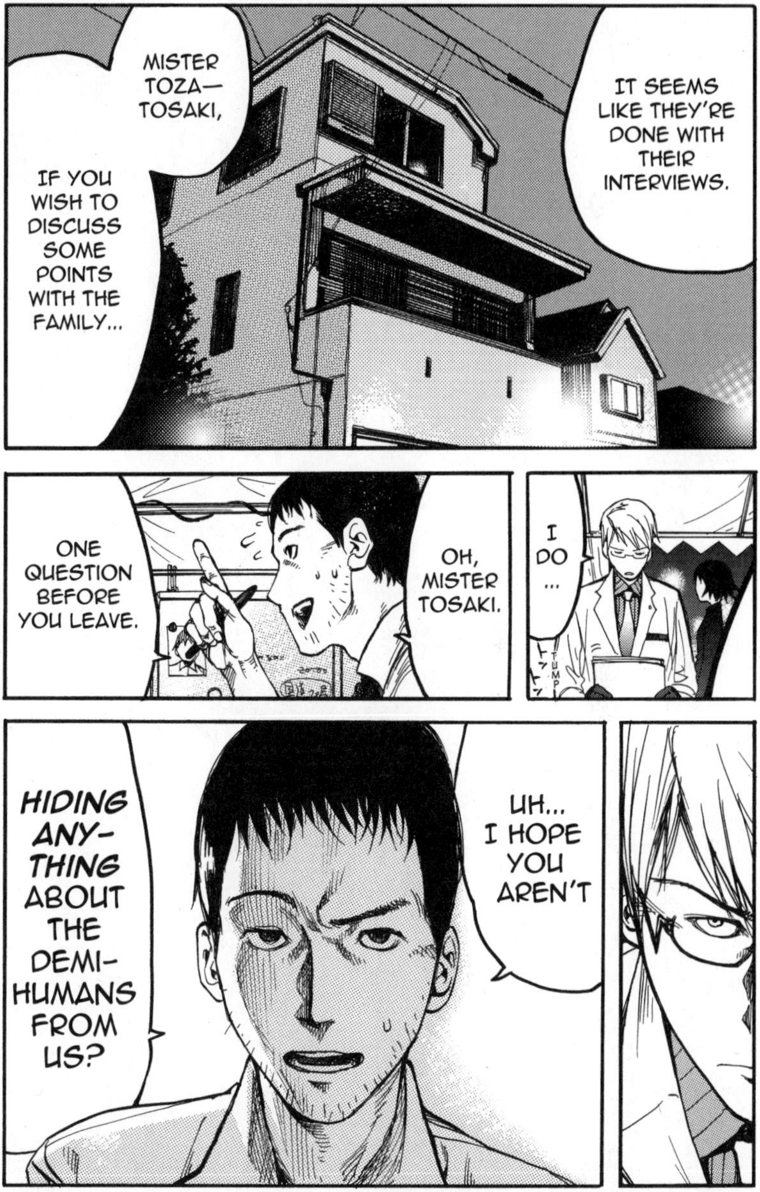
IT SEEMS LIKE THEY'RE DONE WITH THEIR INTERVIEWS.
MISTER TOZA— TOSAKI,
IF YOU WISH TO DISCUSS SOME POINTS WITH THE FAMILY...
I DO ...
TUMP
OH, MISTER TOSAKI.
ONE QUESTION BEFORE YOU LEAVE.
UH... I HOPE YOU AREN'T
HIDING ANY-THING ABOUT THE DEMI-HUMANS FROM US?

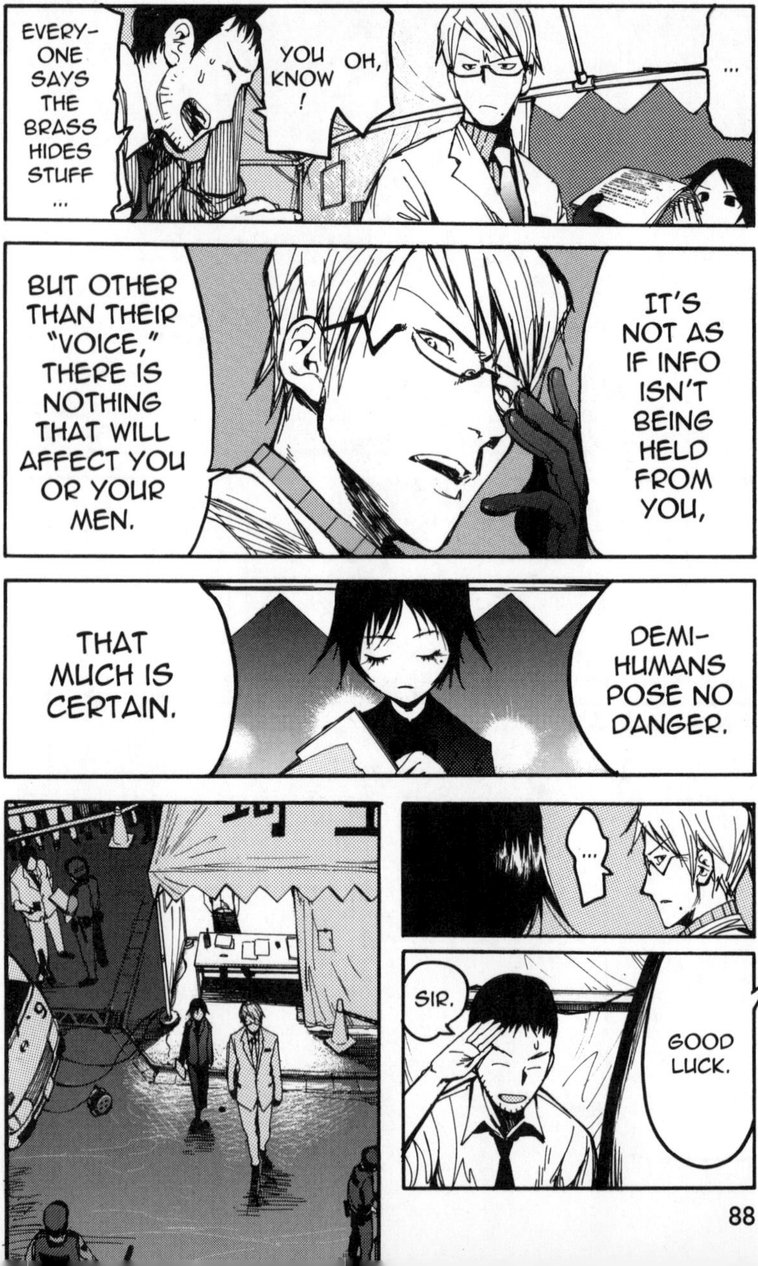
...
OH, YOU KNOW!
EVERYONE SAYS THE BRASS HIDES STUFF...
IT'S NOT AS IF INFO ISN'T BEING HELD FROM YOU,
BUT OTHER THAN THEIR "VOICE," THERE IS NOTHING THAT WILL AFFECT YOU OR YOUR MEN.
DEMI-HUMANS POSE NO DANGER.
THAT MUCH IS CERTAIN.
...
SIR.
GOOD LUCK.

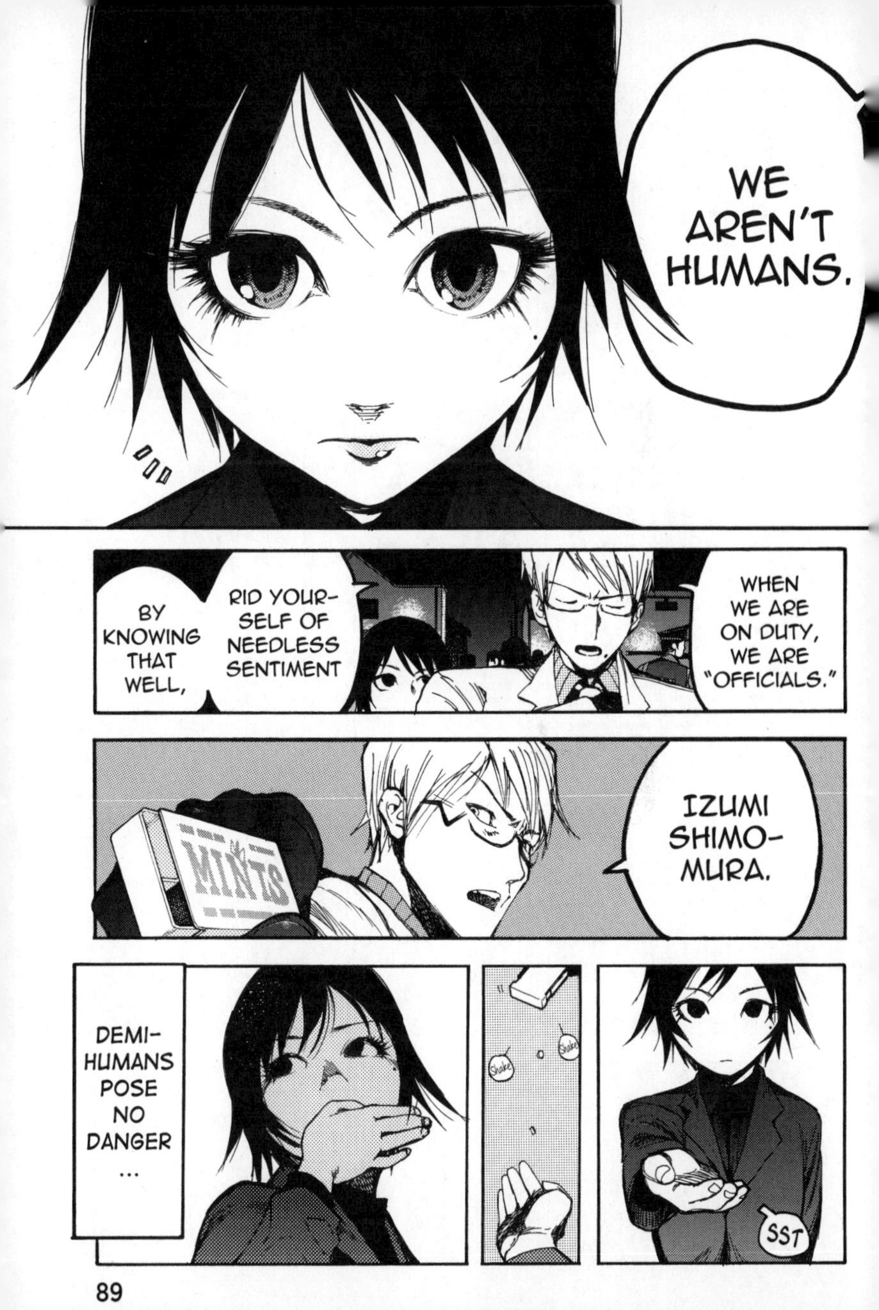
WE AREN'T HUMANS.
WHEN WE ARE ON DUTY, WE ARE "OFFICIALS."
RID YOURSELF OF NEEDLESS SENTIMENT
BY KNOWING THAT WELL,
IZUMI SHIMOMURA.
MINTS
SST
Shake
Shake
DEMI-HUMANS POSE NO DANGER ...

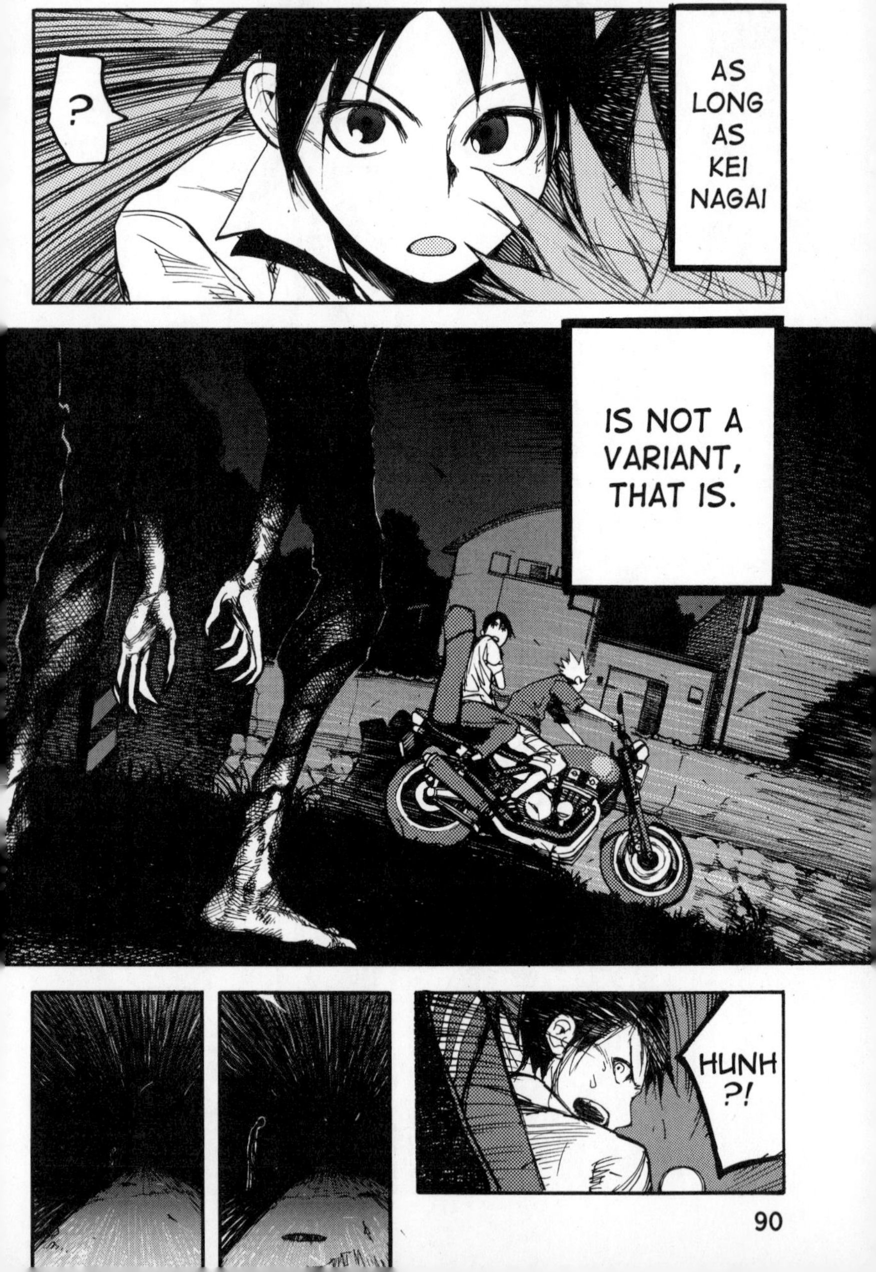
AS LONG AS KEI NAGAI
?
IS NOT A VARIANT, THAT IS.
HUNH ?!

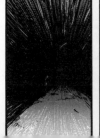

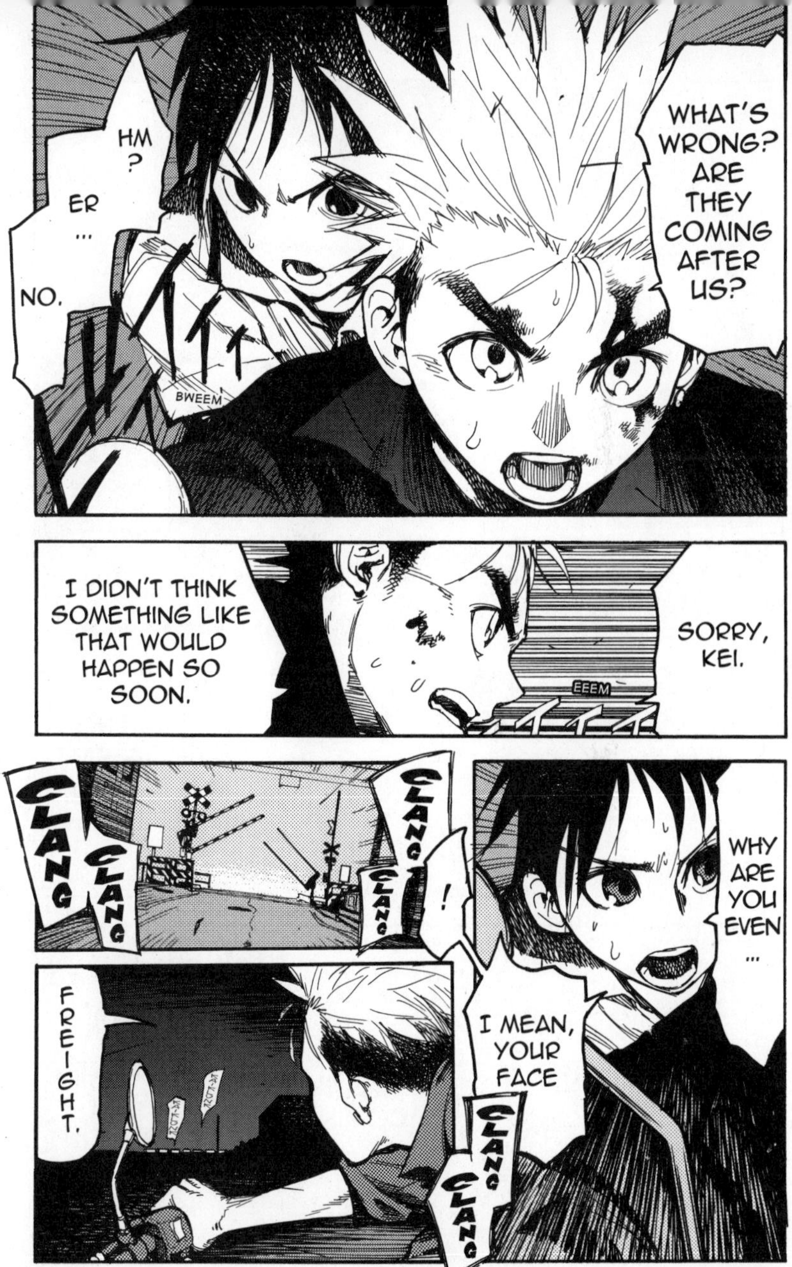
WHAT'S WRONG? ARE THEY COMING AFTER US?
HM?
ER ...
NO.
BWEEM
SORRY, KEI.
I DIDN'T THINK SOMETHING LIKE THAT WOULD HAPPEN SO SOON.
EEEM
WHY ARE YOU EVEN ...
!
I MEAN, YOUR FACE
CLANG CLANG
CLANG CLANG
CLANG CLANG
CLANG CLANG
CLANG
FREIGHT.

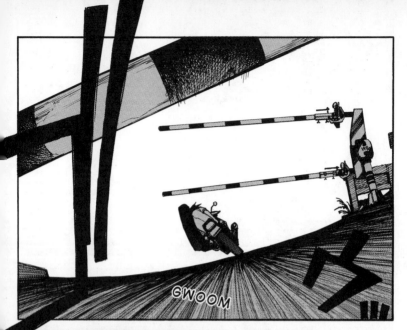

GWOOM

LUCK IS ON OUR SIDE.

SHIT, AND A TRAIN'S COMING. NRAH!!

...

TRACKS?

GAH...

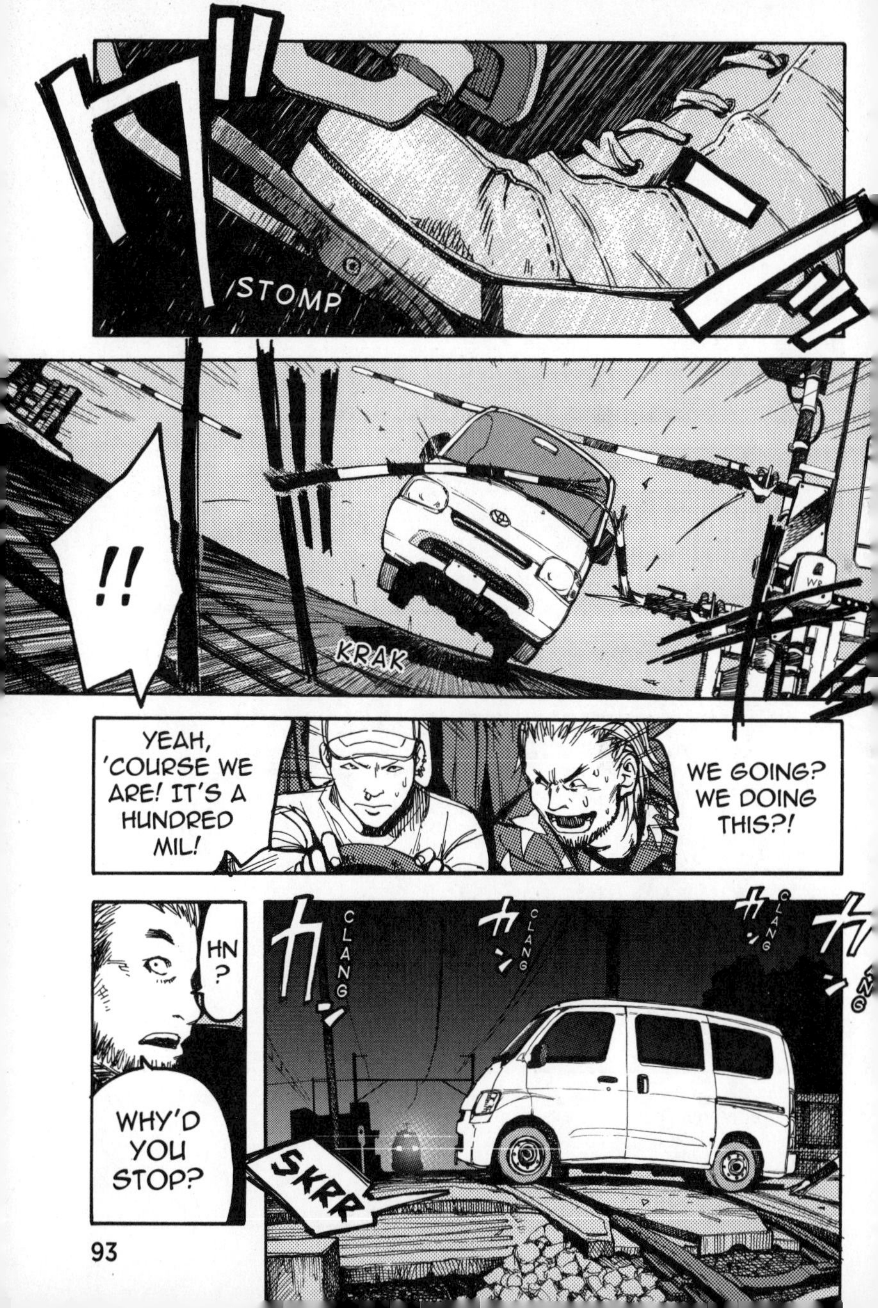
STOMP
!!
KRAK
WE GOING? WE DOING THIS?!
YEAH, 'COURSE WE ARE! IT'S A HUNDRED MIL!
CLANG
CLANG
CLANG
CLANG
SKRR
HN?
WHY'D YOU STOP?

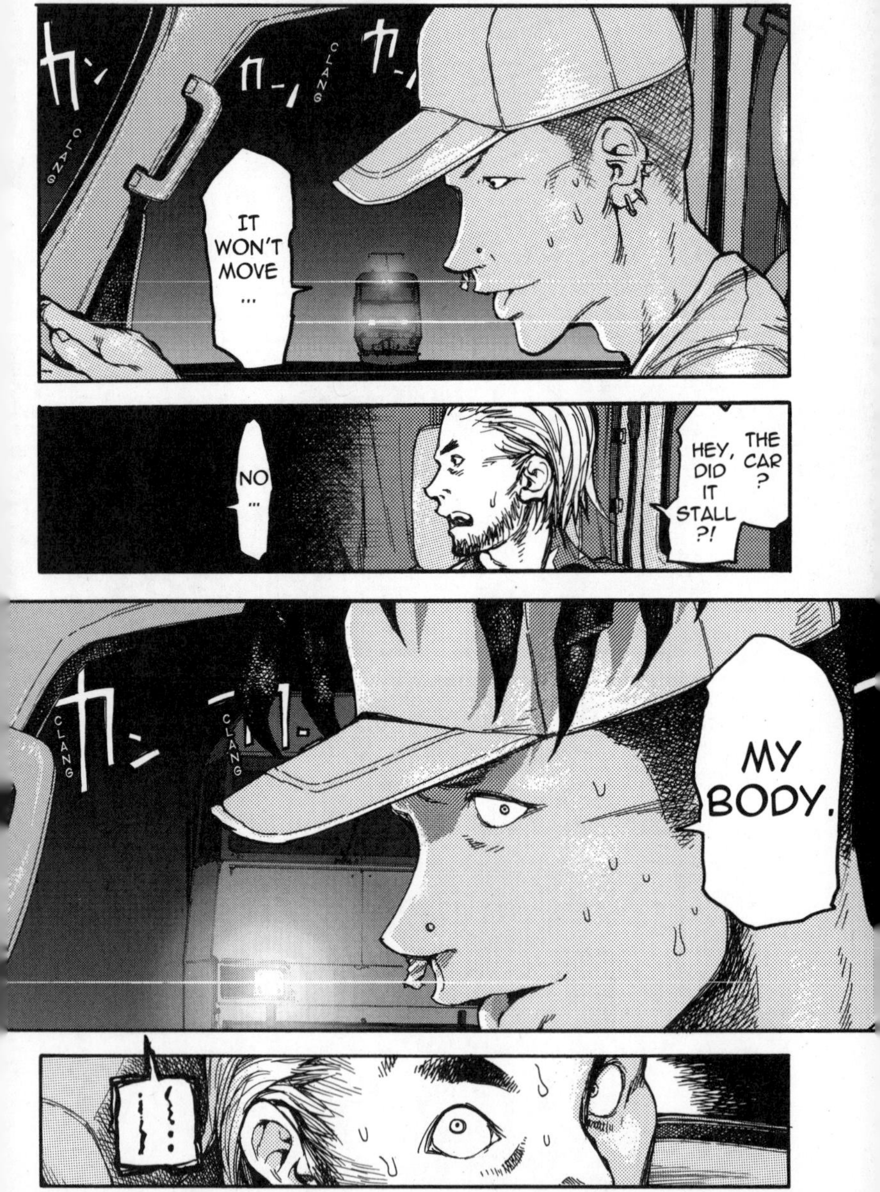
CLANG
CLANG
CLANG
IT WON'T MOVE ...
HEY, DID IT STALL ?! THE CAR ?
NO ...
CLANG
CLANG
MY BODY.
...!!

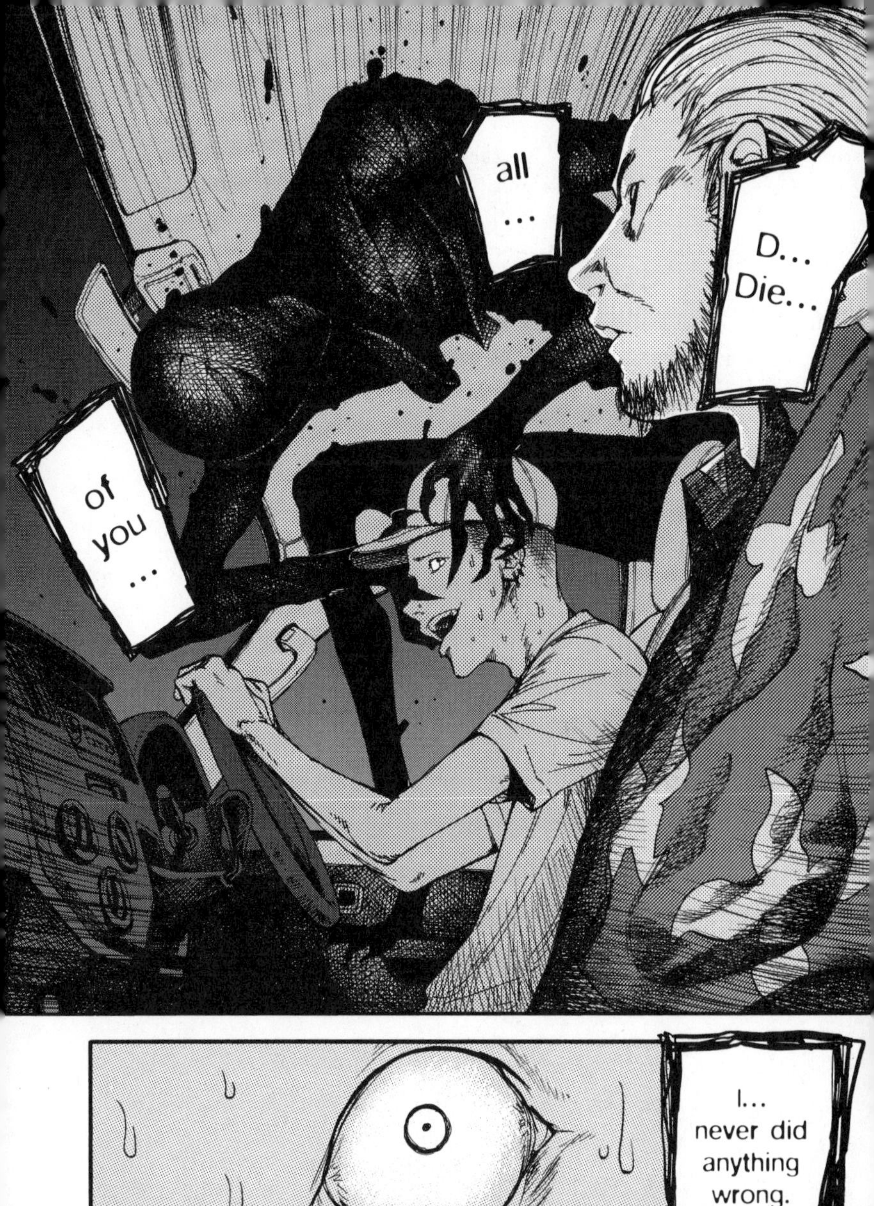
D... Die...
all ...
of you ...
I... never did anything wrong.

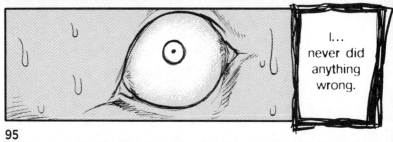

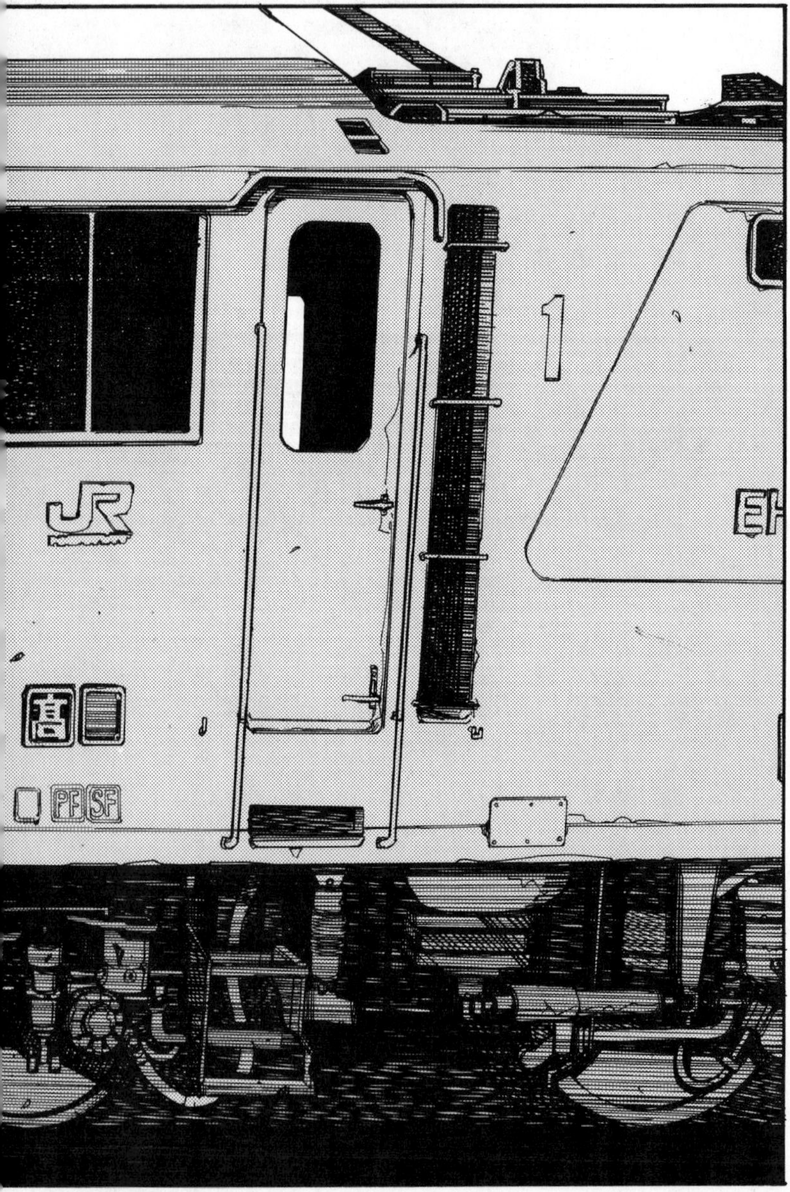
1
EH
高
PF
SF

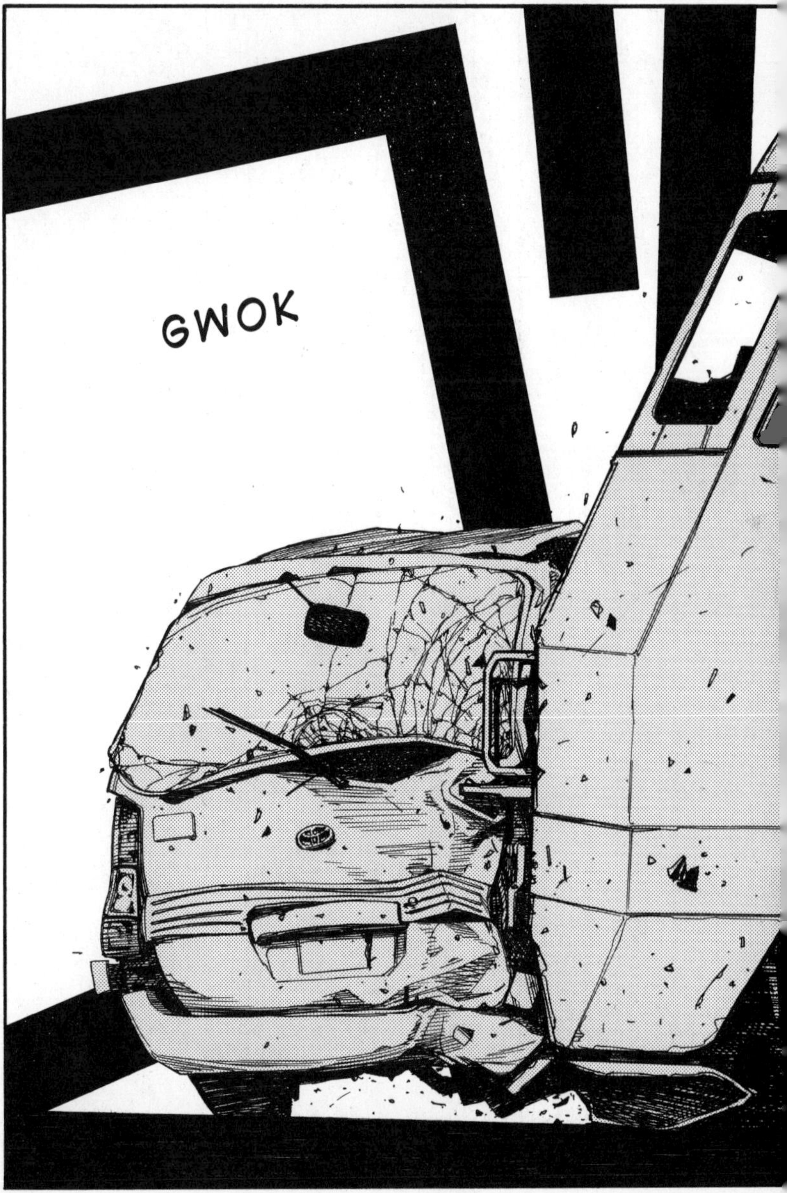
GWOK

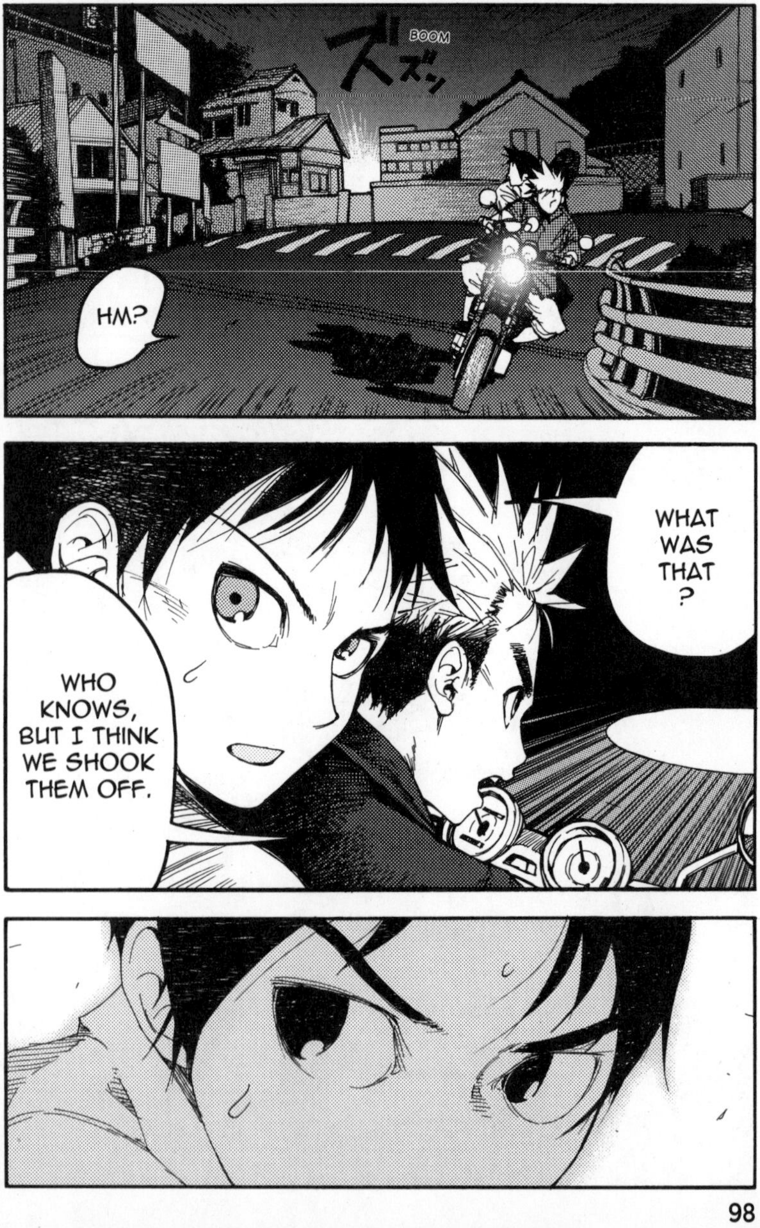
BOOM
ズズッ
HM?
WHAT WAS THAT ?
WHO KNOWS, BUT I THINK WE SHOOK THEM OFF.

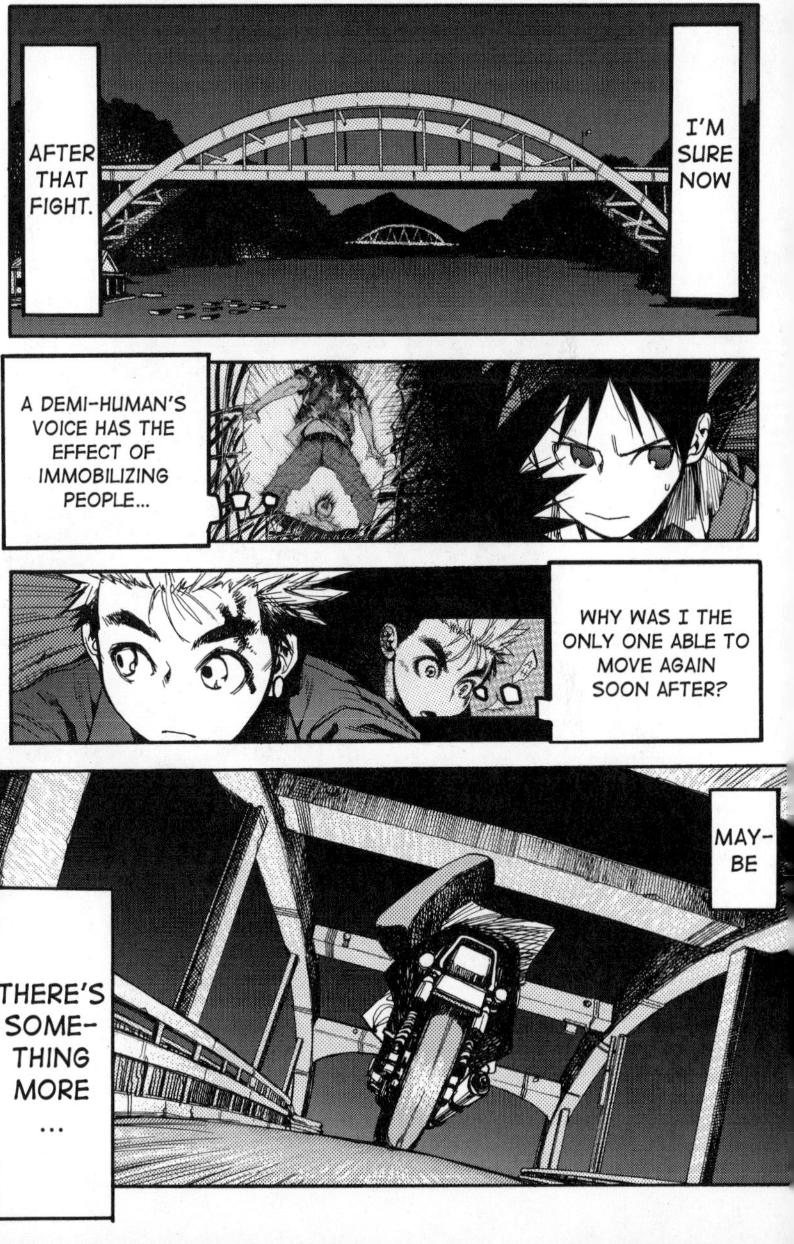
I'M SURE NOW
AFTER THAT FIGHT.
A DEMI-HUMAN'S VOICE HAS THE EFFECT OF IMMOBILIZING PEOPLE...
WHY WAS I THE ONLY ONE ABLE TO MOVE AGAIN SOON AFTER?
MAY-BE
THERE'S SOME-THING MORE ...

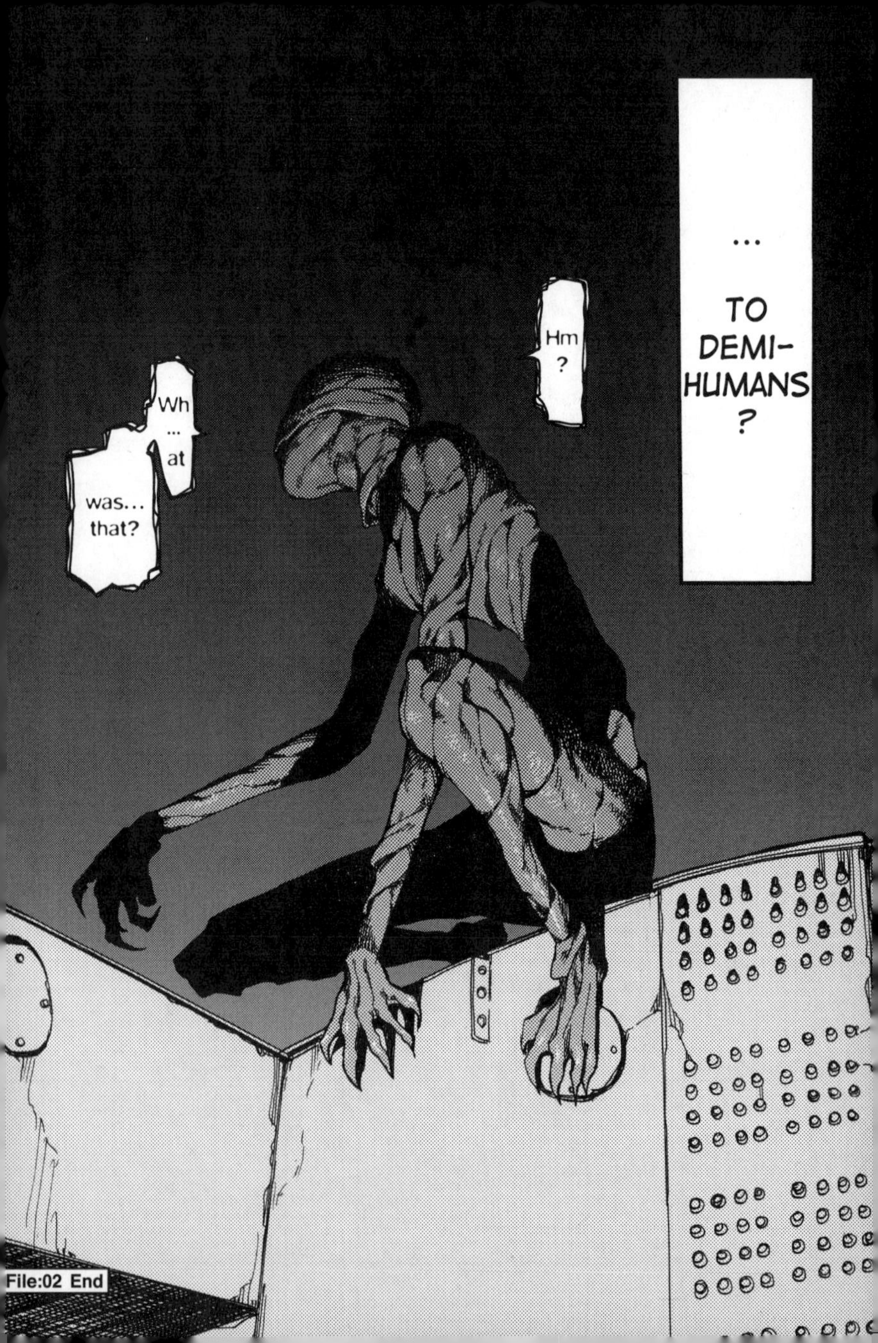
... TO DEMI-HUMANS ?
Hm ?
Wh ... at was... that?
File:02 End

NEED TO STIR

THE DRIFT OF THINGS.

June 16, 03:39

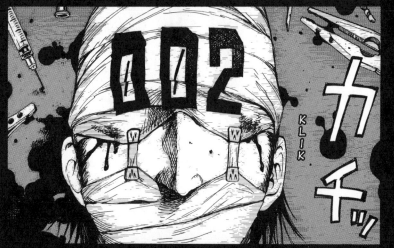

File:03

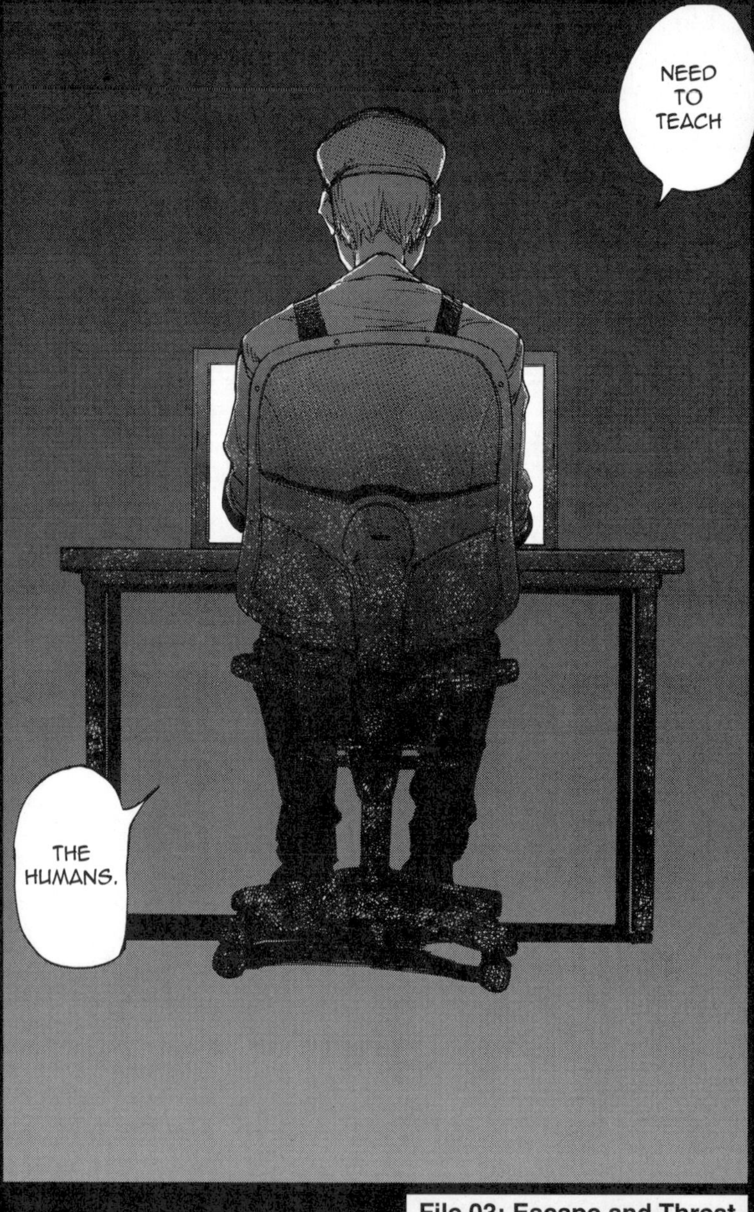
NEED TO TEACH
THE HUMANS.

File 03: Escape and Threat

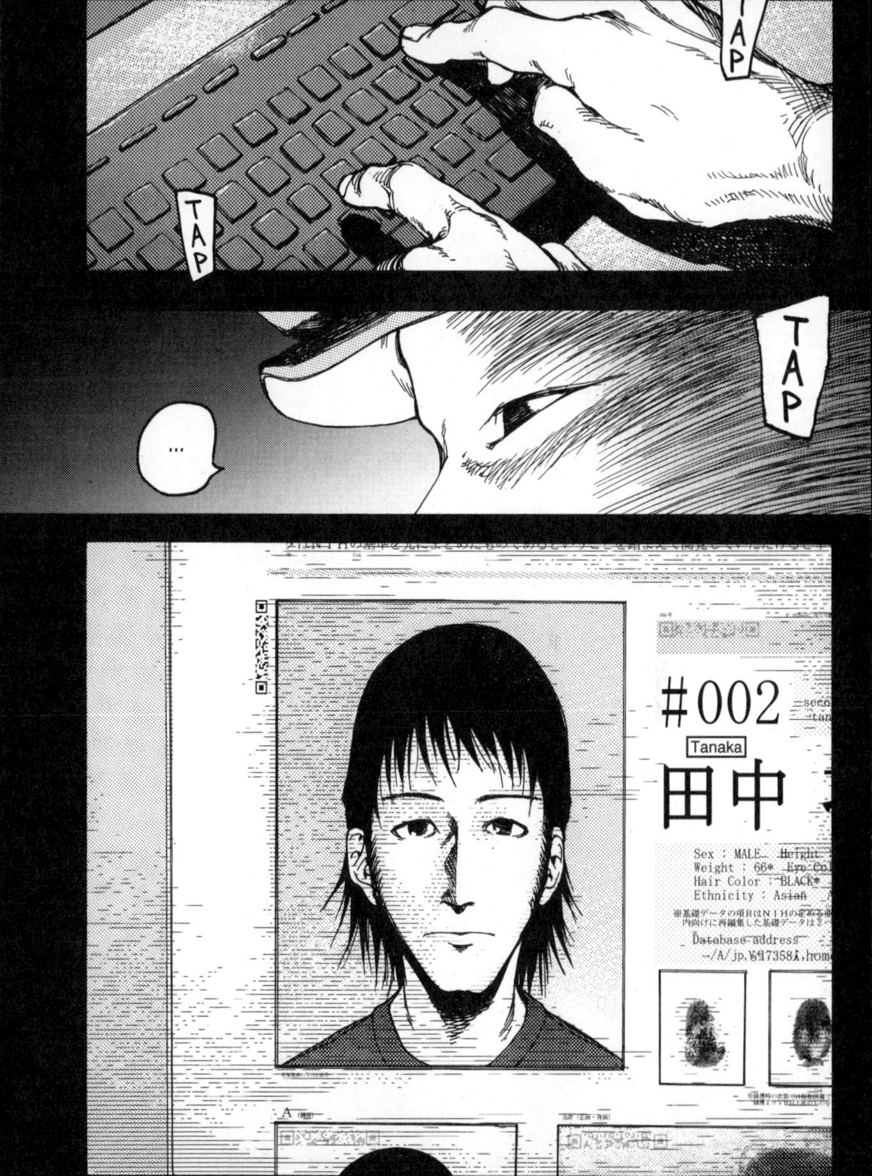

TAP
TAP
...
#002
Tanaka
田中
Sex : MALE
Weight : 66*
Hair Color : BLACK*
Ethnicity : Asian
Database address

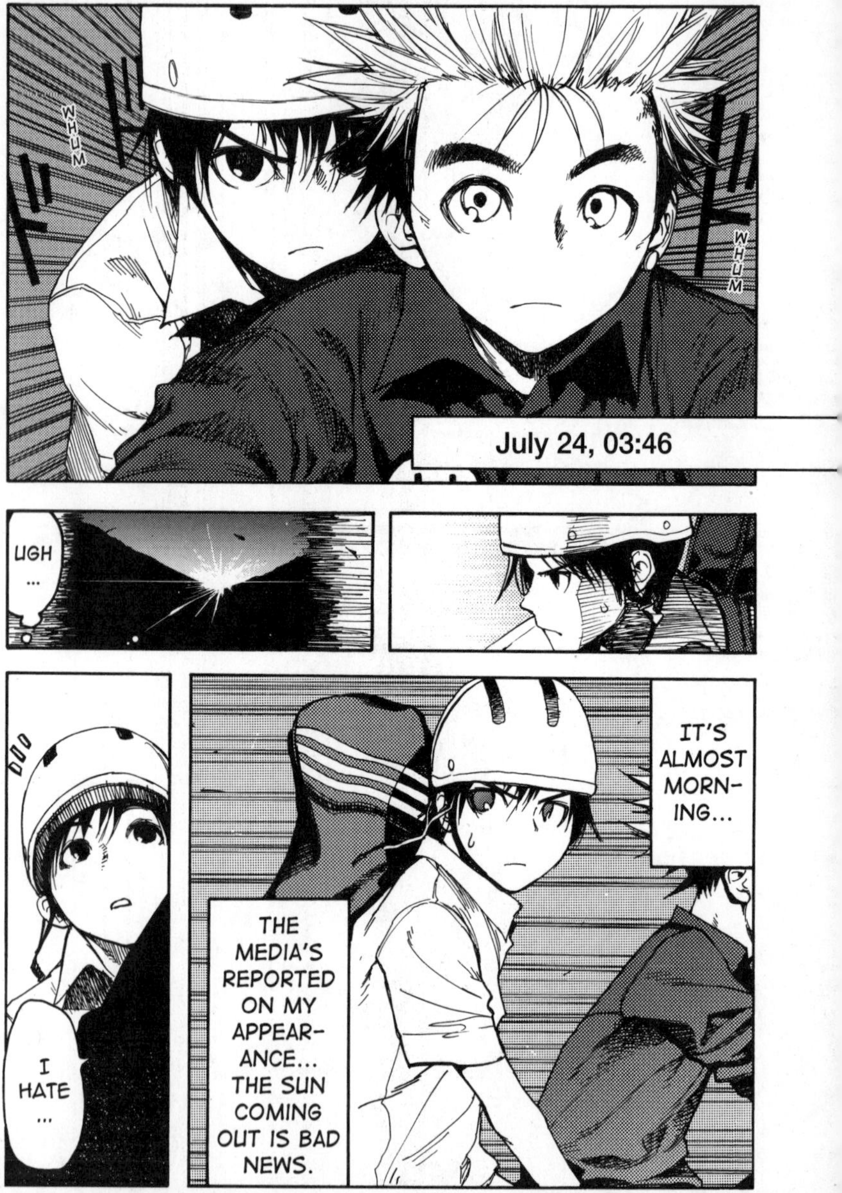
WHUM
WHUM
July 24, 03:46
UGH ...
IT'S ALMOST MORNING...
THE MEDIA'S REPORTED ON MY APPEARANCE... THE SUN COMING OUT IS BAD NEWS.
I HATE ...

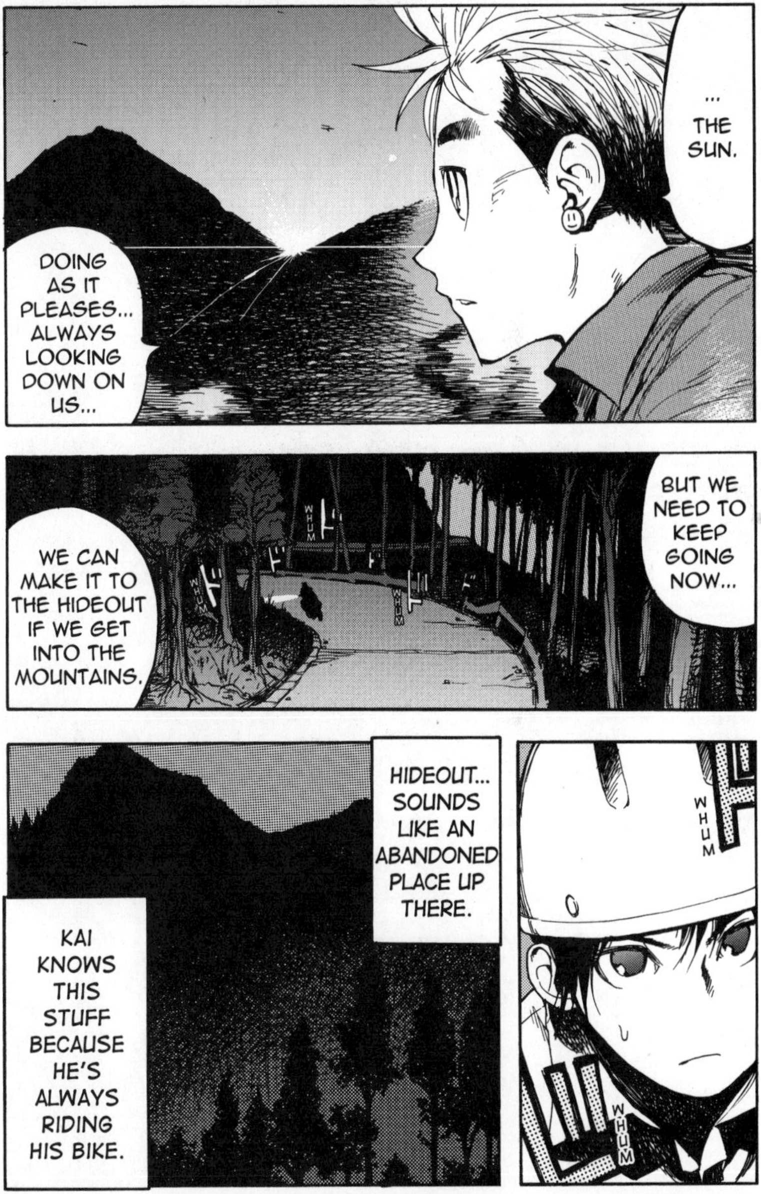
... THE SUN.
DOING AS IT PLEASES... ALWAYS LOOKING DOWN ON US...
BUT WE NEED TO KEEP GOING NOW...
WHUM
WHUM
WHUM
WE CAN MAKE IT TO THE HIDEOUT IF WE GET INTO THE MOUNTAINS.
WHUM
WHUM
HIDEOUT... SOUNDS LIKE AN ABANDONED PLACE UP THERE.
KAI KNOWS THIS STUFF BECAUSE HE'S ALWAYS RIDING HIS BIKE.

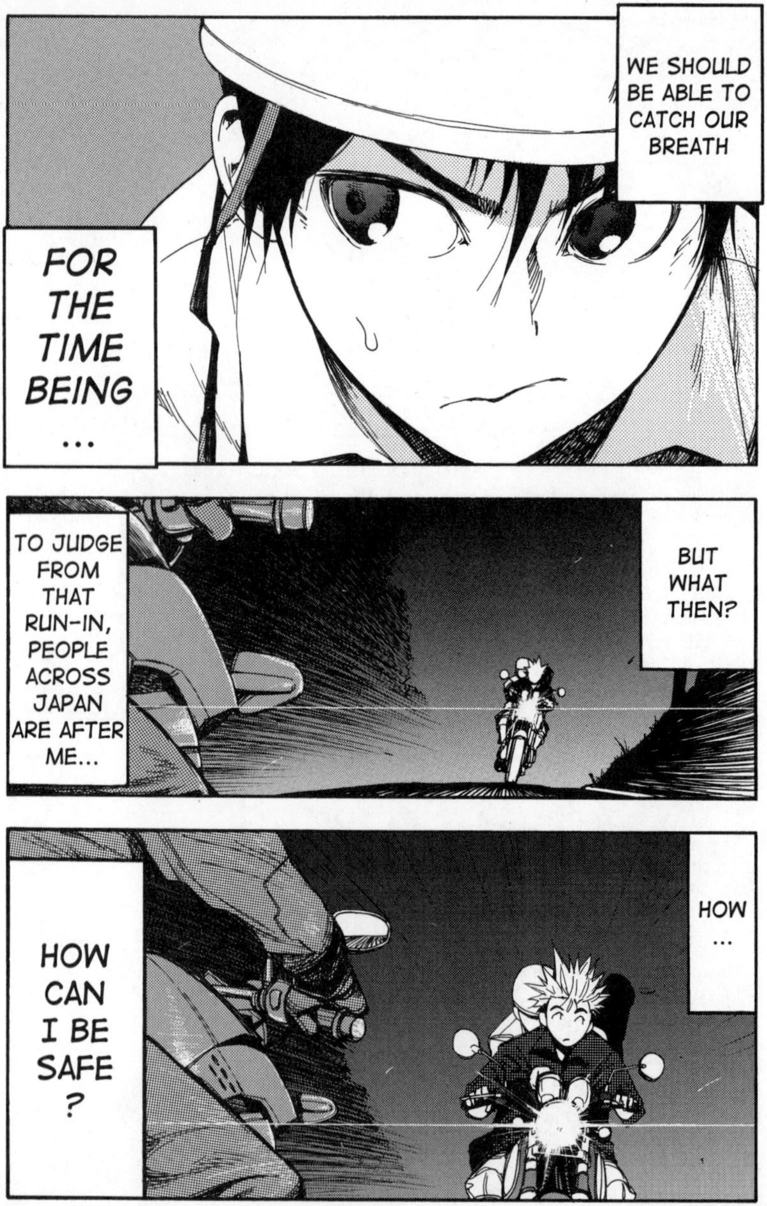
WE SHOULD BE ABLE TO CATCH OUR BREATH
FOR THE TIME BEING ...
BUT WHAT THEN?
TO JUDGE FROM THAT RUN-IN, PEOPLE ACROSS JAPAN ARE AFTER ME...
HOW ...
HOW CAN I BE SAFE ?

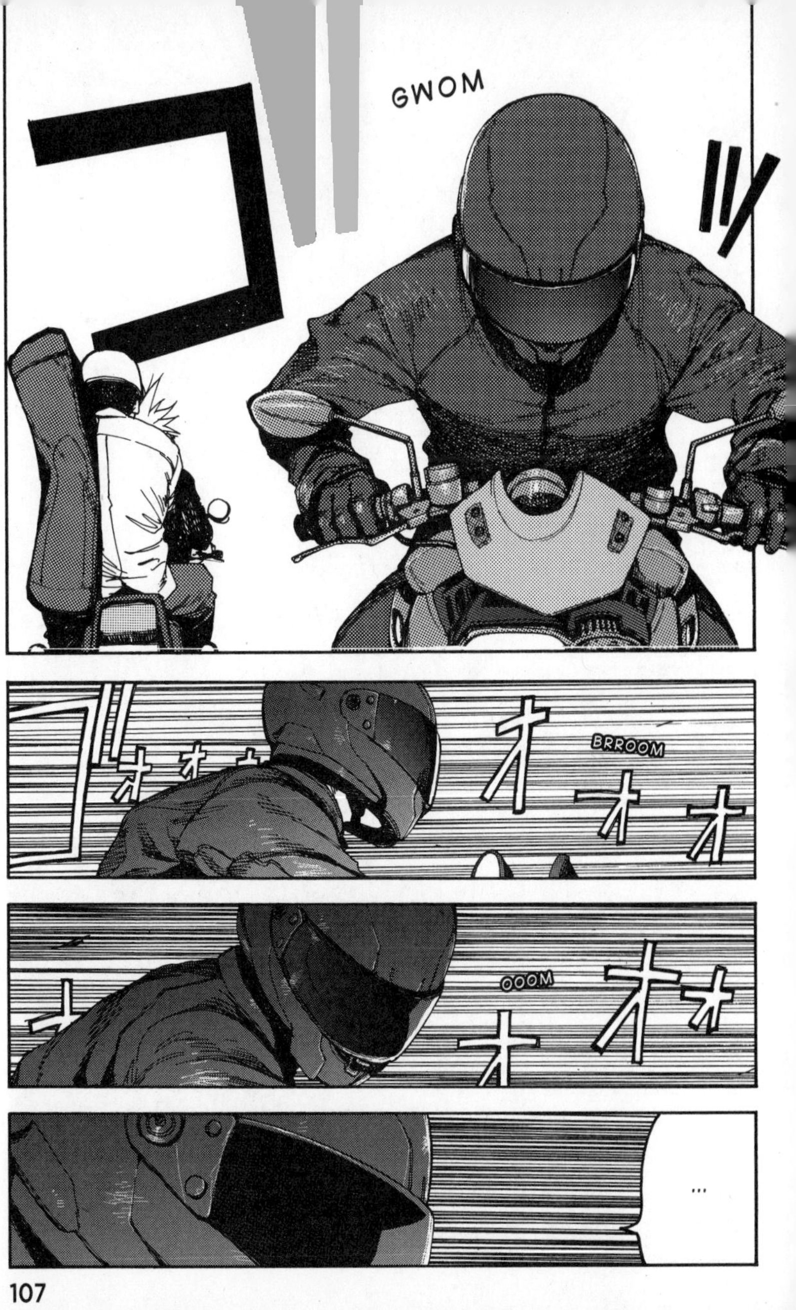
GWOM
BRROOM
OOOM
...

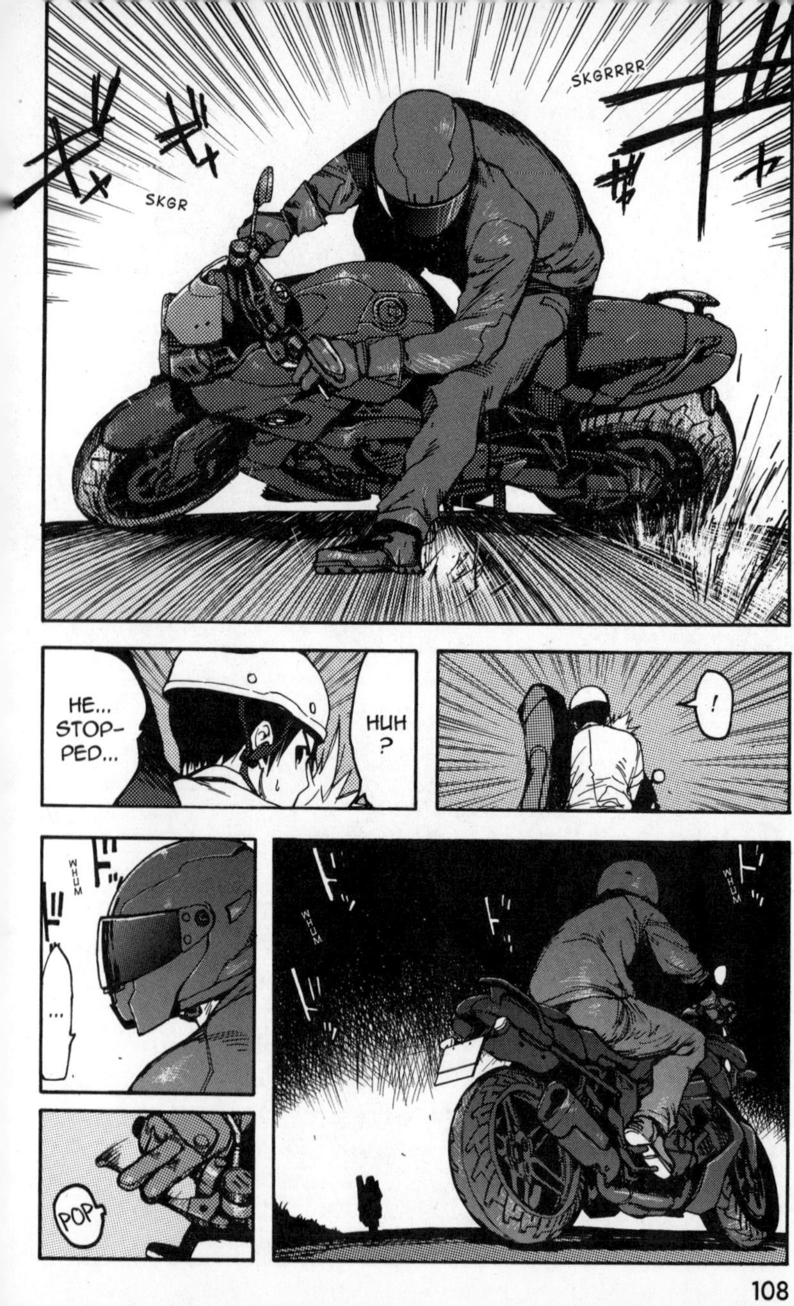
SKGRRRR
SKGR
!
HUH ?
HE... STOP-PED...
WHUM
WHUM
WHUM
...
POP

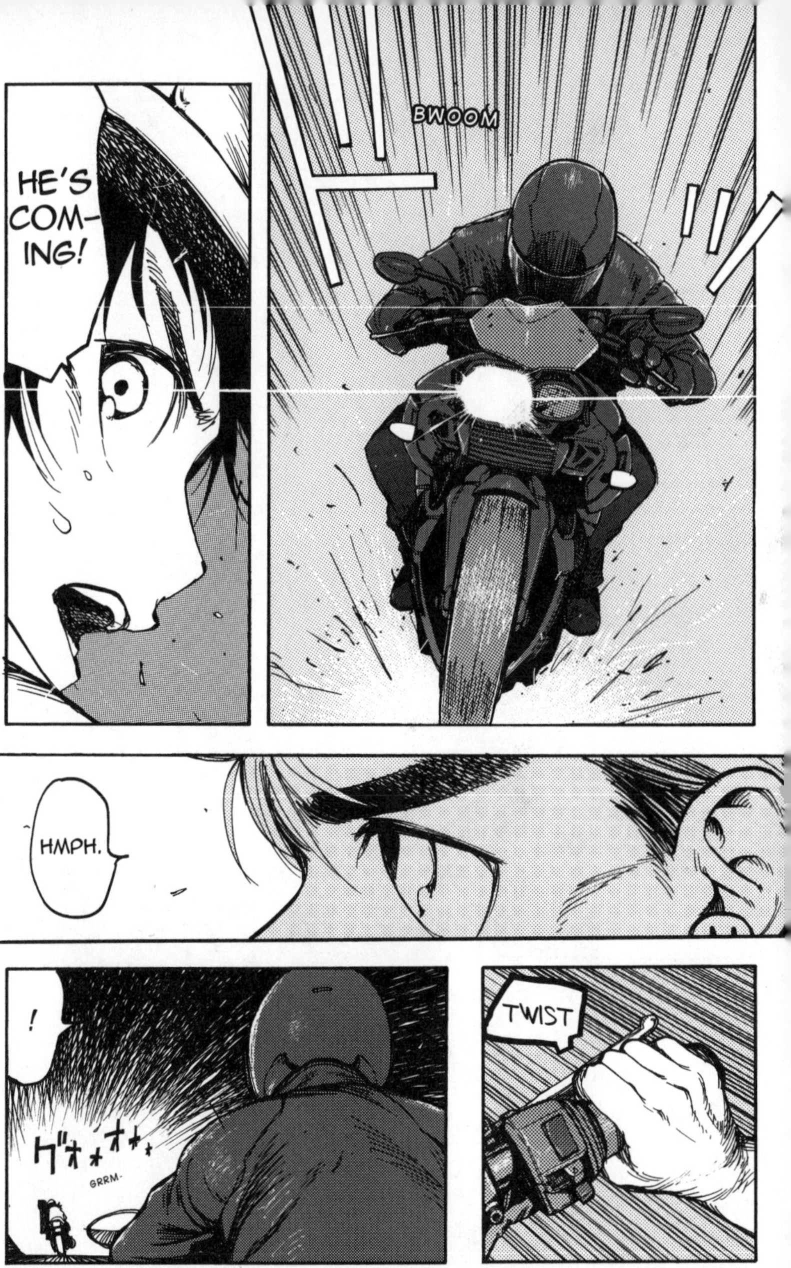
BWOOM
HE'S COMING!
HMPH.
TWIST
!
グオォオォ
GRRM.

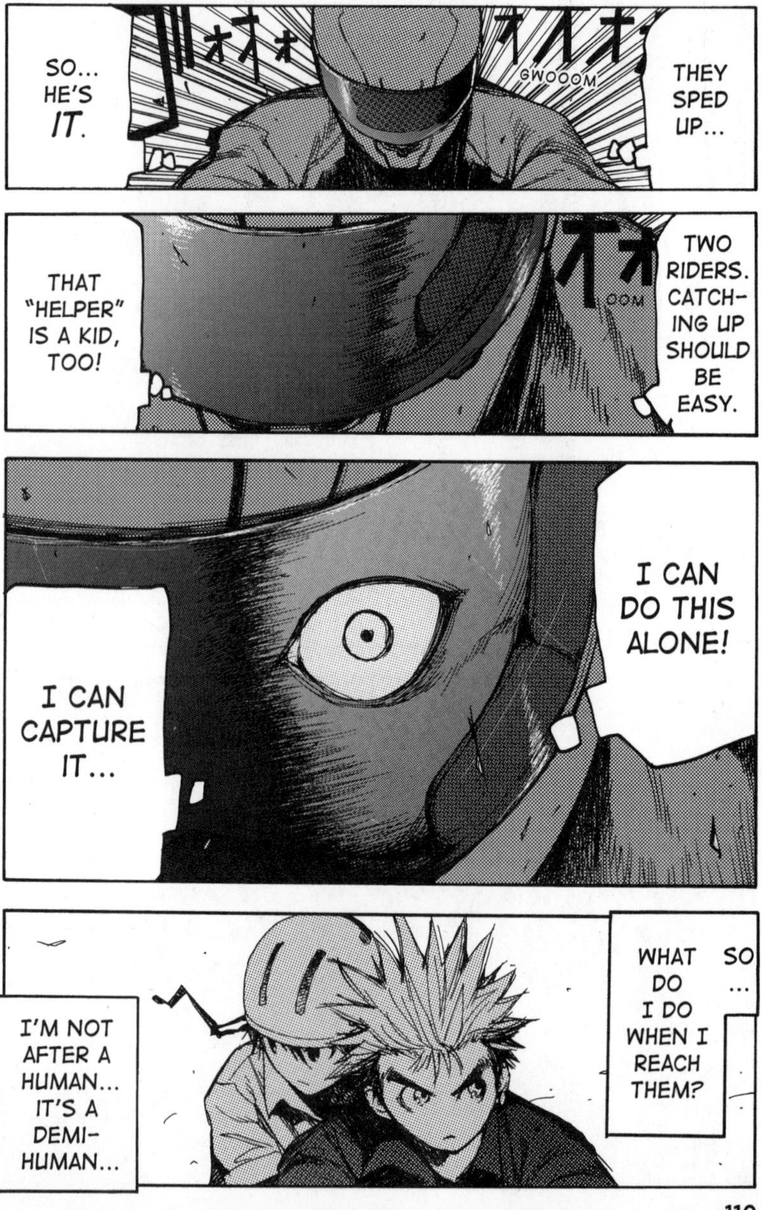
THEY SPED UP...
GWOOOM
SO... HE'S IT.
TWO RIDERS. CATCHING-ING UP SHOULD BE EASY.
OOM
THAT "HELPER" IS A KID, TOO!
I CAN DO THIS ALONE!
I CAN CAPTURE IT...
SO...
WHAT DO I DO WHEN I REACH THEM?
I'M NOT AFTER A HUMAN... IT'S A DEMI-HUMAN...

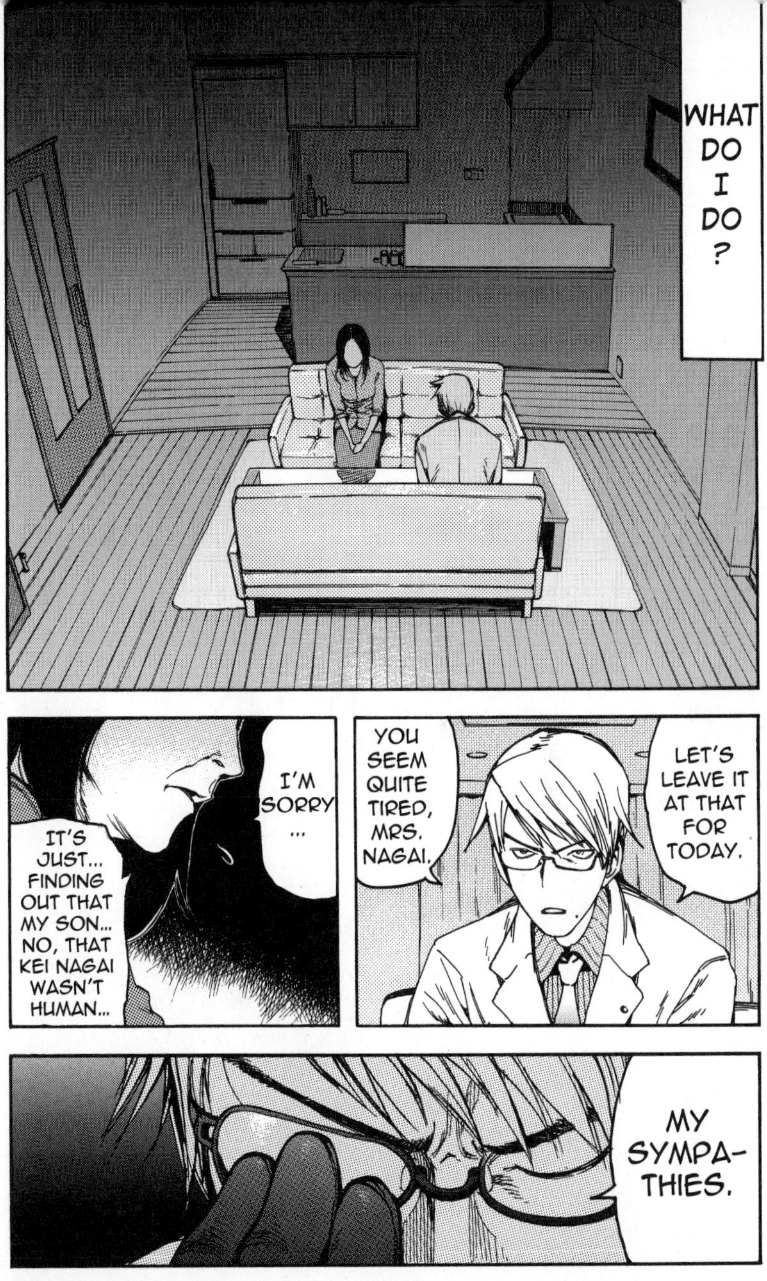
WHAT DO I DO?
LET'S LEAVE IT AT THAT FOR TODAY.
YOU SEEM QUITE TIRED, MRS. NAGAI.
I'M SORRY...
IT'S JUST... FINDING OUT THAT MY SON... NO, THAT KEI NAGAI WASN'T HUMAN...
MY SYMPA-THIES.

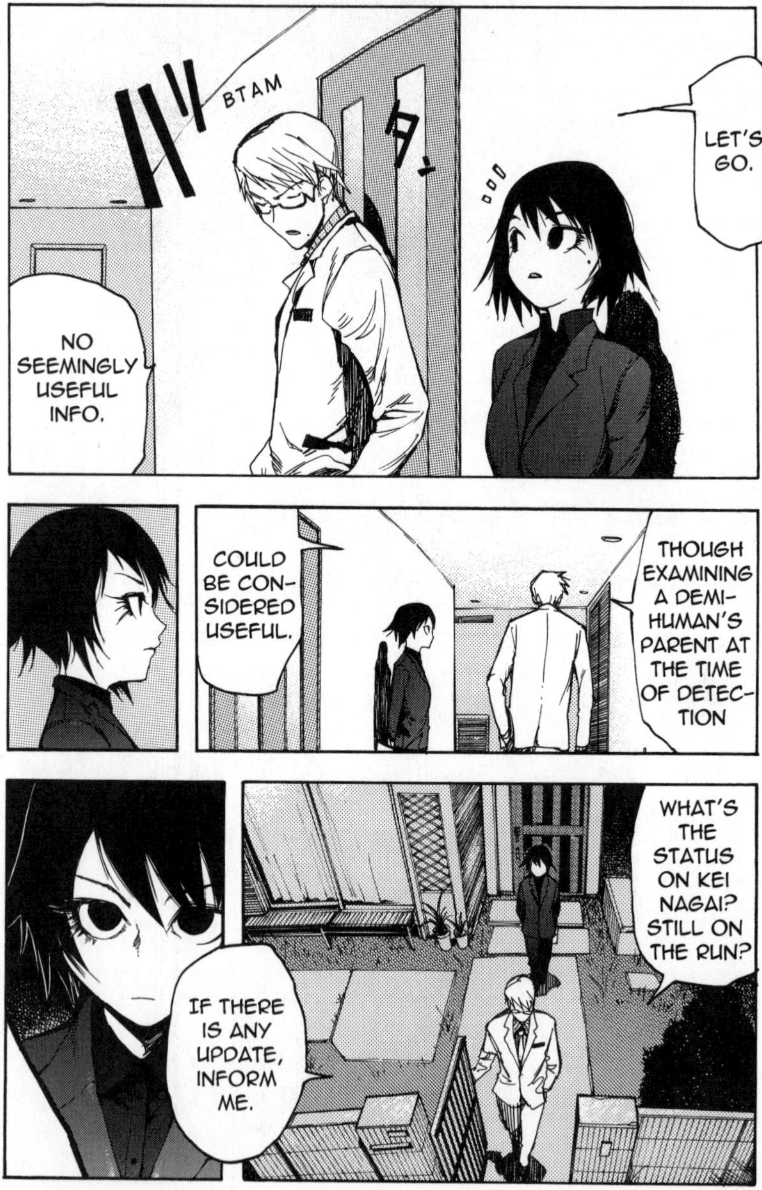
LET'S GO.
BTAM
NO SEEMINGLY USEFUL INFO.
THOUGH EXAMINING A DEMI-HUMAN'S PARENT AT THE TIME OF DETECTION
COULD BE CON-SIDERED USEFUL.
WHAT'S THE STATUS ON KEI NAGAI? STILL ON THE RUN?
IF THERE IS ANY UPDATE, INFORM ME.

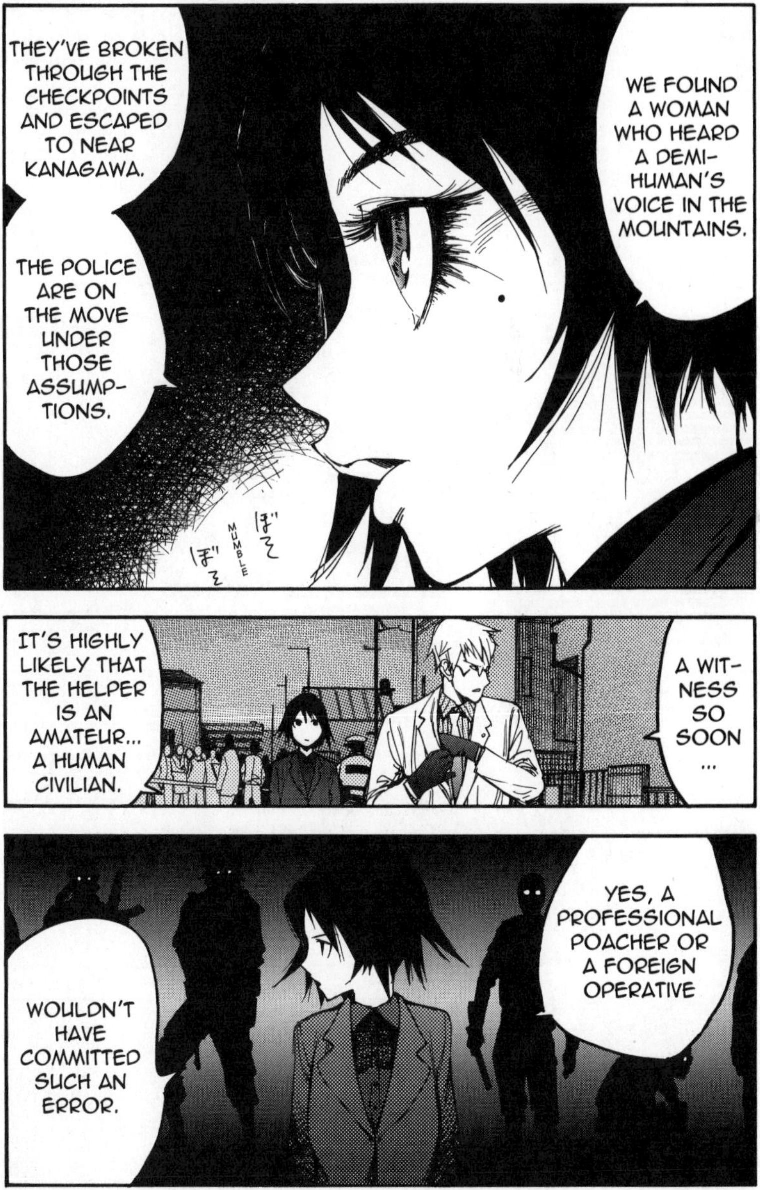
WE FOUND A WOMAN WHO HEARD A DEMI-HUMAN'S VOICE IN THE MOUNTAINS.
THEY'VE BROKEN THROUGH THE CHECKPOINTS AND ESCAPED TO NEAR KANAGAWA.
THE POLICE ARE ON THE MOVE UNDER THOSE ASSUMP-TIONS.
ぼそぼそ
MUMBLE
A WIT-NESS SO SOON ...
IT'S HIGHLY LIKELY THAT THE HELPER IS AN AMATEUR... A HUMAN CIVILIAN.
YES, A PROFESSIONAL POACHER OR A FOREIGN OPERATIVE
WOULDN'T HAVE COMMITTED SUCH AN ERROR.

IF IT'S AN AMATEUR CRIMINAL OUT FOR MONEY, WE SHOULD QUICKLY BE ABLE TO FIND KEI NAGAI.

OF COURSE, THAT IS THE JOB OF THE POLICE... WE—

REALLY?

IS MONEY THE ONLY MOTIVE?

PERSONALLY...

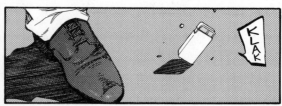

KLAK

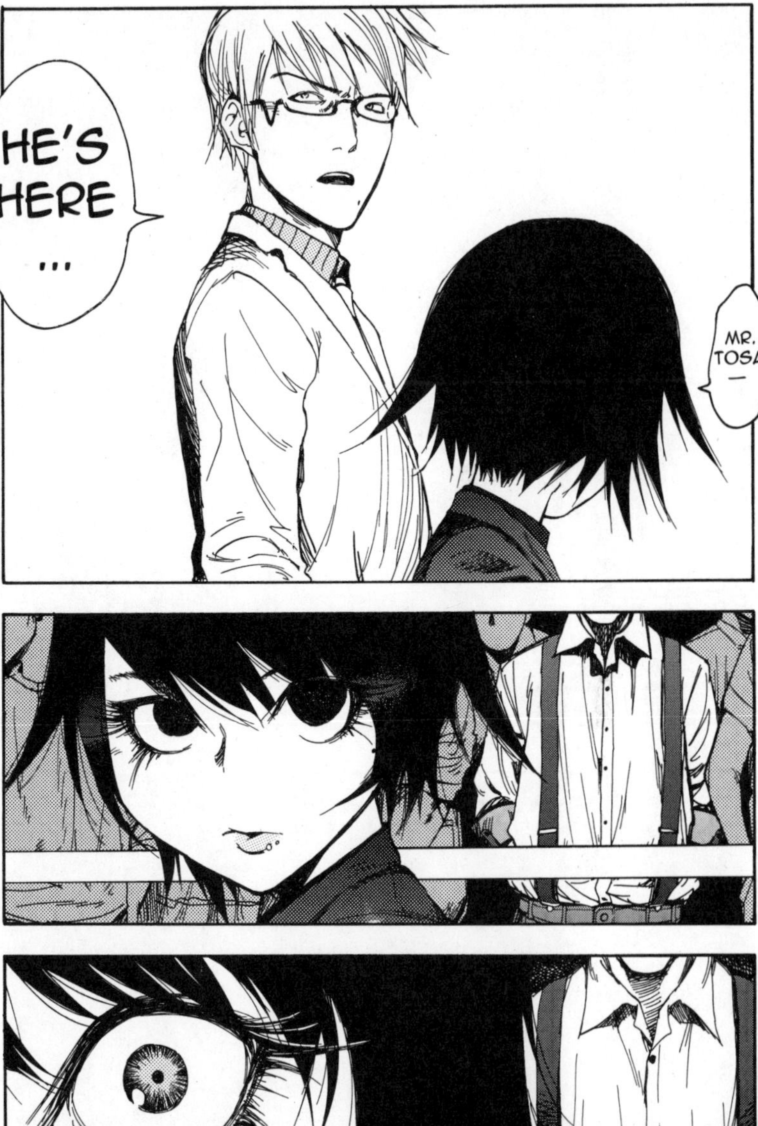
MR. TOSA —
HE'S HERE ...

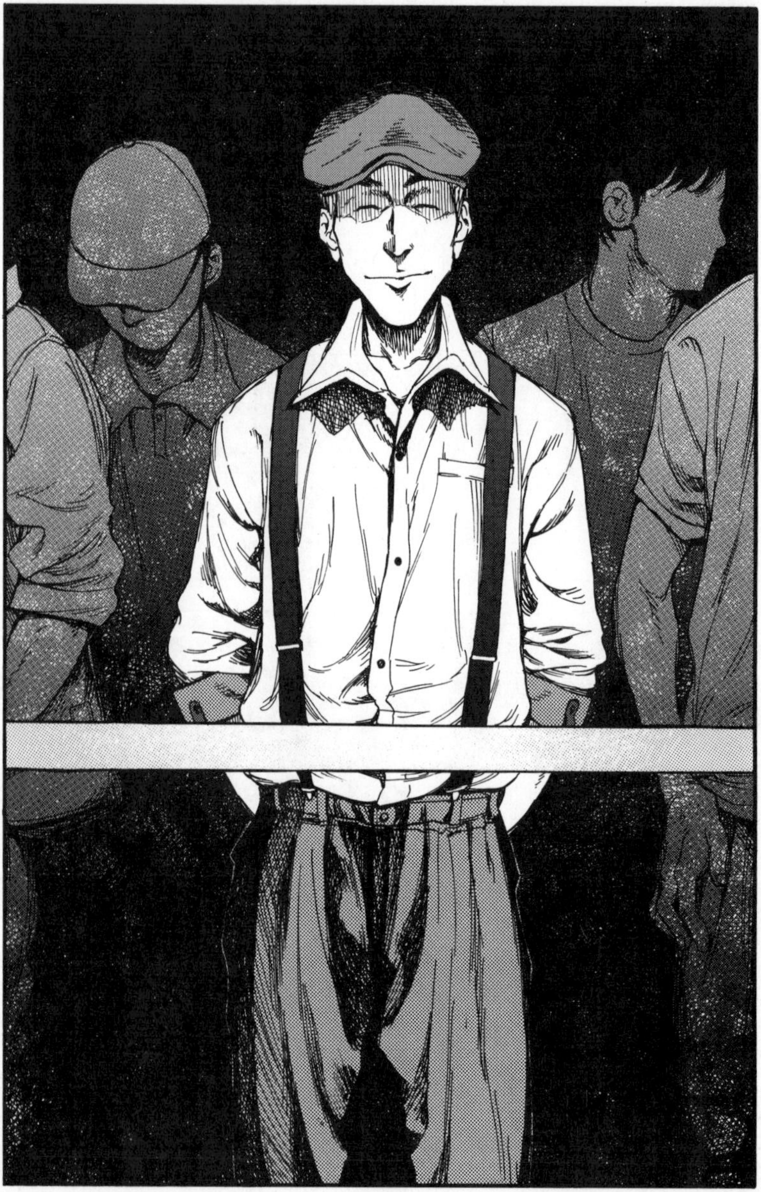

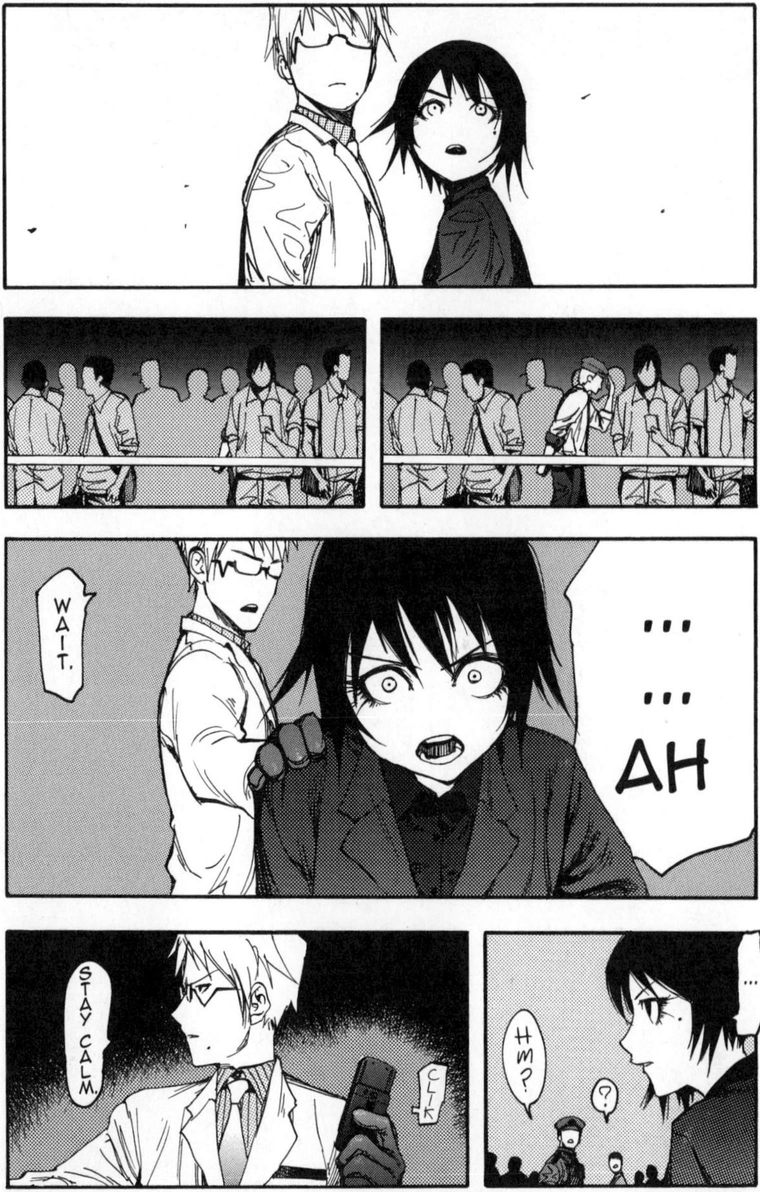
... ... AH
WAIT.
...
HM?
?
STAY CALM.
CLIK

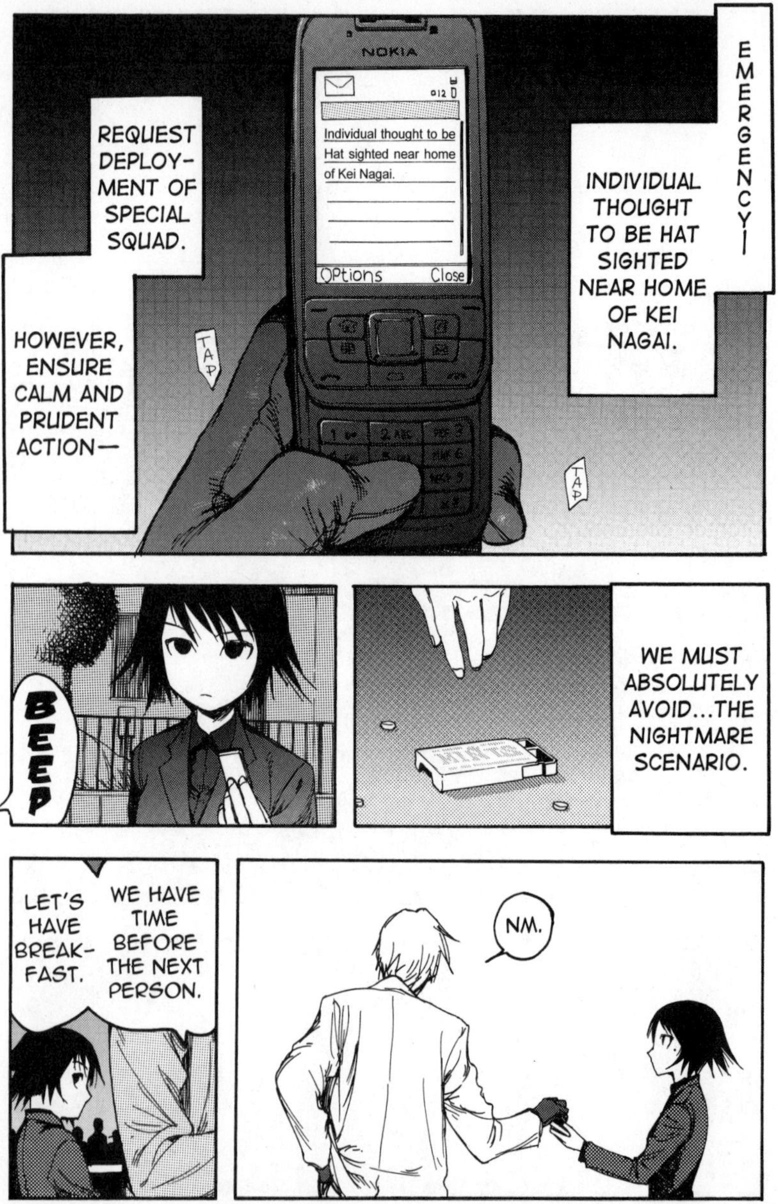

EMERGENCY!
INDIVIDUAL THOUGHT TO BE HAT SIGHTED NEAR HOME OF KEI NAGAI.
NOKIA
Individual thought to be Hat sighted near home of Kei Nagai.
Options
Close
REQUEST DEPLOYMENT OF SPECIAL SQUAD.
TAP
HOWEVER, ENSURE CALM AND PRUDENT ACTION—
TAP
WE MUST ABSOLUTELY AVOID...THE NIGHTMARE SCENARIO.
BEEP
NM.
WE HAVE TIME BEFORE THE NEXT PERSON.
LET'S HAVE BREAK-FAST.

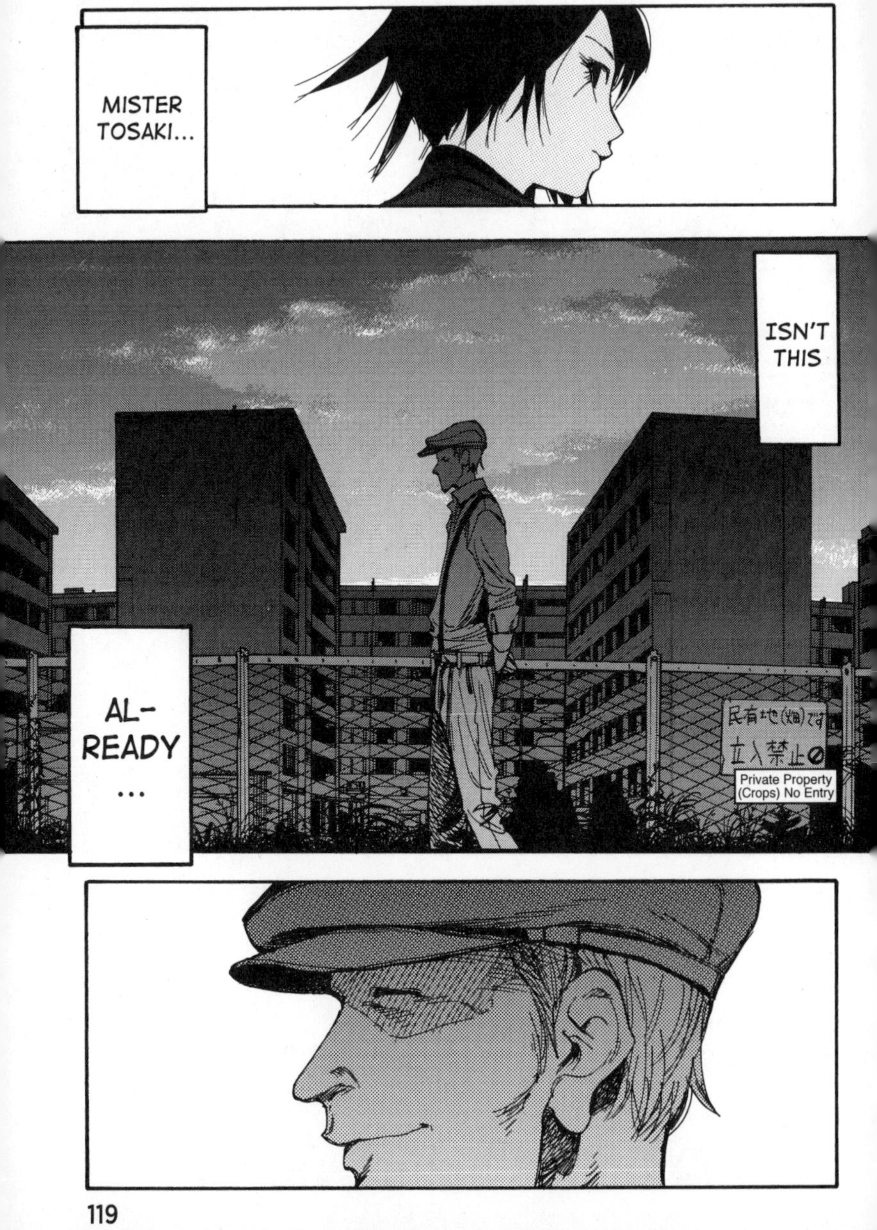
MISTER TOSAKI...
ISN'T THIS
AL-READY ...
民有地(畑)です
立入禁止
Private Property (Crops) No Entry

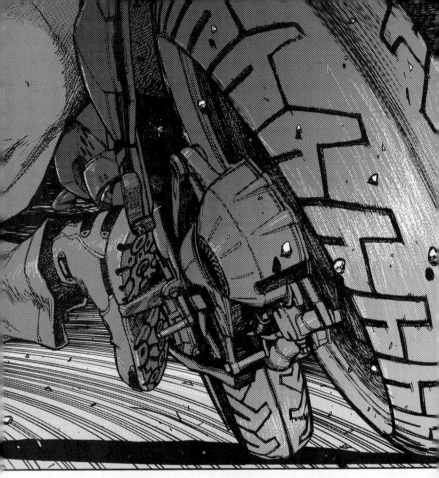

KEI.

...

KAI...
HE'S
CATCH-
ING
UP!

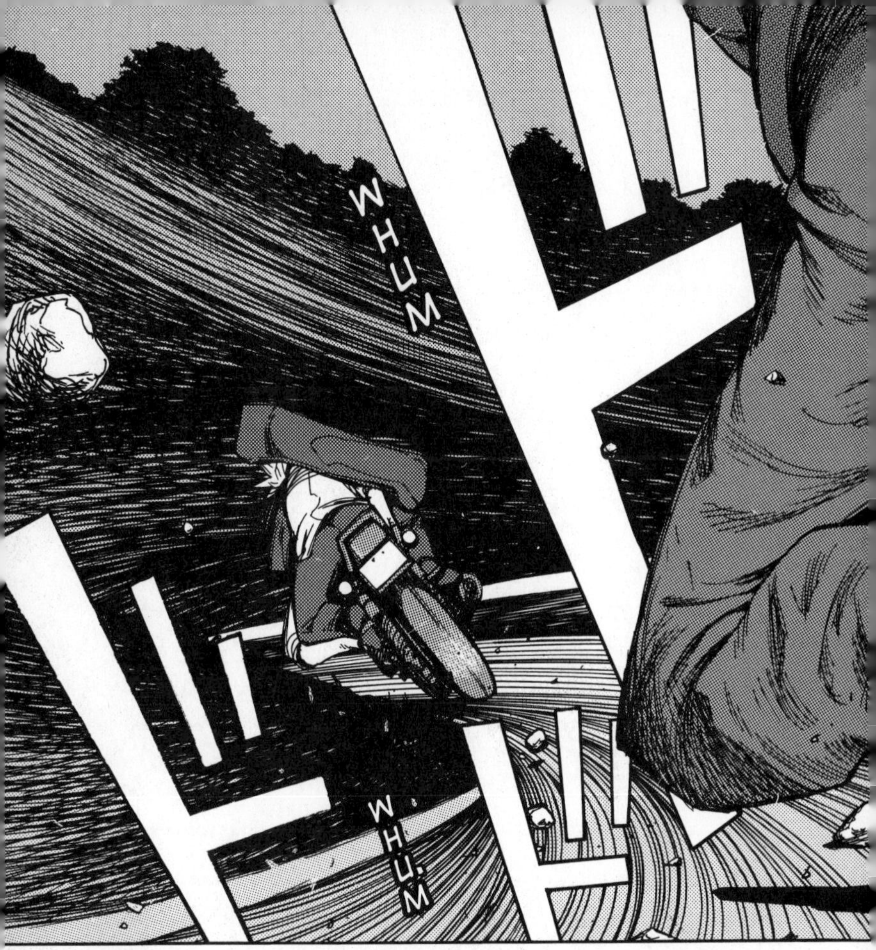
WHUM
WHUM

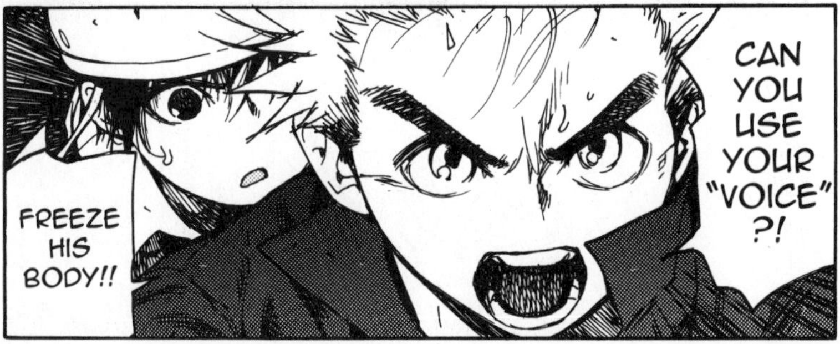
CAN YOU USE YOUR "VOICE" ?!
FREEZE HIS BODY!!

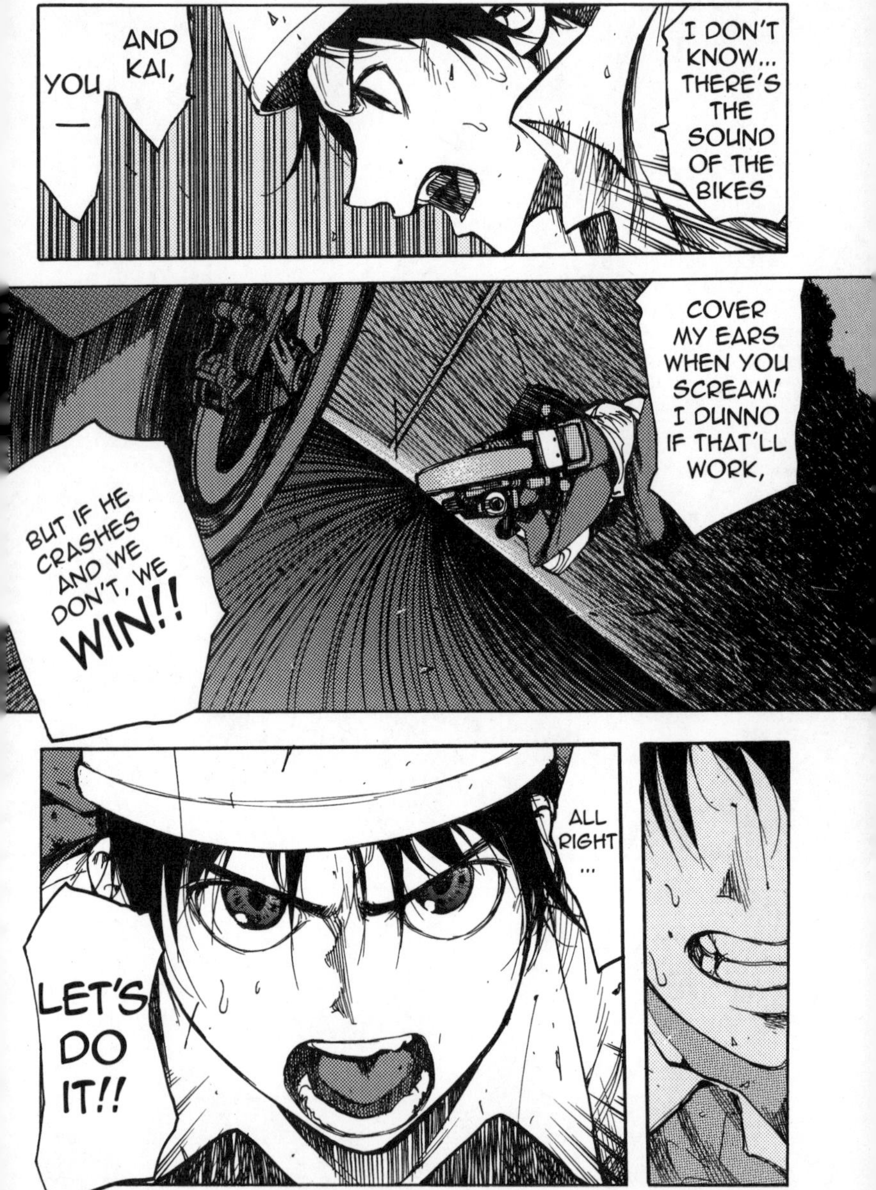
I DON'T KNOW... THERE'S THE SOUND OF THE BIKES
AND KAI,
YOU —
COVER MY EARS WHEN YOU SCREAM! I DUNNO IF THAT'LL WORK,
BUT IF HE CRASHES AND WE DON'T, WE WIN!!
ALL RIGHT ...
LET'S DO IT!!

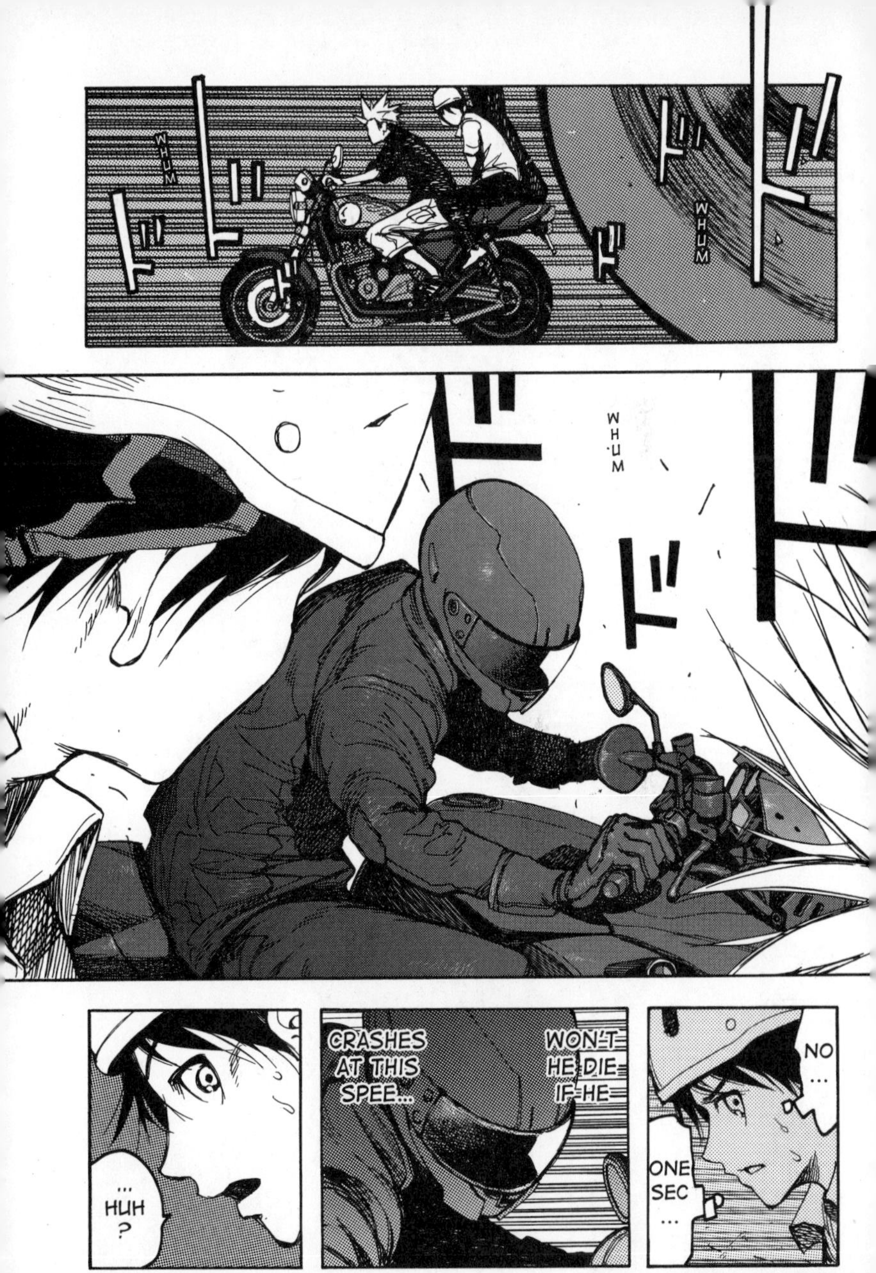
WHUM
WHUM
WHUM
NO ...
ONE SEC ...
WON'T HE DIE IF HE
CRASHES AT THIS SPEE...
... HUH ?

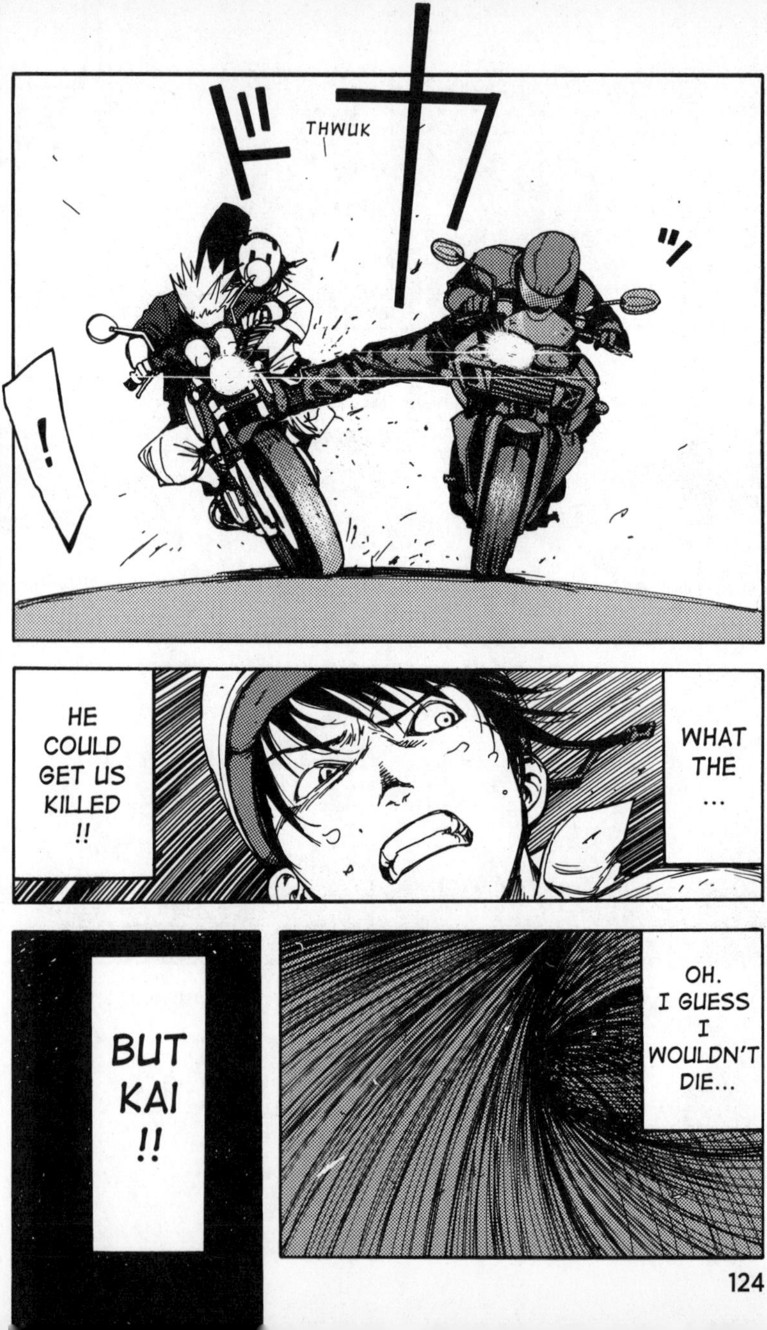
ドカ
THWUK
ッ
!
WHAT THE ...
HE COULD GET US KILLED !!
OH. I GUESS I WOULDN'T DIE...
BUT KAI !!

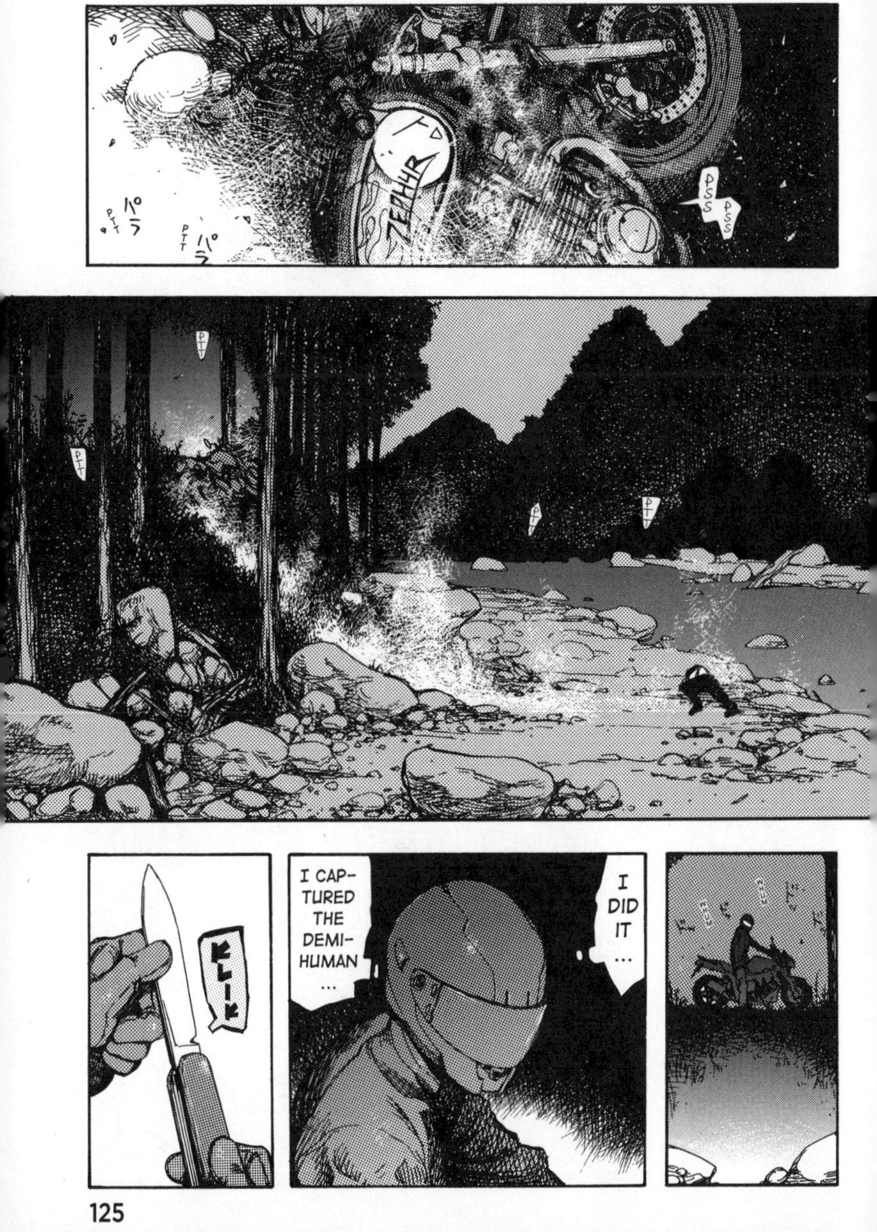
ZEPHYR
PSS PSS
PTT パラ
PTT パラ
PTT
PTT
PTT
PTT
I DID IT ...
I CAPTURED THE DEMI-HUMAN ...
KLIK

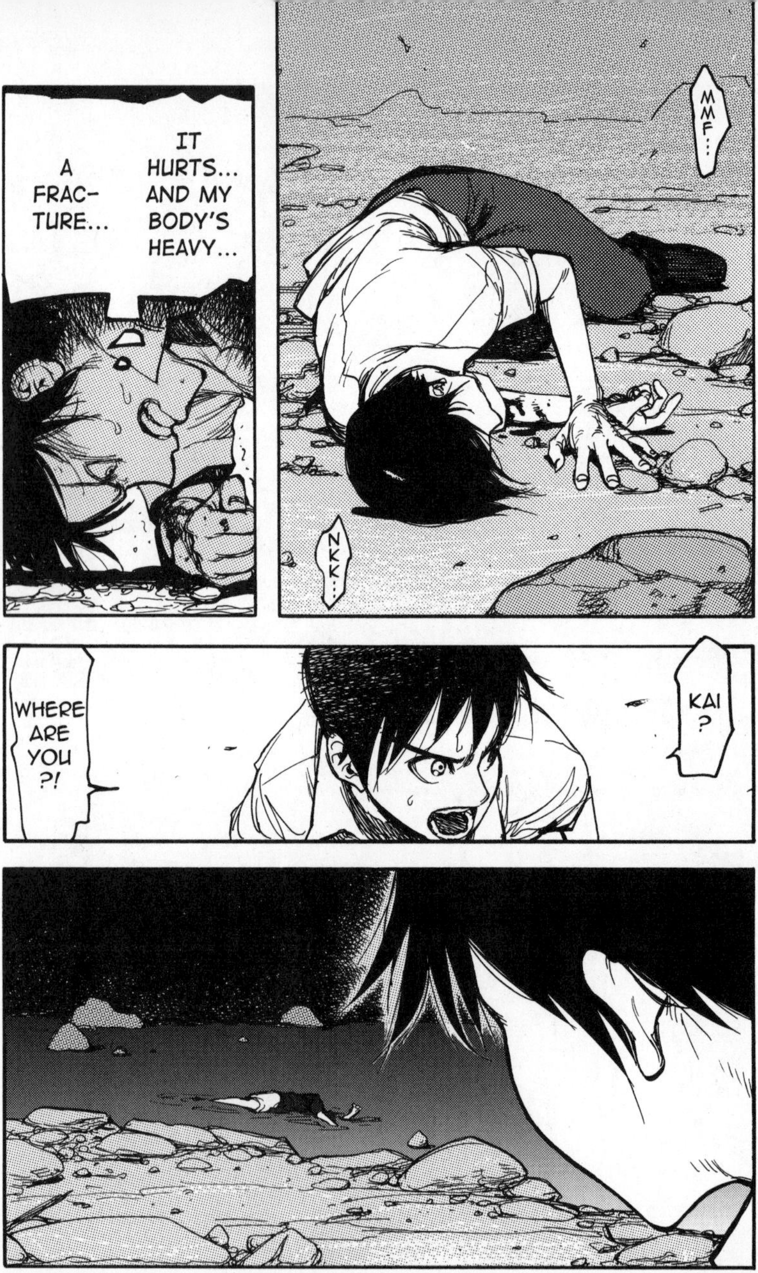
MMF...
NKK...
IT HURTS... AND MY BODY'S HEAVY...
A FRAC-TURE...
KAI?
WHERE ARE YOU?!

KA...

SHUT UP AND DON'T MOVE.

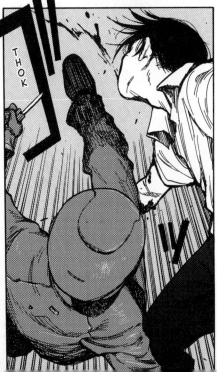

THOK

OUCH!!

OWW...

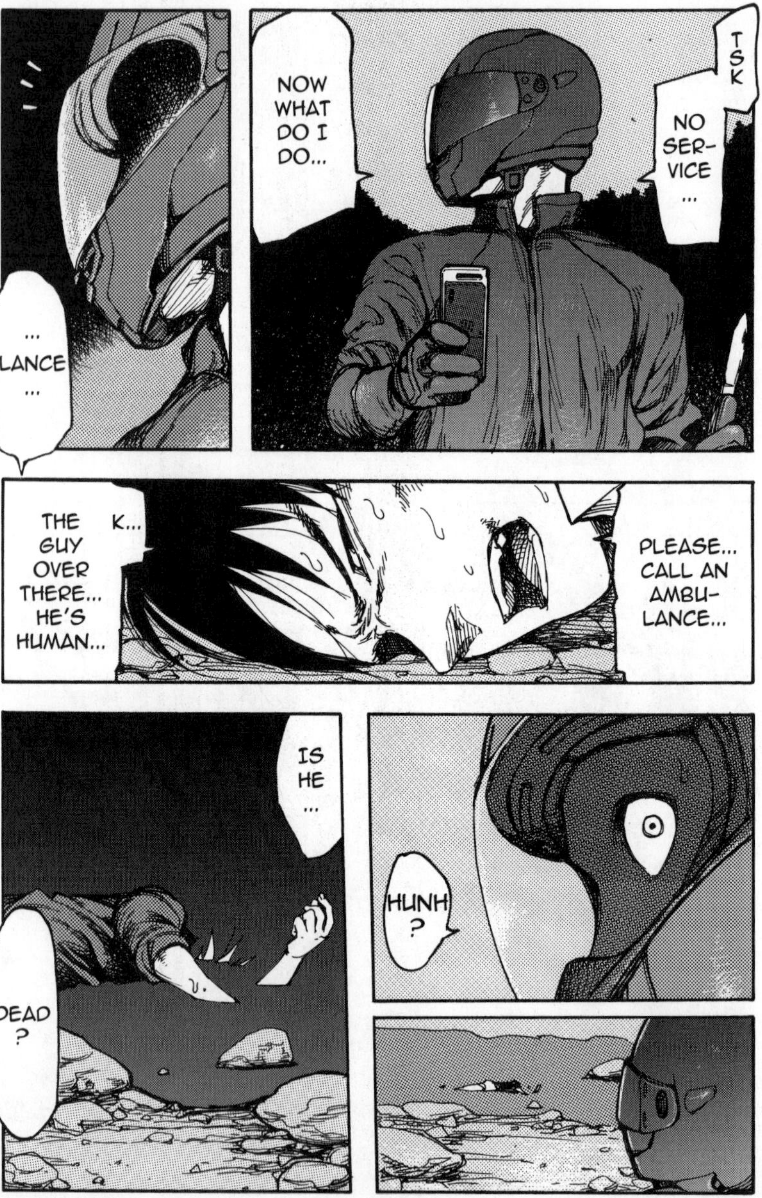
TSK
NO SER-VICE ...
NOW WHAT DO I DO...
... LANCE ...
PLEASE... CALL AN AMBU-LANCE...
K...
THE GUY OVER THERE... HE'S HUMAN...
HUNH ?
IS HE ...
DEAD ?

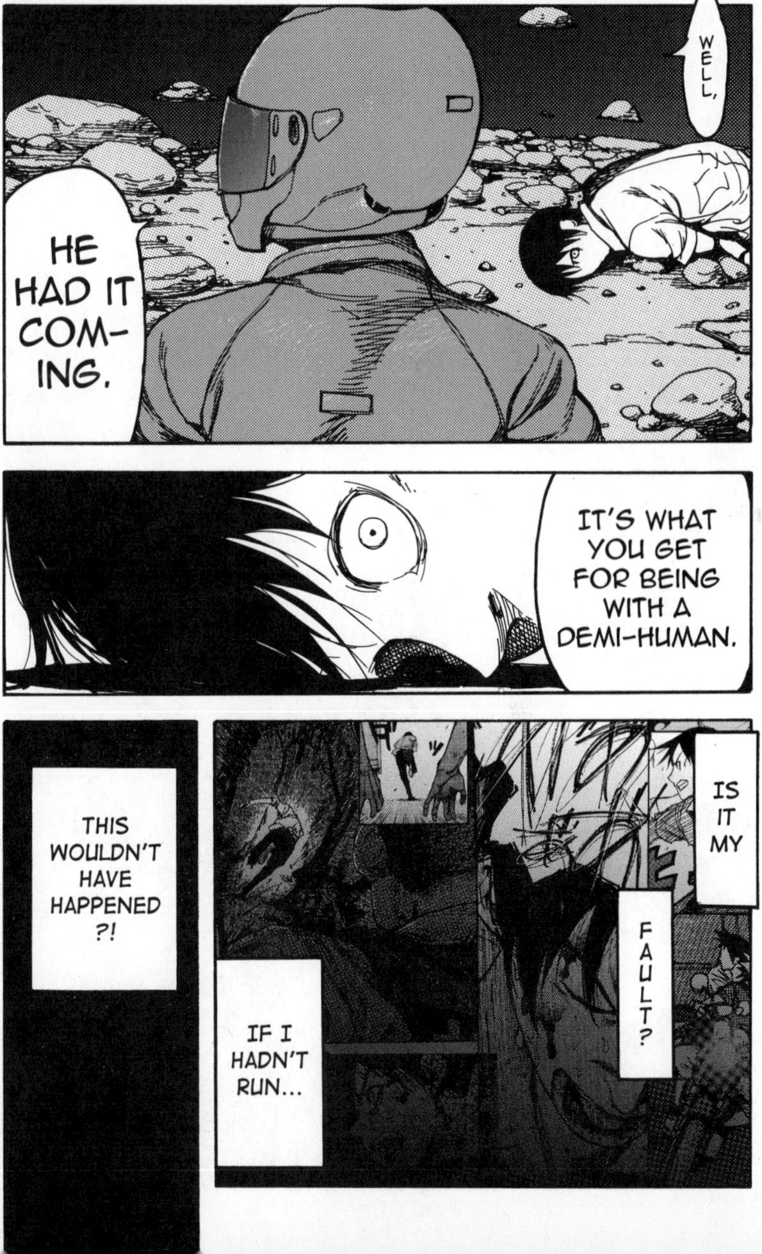
WELL,
HE HAD IT COMING.
IT'S WHAT YOU GET FOR BEING WITH A DEMI-HUMAN.
IS IT MY FAULT?
IF I HADN'T RUN...
THIS WOULDN'T HAVE HAPPENED?!

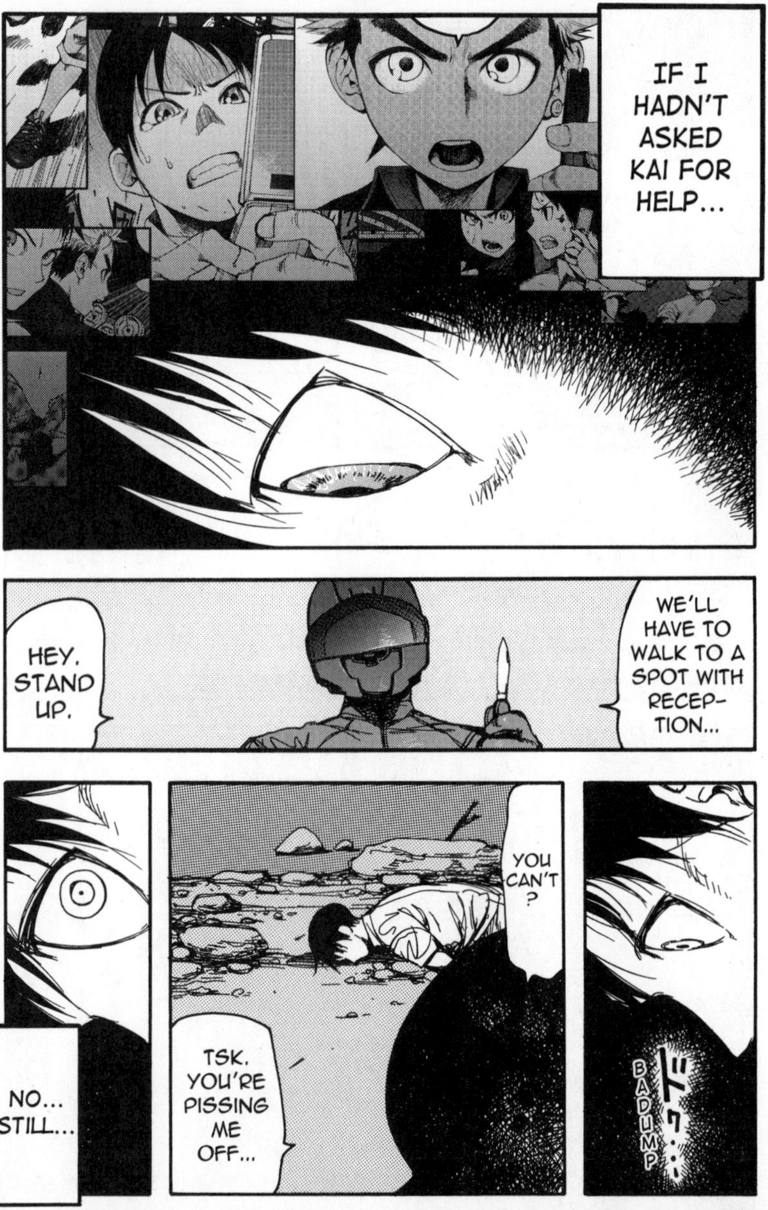
IF I HADN'T ASKED KAI FOR HELP...
WE'LL HAVE TO WALK TO A SPOT WITH RECEP-TION...
HEY. STAND UP.
BADUMP
YOU CAN'T?
TSK. YOU'RE PISSING ME OFF...
NO... STILL...

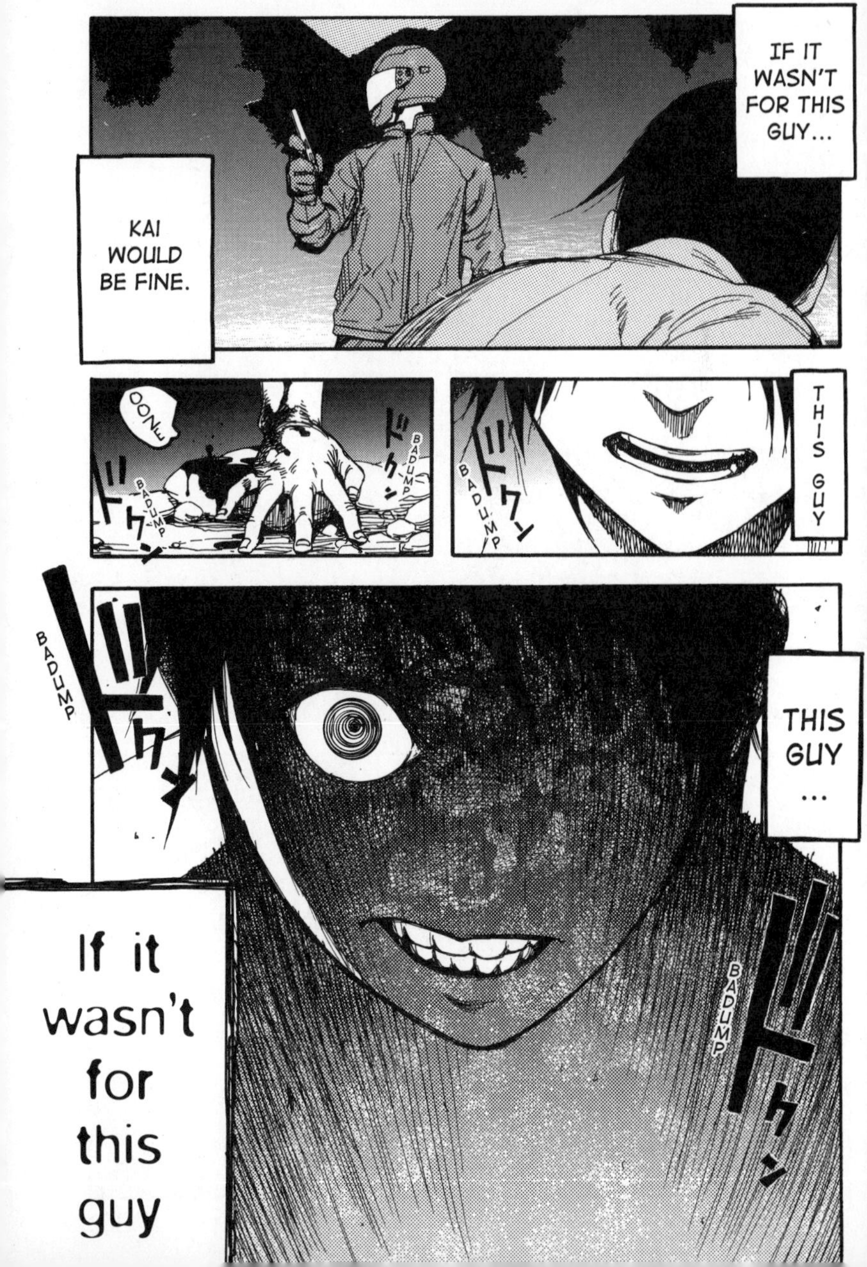
IF IT WASN'T FOR THIS GUY...
KAI WOULD BE FINE.
THIS GUY
BADUMP
DONE
BADUMP
BADUMP
THIS GUY ...
BADUMP
BADUMP
If it wasn't for this guy

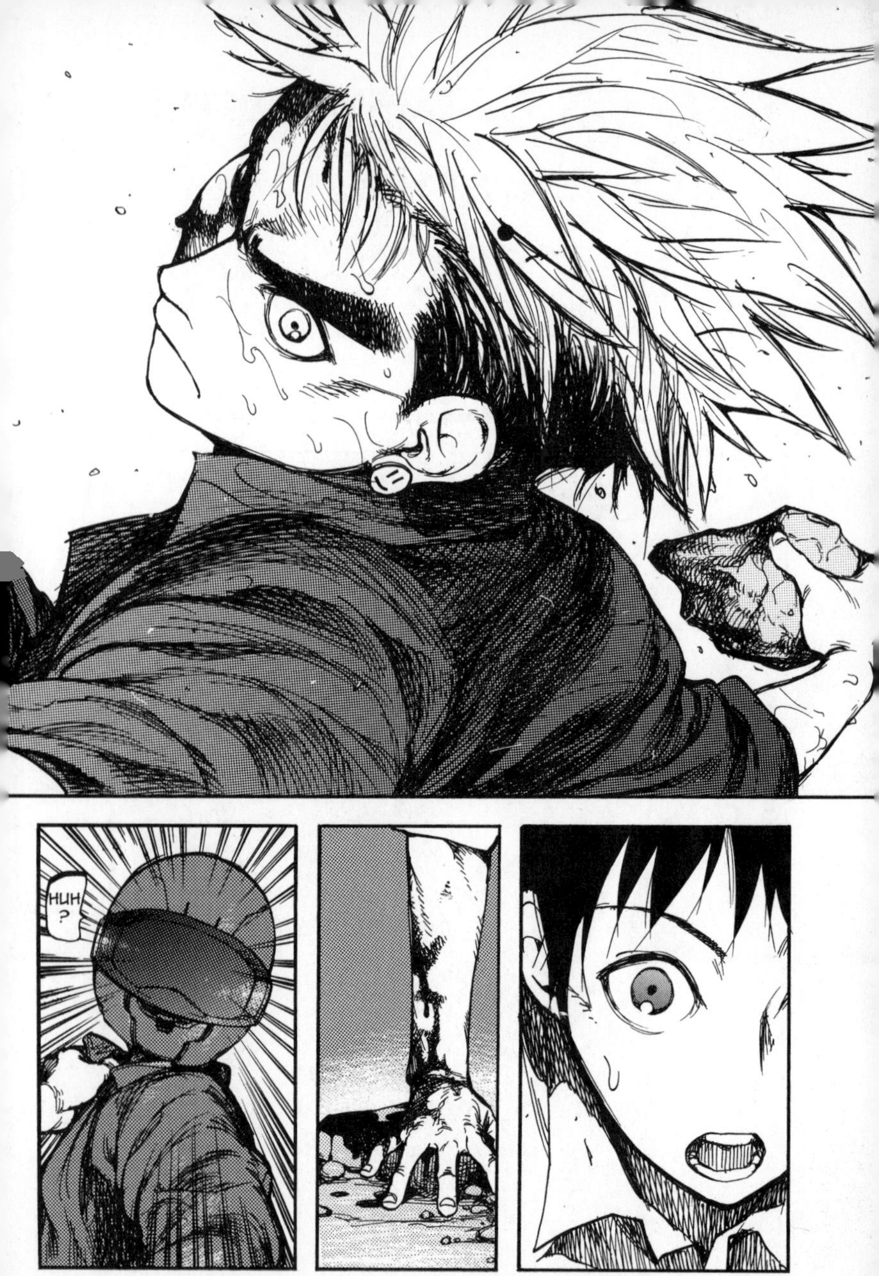
HUH
?

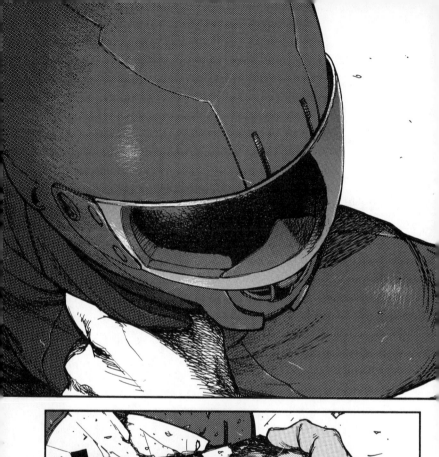

GWOK

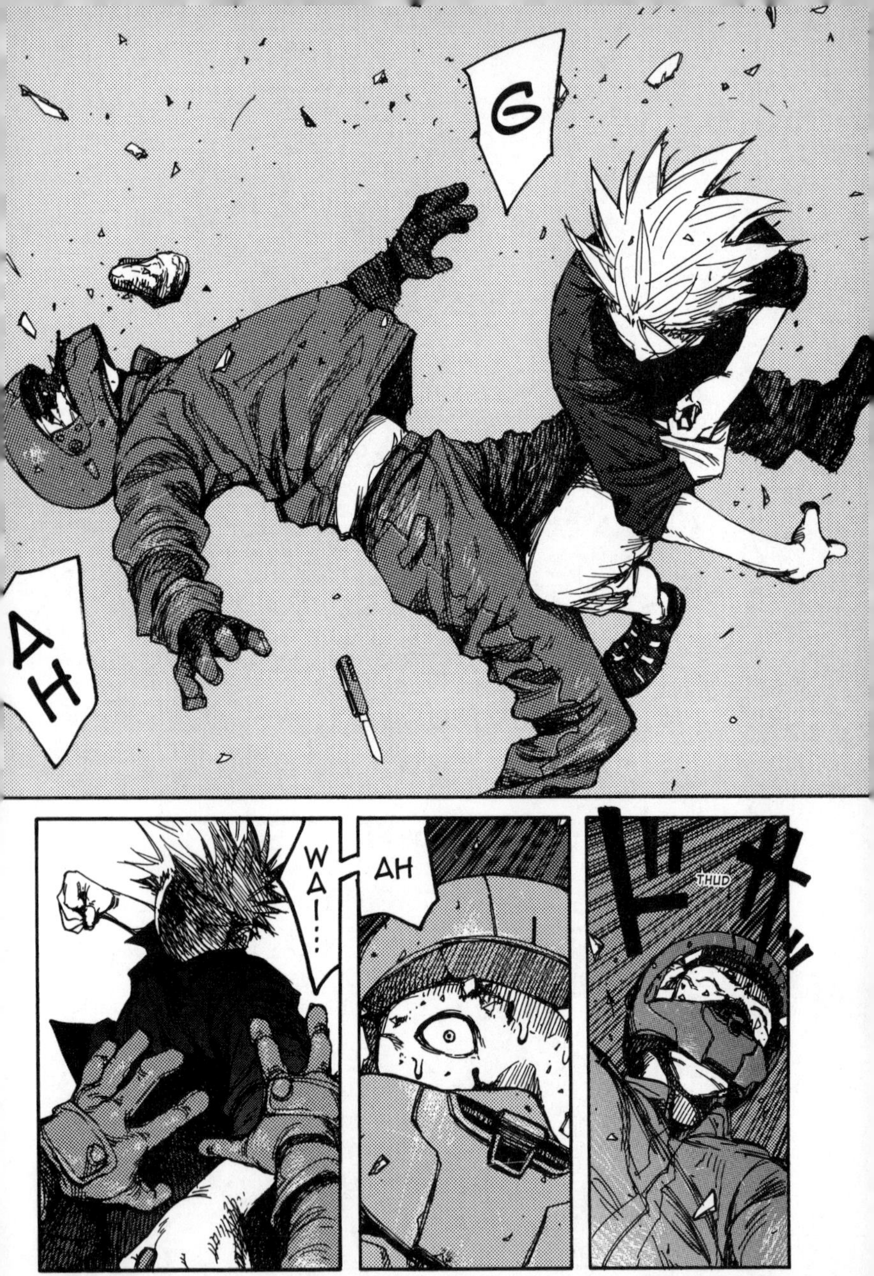
G
AH
THUD
AH
WAI...!

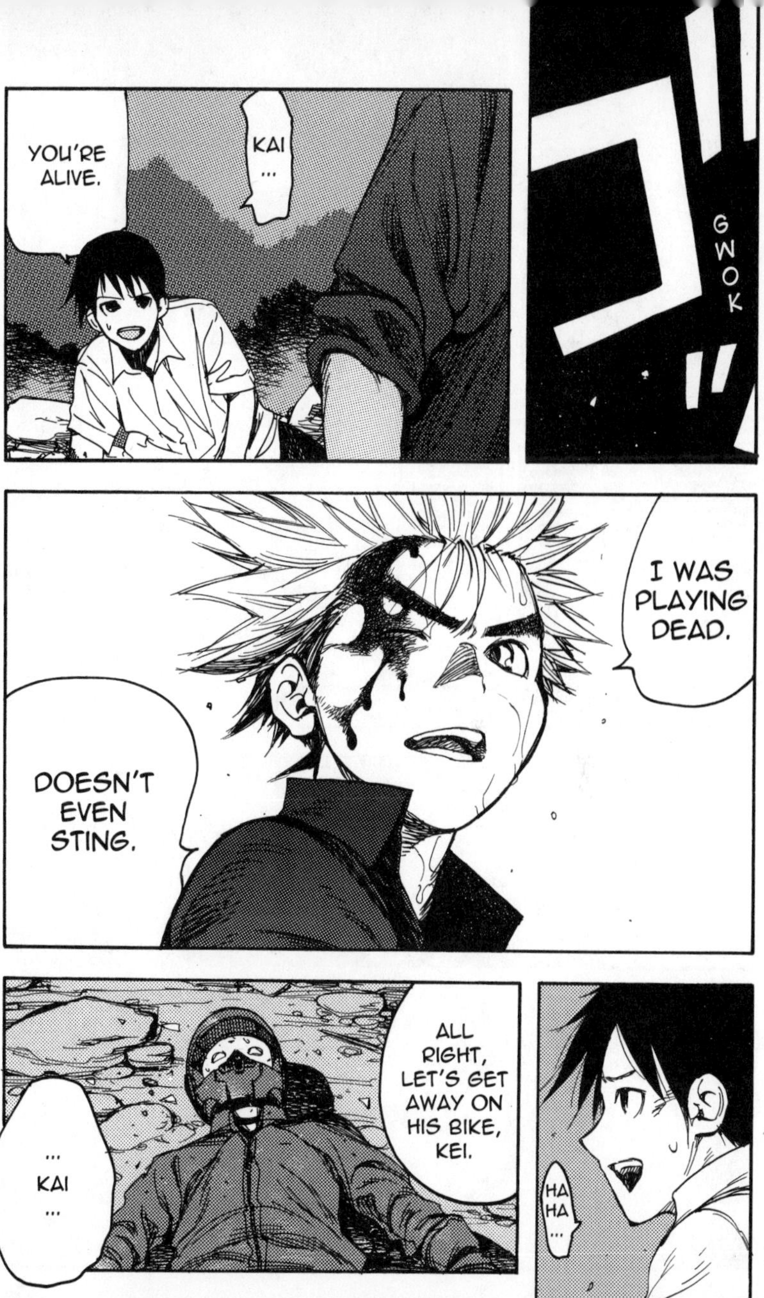
GWOK
KAI ...
YOU'RE ALIVE.
I WAS PLAYING DEAD.
DOESN'T EVEN STING.
HA HA ...
ALL RIGHT, LET'S GET AWAY ON HIS BIKE, KEI.
... KAI ...

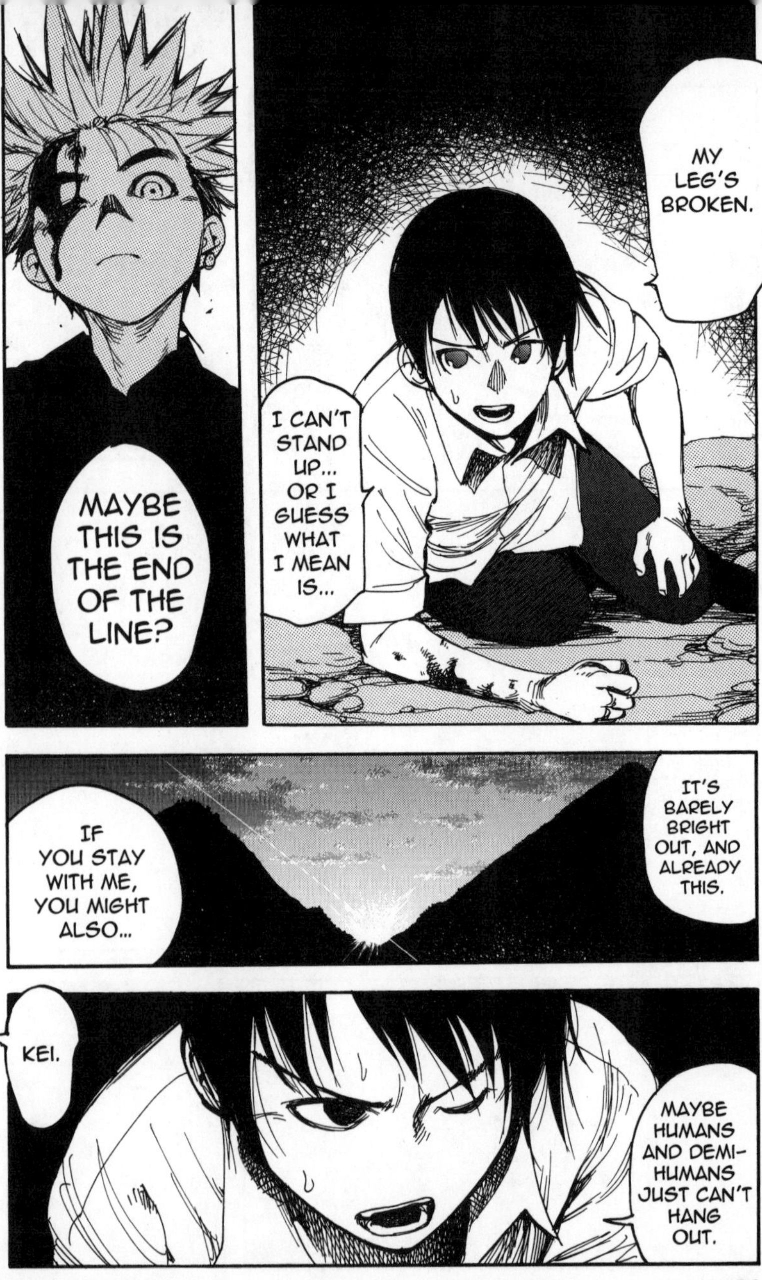
MY LEG'S BROKEN.
I CAN'T STAND UP... OR I GUESS WHAT I MEAN IS...
MAYBE THIS IS THE END OF THE LINE?
IT'S BARELY BRIGHT OUT, AND ALREADY THIS.
IF YOU STAY WITH ME, YOU MIGHT ALSO...
MAYBE HUMANS AND DEMI-HUMANS JUST CAN'T HANG OUT.
KEI.

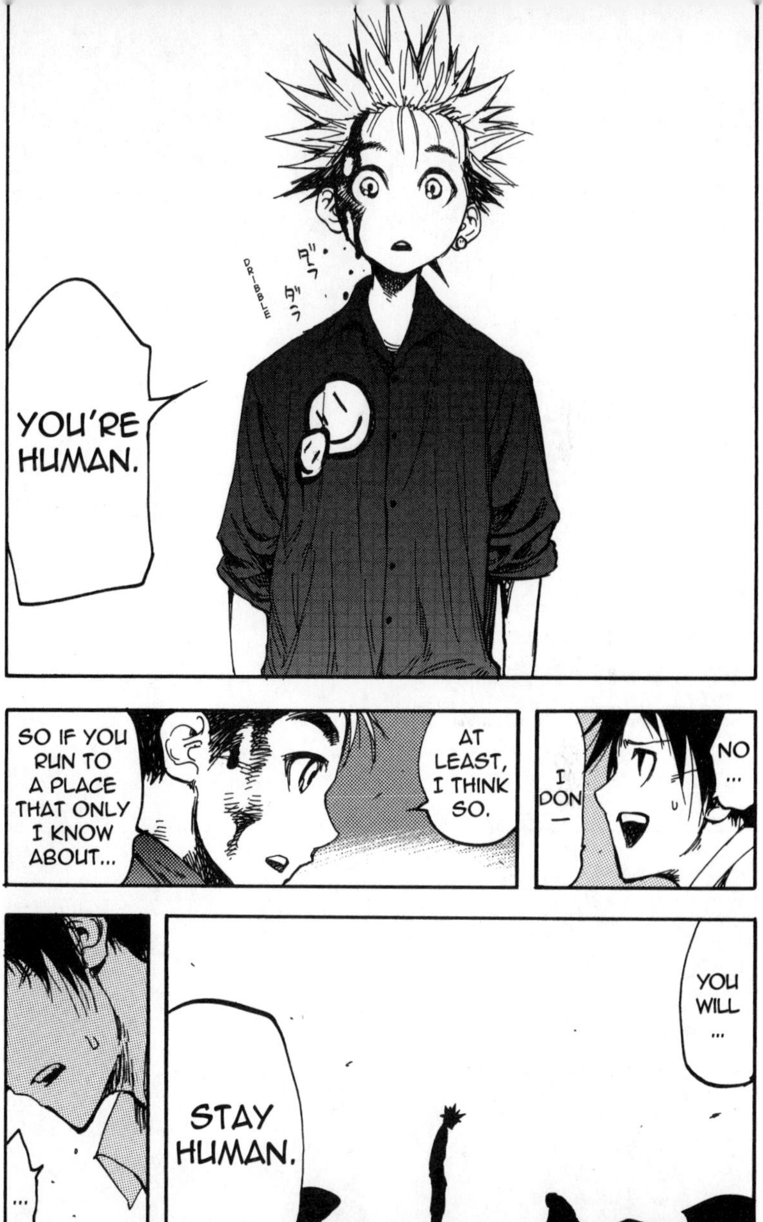
ダラ ダラ
DRIBBLE
YOU'RE HUMAN.
NO...
I DON—
AT LEAST, I THINK SO.
SO IF YOU RUN TO A PLACE THAT ONLY I KNOW ABOUT...
YOU WILL...
STAY HUMAN.
...

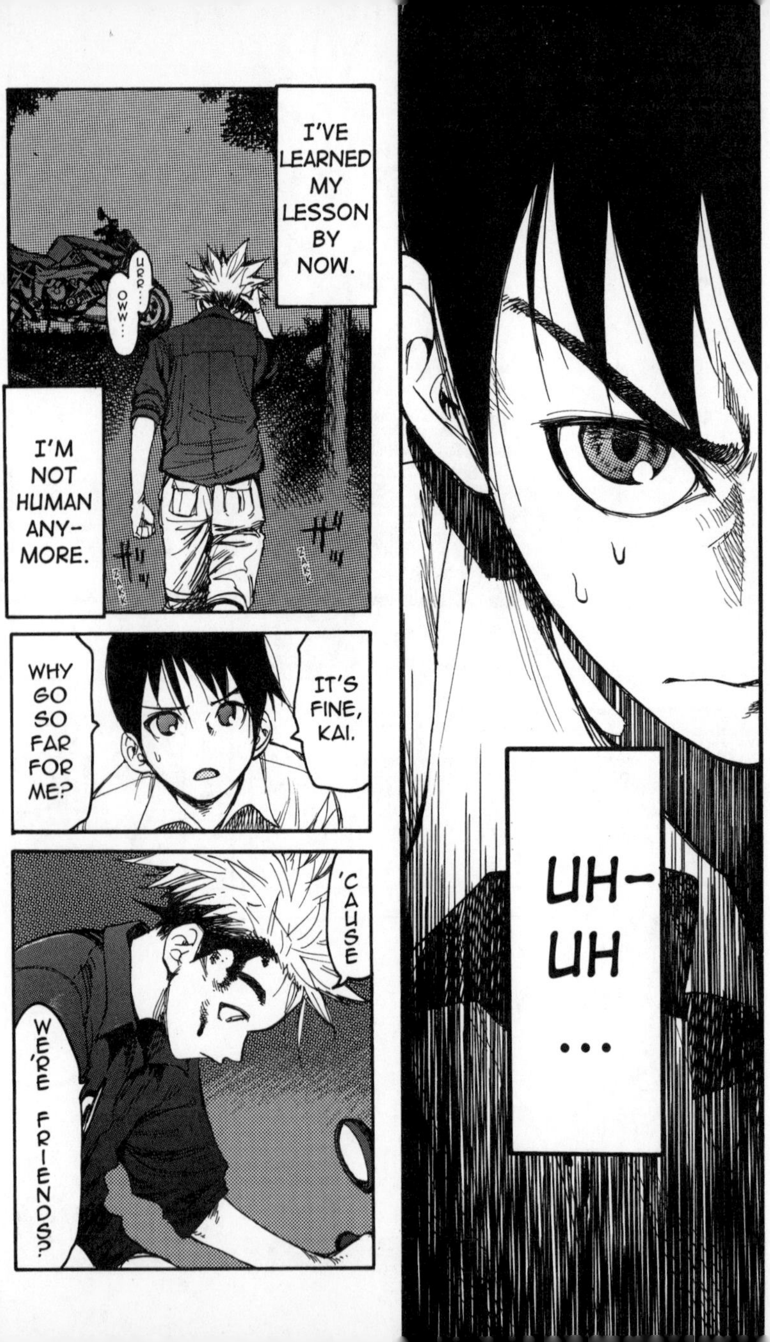
UH-UH ...
I'VE LEARNED MY LESSON BY NOW.
URR... OWW...
I'M NOT HUMAN ANYMORE.
ZAKK
ZAKK
IT'S FINE, KAI.
WHY GO SO FAR FOR ME?
'CAUSE
WE'RE FRIENDS?

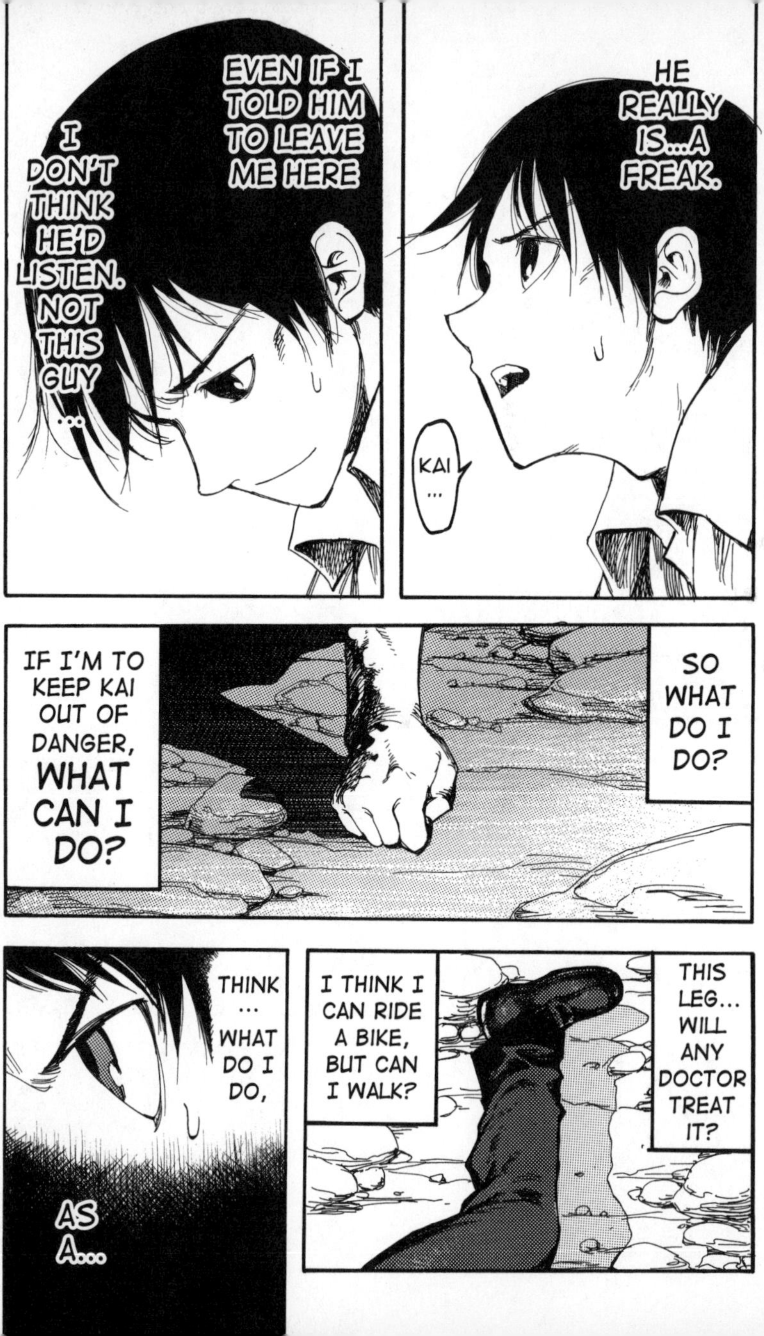
HE REALLY IS...A FREAK.
KAI ...
EVEN IF I TOLD HIM TO LEAVE ME HERE
I DON'T THINK HE'D LISTEN. NOT THIS GUY ...
SO WHAT DO I DO?
IF I'M TO KEEP KAI OUT OF DANGER, WHAT CAN I DO?
THIS LEG... WILL ANY DOCTOR TREAT IT?
I THINK I CAN RIDE A BIKE, BUT CAN I WALK?
THINK ... WHAT DO I DO,
AS A...

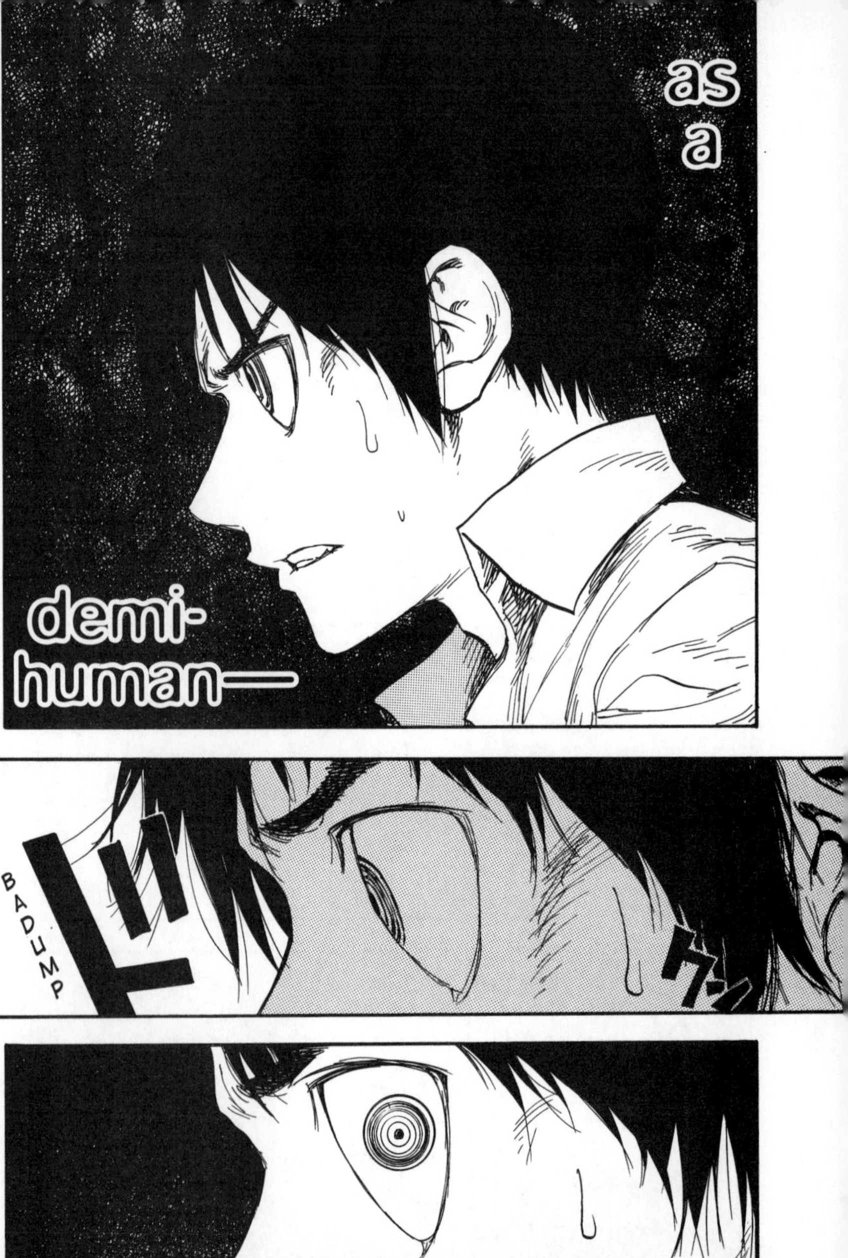
as a
demi-human—
BADUMP

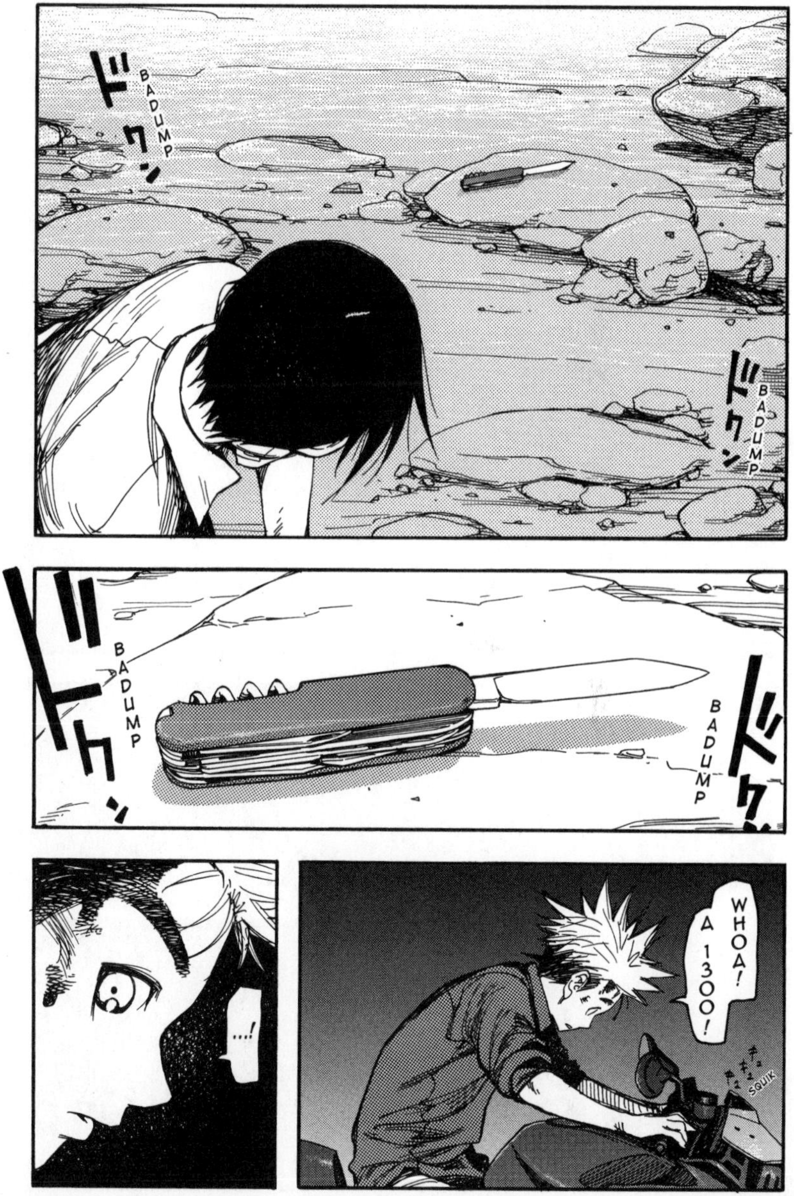
BADUMP
BADUMP
BADUMP
BADUMP
WHOA! A 1300!
SQUIK
...!

KE...

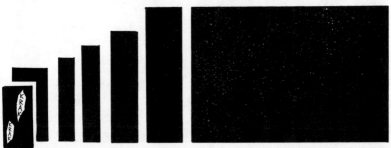

KRAK
KRAK

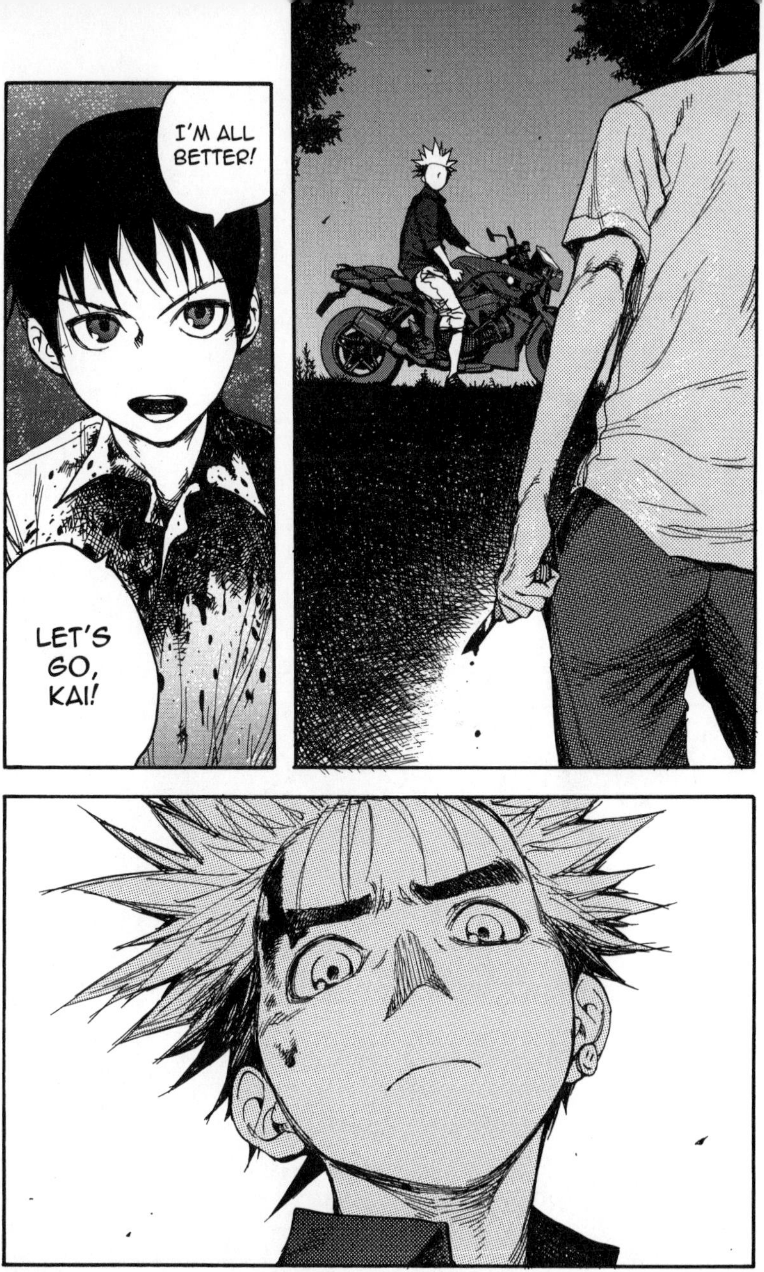
I'M ALL BETTER!
LET'S GO, KAI!

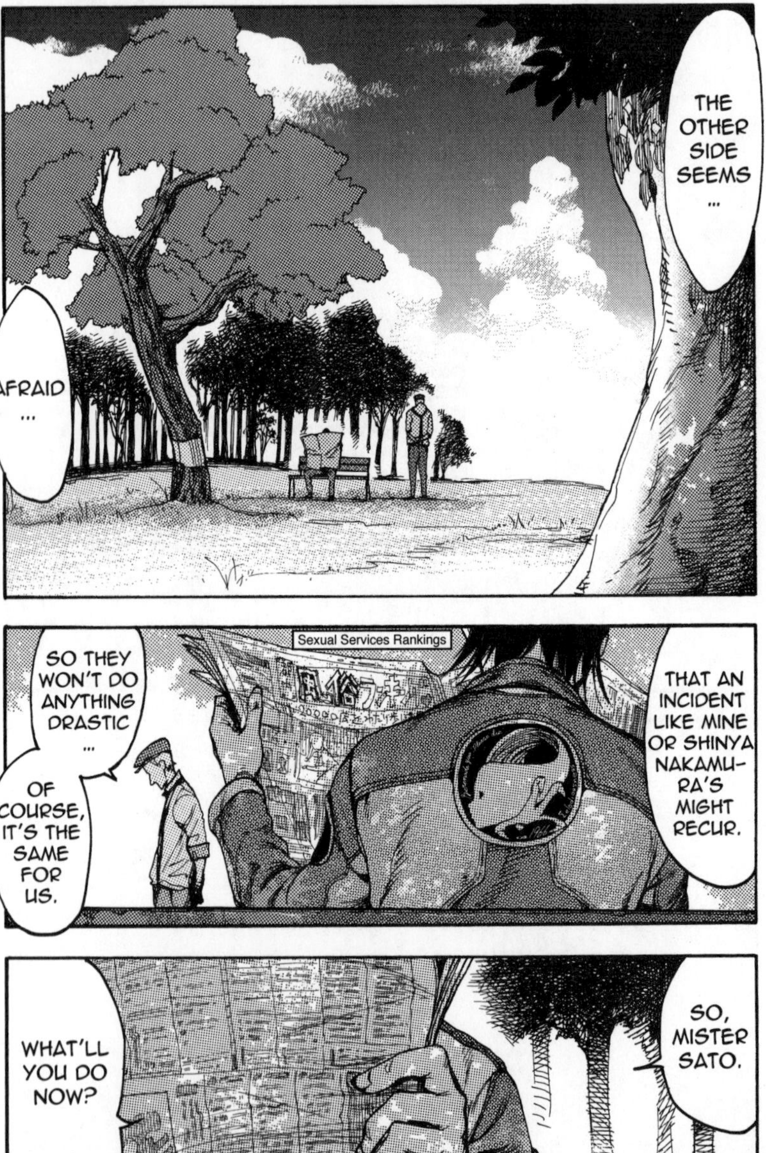
THE OTHER SIDE SEEMS ...
AFRAID ...
THAT AN INCIDENT LIKE MINE OR SHINYA NAKAMURA'S MIGHT RECUR.
Sexual Services Rankings
SO THEY WON'T DO ANYTHING DRASTIC ...
OF COURSE, IT'S THE SAME FOR US.
SO, MISTER SATO.
WHAT'LL YOU DO NOW?

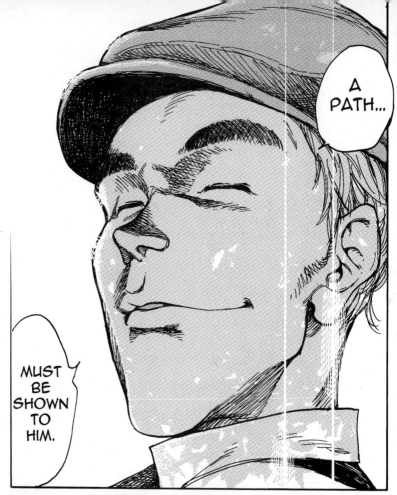

A PATH...
MUST BE SHOWN TO HIM.
JOINING UP WITH KEI NAGAI WILL BE THE FIRST STEP...
パサッ FLAP
WILL YOU HELP ME,

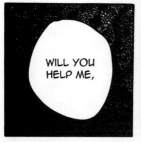

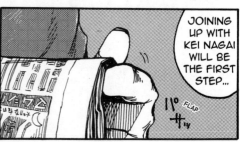

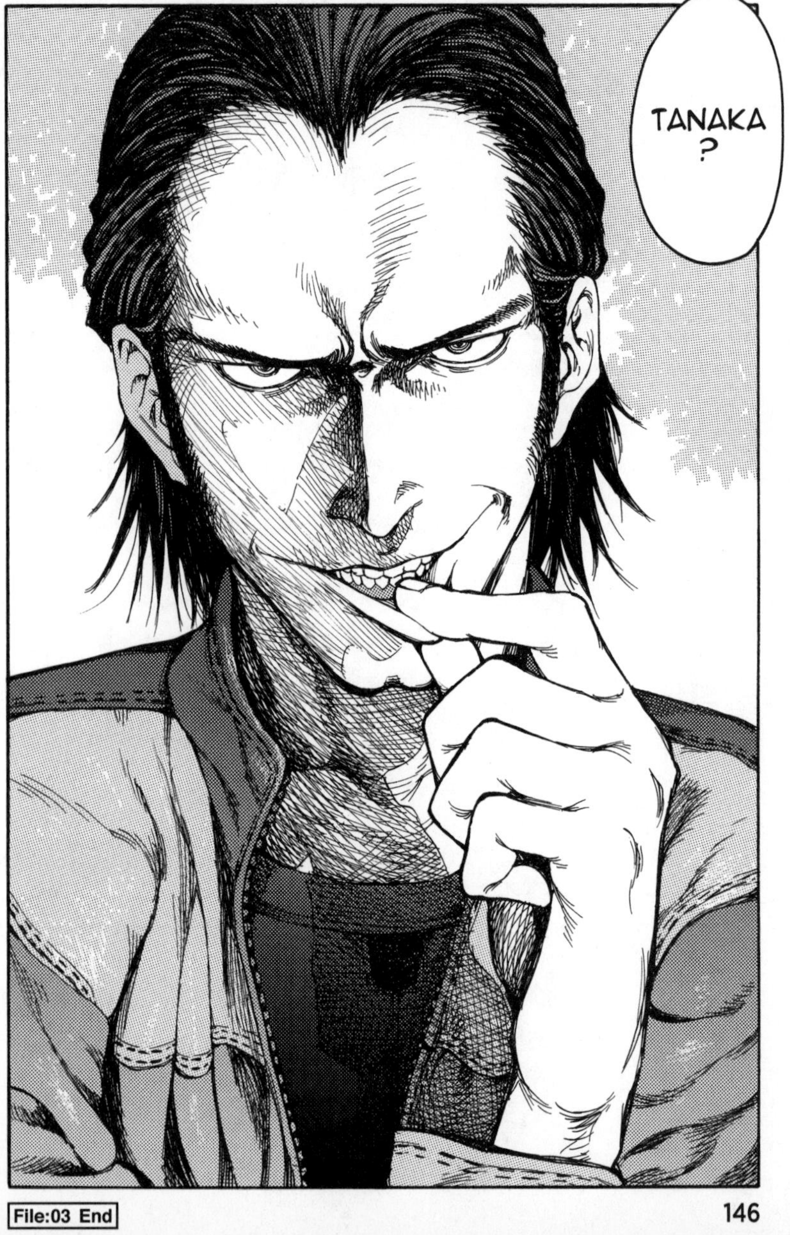
TANAKA
?

File:03 End

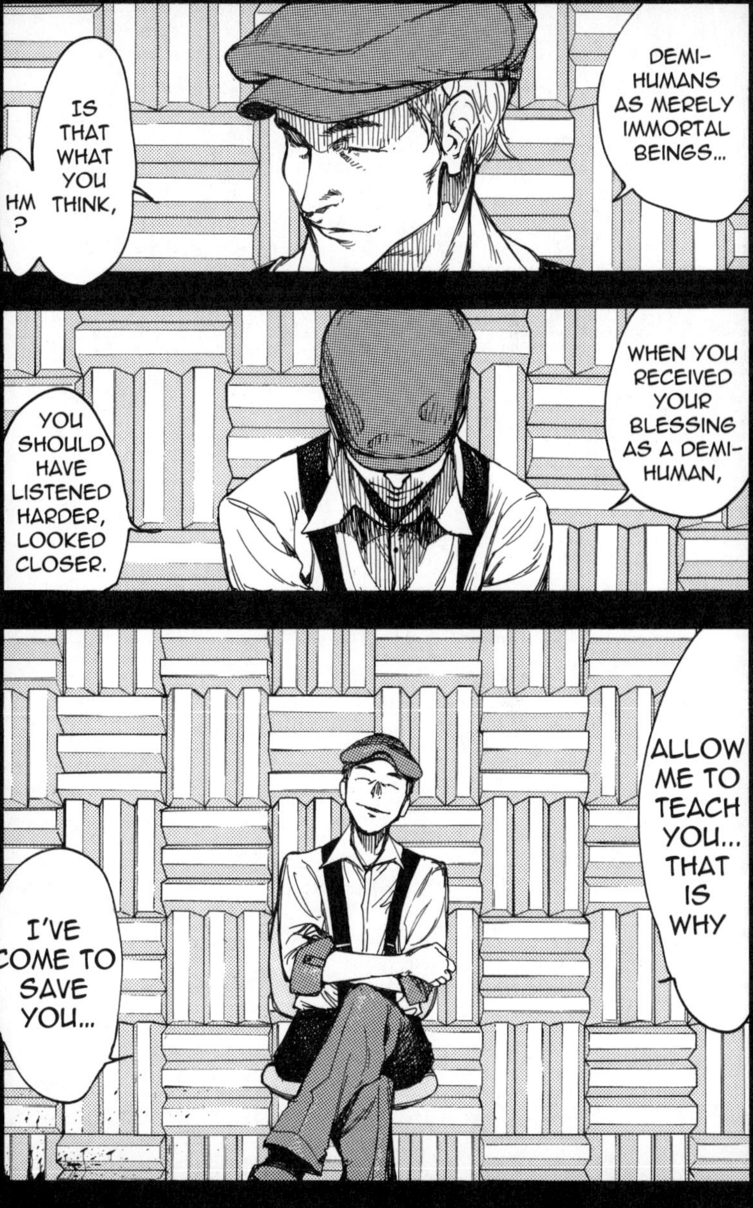
DEMI-HUMANS AS MERELY IMMORTAL BEINGS...
IS THAT WHAT YOU THINK, HM?
WHEN YOU RECEIVED YOUR BLESSING AS A DEMI-HUMAN,
YOU SHOULD HAVE LISTENED HARDER, LOOKED CLOSER.
ALLOW ME TO TEACH YOU... THAT IS WHY
I'VE COME TO SAVE YOU...

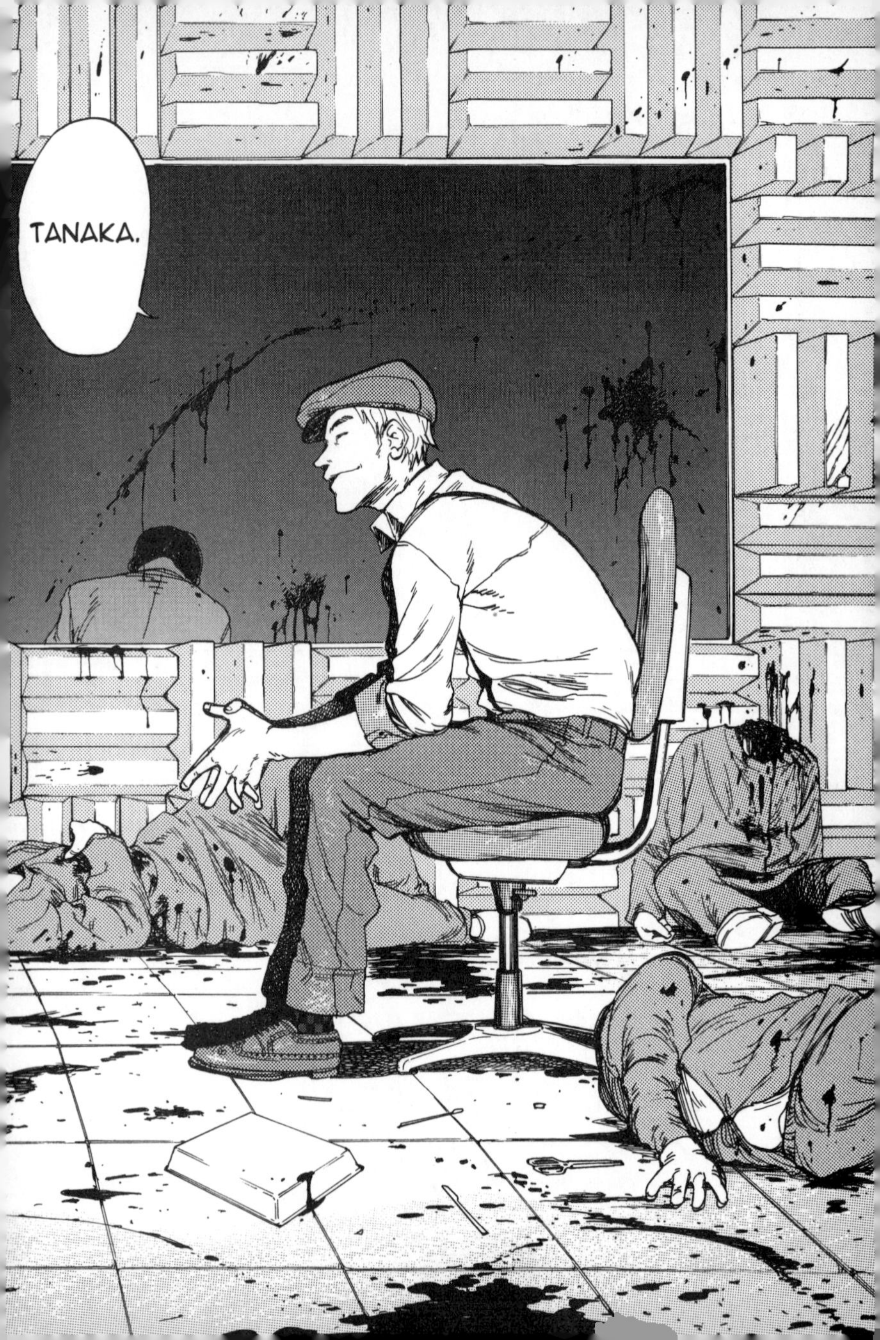
TANAKA.

File 04: Interrogation and Aid

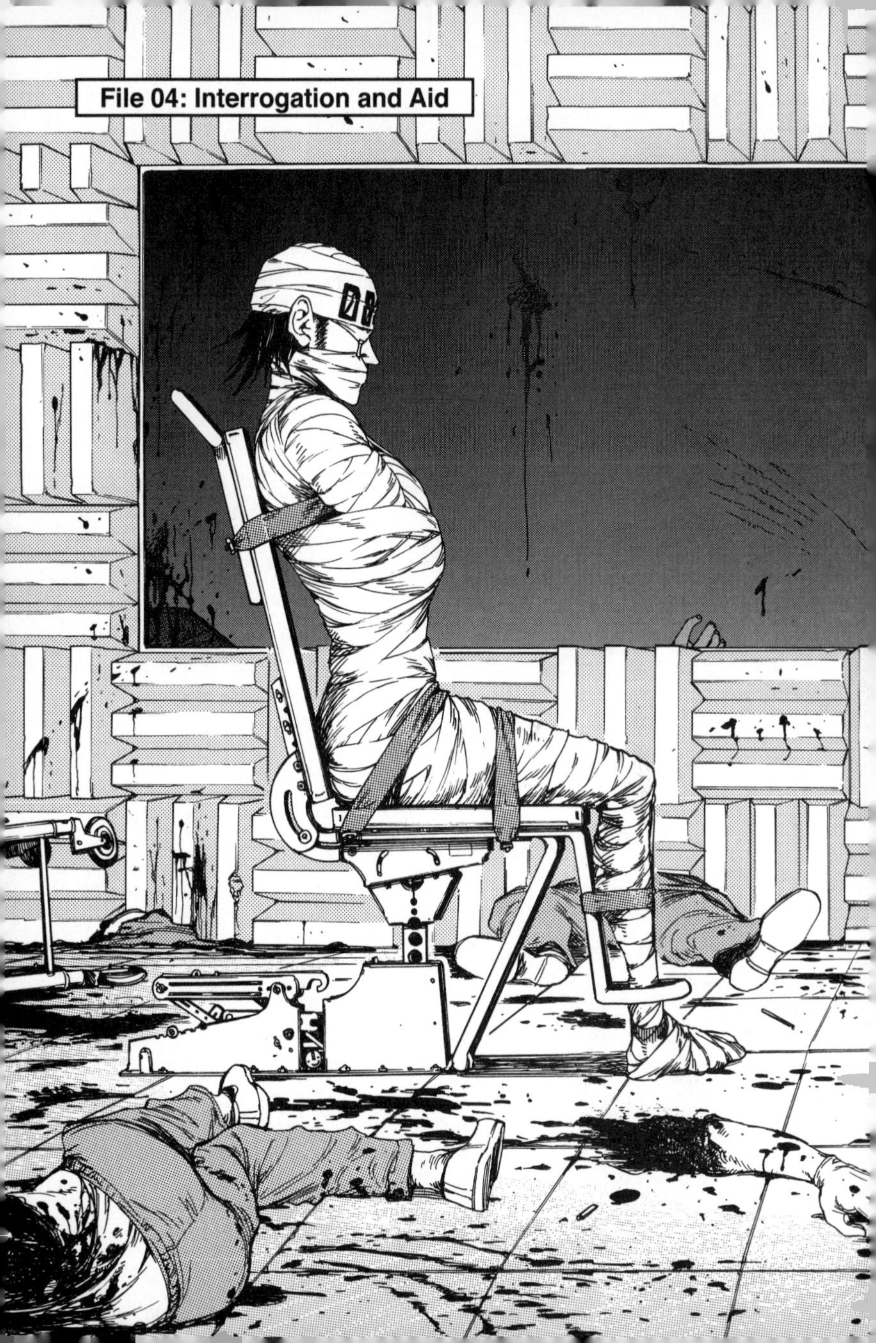

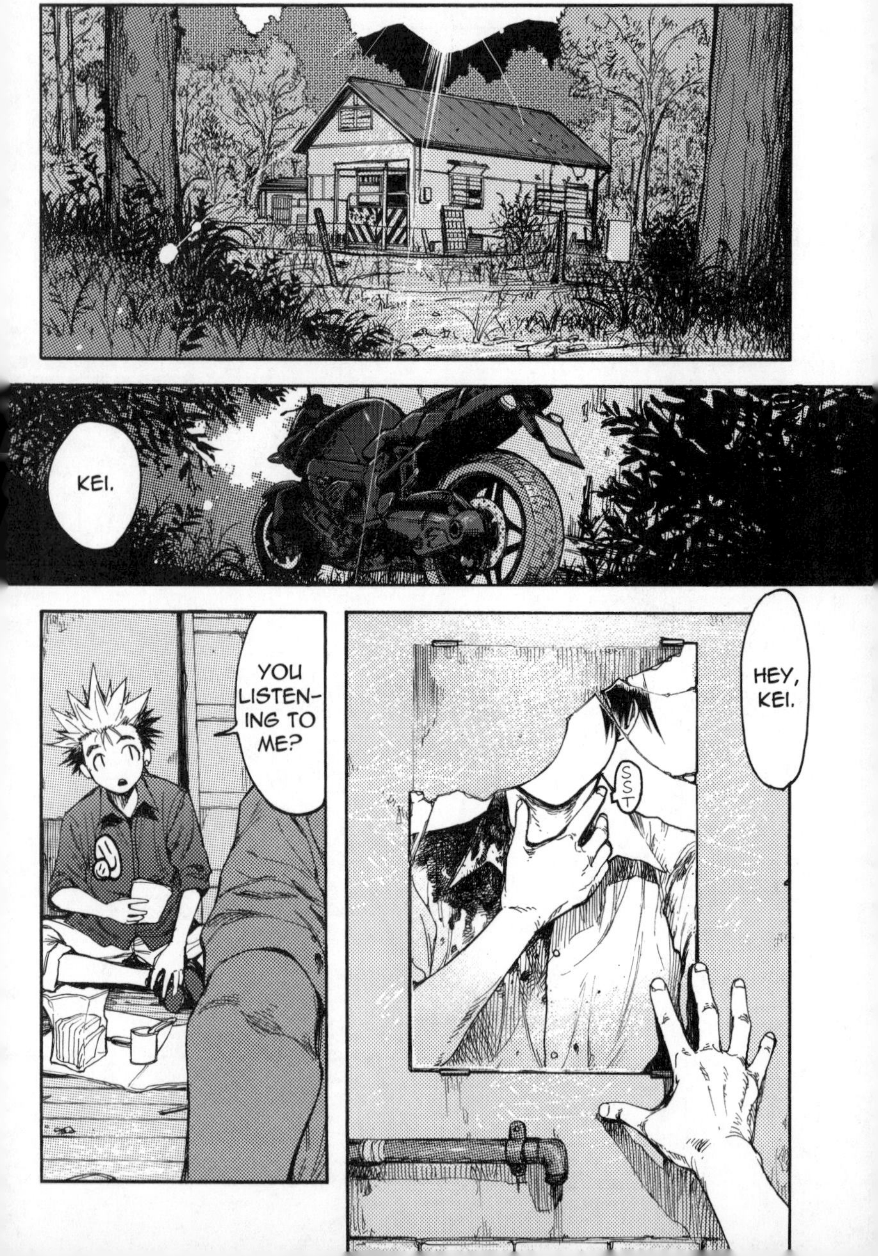
KEI.
HEY, KEI.
SST
YOU LISTEN-ING TO ME?

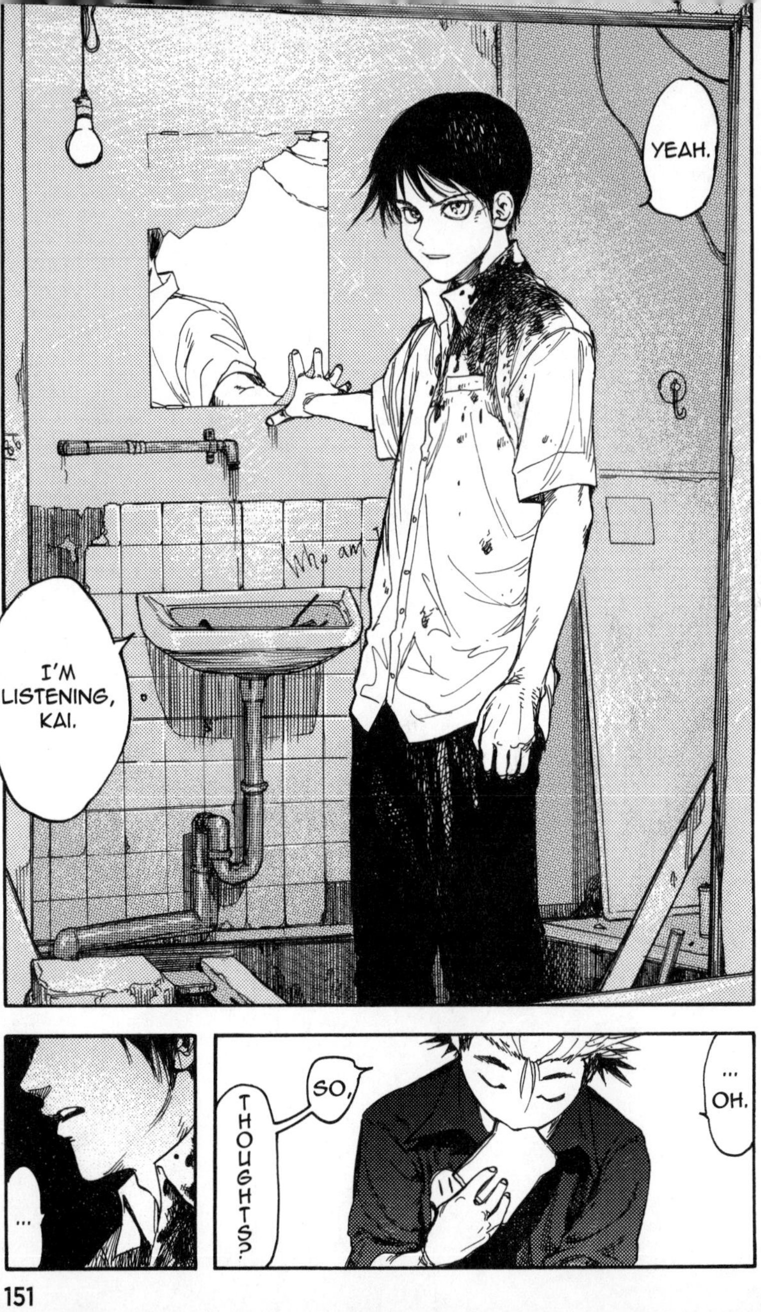
YEAH.
Who am
I'M LISTENING, KAI.
... OH.
SO,
THOUGHTS?
...

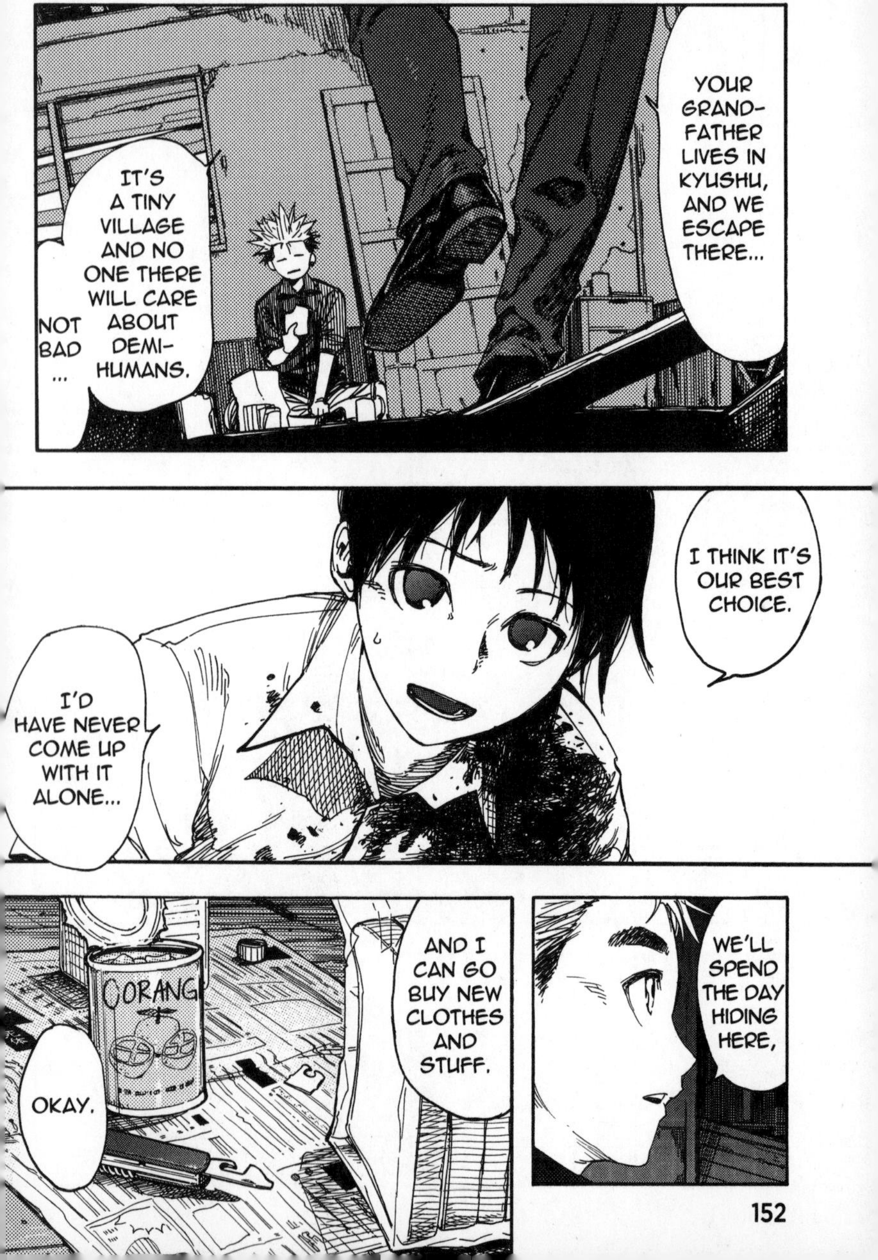
YOUR GRANDFATHER LIVES IN KYUSHU, AND WE ESCAPE THERE...
IT'S A TINY VILLAGE AND NO ONE THERE WILL CARE ABOUT DEMI-HUMANS.
NOT BAD ...
I THINK IT'S OUR BEST CHOICE.
I'D HAVE NEVER COME UP WITH IT ALONE...
WE'LL SPEND THE DAY HIDING HERE,
AND I CAN GO BUY NEW CLOTHES AND STUFF.
OKAY.

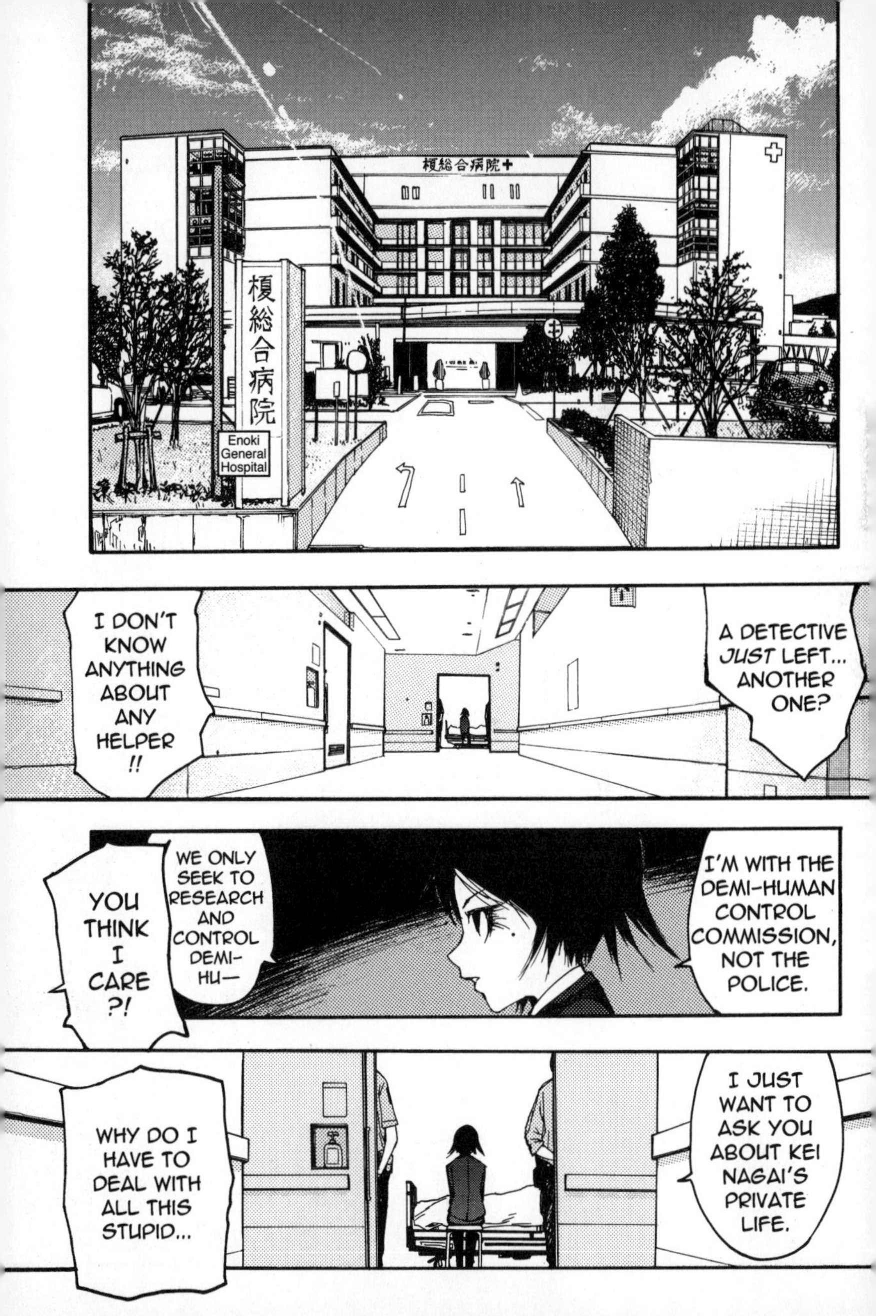
榎総合病院
榎総合病院
Enoki General Hospital
A DETECTIVE *JUST* LEFT... ANOTHER ONE?
I DON'T KNOW ANYTHING ABOUT ANY HELPER !!
I'M WITH THE DEMI-HUMAN CONTROL COMMISSION, NOT THE POLICE.
WE ONLY SEEK TO RESEARCH AND CONTROL DEMI-HU—
YOU THINK I CARE ?!
I JUST WANT TO ASK YOU ABOUT KEI NAGAI'S PRIVATE LIFE.
WHY DO I HAVE TO DEAL WITH ALL THIS STUPID...

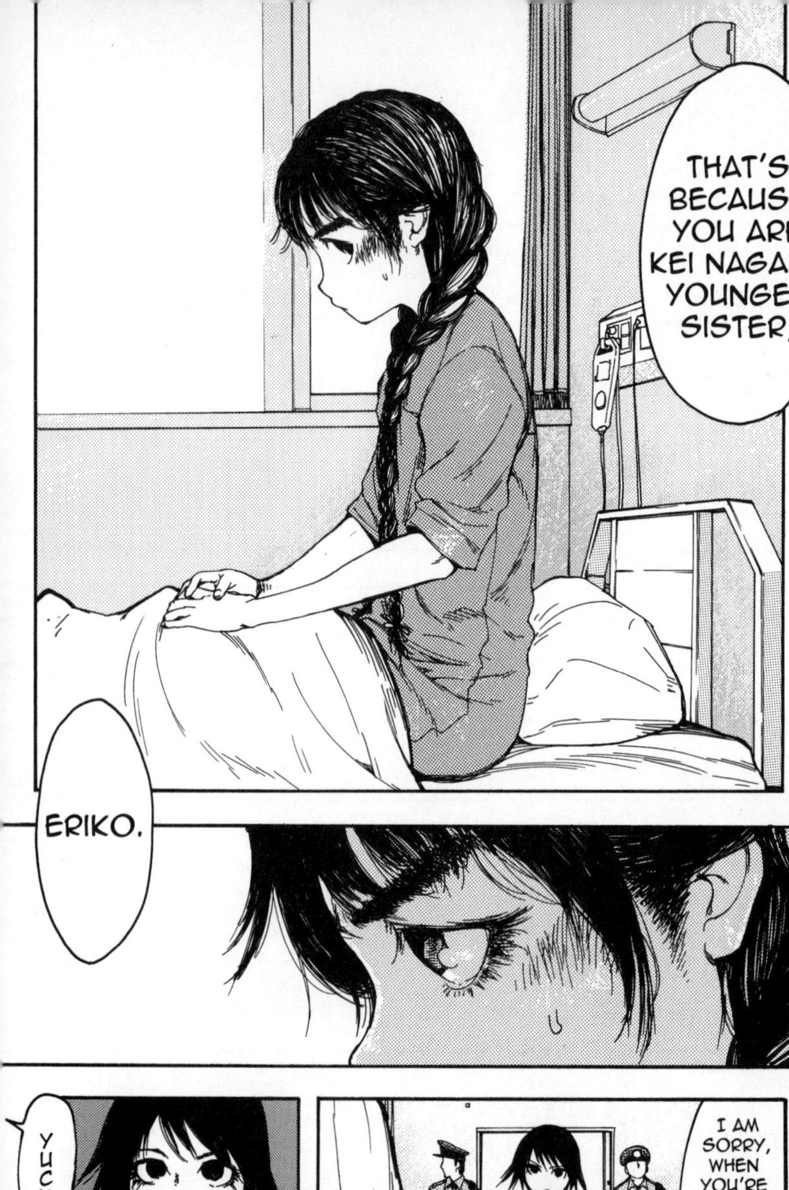
THAT'S BECAUSE YOU ARE KEI NAGAI'S YOUNGER SISTER,
ERIKO.
I AM SORRY, WHEN YOU'RE TRYING TO GET BETTER...
YUCK.

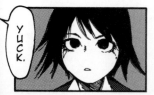

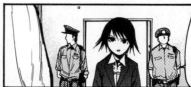

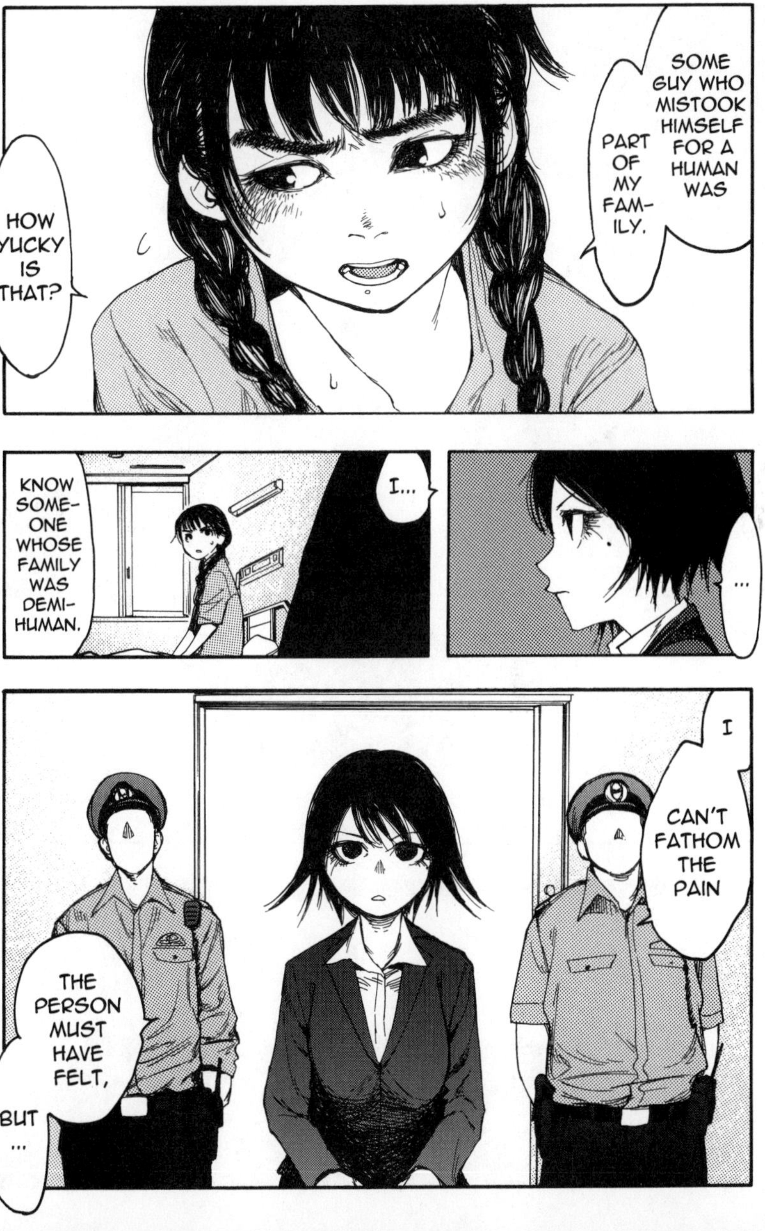
SOME GUY WHO MISTOOK HIMSELF FOR A HUMAN WAS PART OF MY FAM-ILY.
HOW YUCKY IS THAT?
...
I...
KNOW SOME-ONE WHOSE FAMILY WAS DEMI-HUMAN.
I CAN'T FATHOM THE PAIN
THE PERSON MUST HAVE FELT,
BUT ...

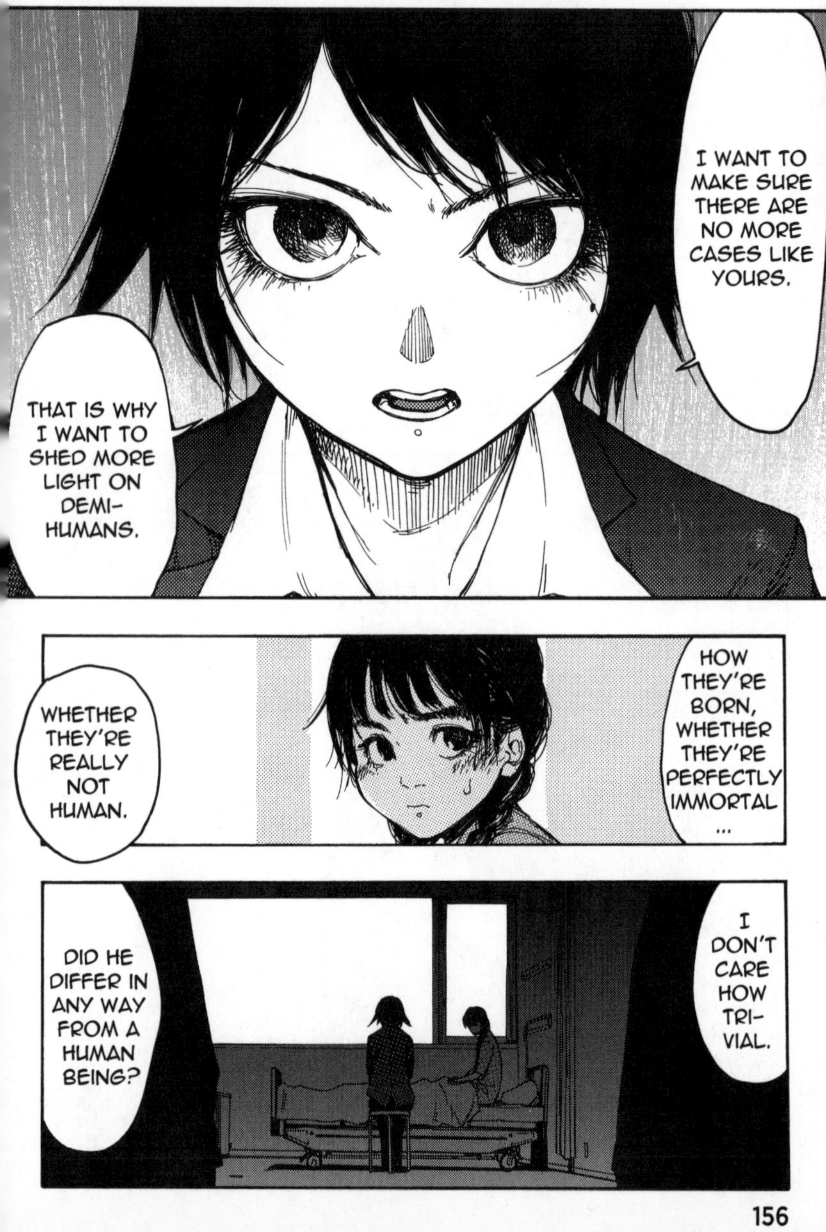
I WANT TO MAKE SURE THERE ARE NO MORE CASES LIKE YOURS.
THAT IS WHY I WANT TO SHED MORE LIGHT ON DEMI-HUMANS.
HOW THEY'RE BORN, WHETHER THEY'RE PERFECTLY IMMORTAL ...
WHETHER THEY'RE REALLY NOT HUMAN.
I DON'T CARE HOW TRI-VIAL.
DID HE DIFFER IN ANY WAY FROM A HUMAN BEING?

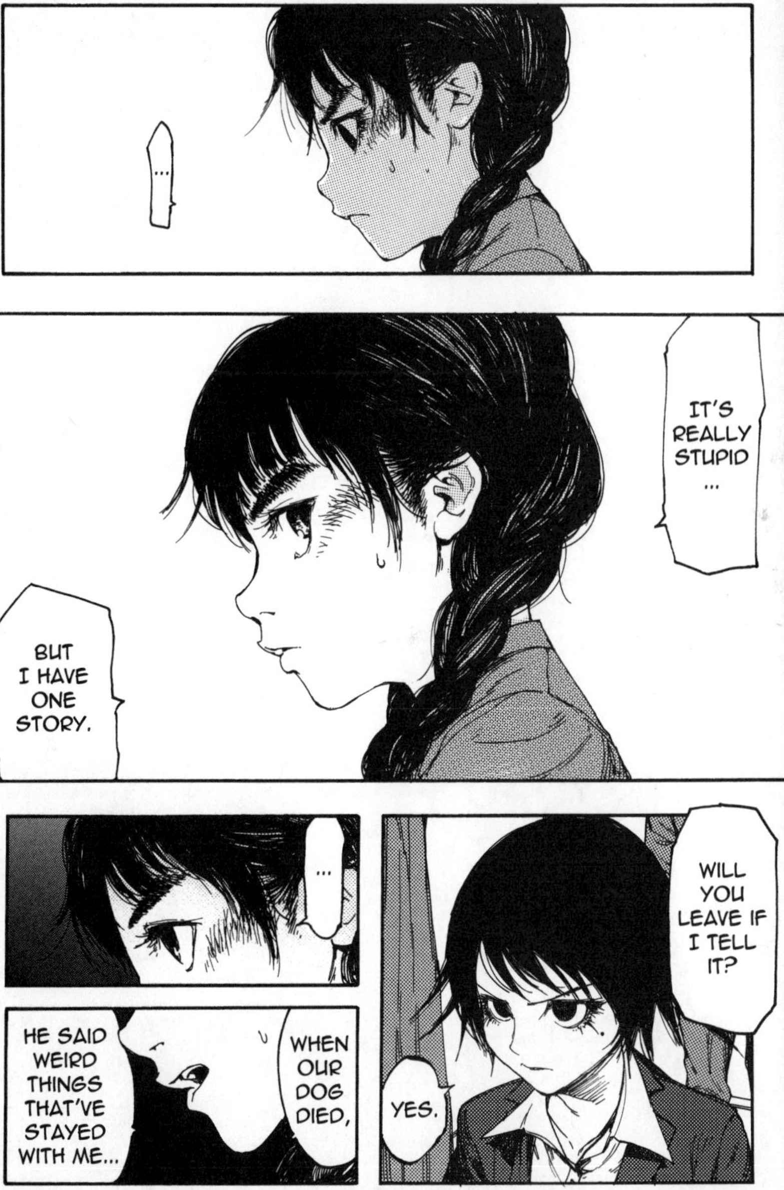
...
IT'S REALLY STUPID ...
BUT I HAVE ONE STORY.
WILL YOU LEAVE IF I TELL IT?
YES.
...
WHEN OUR DOG DIED,
HE SAID WEIRD THINGS THAT'VE STAYED WITH ME...

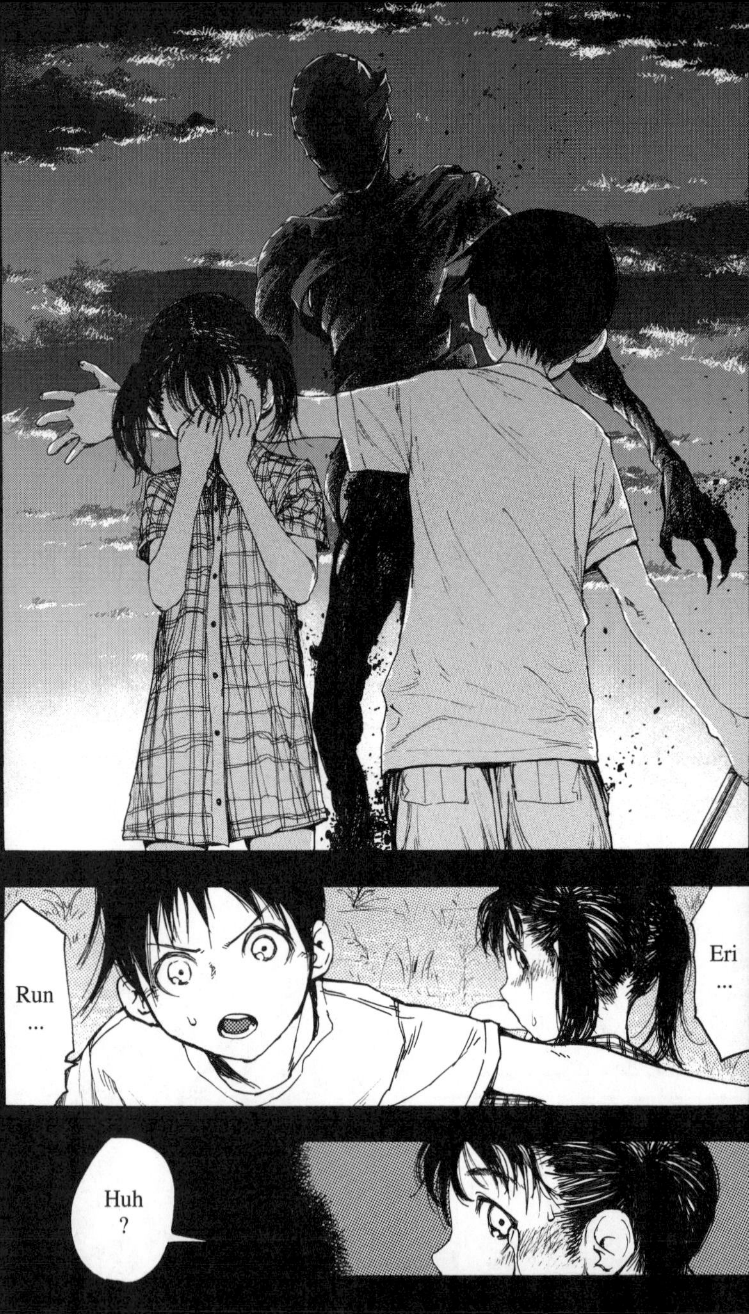
Eri ...
Run ...
Huh ?

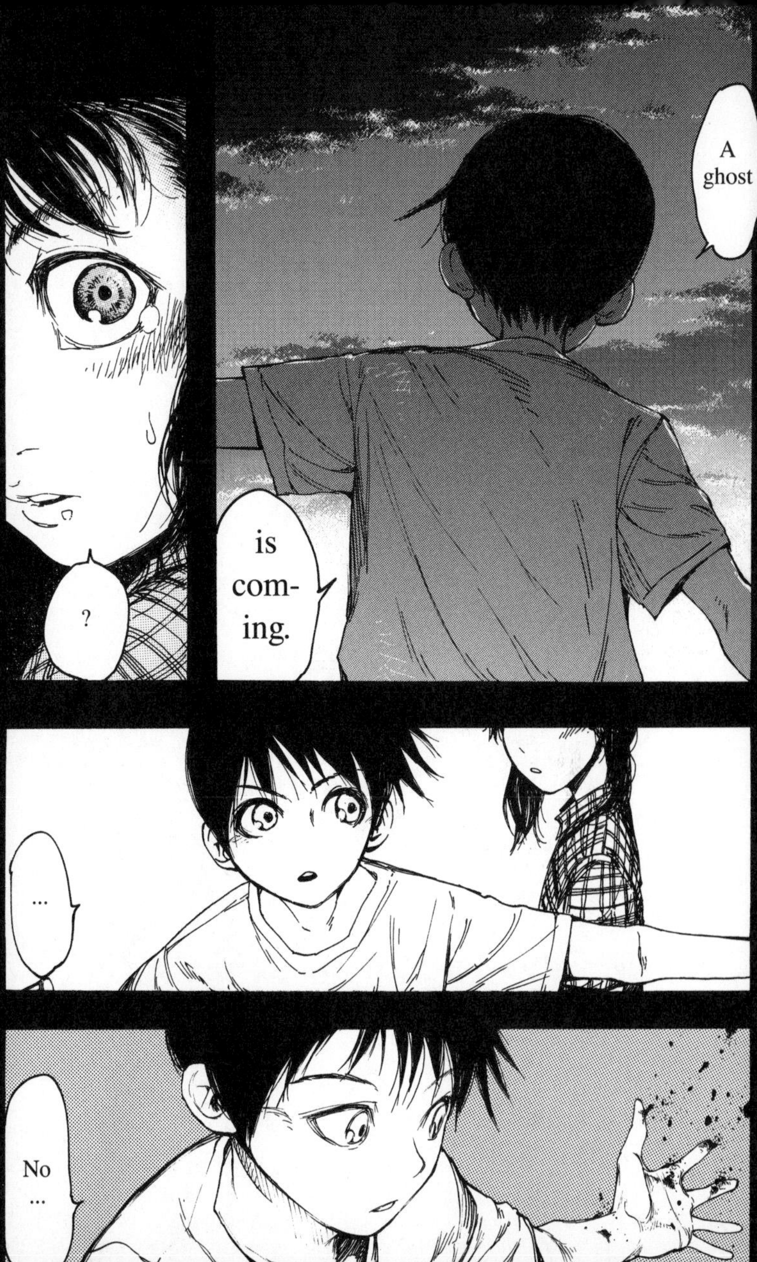
A ghost
is coming.
?
...
No ...

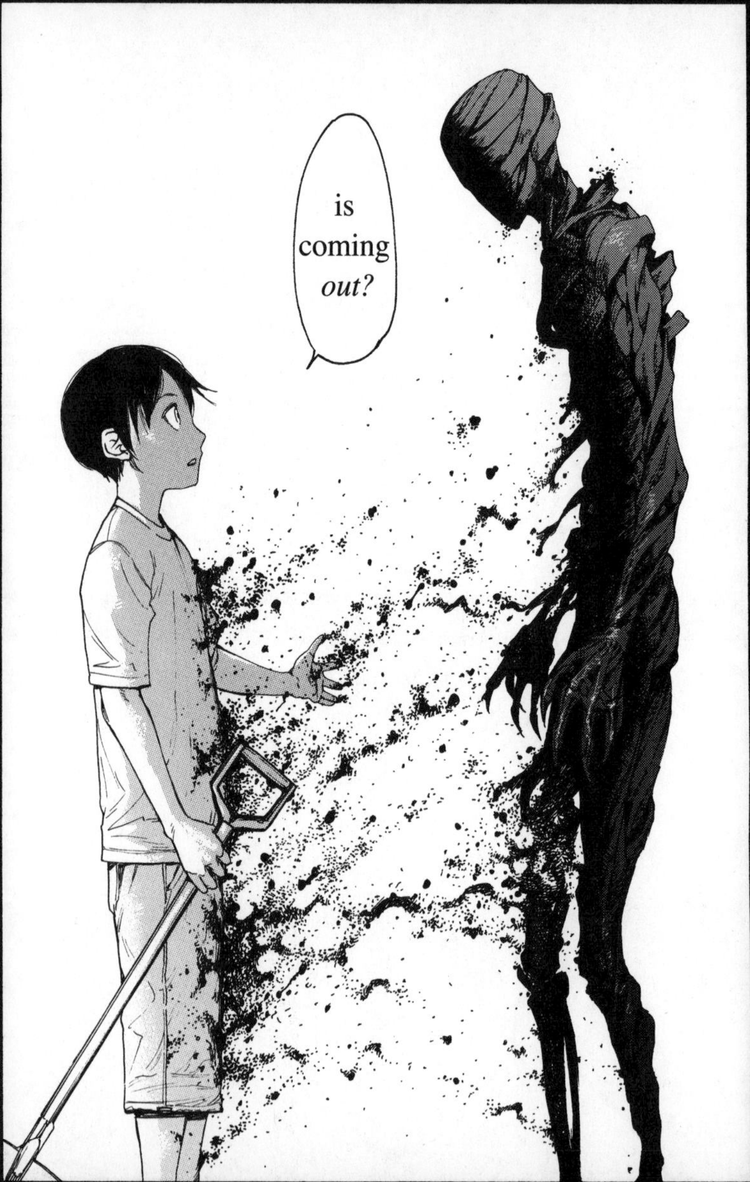
is coming *out?*

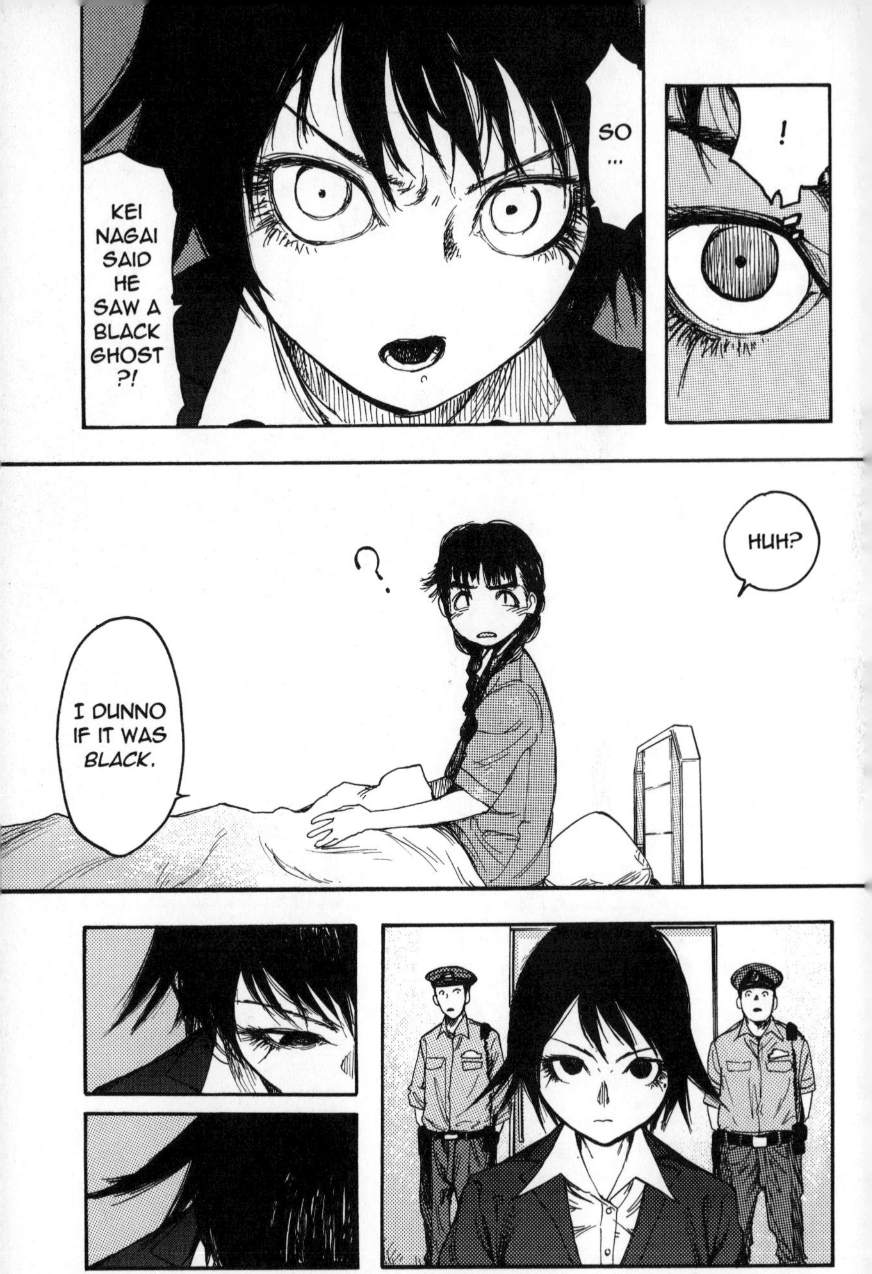
!
SO ...
KEI NAGAI SAID HE SAW A BLACK GHOST?!
HUH?
I DUNNO IF IT WAS BLACK.

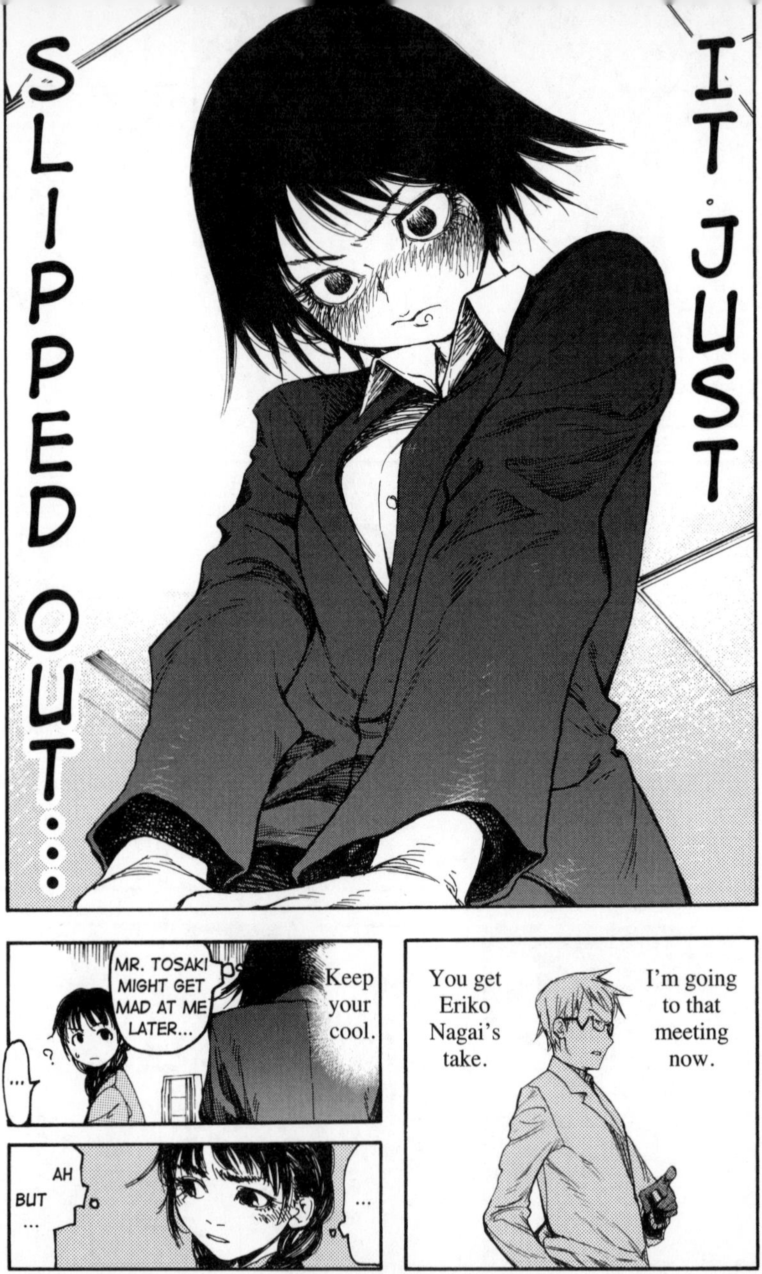
IT JUST
SLIPPED OUT...
I'm going to that meeting now.
You get Eriko Nagai's take.
Keep your cool.
MR. TOSAKI MIGHT GET MAD AT ME LATER...
...
...
AH BUT ...

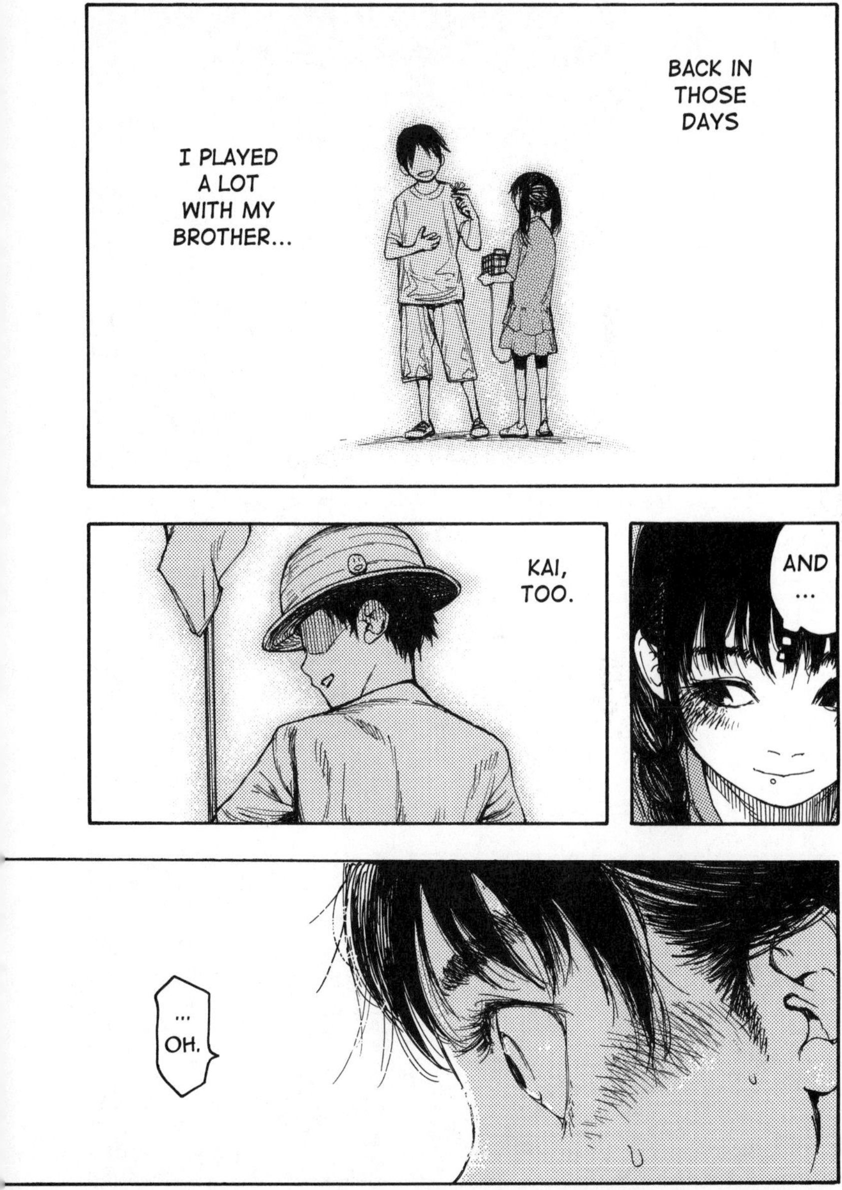
BACK IN THOSE DAYS
I PLAYED A LOT WITH MY BROTHER...
AND ...
KAI, TOO.
... OH.

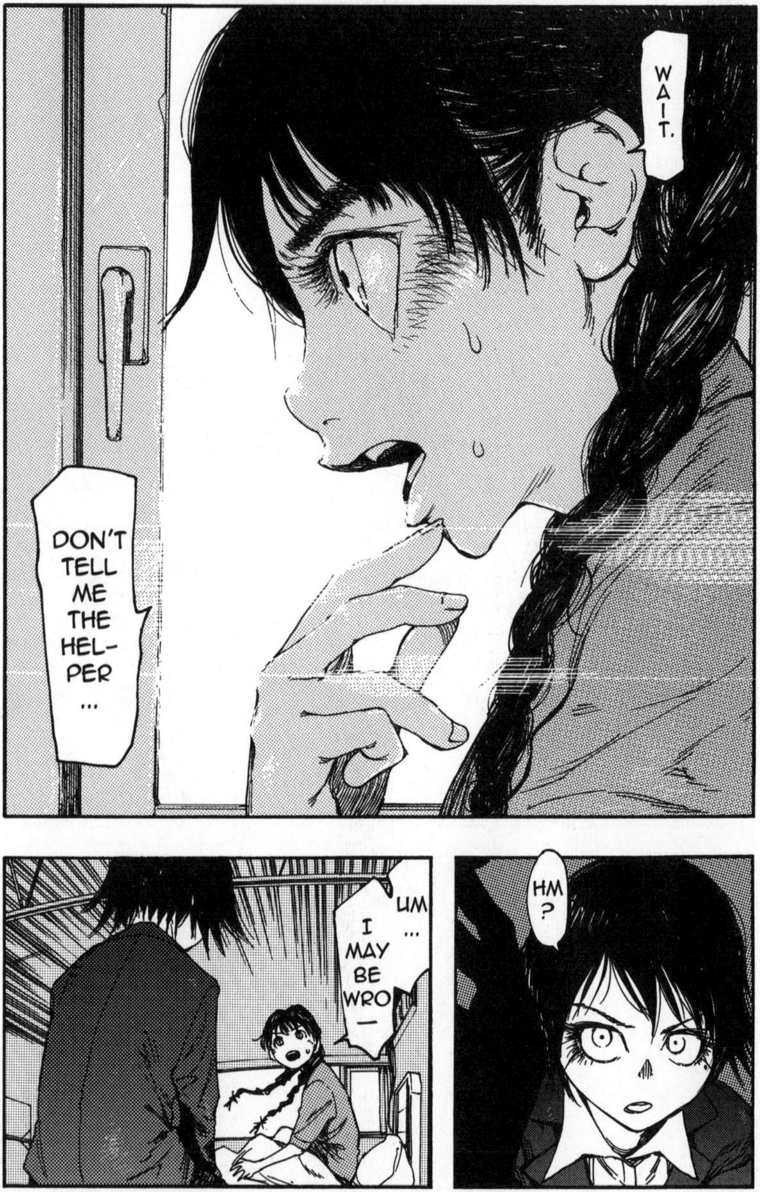
WAIT.
DON'T TELL ME THE HEL-PER ...
HM?
UM ... I MAY BE WRO—

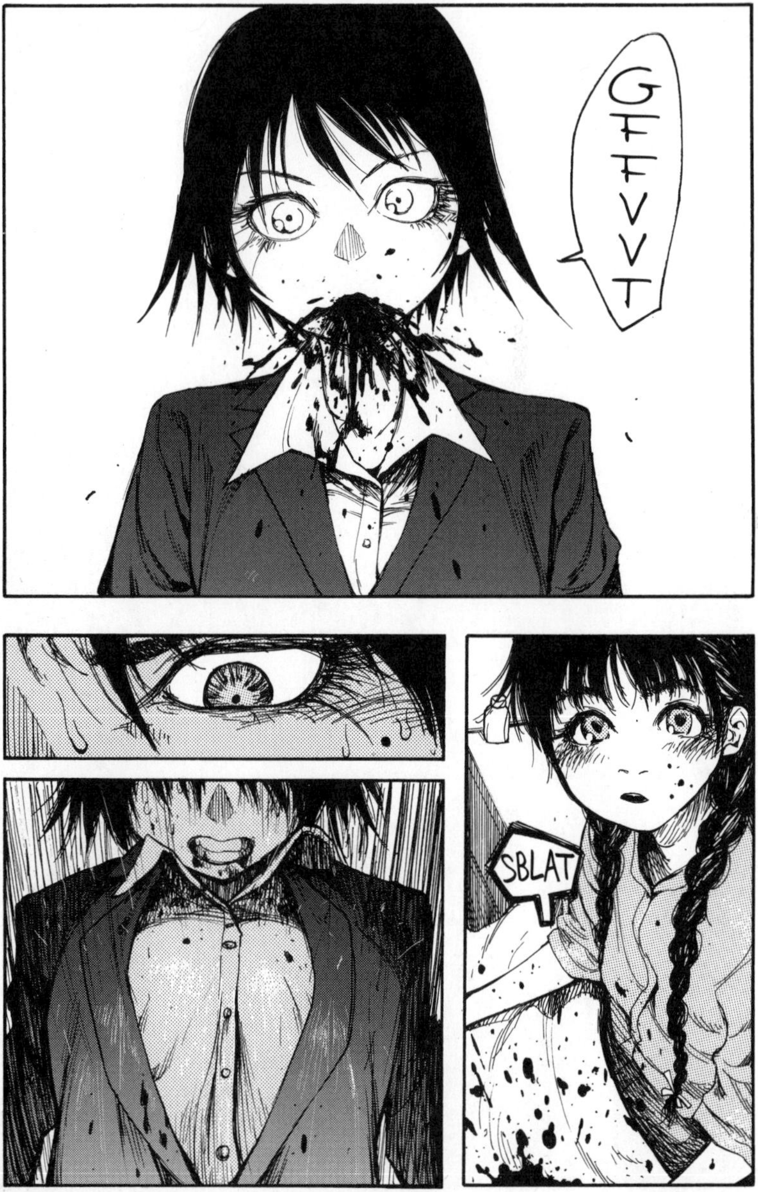
GFFVVT
SBLAT

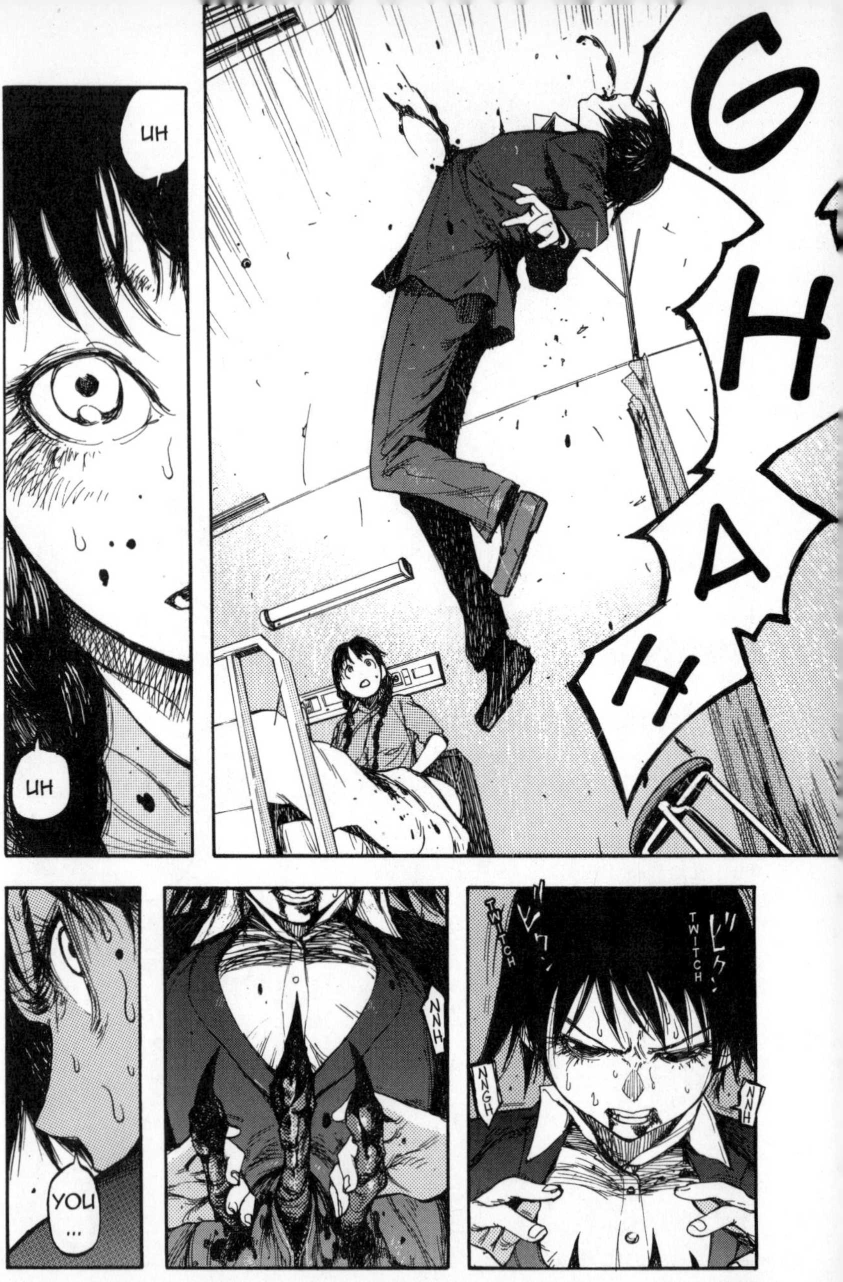
GHAH
UH
UH
TWITCH
TWITCH
NNH
NNGH
NNH
YOU
...

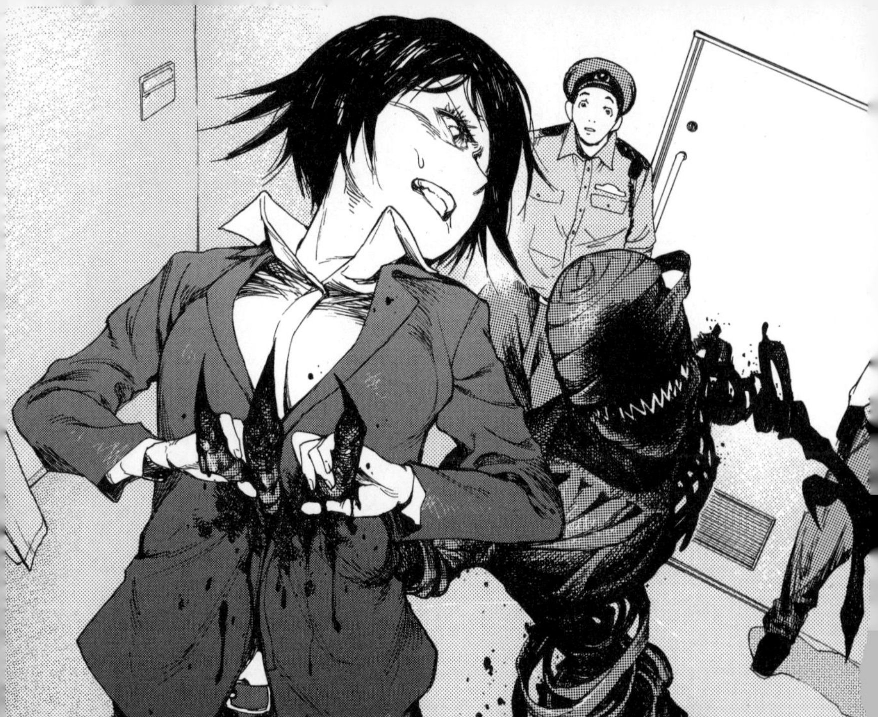

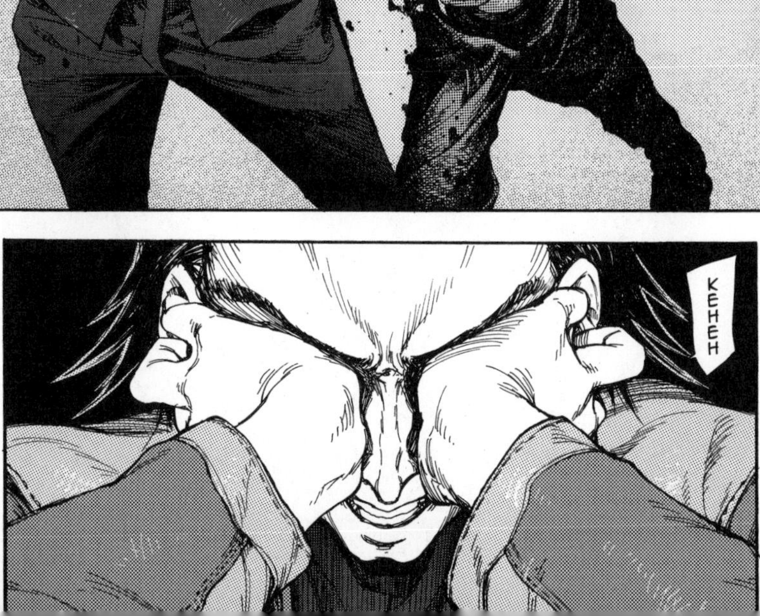
KEHEH

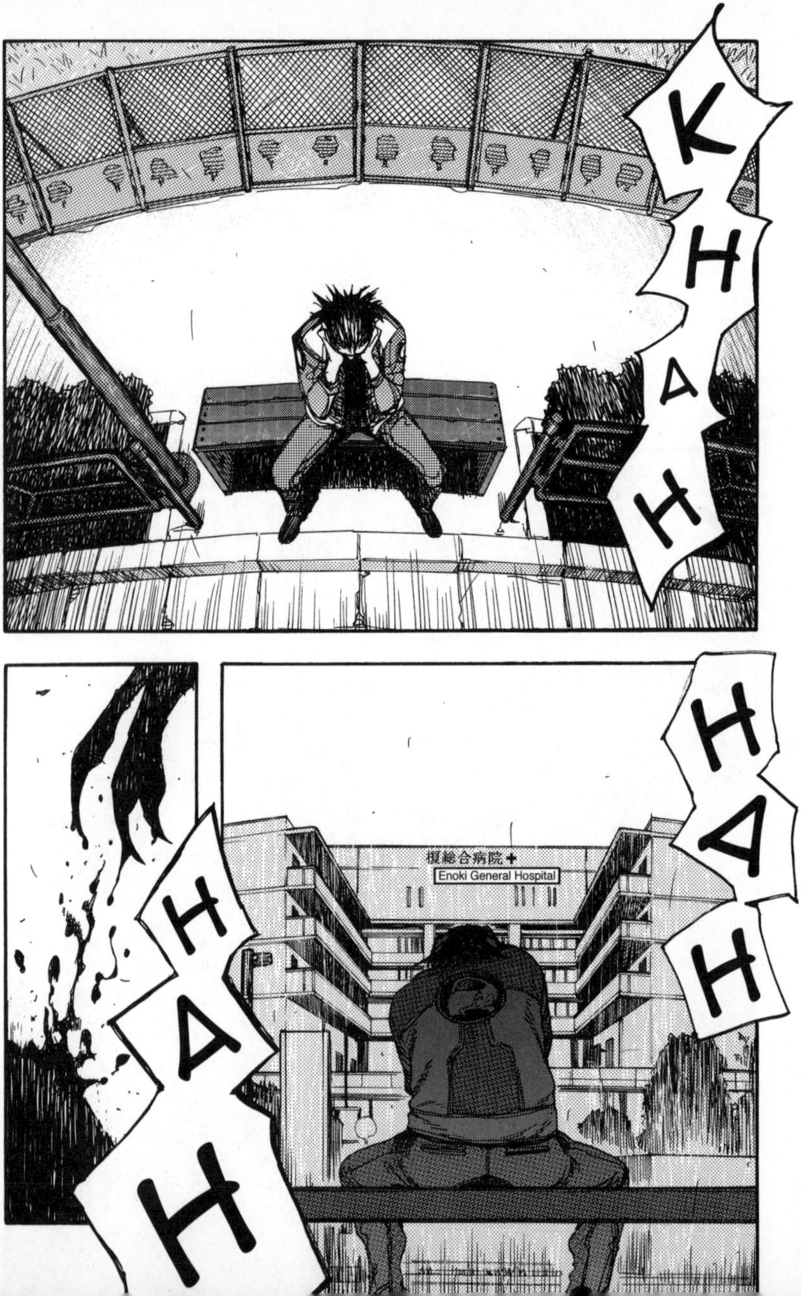
KHAH
榎総合病院
Enoki General Hospital
HAH
HAH

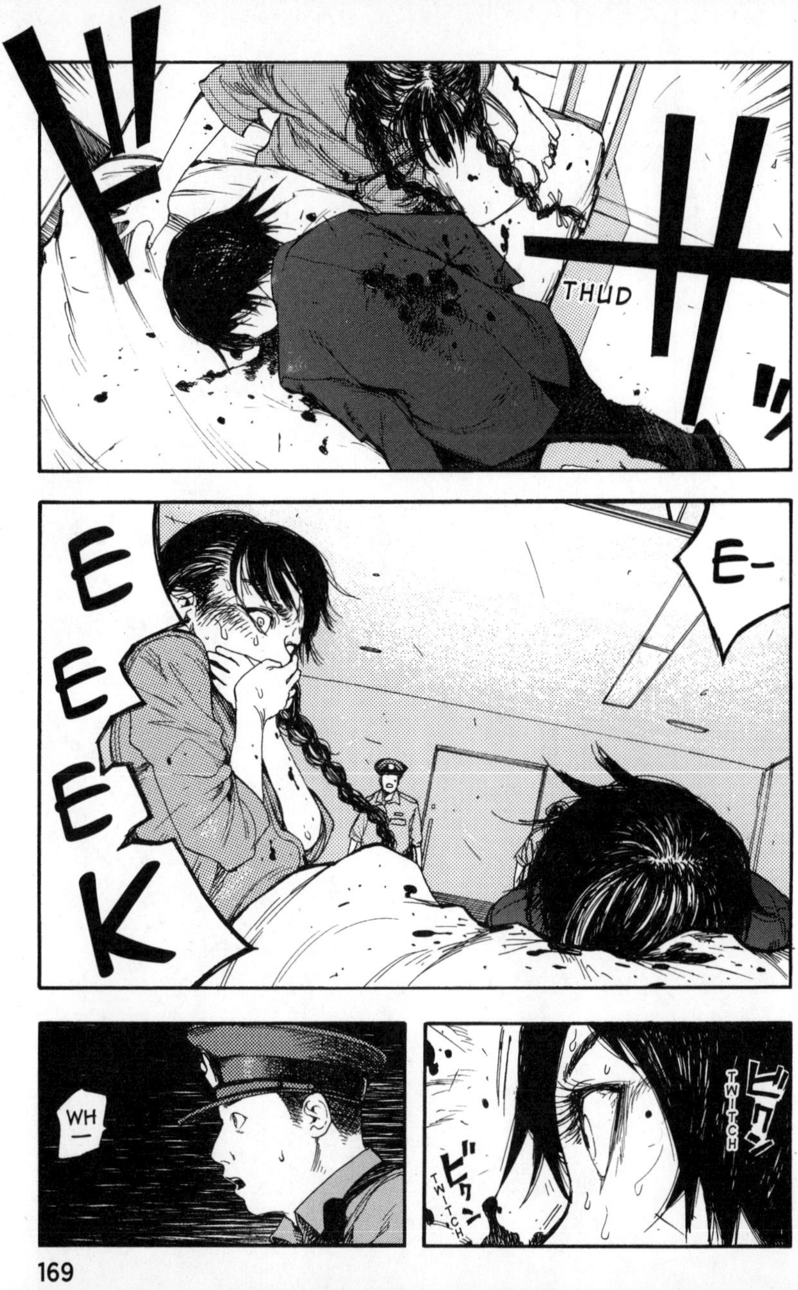
ドサッ
THUD
E–
EEEEK
ビクッ
TWITCH
ビクン
TWITCH
WH—

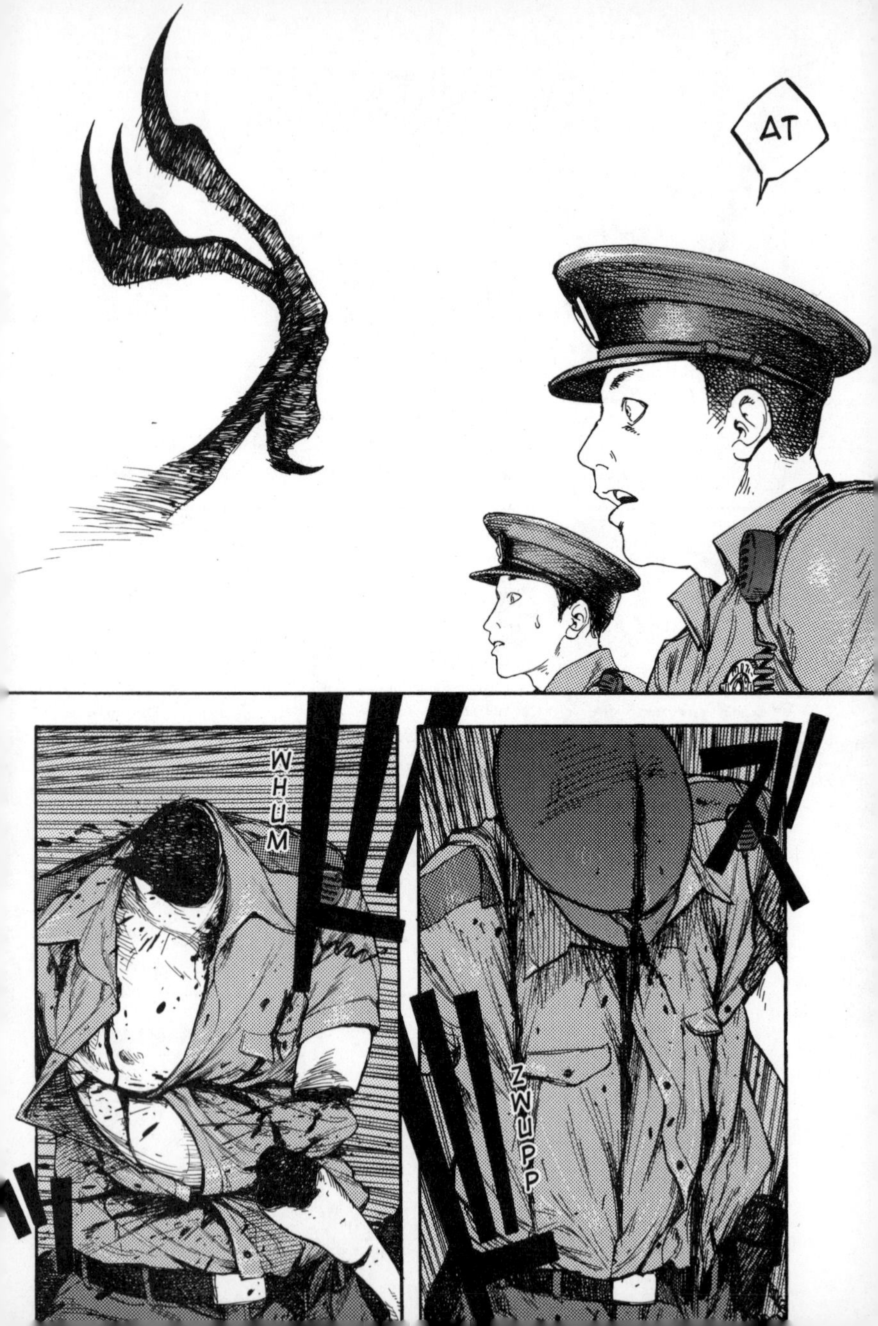
AT
ZWUPP
WHUM

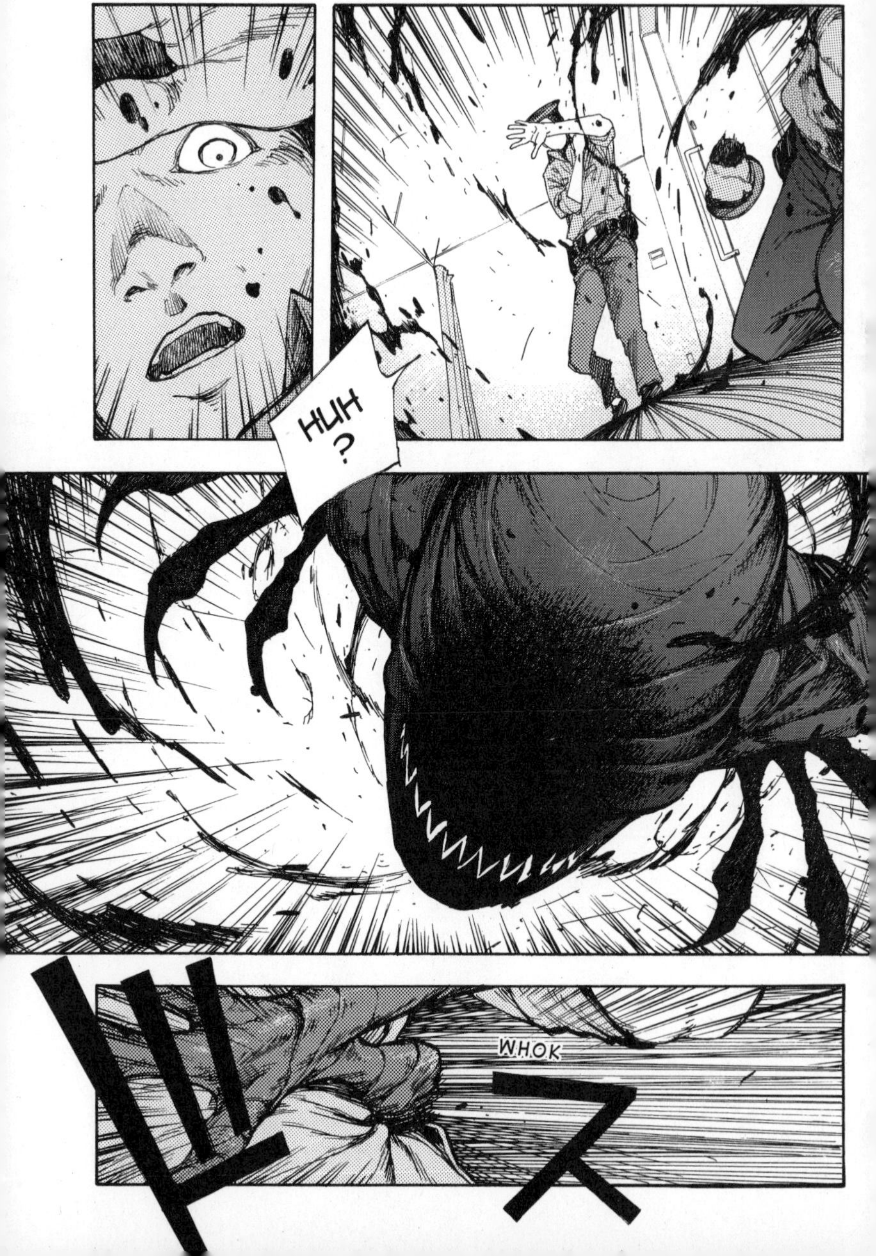
HUH
?
WHOK

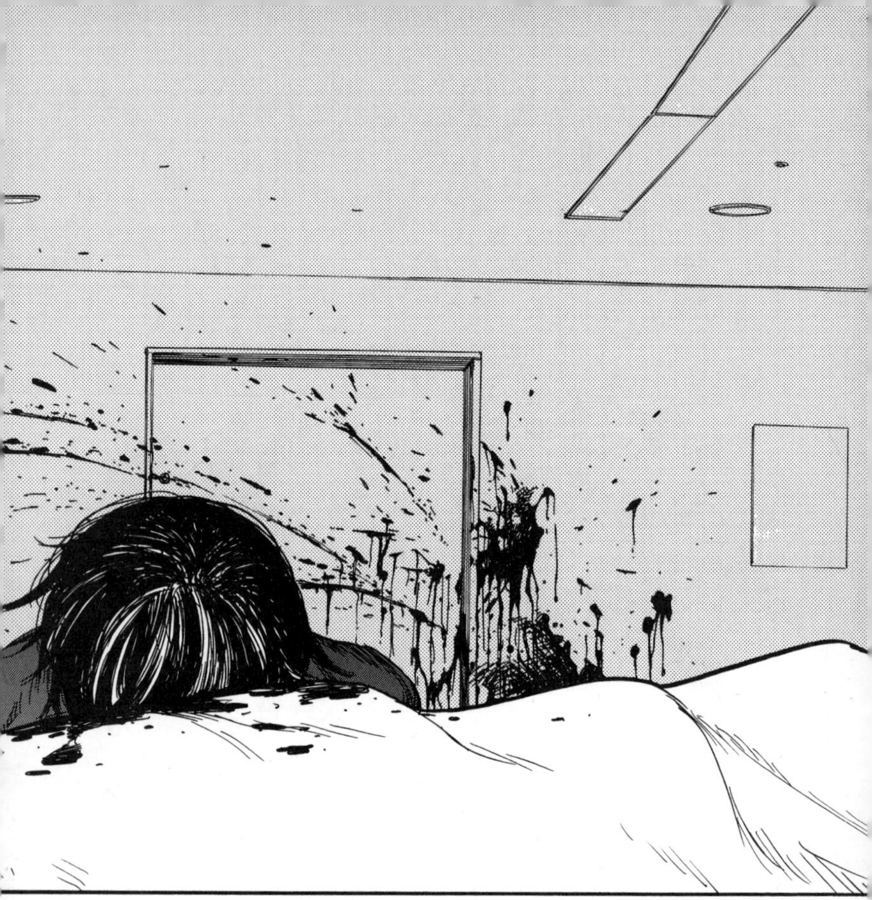

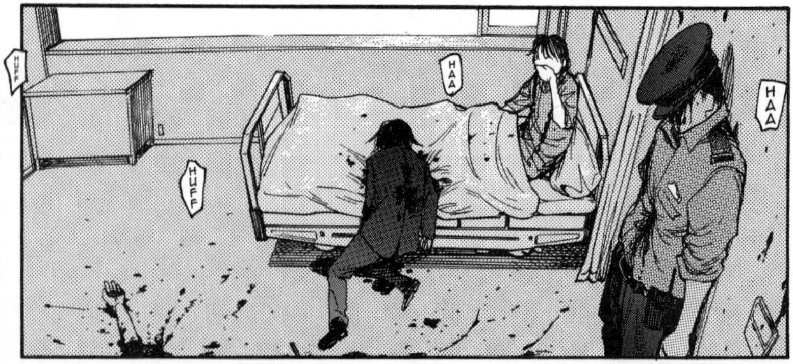
HAA
HAA
HUFF
HUFF

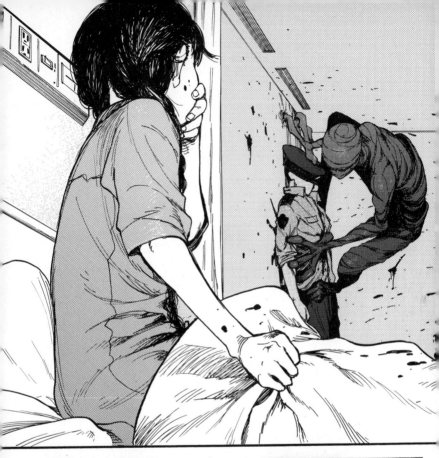

HUFF

HUFF

...

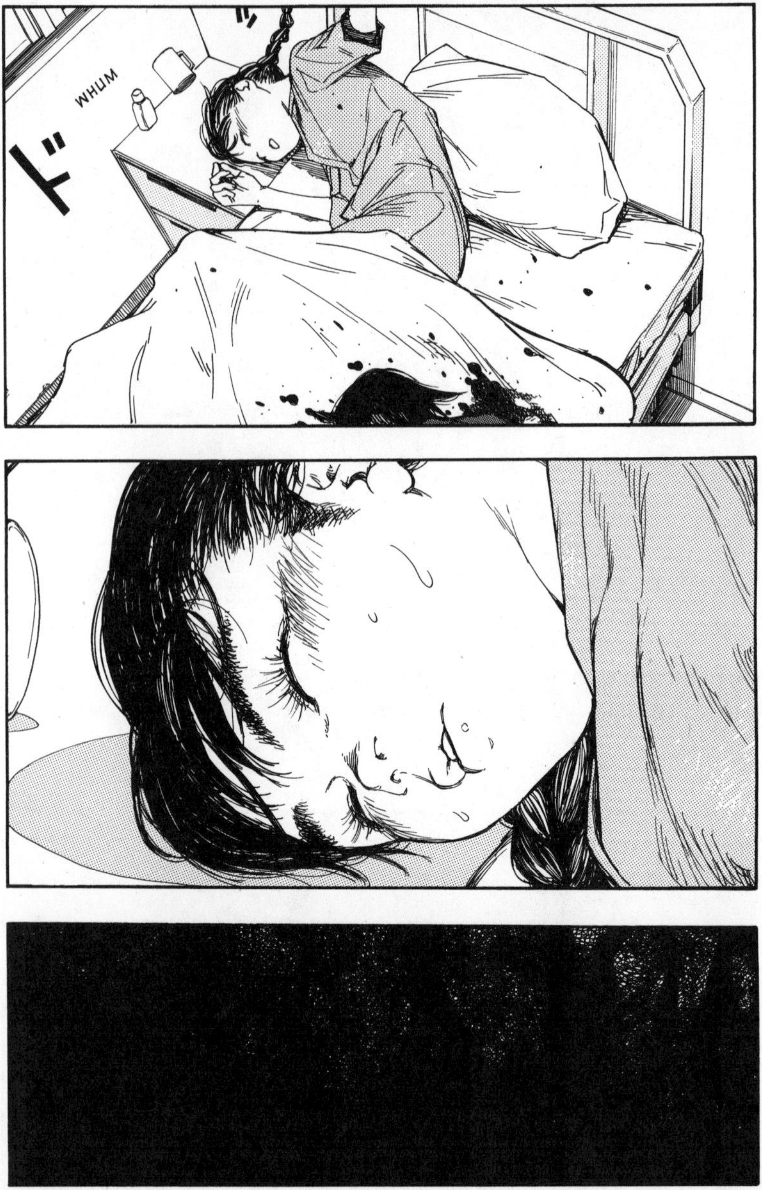
ド
WHUM

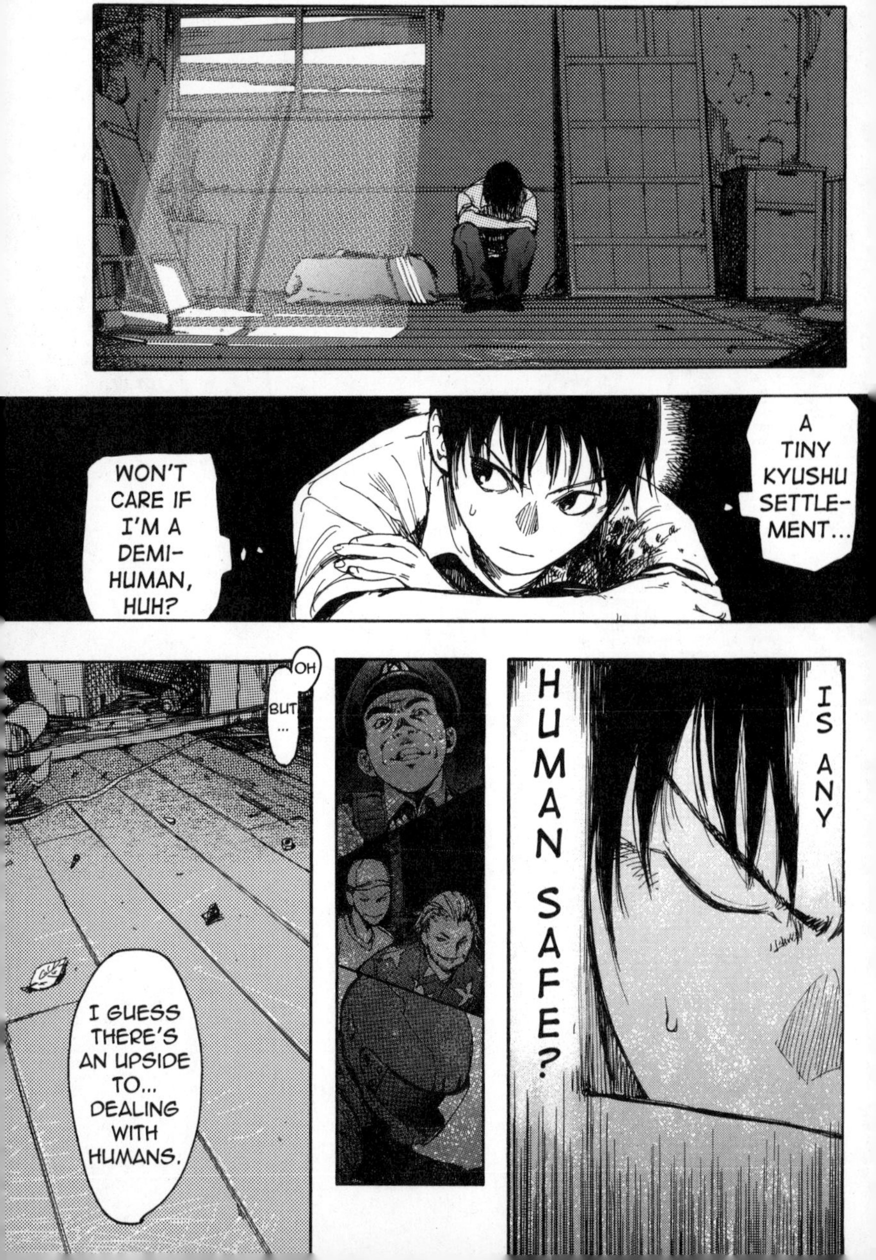
A TINY KYUSHU SETTLE-MENT...
WON'T CARE IF I'M A DEMI-HUMAN, HUH?
IS ANY HUMAN SAFE?
OH BUT...
I GUESS THERE'S AN UPSIDE TO... DEALING WITH HUMANS.

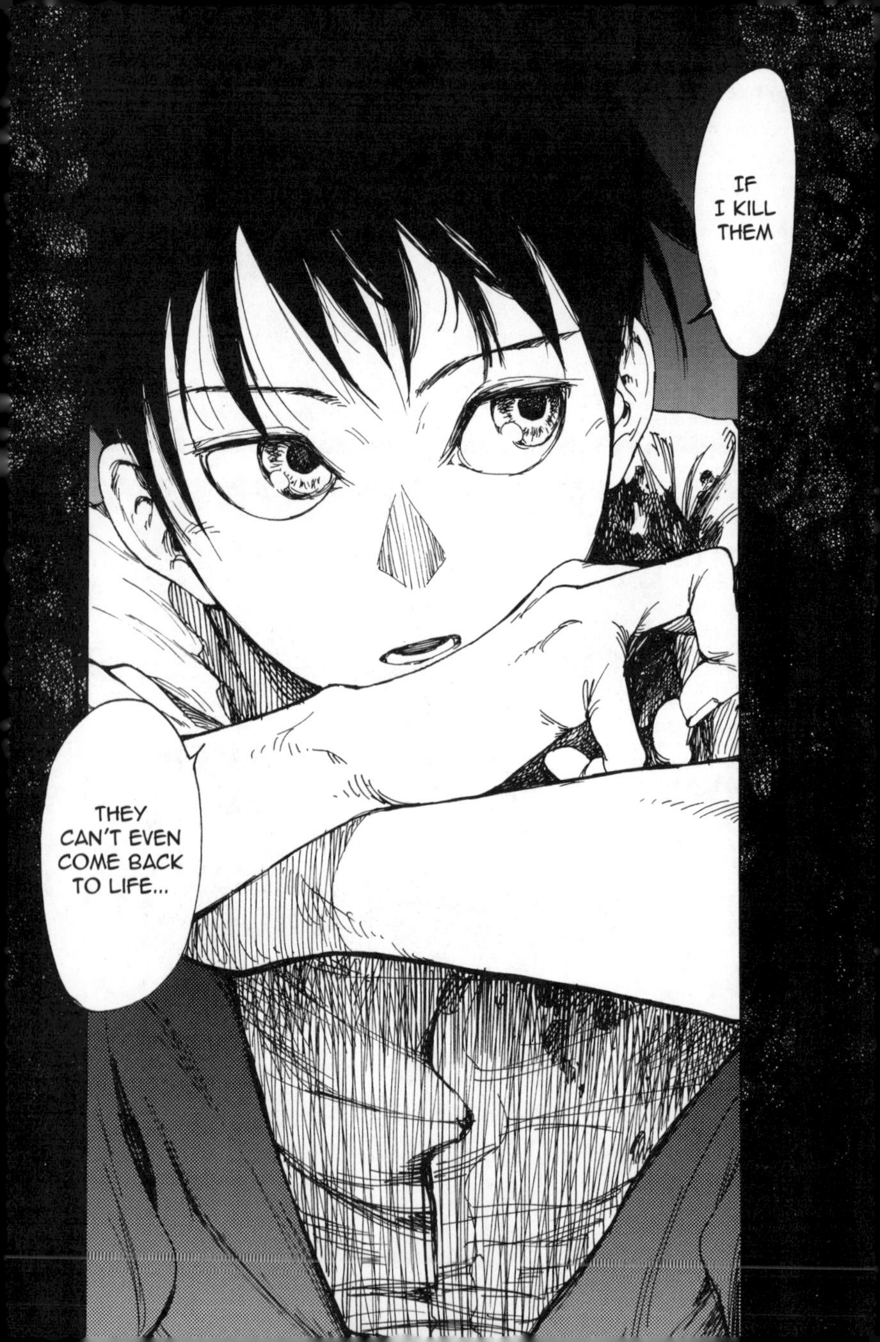
IF I KILL THEM
THEY CAN'T EVEN COME BACK TO LIFE...

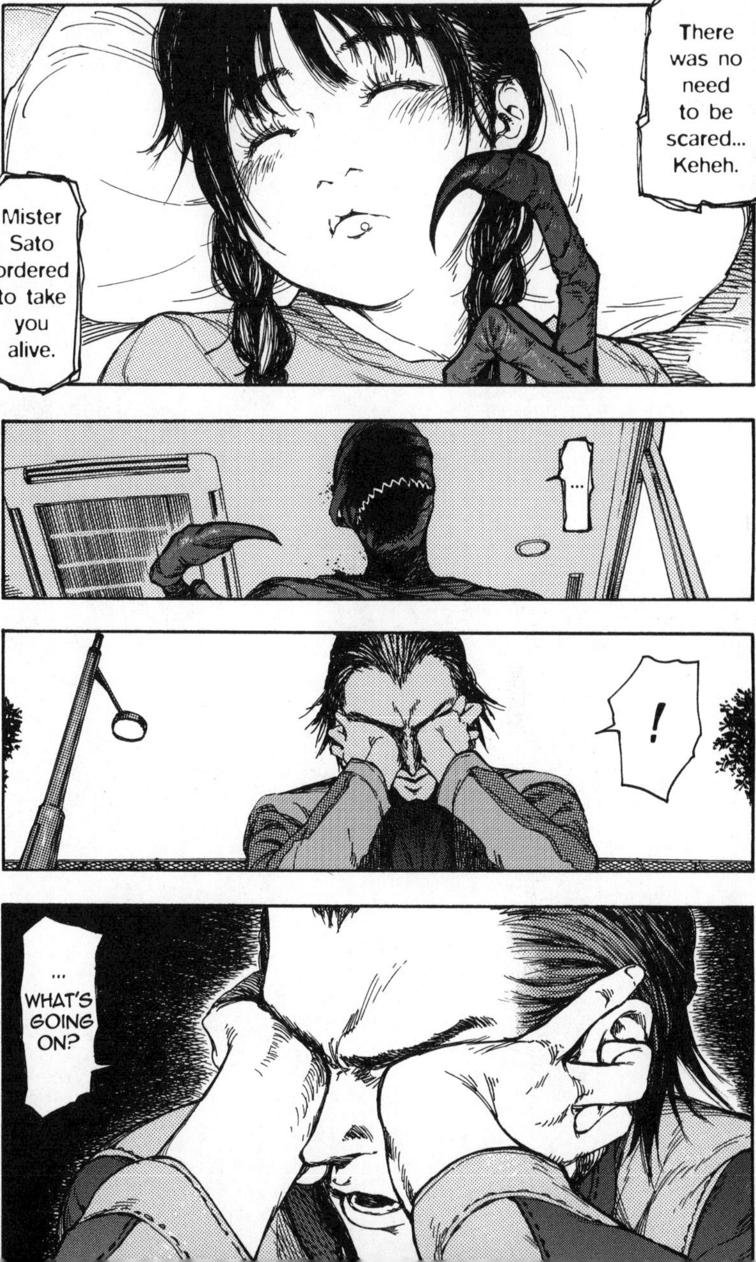
There was no need to be scared... Keheh.
Mister Sato ordered to take you alive.
...
!
... WHAT'S GOING ON?

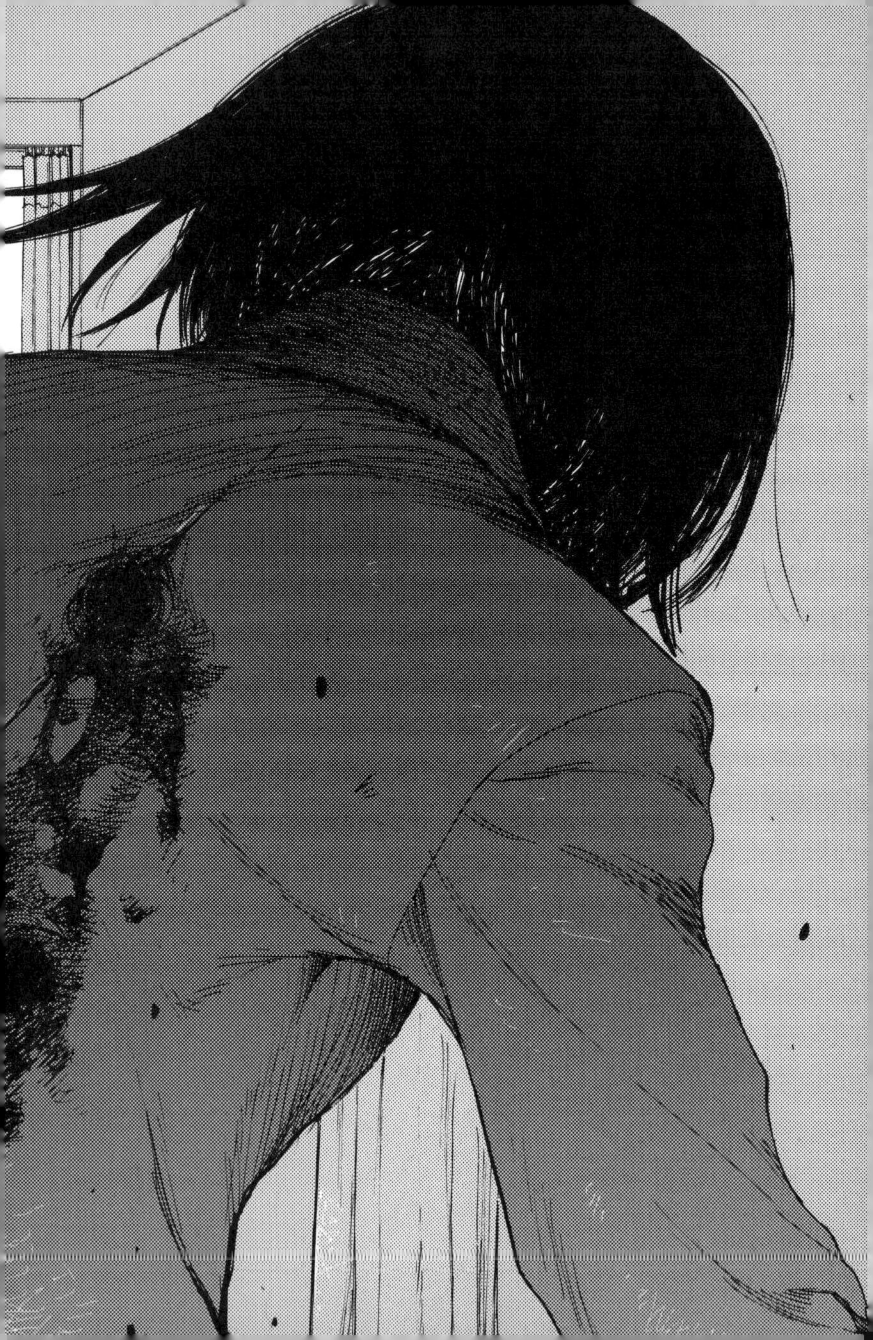

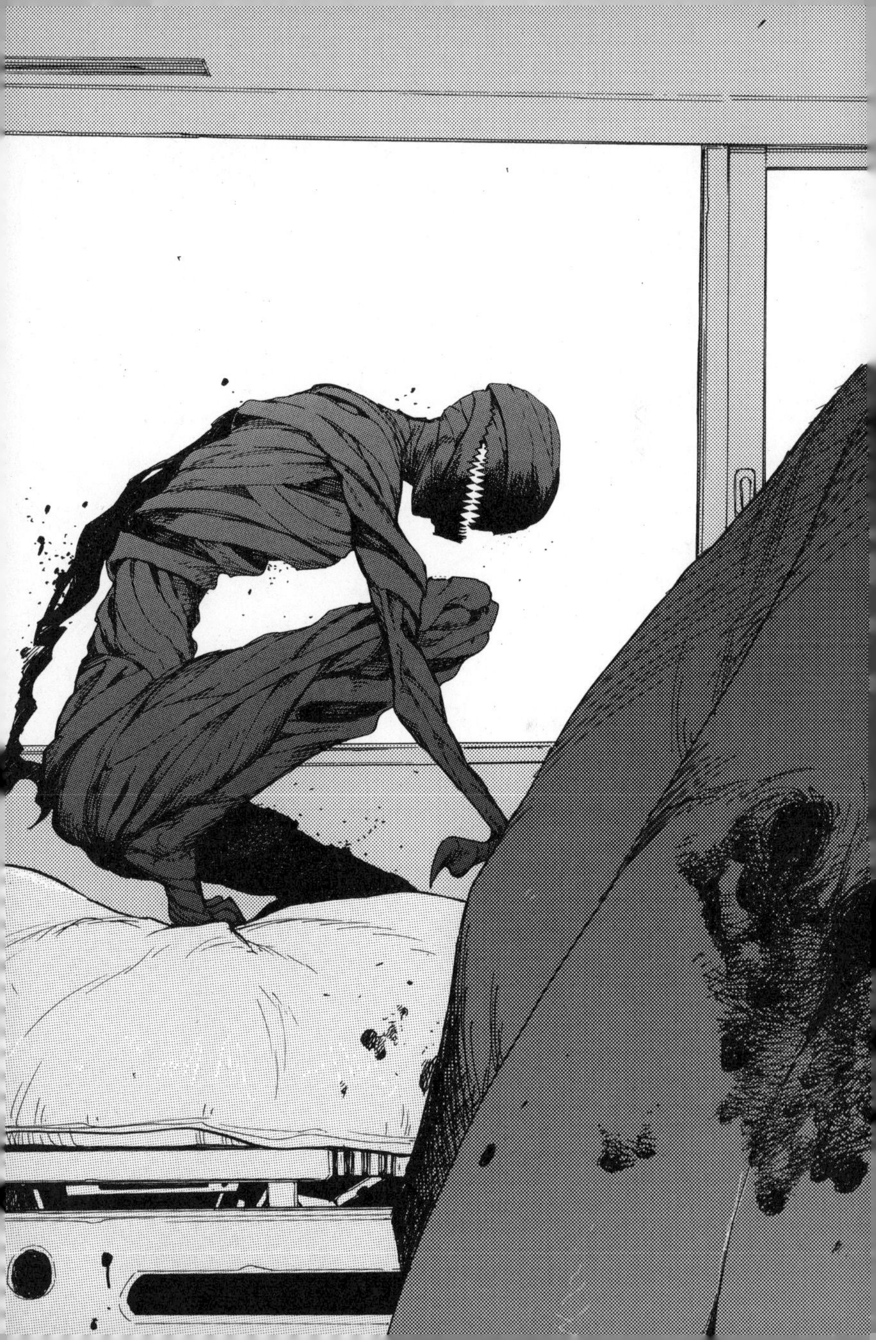

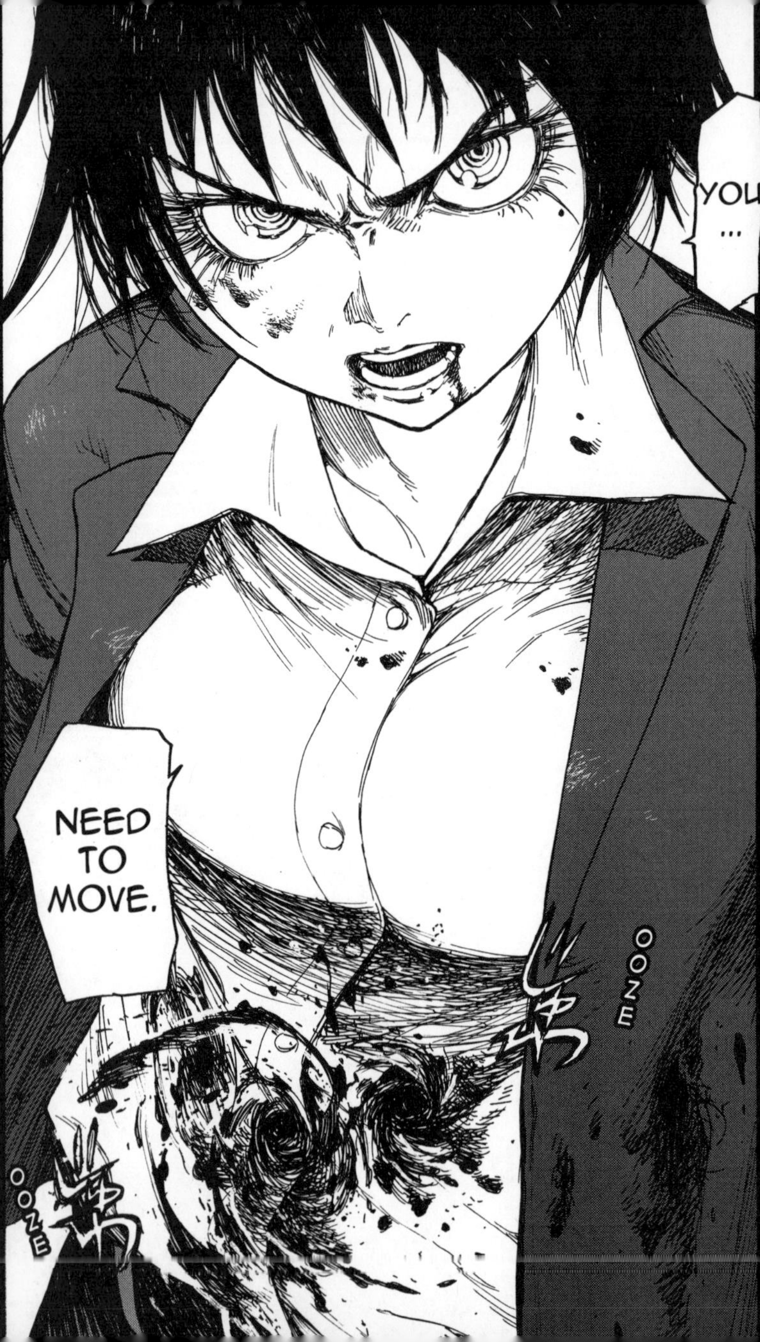
YOU ...
NEED TO MOVE.
OOZE
OOZE

Acting like a human,
were you?
RUB
RUB
SO ...
I'M A
DEMI-HUMAN ...

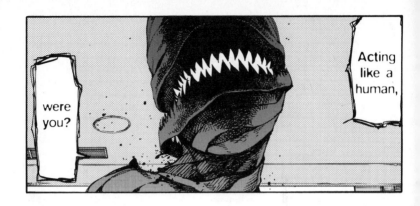

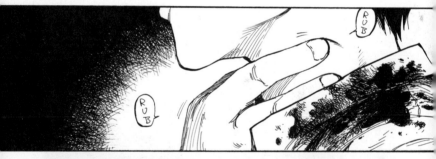

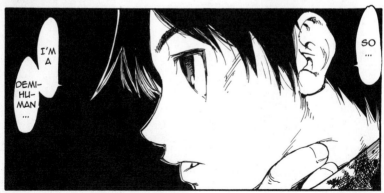

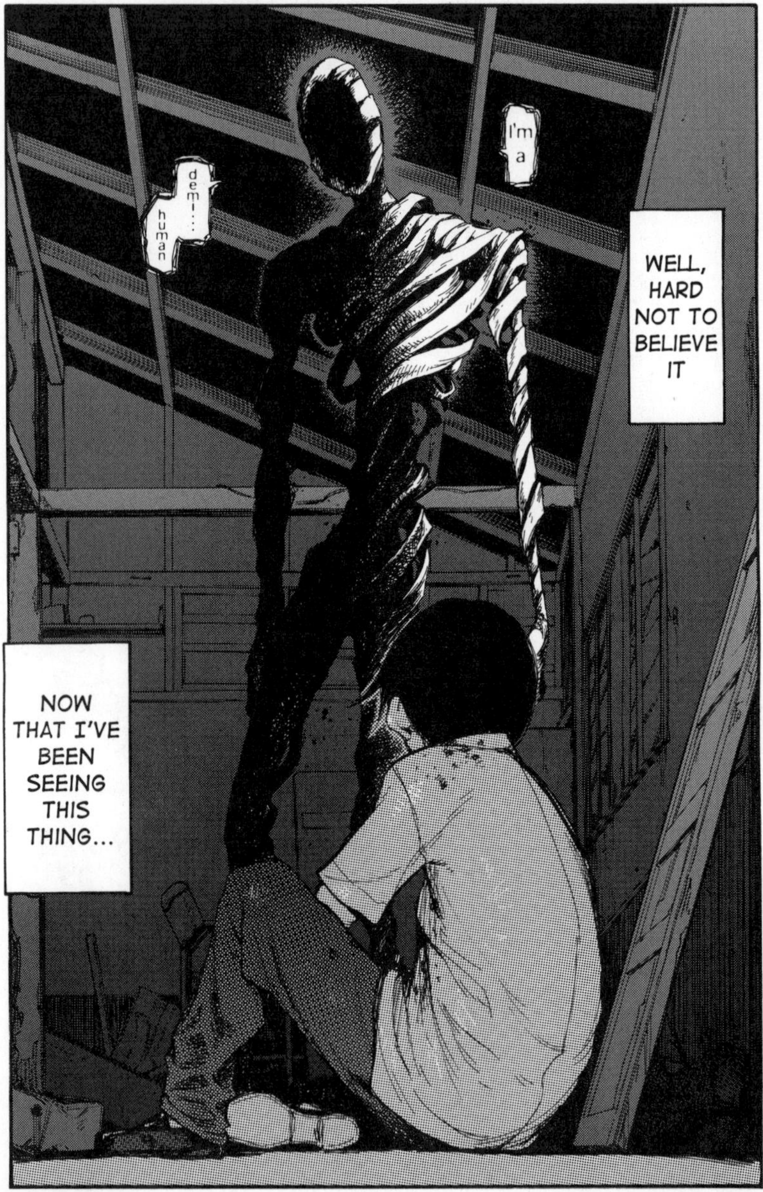
I'm a
demi... human
WELL, HARD NOT TO BELIEVE IT
NOW THAT I'VE BEEN SEEING THIS THING...

File:04 End

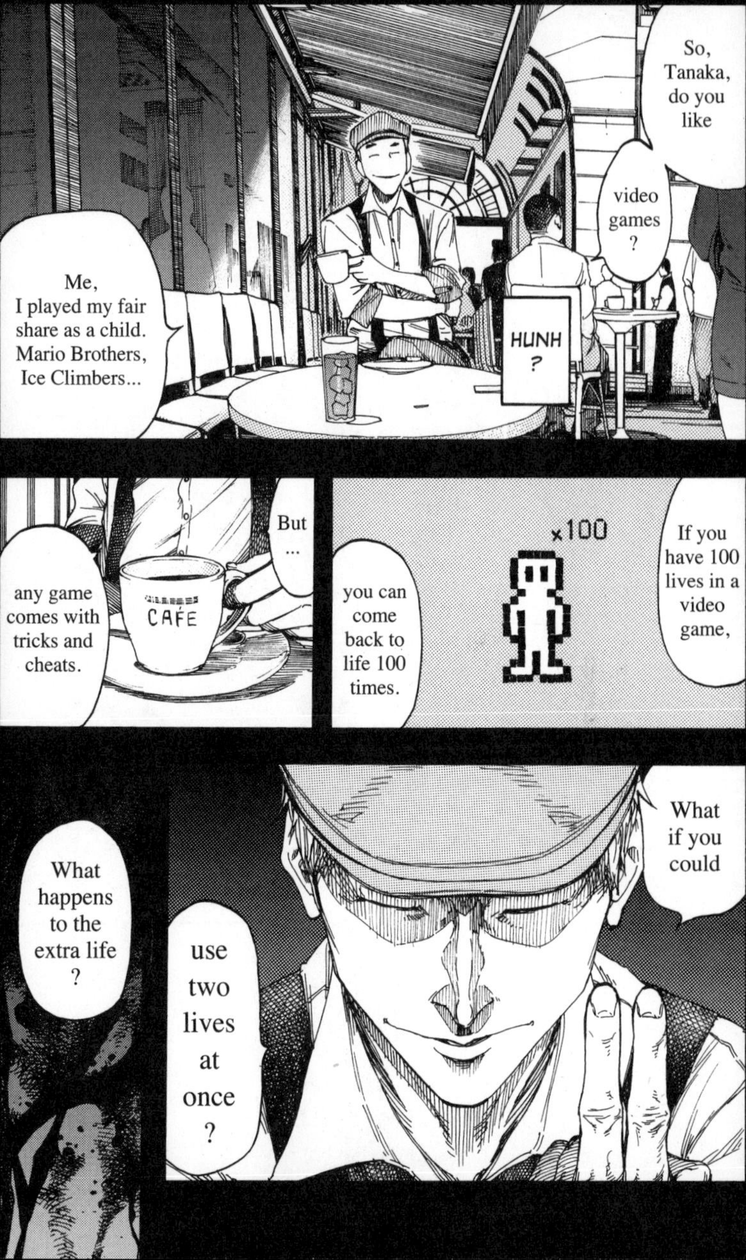
So, Tanaka, do you like
video games ?
HUNH ?
Me, I played my fair share as a child. Mario Brothers, Ice Climbers...
If you have 100 lives in a video game,
×100
you can come back to life 100 times.
But ...
CAFÉ
any game comes with tricks and cheats.
What if you could
use two lives at once ?
What happens to the extra life ?

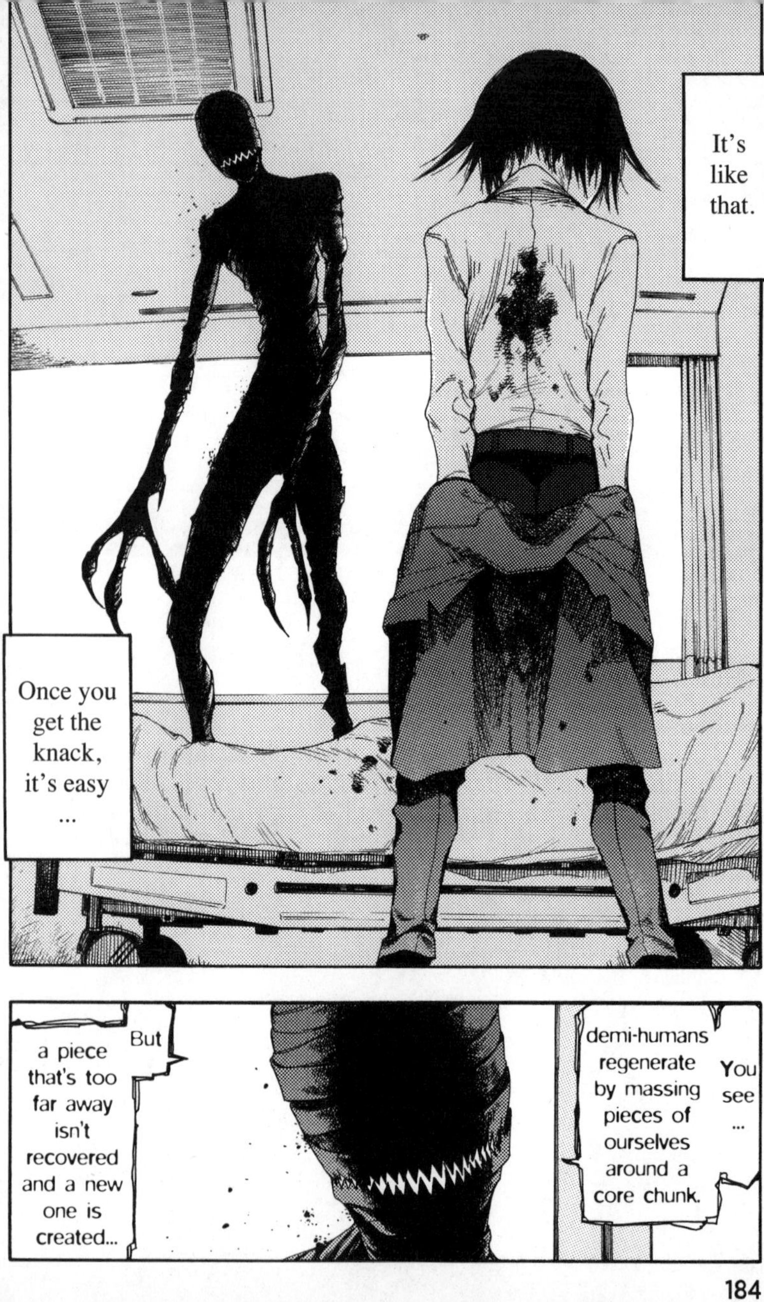
It's like that.
Once you get the knack, it's easy ...
You see ...
demi-humans regenerate by massing pieces of ourselves around a core chunk.
But
a piece that's too far away isn't recovered and a new one is created...

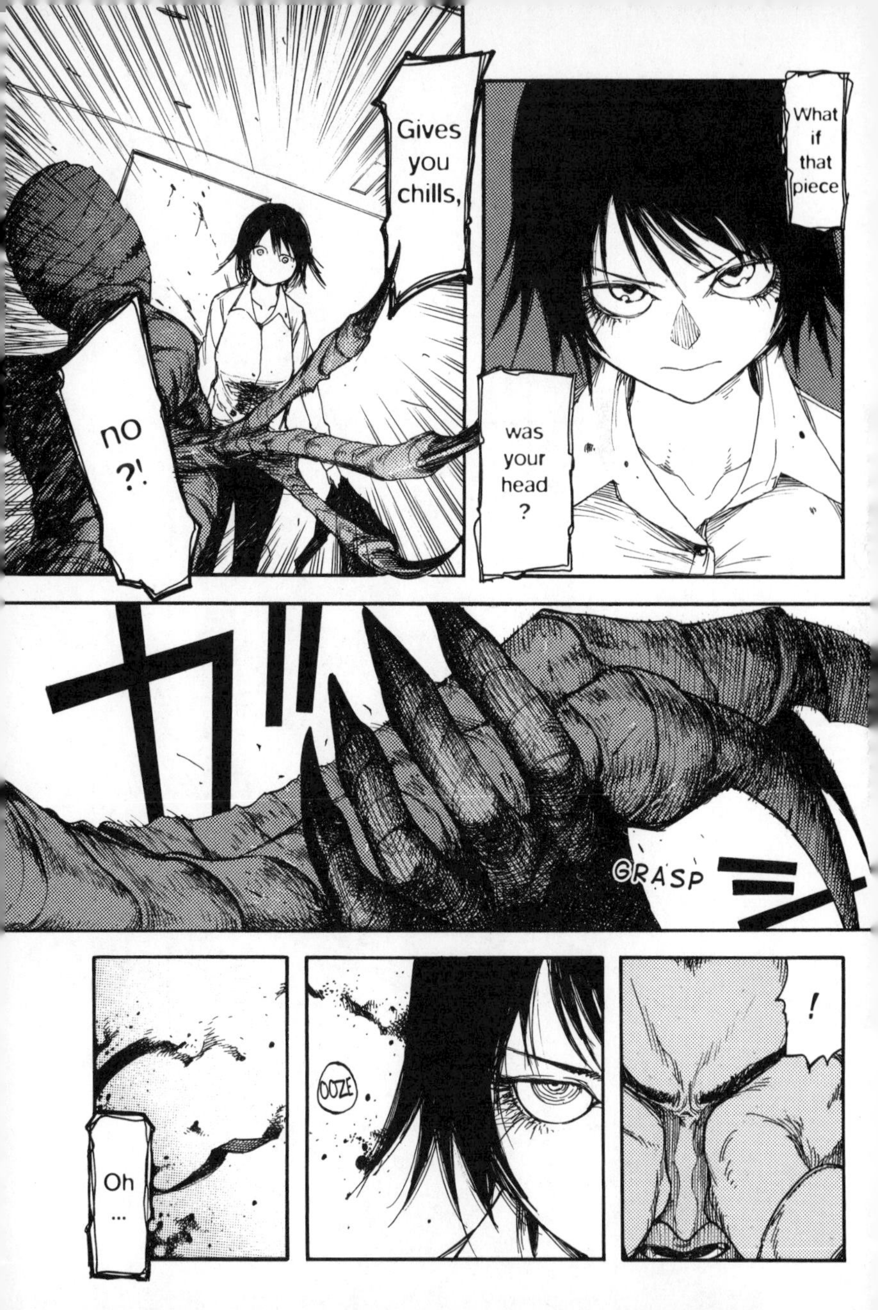
What if that piece
was your head ?
Gives you chills,
no ?!
GRASP
!
OOZE
Oh ...

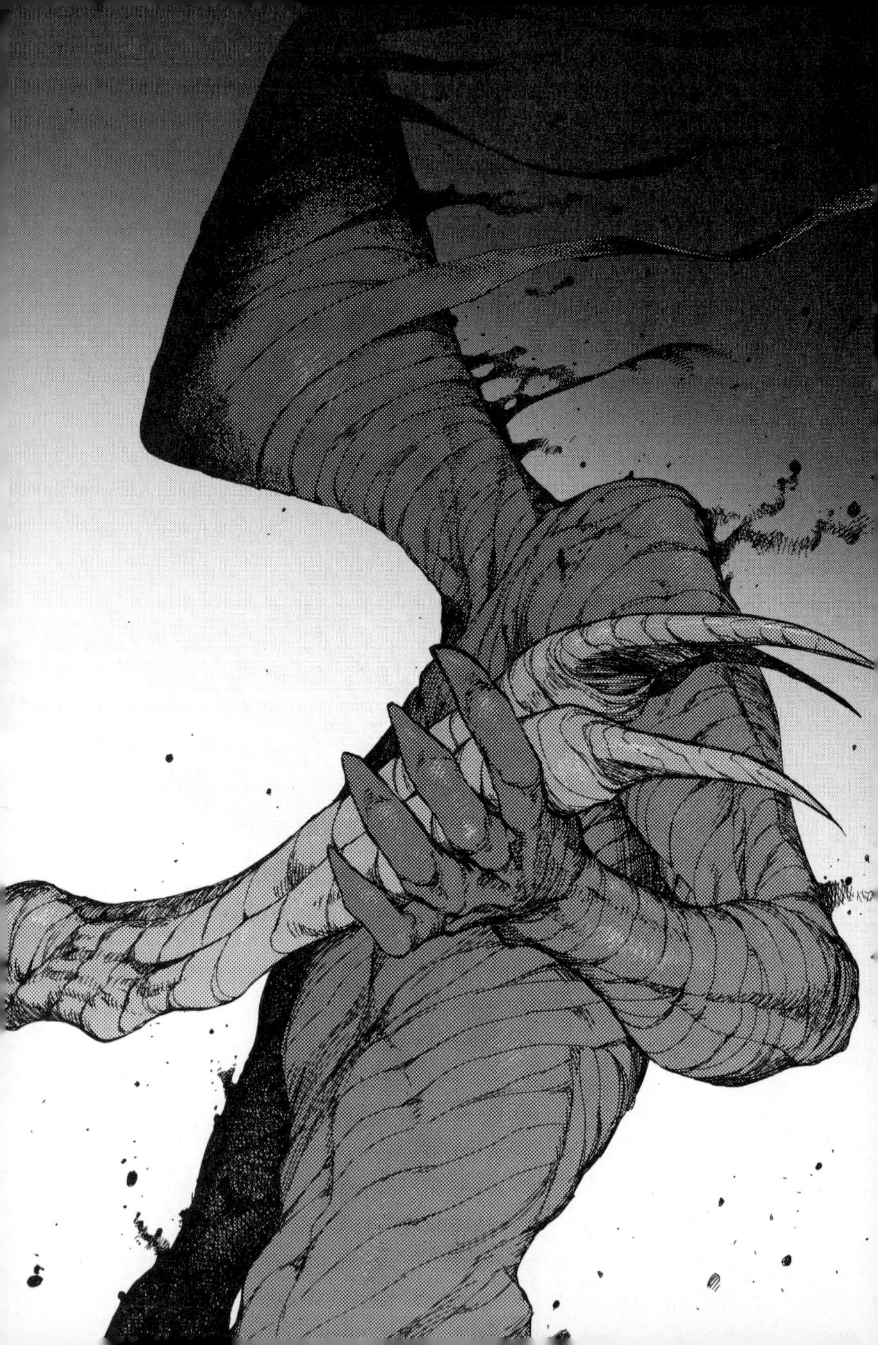

File 05: Emergence and Organization

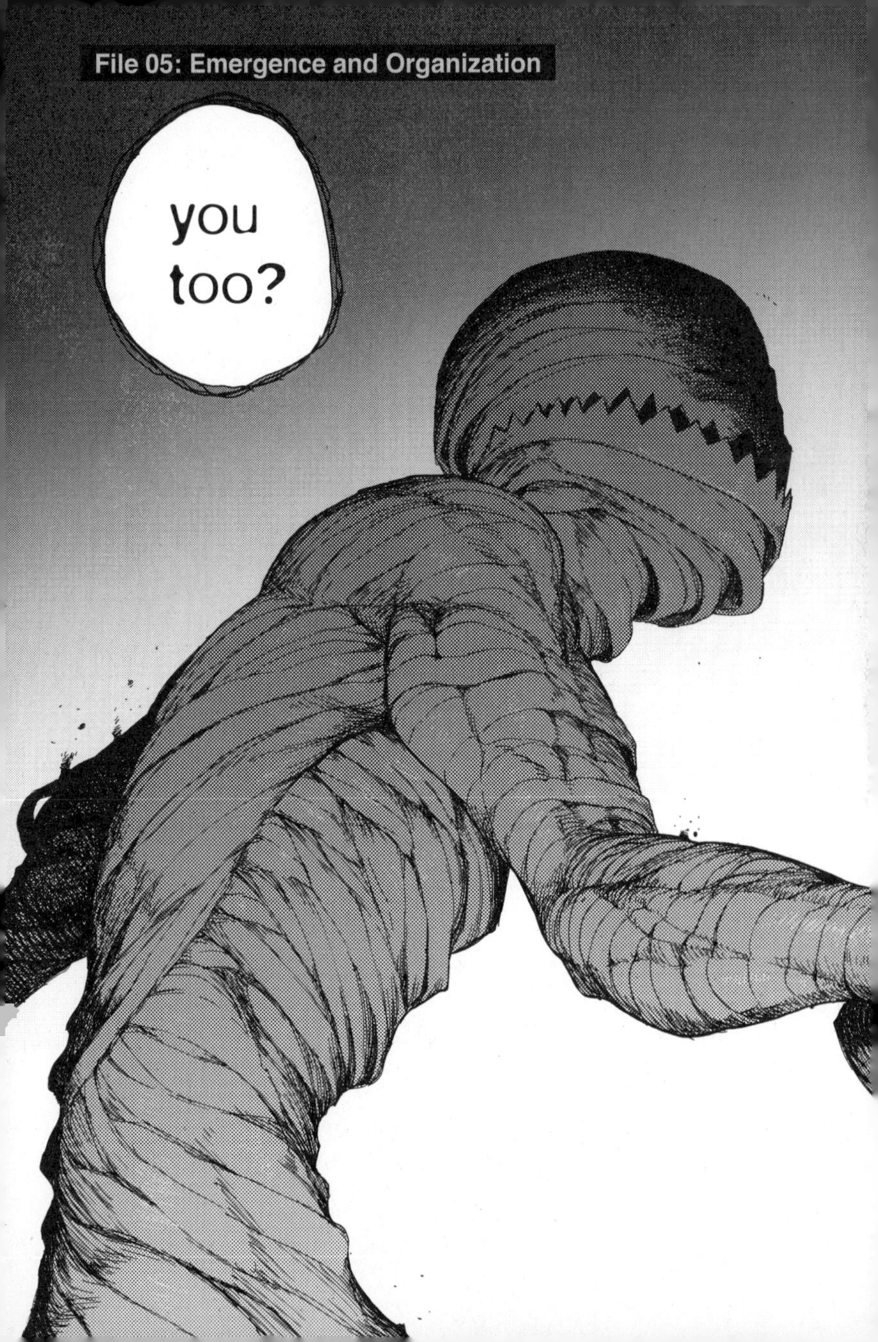
you too?

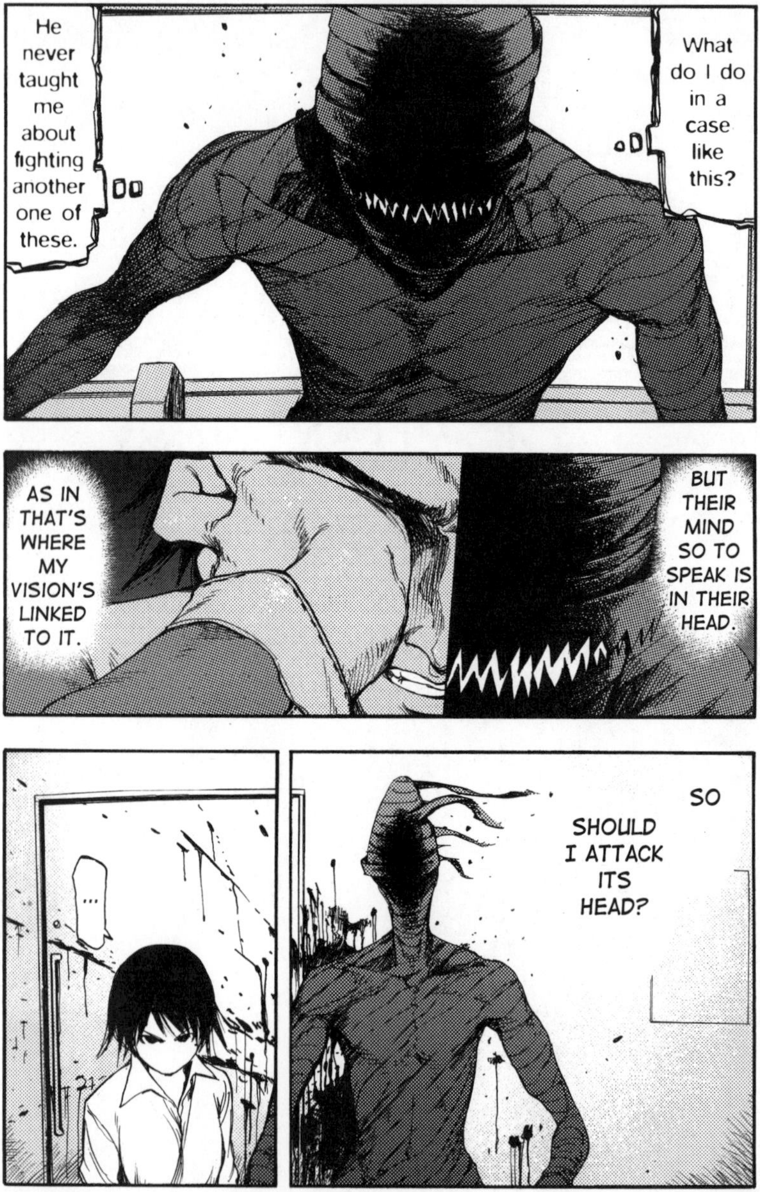
What do I do in a case like this?
He never taught me about fighting another one of these.
BUT THEIR MIND SO TO SPEAK IS IN THEIR HEAD.
AS IN THAT'S WHERE MY VISION'S LINKED TO IT.
SO SHOULD I ATTACK ITS HEAD?
...

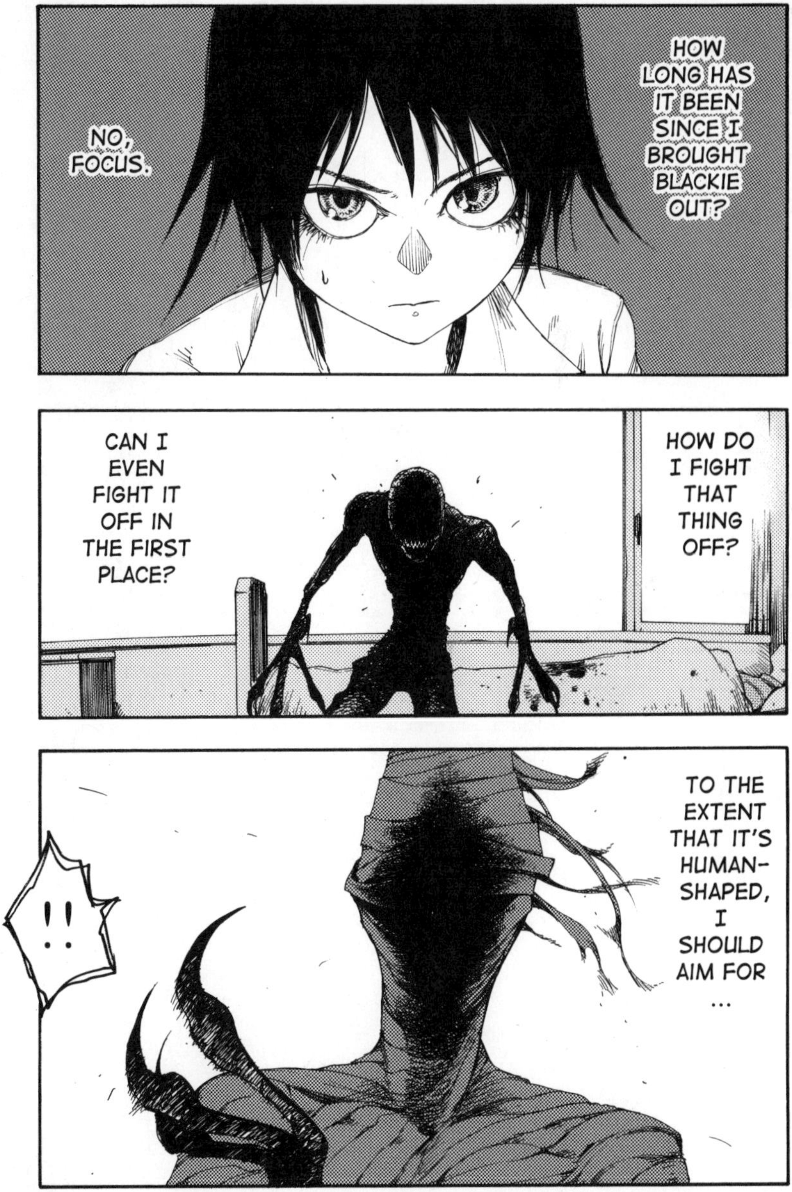
HOW LONG HAS IT BEEN SINCE I BROUGHT BLACKIE OUT?
NO, FOCUS.
HOW DO I FIGHT THAT THING OFF?
CAN I EVEN FIGHT IT OFF IN THE FIRST PLACE?
TO THE EXTENT THAT IT'S HUMAN-SHAPED, I SHOULD AIM FOR ...
!!

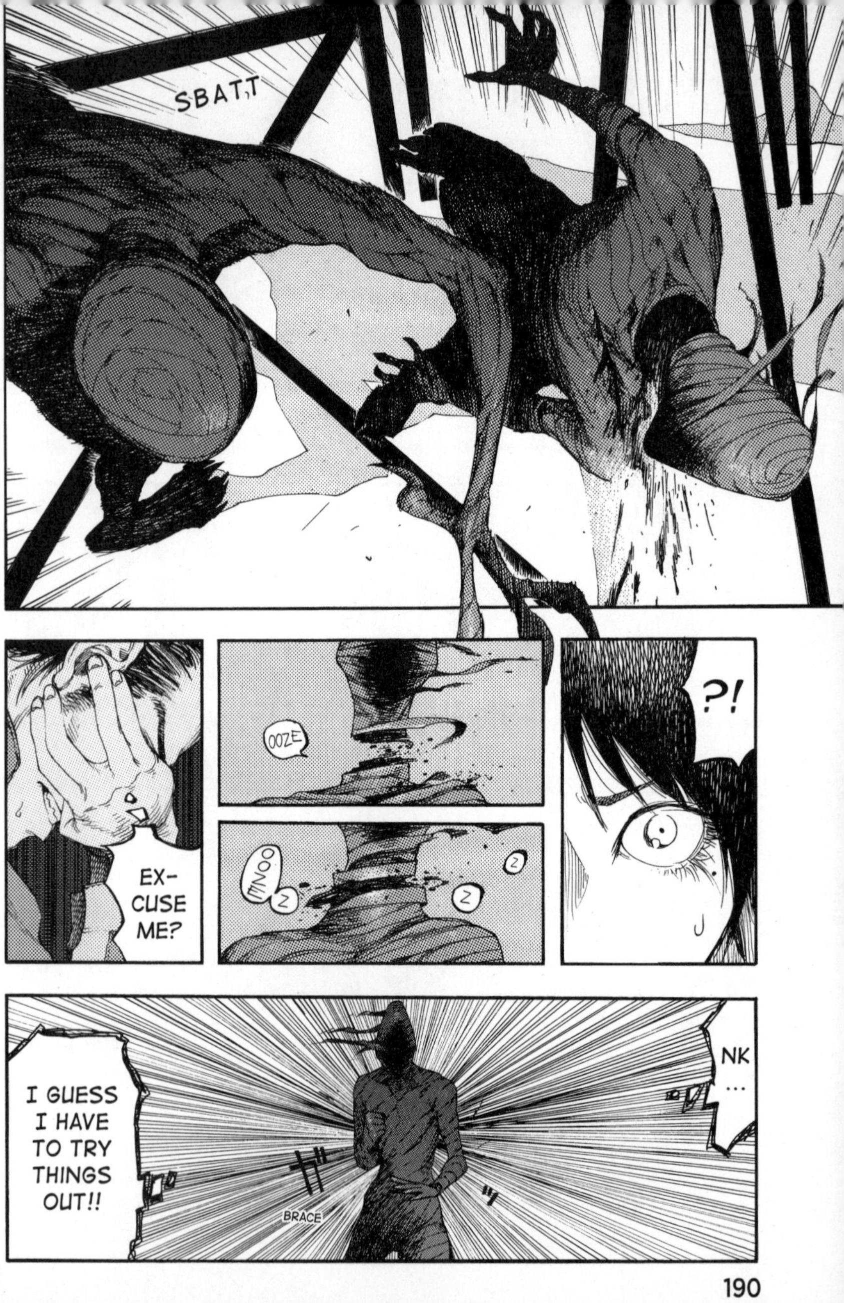
SBATT
?!
OOZE
OOZE
Z
Z
Z
EX-CUSE ME?
NK...
I GUESS I HAVE TO TRY THINGS OUT!!
BRACE

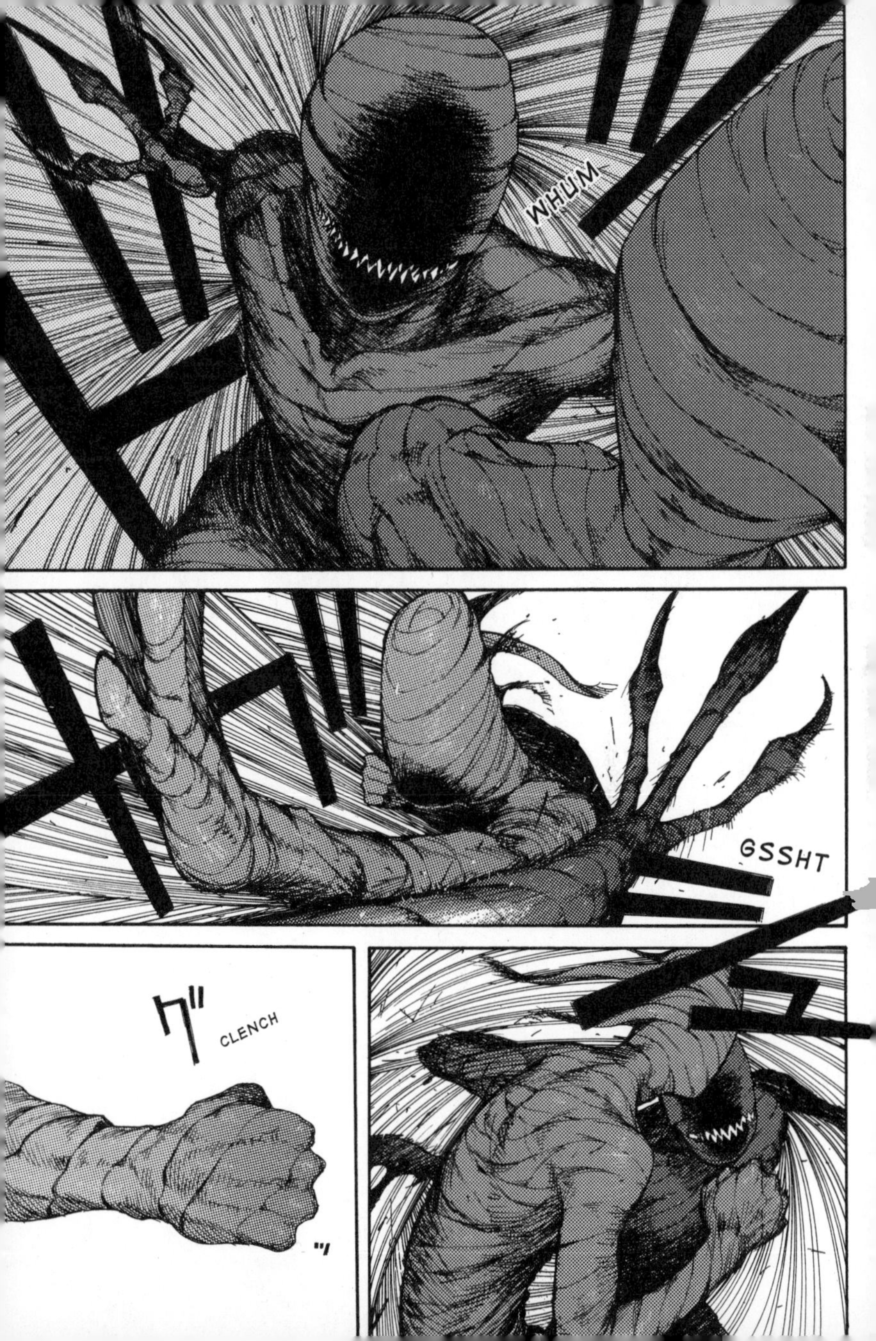
WHUM
GSSHT
グ
CLENCH

GWOK

Wh...

at
?!

?!

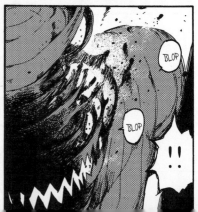

BLOP

BLOP

!!

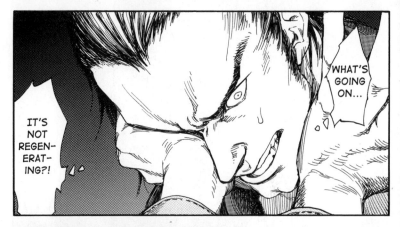

WHAT'S GOING ON...

IT'S NOT REGENERATING?!

I'M... LOSING MY LINK...

MY VISION IS

HAZY...

!

NO...

PUL-VERIZED

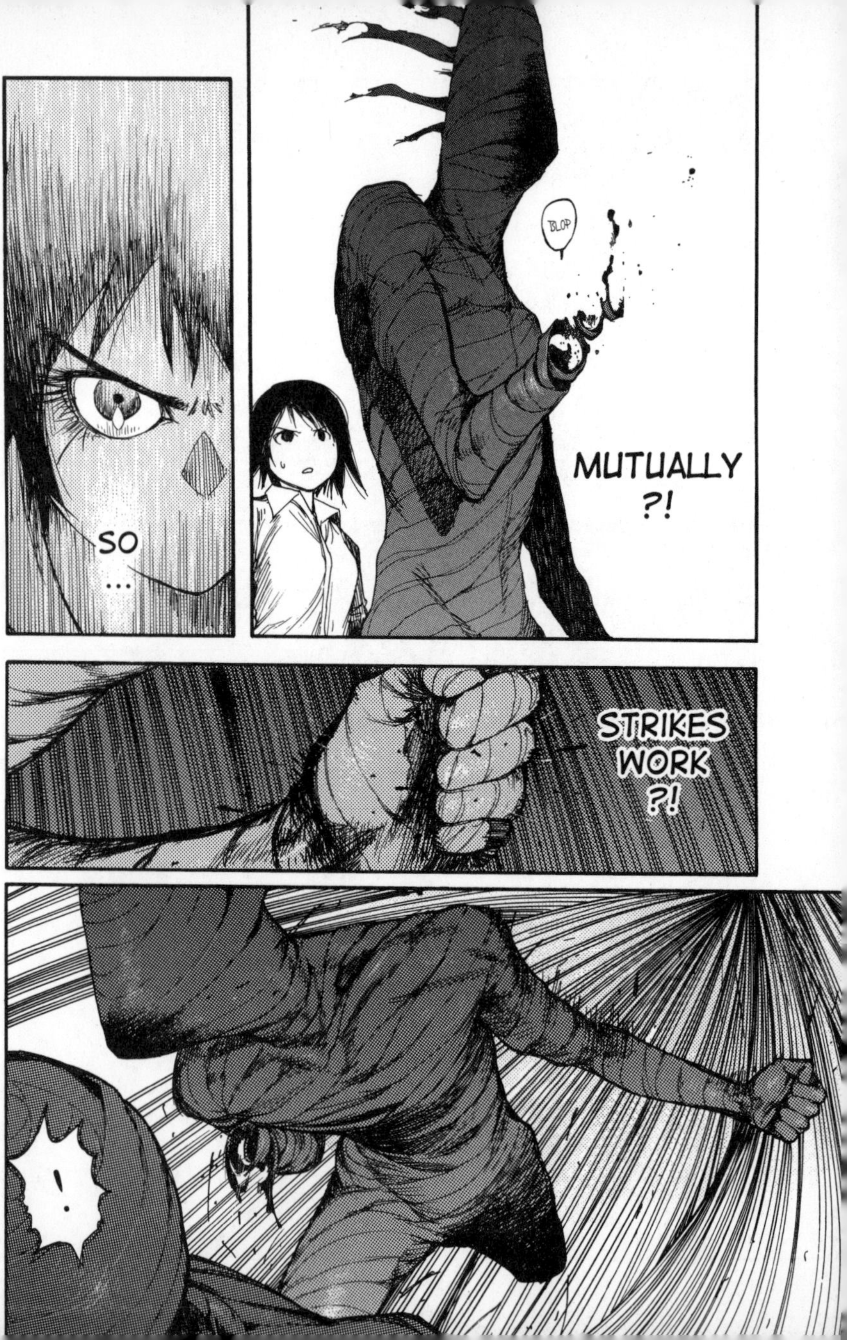
BLOP
MUTUALLY ?!
SO ...
STRIKES WORK ?!
!

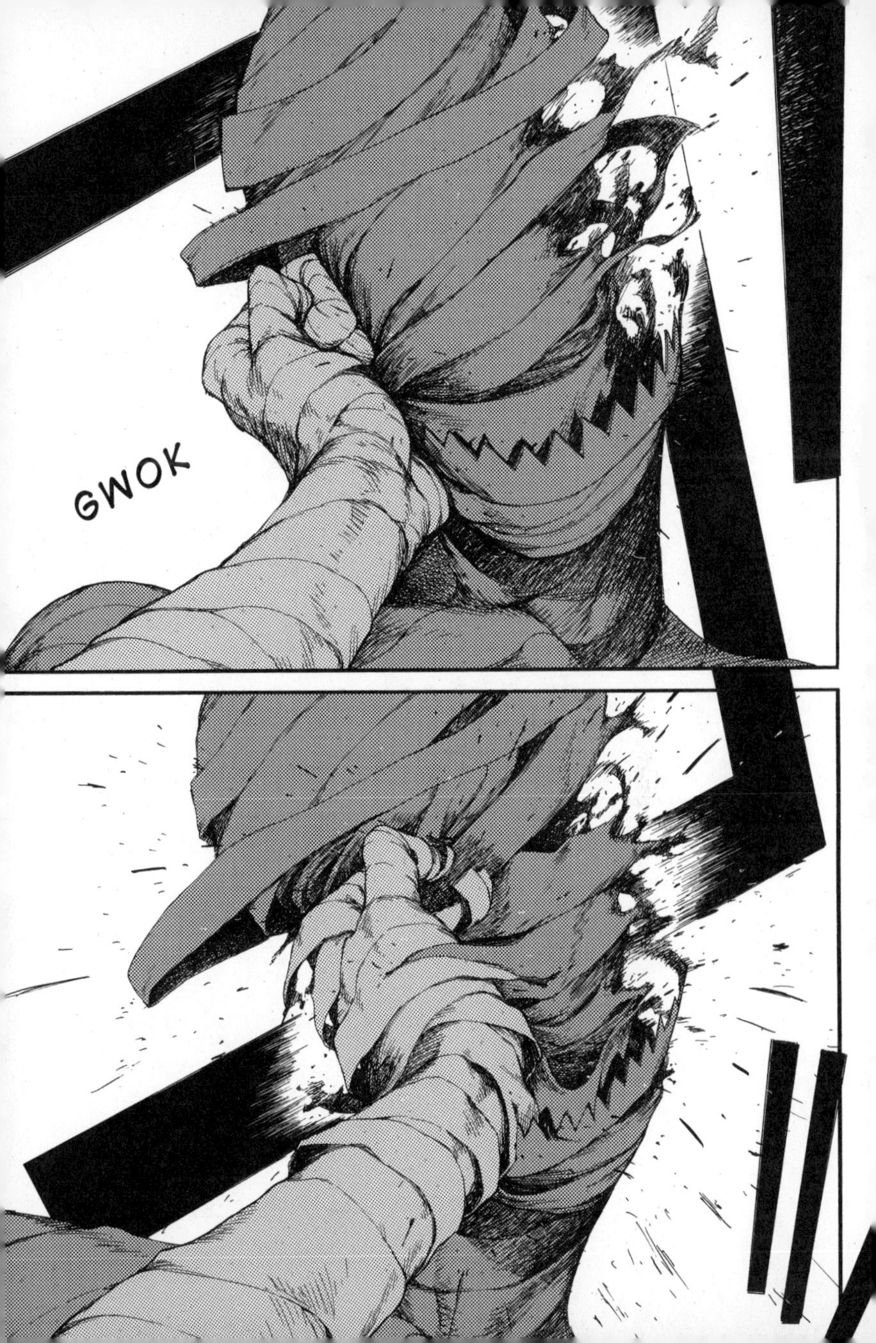
GWOK

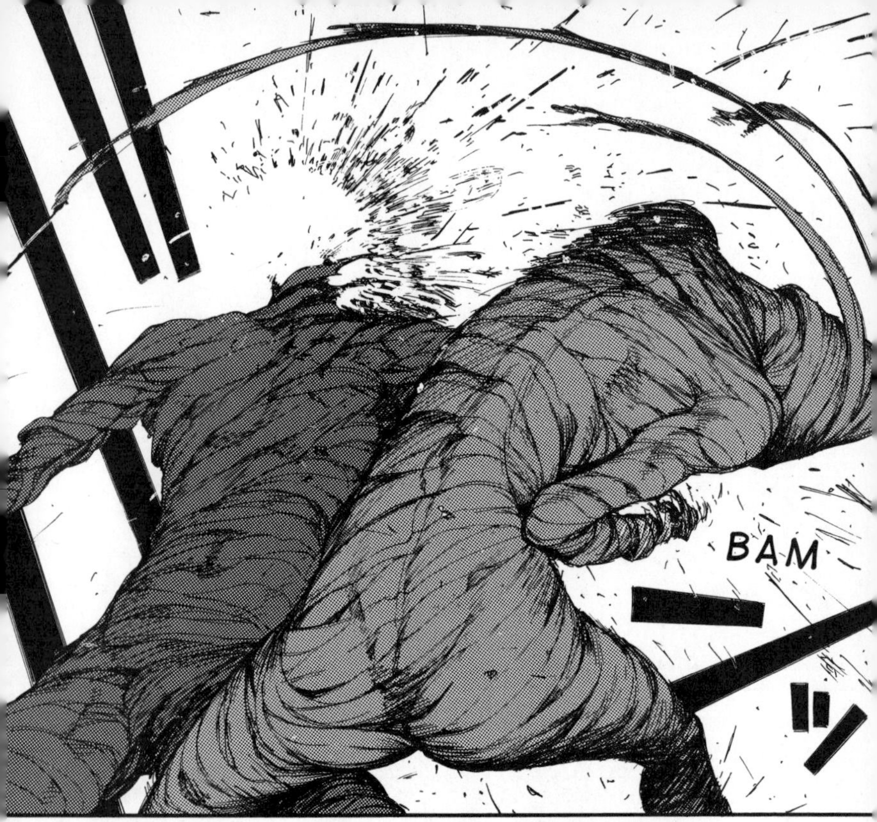
BAM

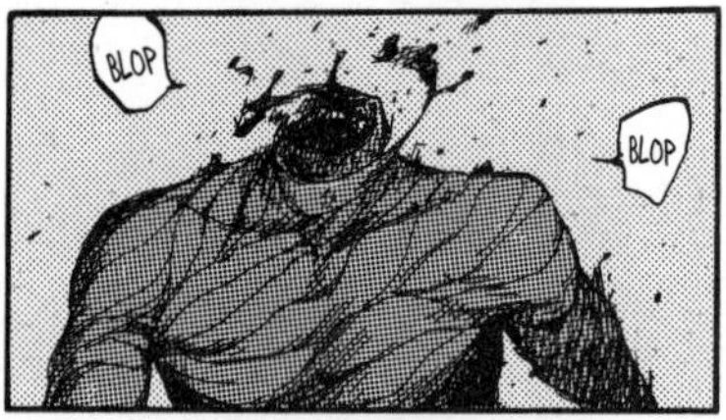
BLOP
BLOP

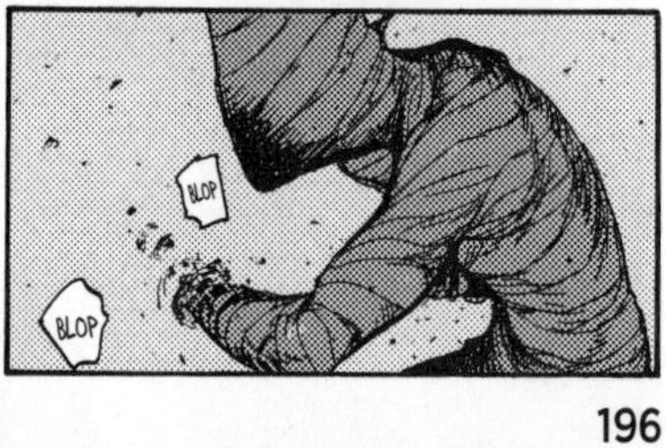
BLOP
BLOP

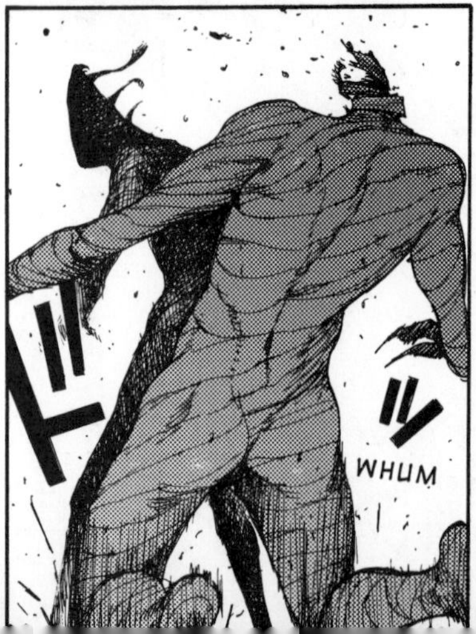
WHUM

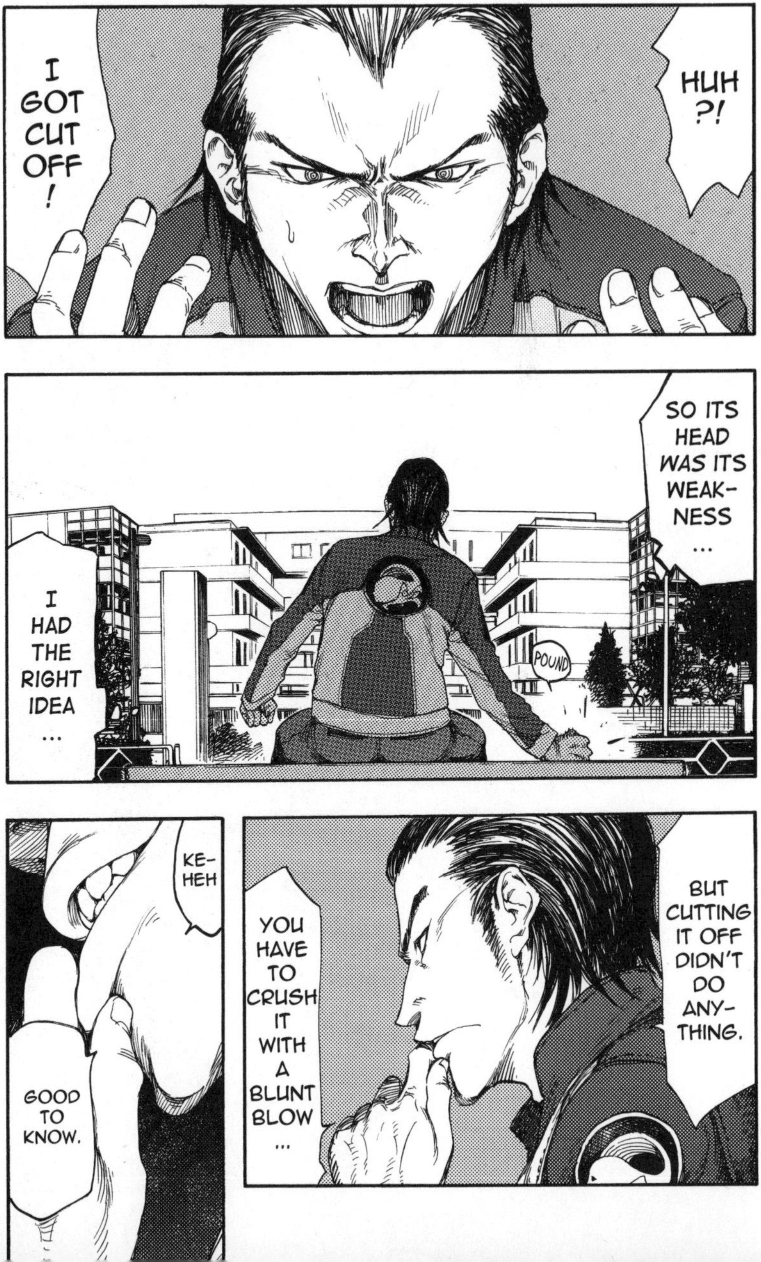
HUH ?!
I GOT CUT OFF !
SO ITS HEAD WAS ITS WEAK- NESS ...
POUND
I HAD THE RIGHT IDEA ...
BUT CUTTING IT OFF DIDN'T DO ANY- THING.
YOU HAVE TO CRUSH IT WITH A BLUNT BLOW ...
KE- HEH
GOOD TO KNOW.

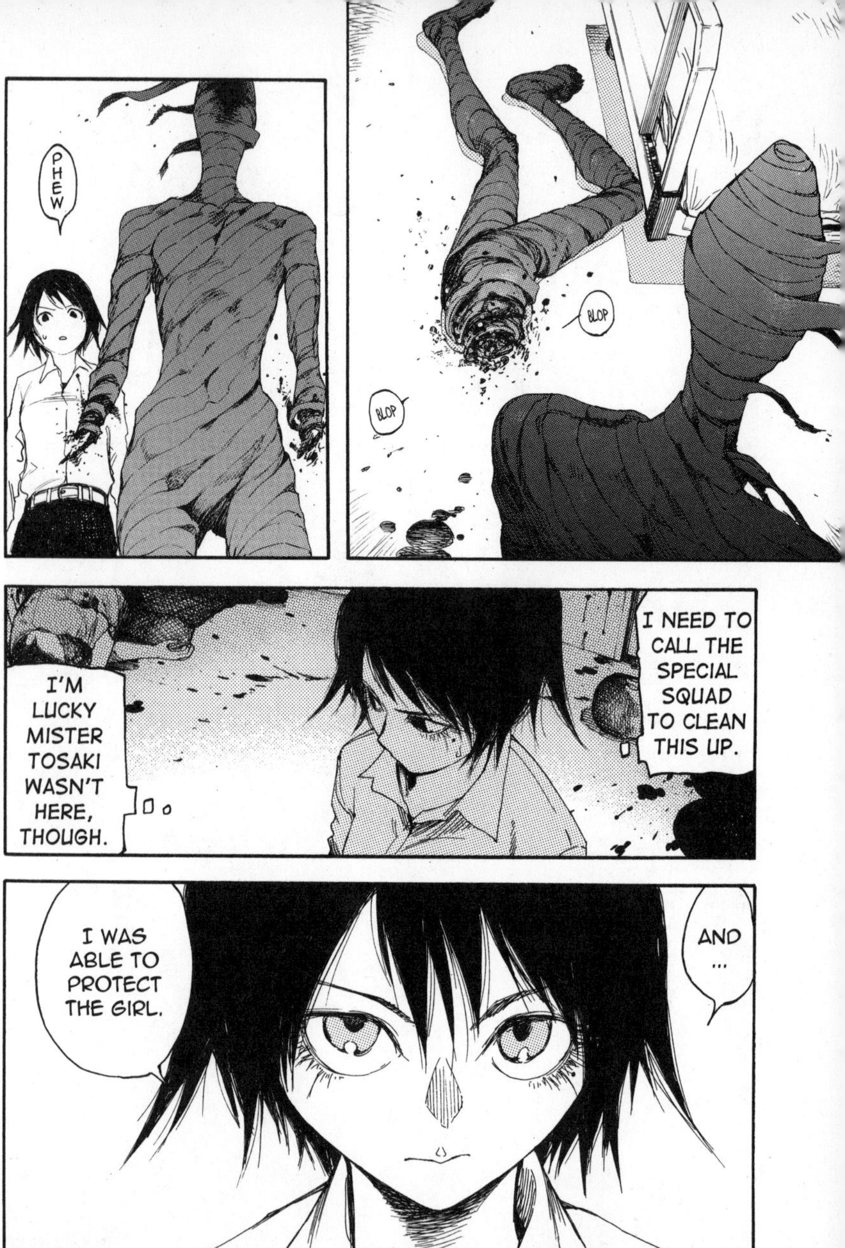
BLOP
BLOP
PHEW
I NEED TO CALL THE SPECIAL SQUAD TO CLEAN THIS UP.
I'M LUCKY MISTER TOSAKI WASN'T HERE, THOUGH.
AND ...
I WAS ABLE TO PROTECT THE GIRL.

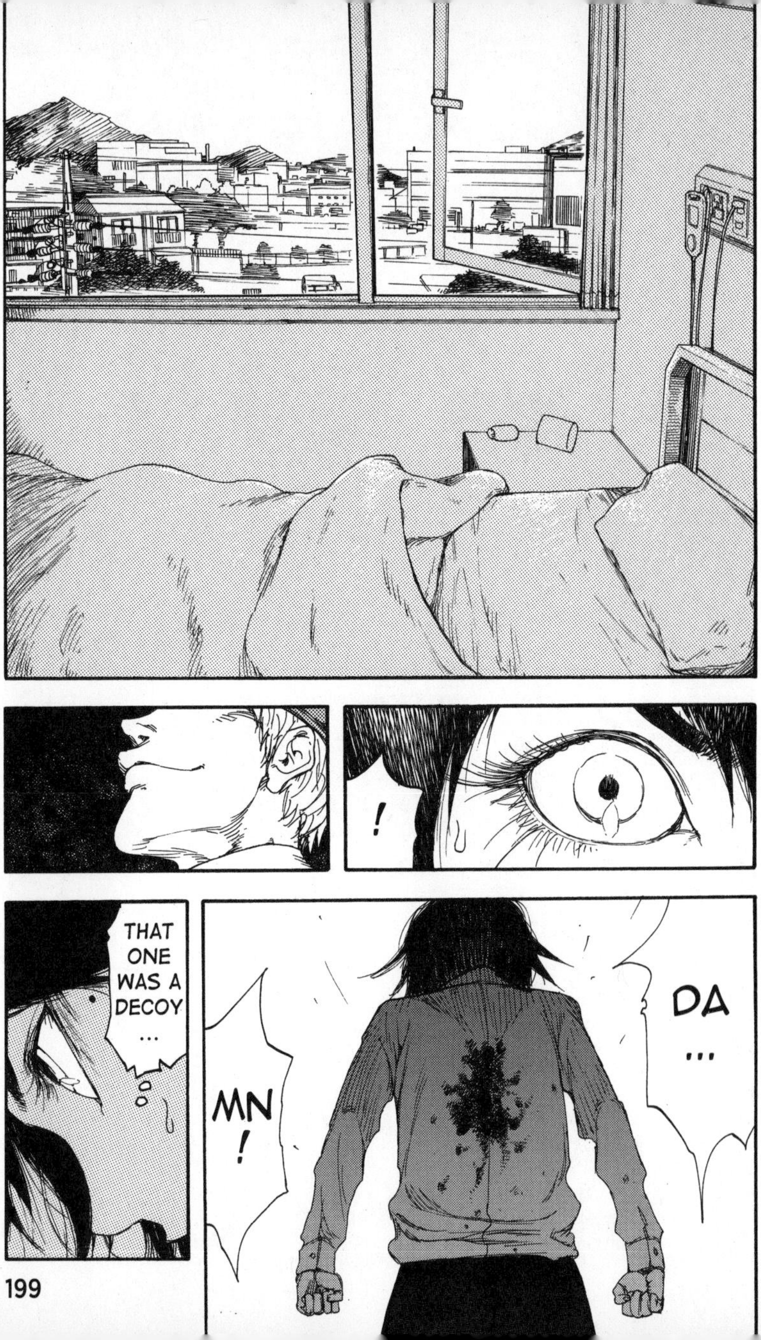
!
DA ...
MN !
THAT ONE WAS A DECOY ...

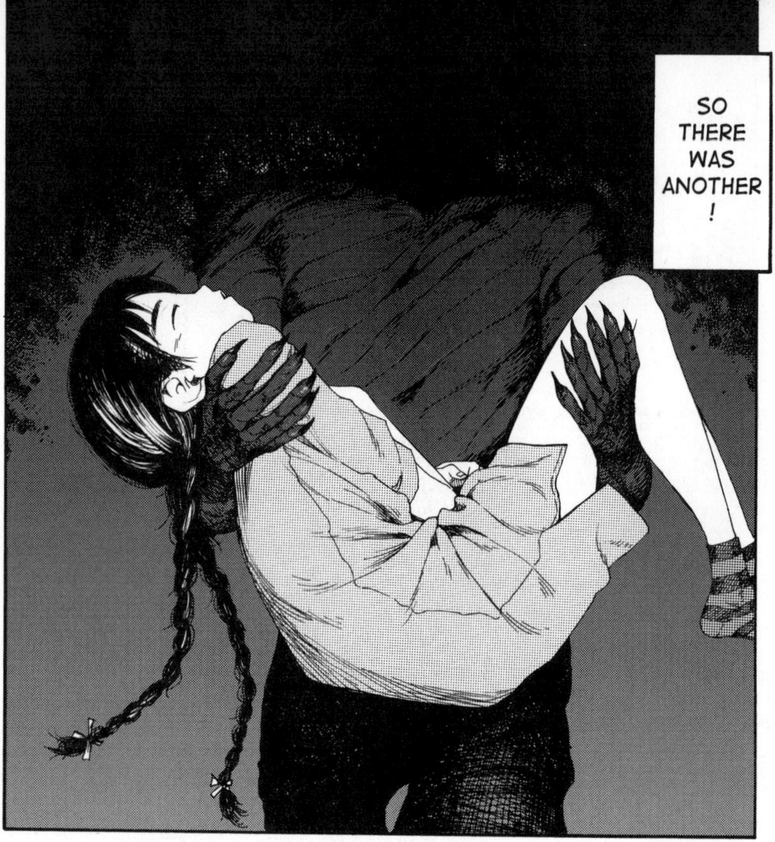
SO THERE WAS ANOTHER!

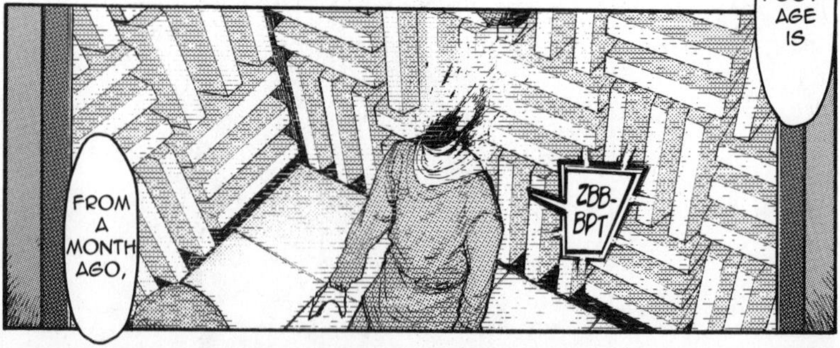
THIS FOOT-AGE IS
ZBB-BPT
FROM A MONTH AGO,

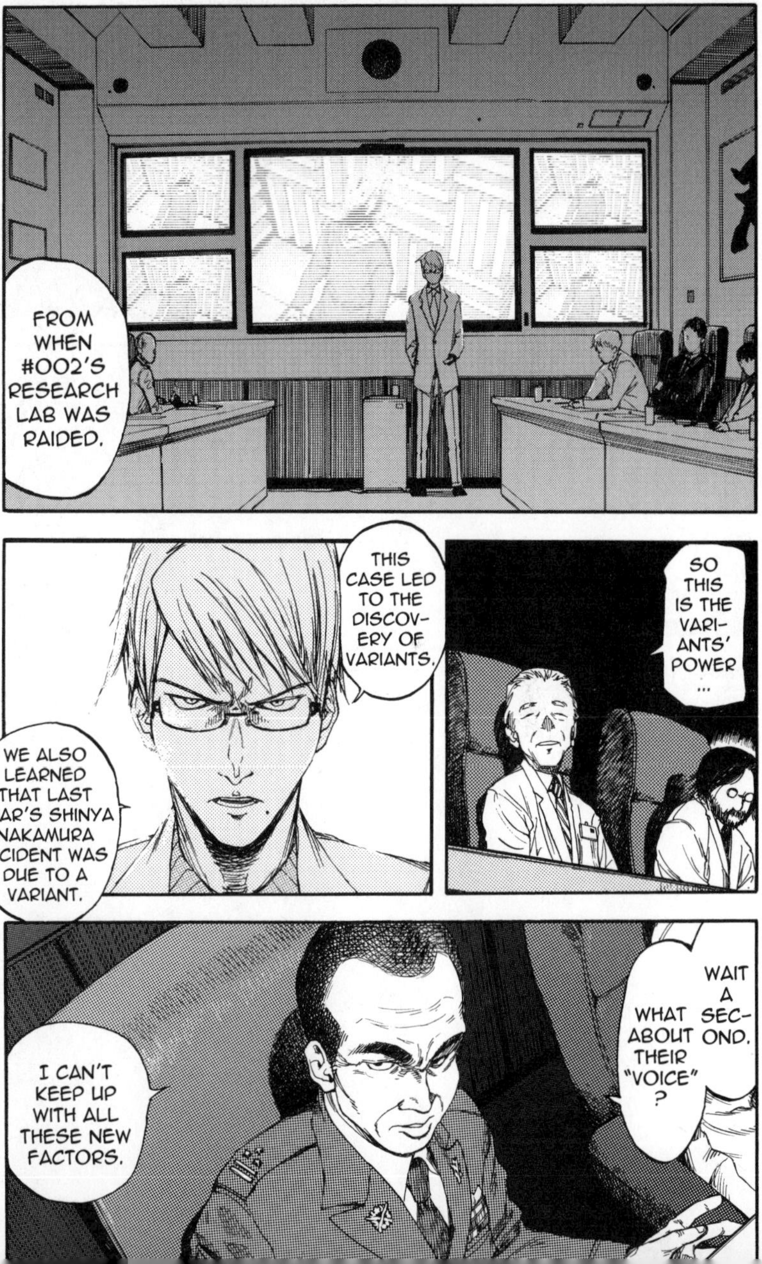
FROM WHEN #002'S RESEARCH LAB WAS RAIDED.
SO THIS IS THE VARIANTS' POWER...
THIS CASE LED TO THE DISCOVERY OF VARIANTS.
WE ALSO LEARNED THAT LAST YEAR'S SHINYA NAKAMURA INCIDENT WAS DUE TO A VARIANT.
WAIT A SECOND. WHAT ABOUT THEIR "VOICE"?
I CAN'T KEEP UP WITH ALL THESE NEW FACTORS.

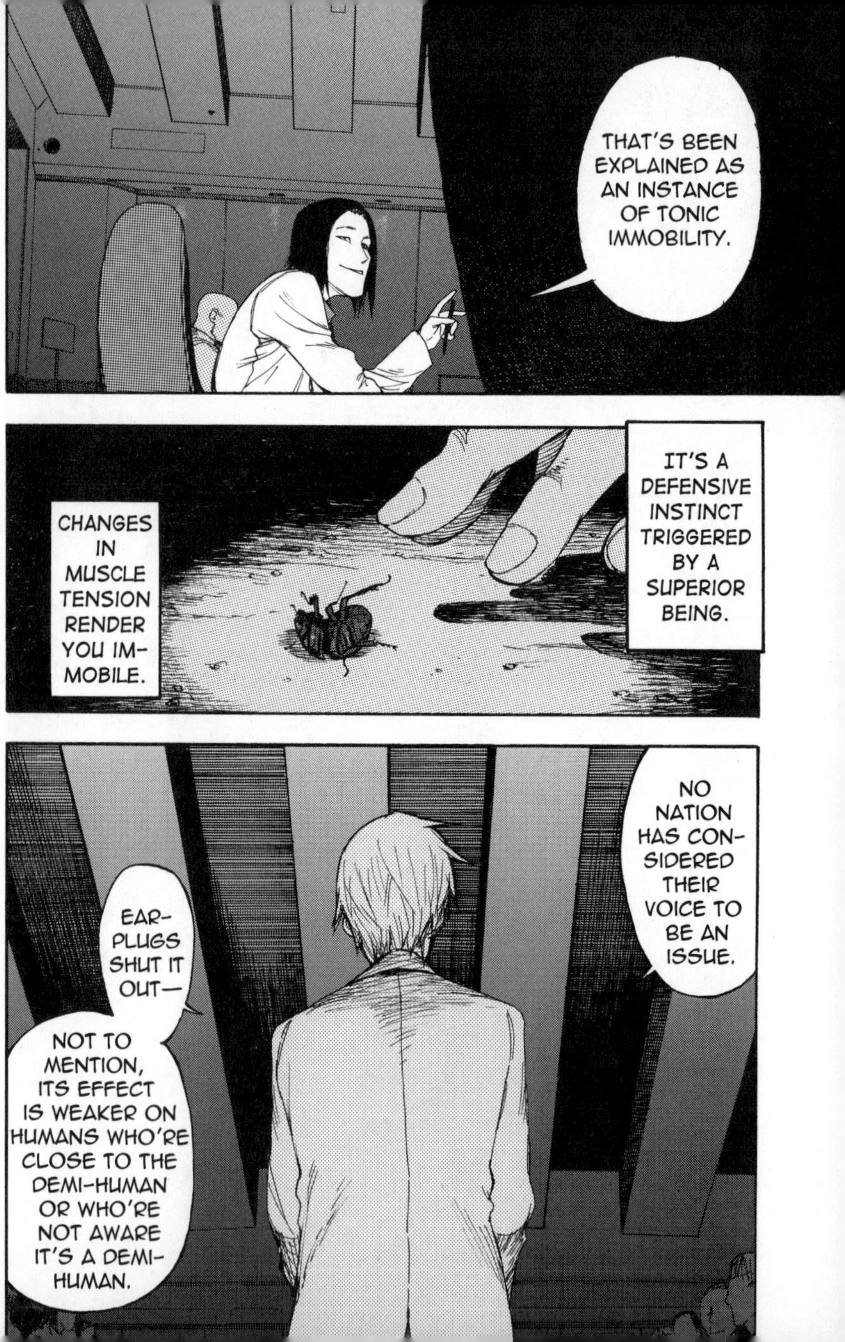
THAT'S BEEN EXPLAINED AS AN INSTANCE OF TONIC IMMOBILITY.
IT'S A DEFENSIVE INSTINCT TRIGGERED BY A SUPERIOR BEING.
CHANGES IN MUSCLE TENSION RENDER YOU IM-MOBILE.
NO NATION HAS CON-SIDERED THEIR VOICE TO BE AN ISSUE.
EAR-PLUGS SHUT IT OUT—
NOT TO MENTION, ITS EFFECT IS WEAKER ON HUMANS WHO'RE CLOSE TO THE DEMI-HUMAN OR WHO'RE NOT AWARE IT'S A DEMI-HUMAN.

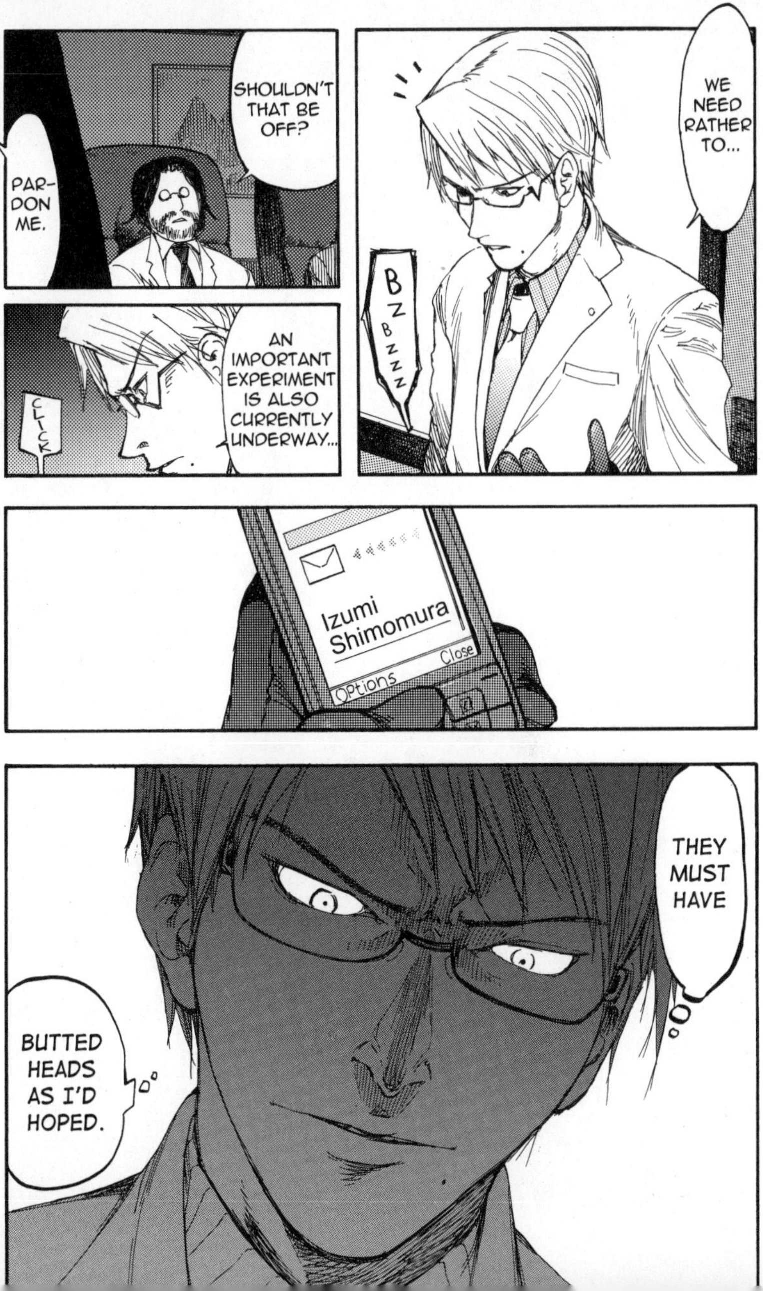
WE NEED RATHER TO...
BZZZZ
SHOULDN'T THAT BE OFF?
PARDON ME.
AN IMPORTANT EXPERIMENT IS ALSO CURRENTLY UNDERWAY...
CLICK
Izumi Shimomura
Close
Options
THEY MUST HAVE
BUTTED HEADS AS I'D HOPED.

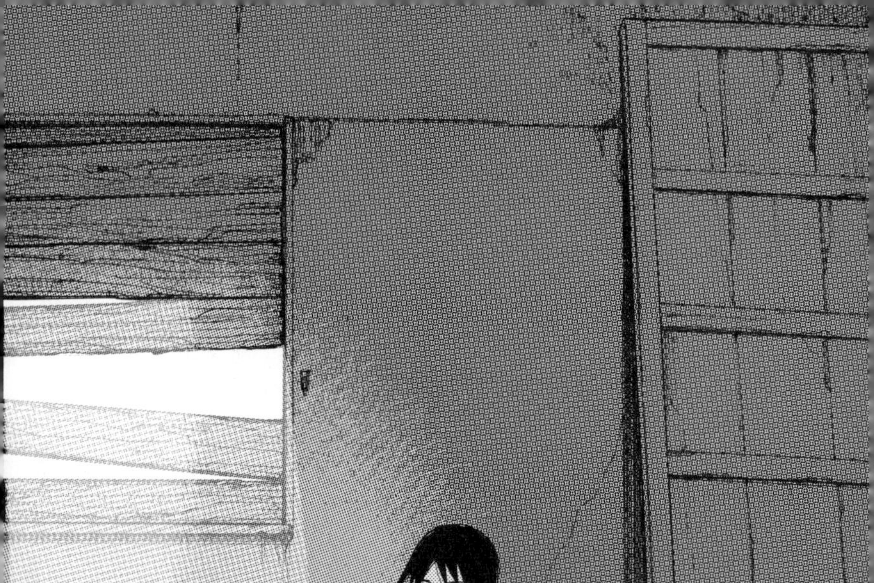
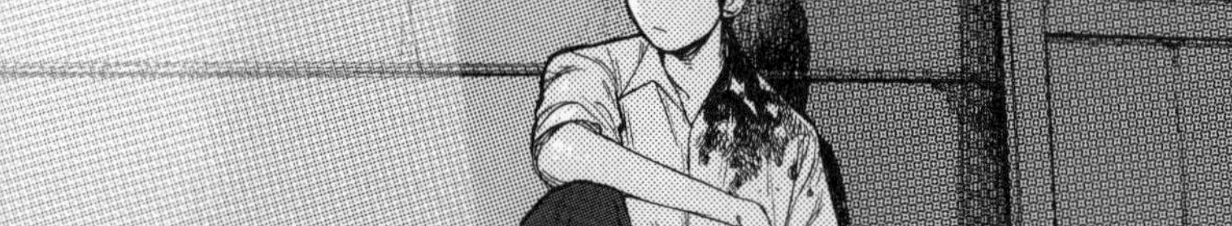

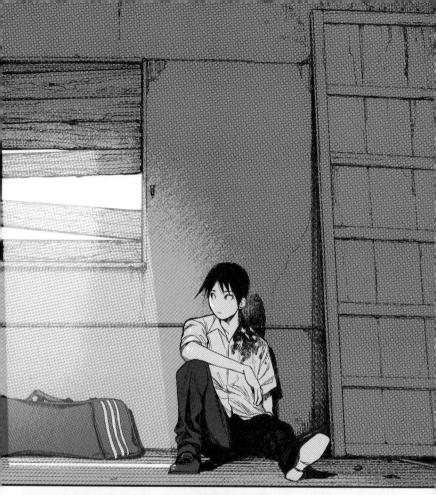

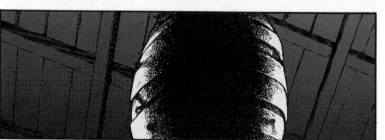

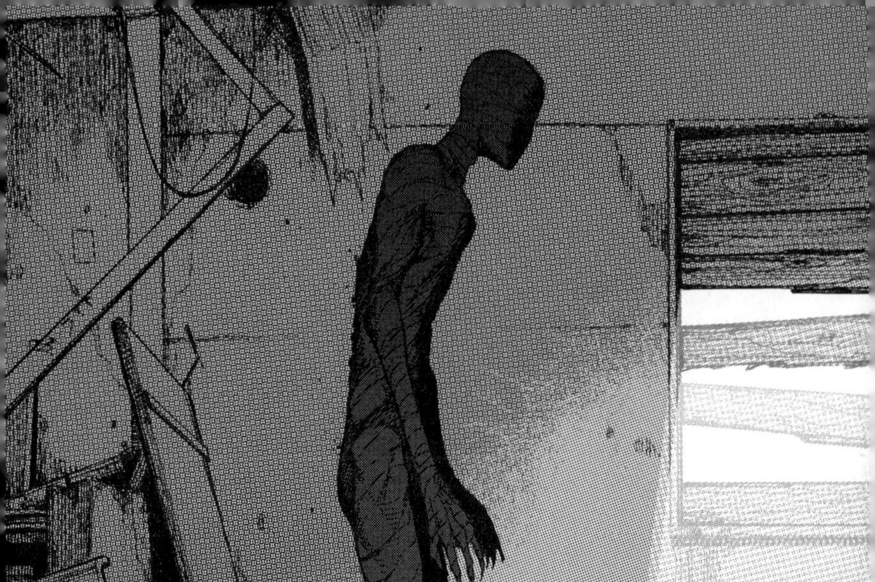

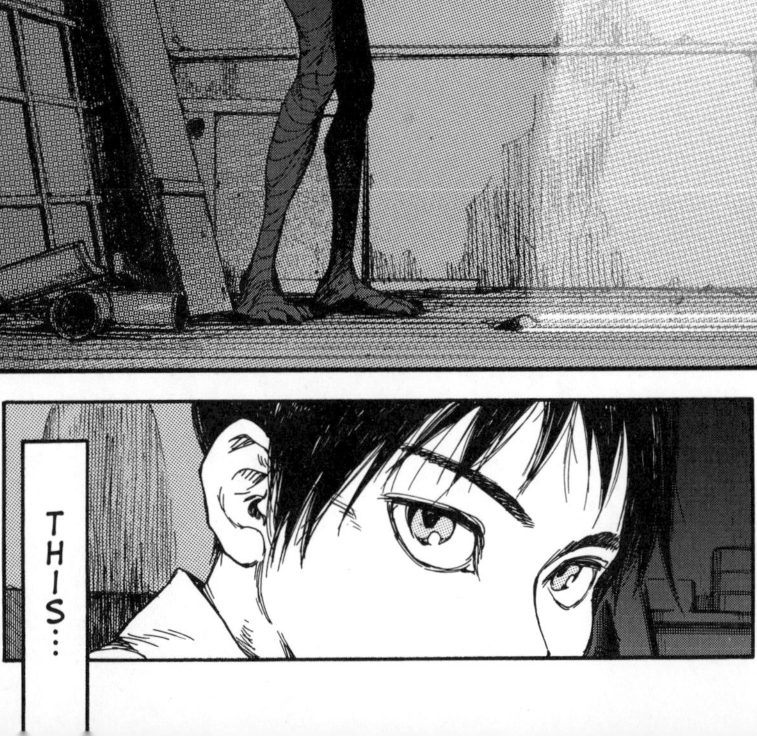
THIS...

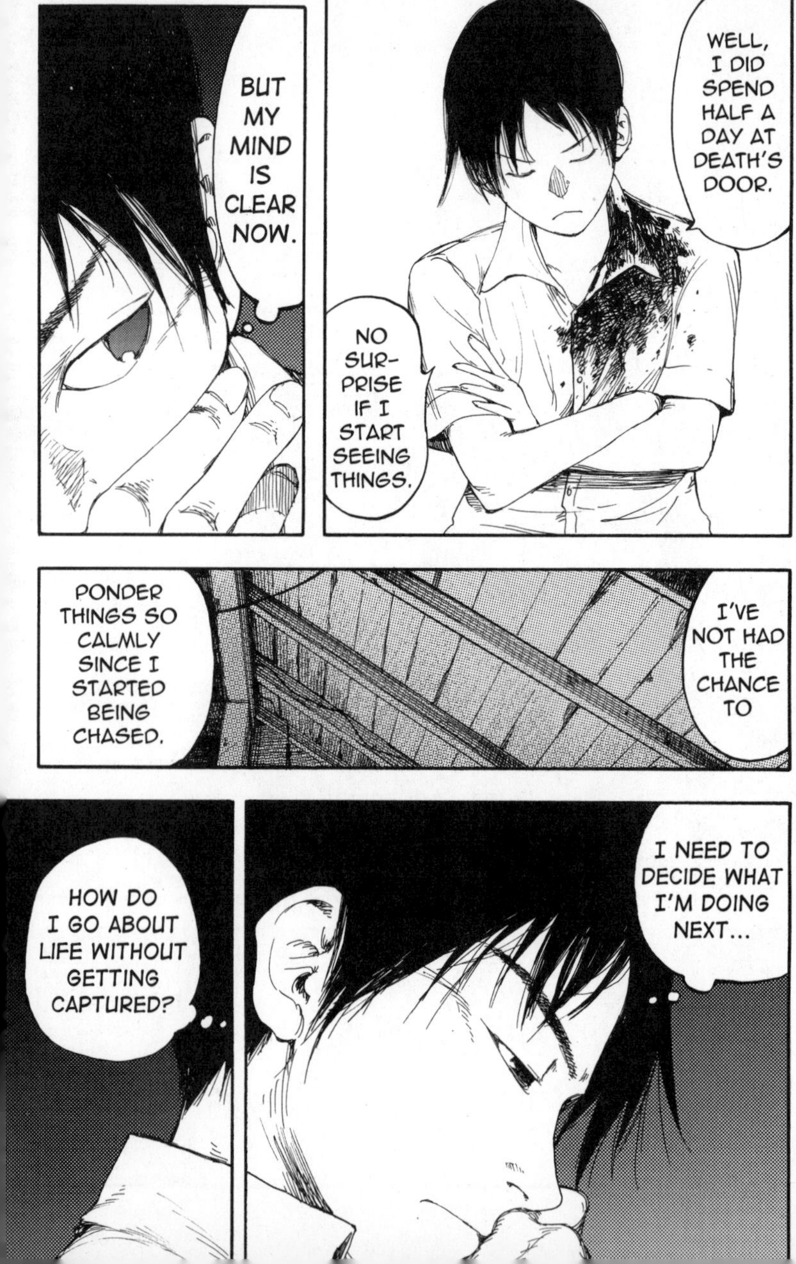
WELL, I DID SPEND HALF A DAY AT DEATH'S DOOR.
NO SURPRISE IF I START SEEING THINGS.
BUT MY MIND IS CLEAR NOW.
I'VE NOT HAD THE CHANCE TO
PONDER THINGS SO CALMLY SINCE I STARTED BEING CHASED.
I NEED TO DECIDE WHAT I'M DOING NEXT...
HOW DO I GO ABOUT LIFE WITHOUT GETTING CAPTURED?

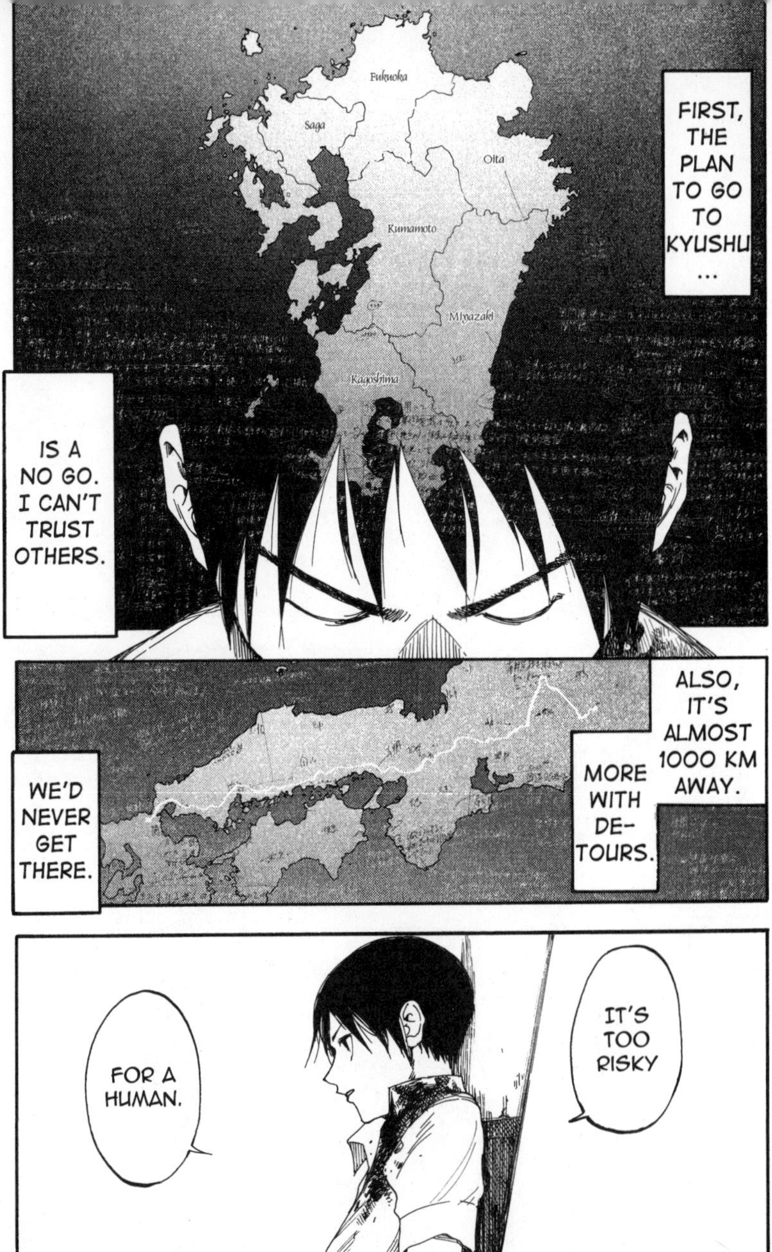
FIRST, THE PLAN TO GO TO KYUSHU ...
Fukuoka
Saga
Oita
Kumamoto
Miyazaki
Kagoshima
IS A NO GO. I CAN'T TRUST OTHERS.
ALSO, IT'S ALMOST 1000 KM AWAY.
MORE WITH DE-TOURS.
WE'D NEVER GET THERE.
IT'S TOO RISKY
FOR A HUMAN.

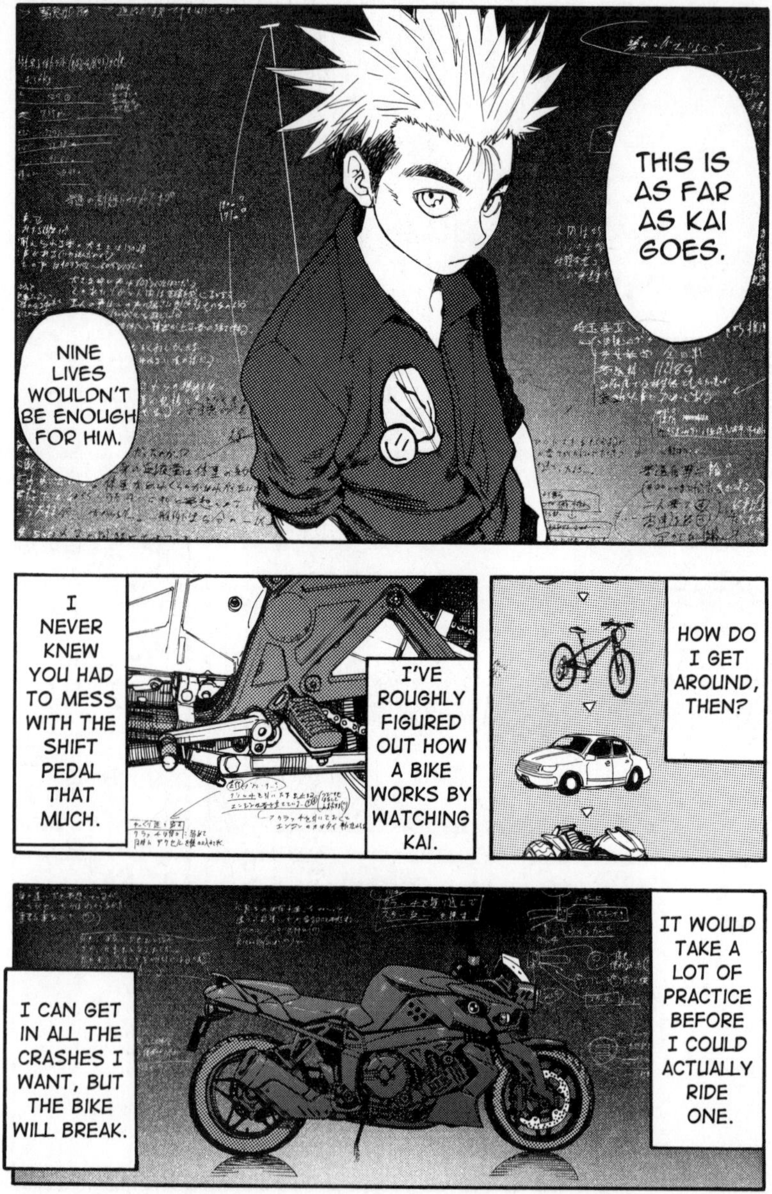
THIS IS AS FAR AS KAI GOES.
NINE LIVES WOULDN'T BE ENOUGH FOR HIM.
HOW DO I GET AROUND, THEN?
I'VE ROUGHLY FIGURED OUT HOW A BIKE WORKS BY WATCHING KAI.
I NEVER KNEW YOU HAD TO MESS WITH THE SHIFT PEDAL THAT MUCH.
IT WOULD TAKE A LOT OF PRACTICE BEFORE I COULD ACTUALLY RIDE ONE.
I CAN GET IN ALL THE CRASHES I WANT, BUT THE BIKE WILL BREAK.

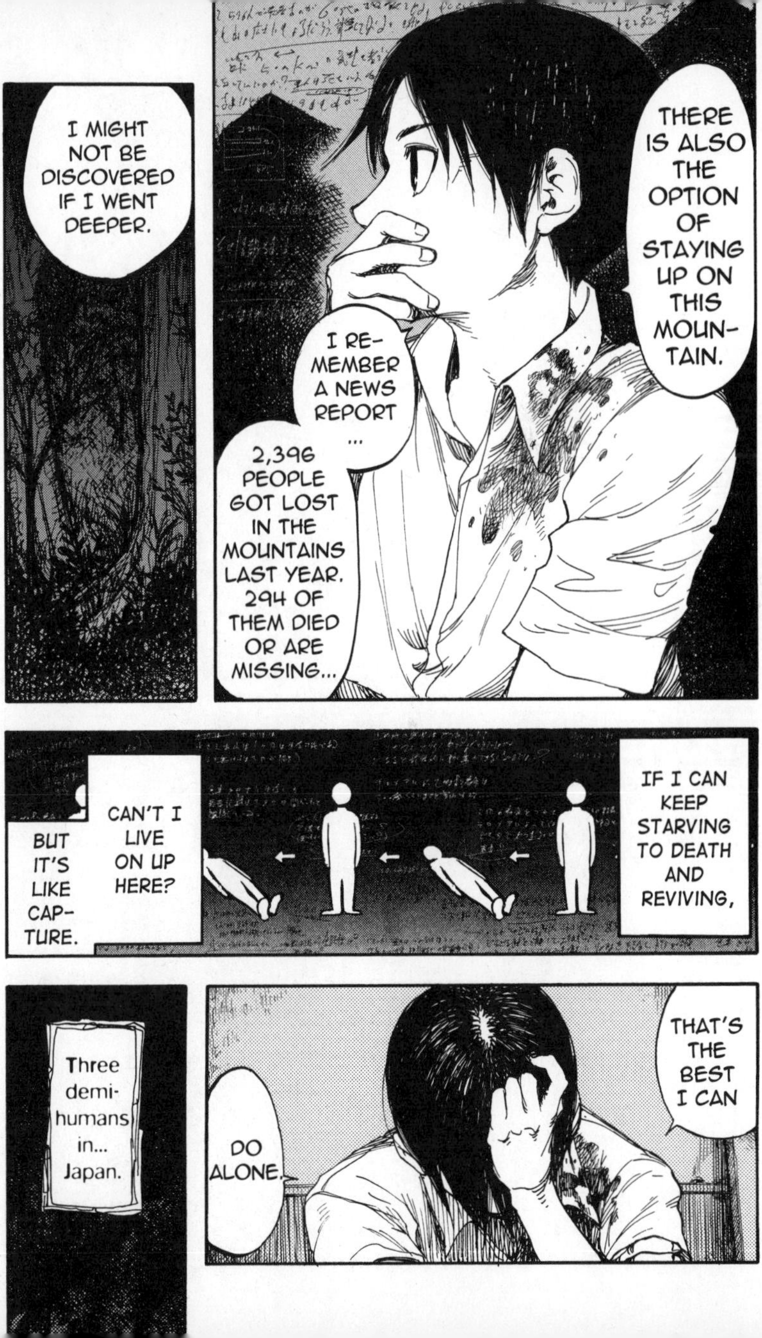
THERE IS ALSO THE OPTION OF STAYING UP ON THIS MOUN-TAIN.
I RE-MEMBER A NEWS REPORT ...
2,396 PEOPLE GOT LOST IN THE MOUNTAINS LAST YEAR. 294 OF THEM DIED OR ARE MISSING...
I MIGHT NOT BE DISCOVERED IF I WENT DEEPER.
IF I CAN KEEP STARVING TO DEATH AND REVIVING,
CAN'T I LIVE ON UP HERE?
BUT IT'S LIKE CAP-TURE.
THAT'S THE BEST I CAN
DO ALONE.
Three demi-humans in... Japan.

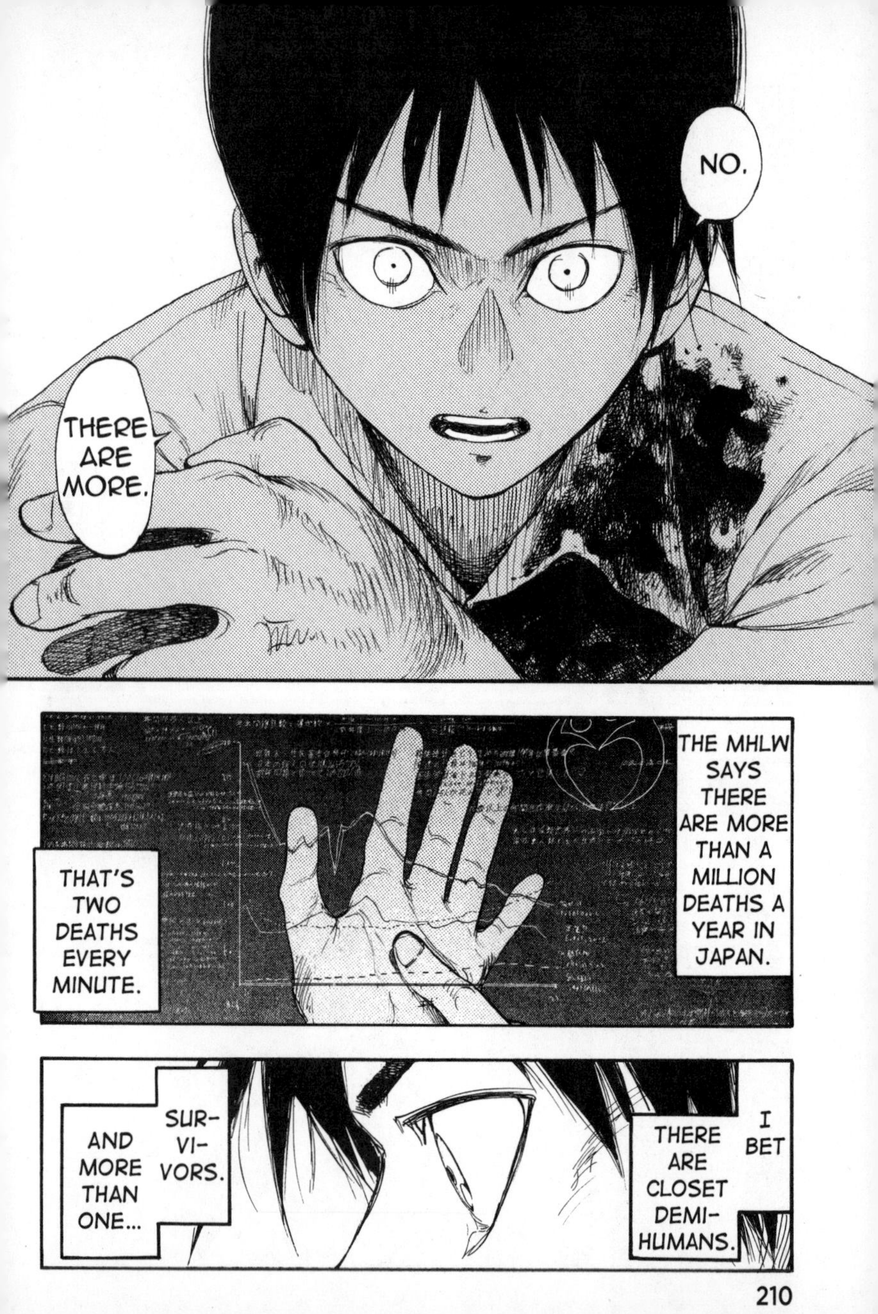
NO.
THERE ARE MORE.
THE MHLW SAYS THERE ARE MORE THAN A MILLION DEATHS A YEAR IN JAPAN.
THAT'S TWO DEATHS EVERY MINUTE.
I BET
THERE ARE CLOSET DEMI-HUMANS.
SURVIVORS.
AND MORE THAN ONE...

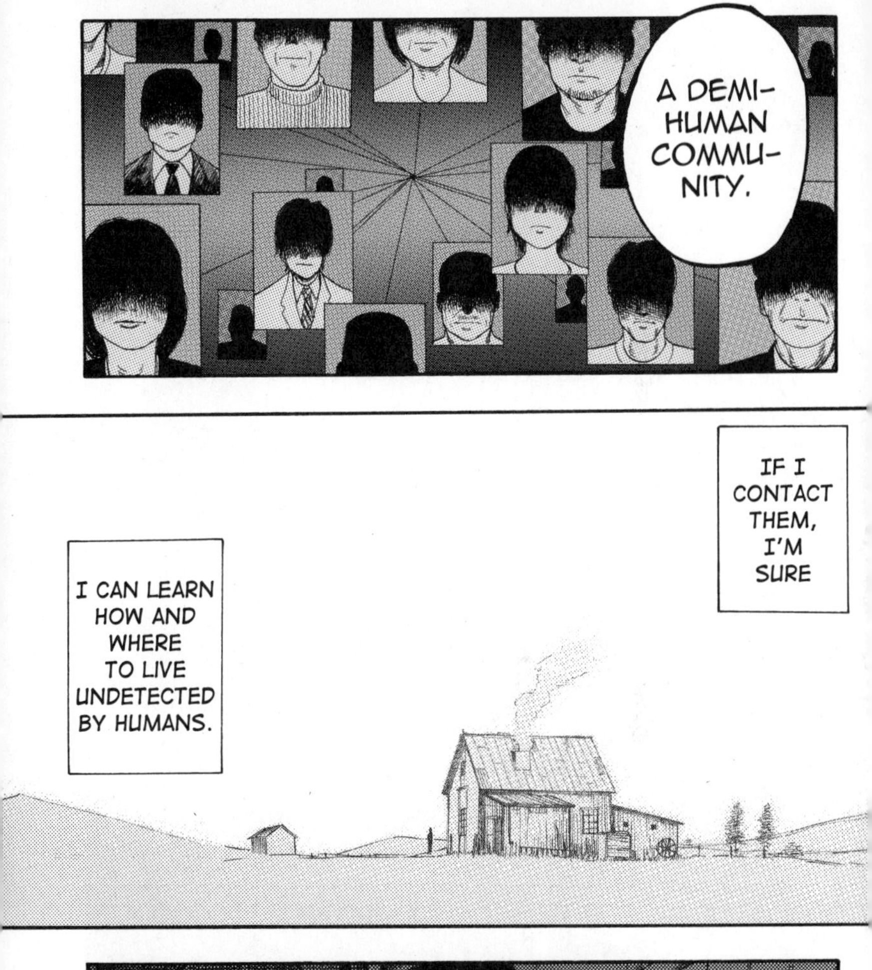
A DEMI-HUMAN COMMUNITY.
IF I CONTACT THEM, I'M SURE
I CAN LEARN HOW AND WHERE TO LIVE UNDETECTED BY HUMANS.
KEI?

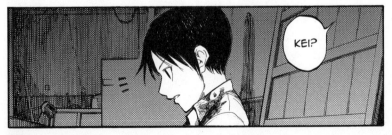

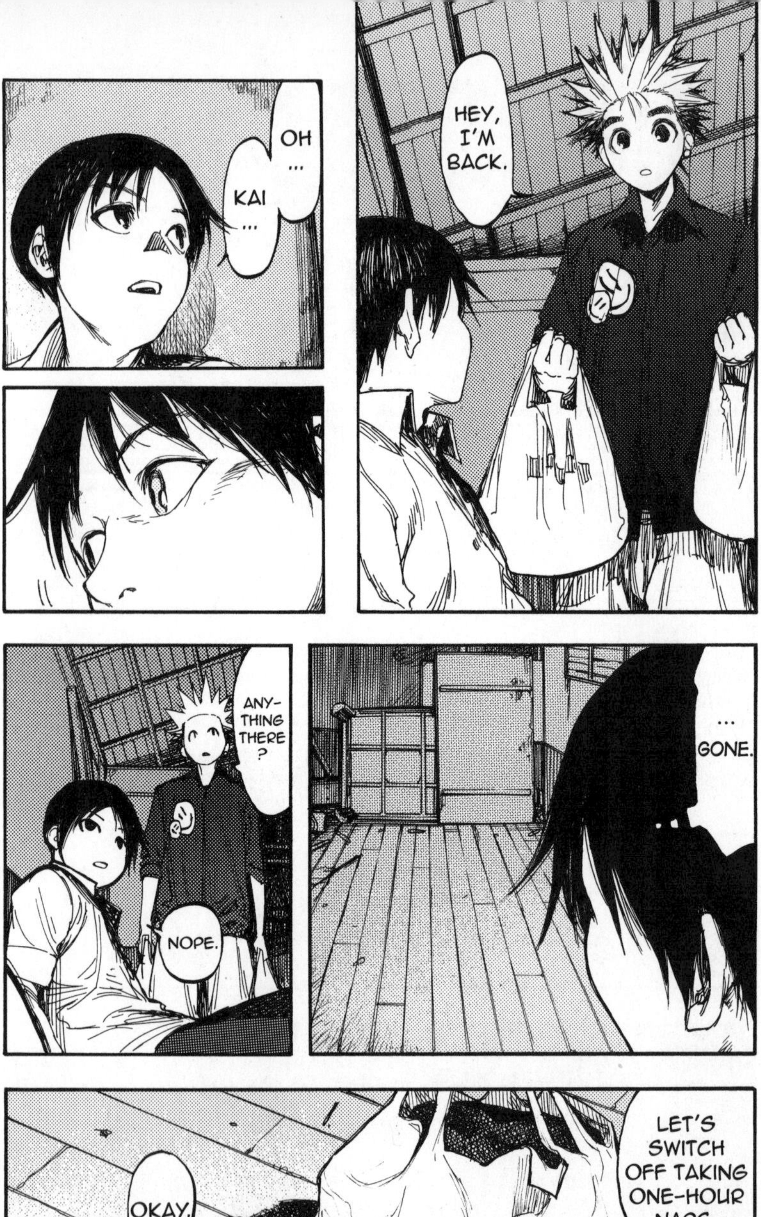
HEY, I'M BACK.
OH ... KAI ...
... GONE.
ANY-THING THERE?
NOPE.
LET'S SWITCH OFF TAKING ONE-HOUR NAPS.
OKAY.

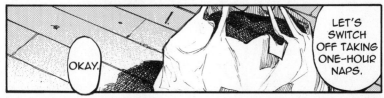

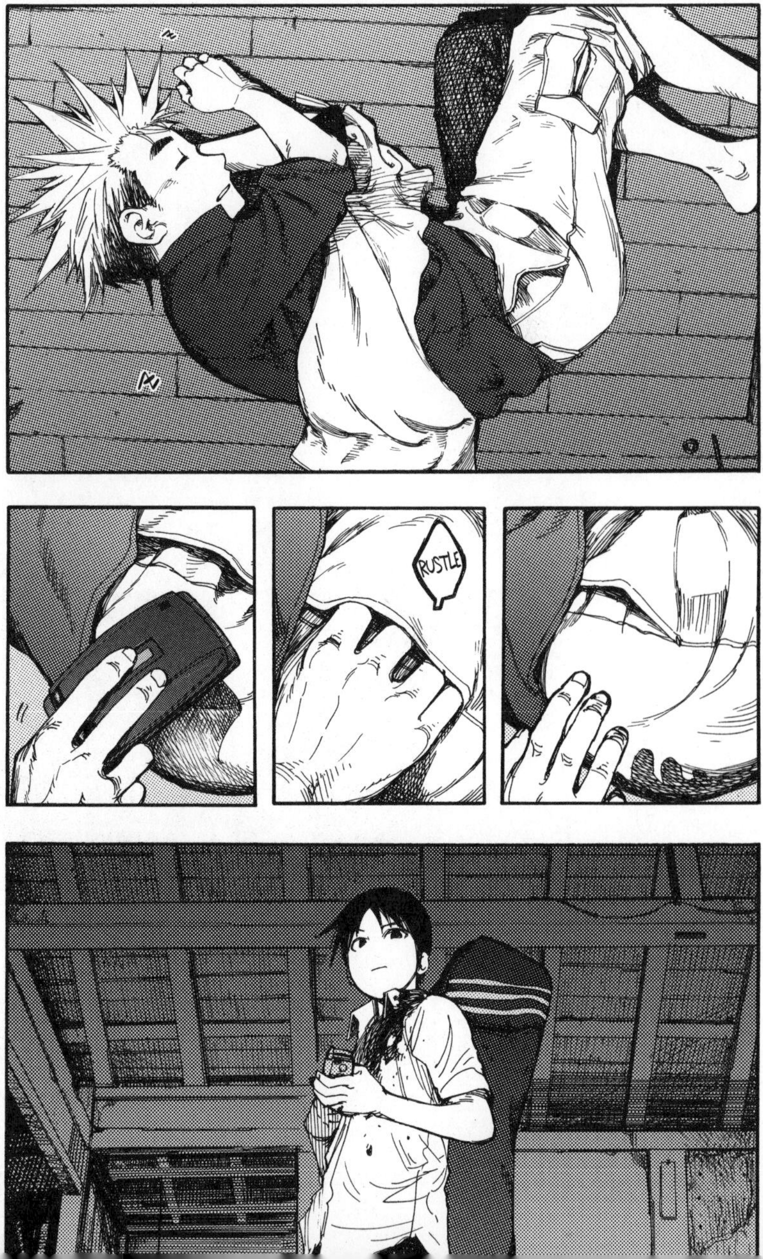
RUSTLE

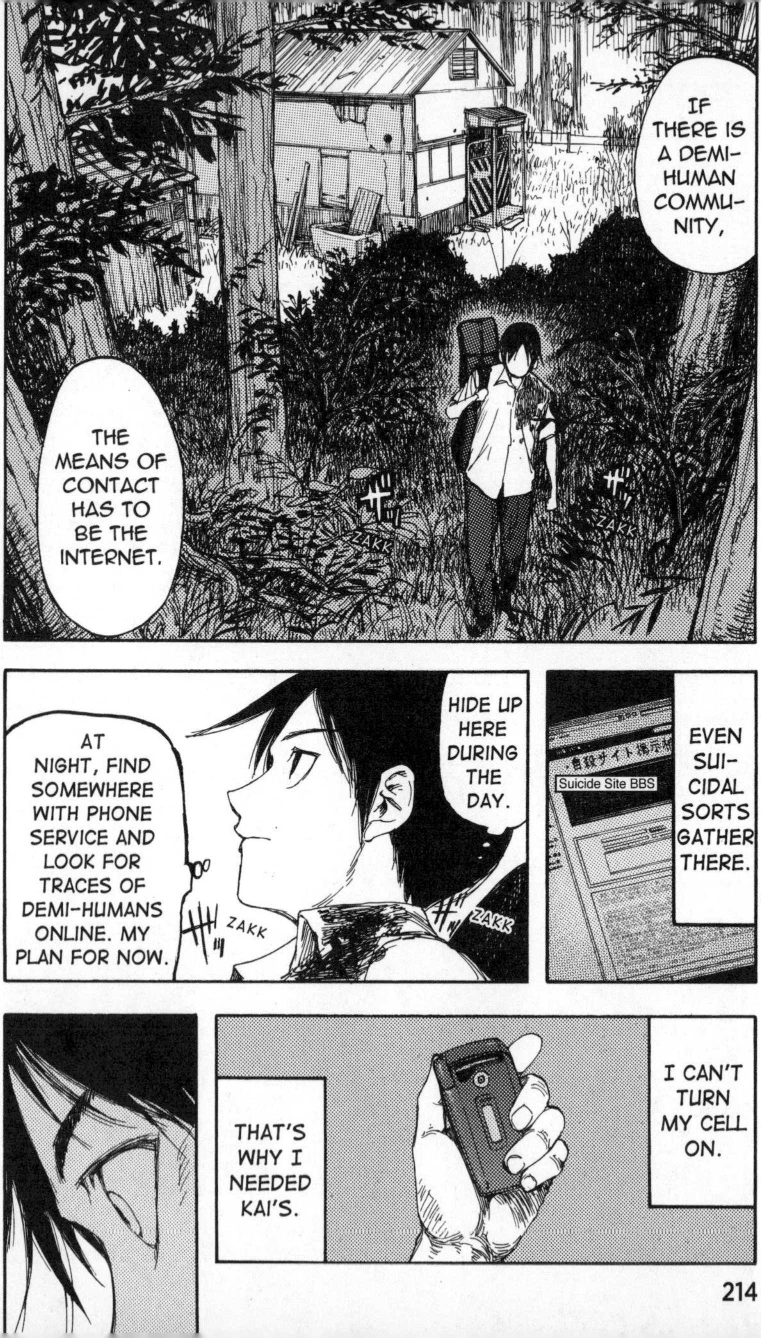
IF THERE IS A DEMI-HUMAN COMMUNITY,
THE MEANS OF CONTACT HAS TO BE THE INTERNET.
ZAKK
ZAKK
EVEN SUICIDAL SORTS GATHER THERE.
Suicide Site BBS
HIDE UP HERE DURING THE DAY.
AT NIGHT, FIND SOMEWHERE WITH PHONE SERVICE AND LOOK FOR TRACES OF DEMI-HUMANS ONLINE. MY PLAN FOR NOW.
ZAKK
ZAKK
I CAN'T TURN MY CELL ON.
THAT'S WHY I NEEDED KAI'S.

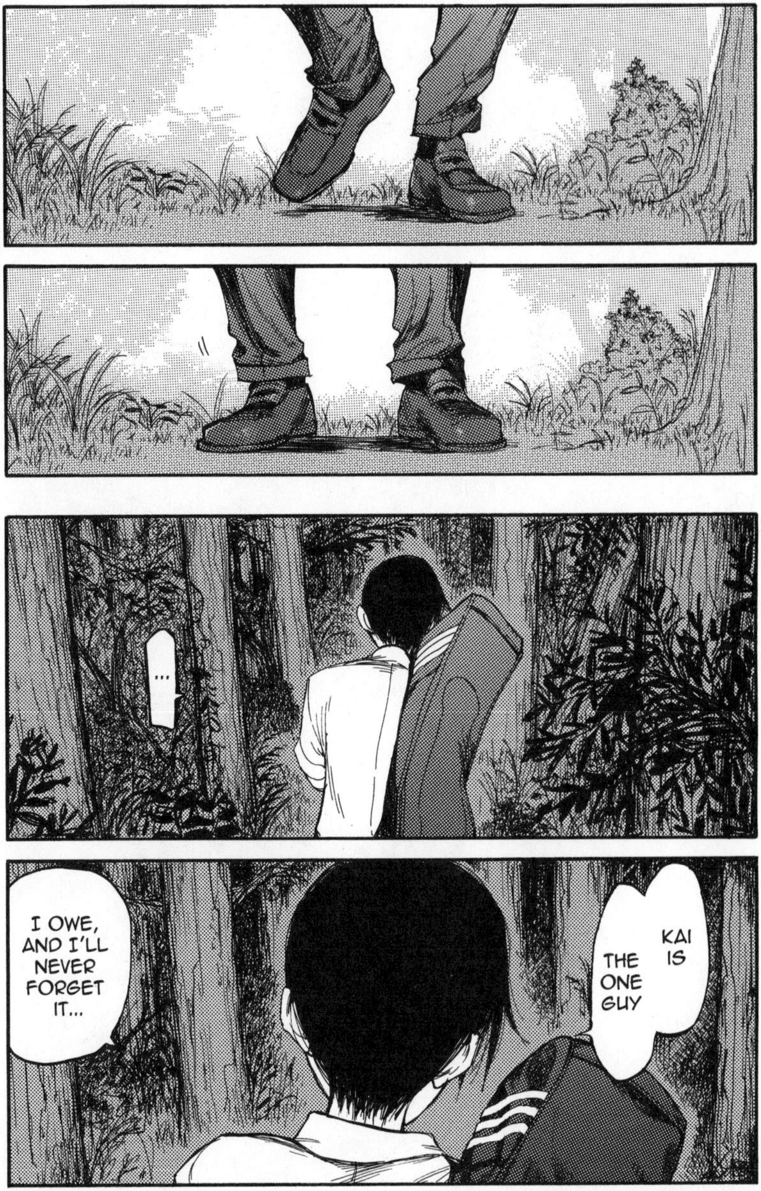
...
KAI IS THE ONE GUY
I OWE, AND I'LL NEVER FORGET IT...

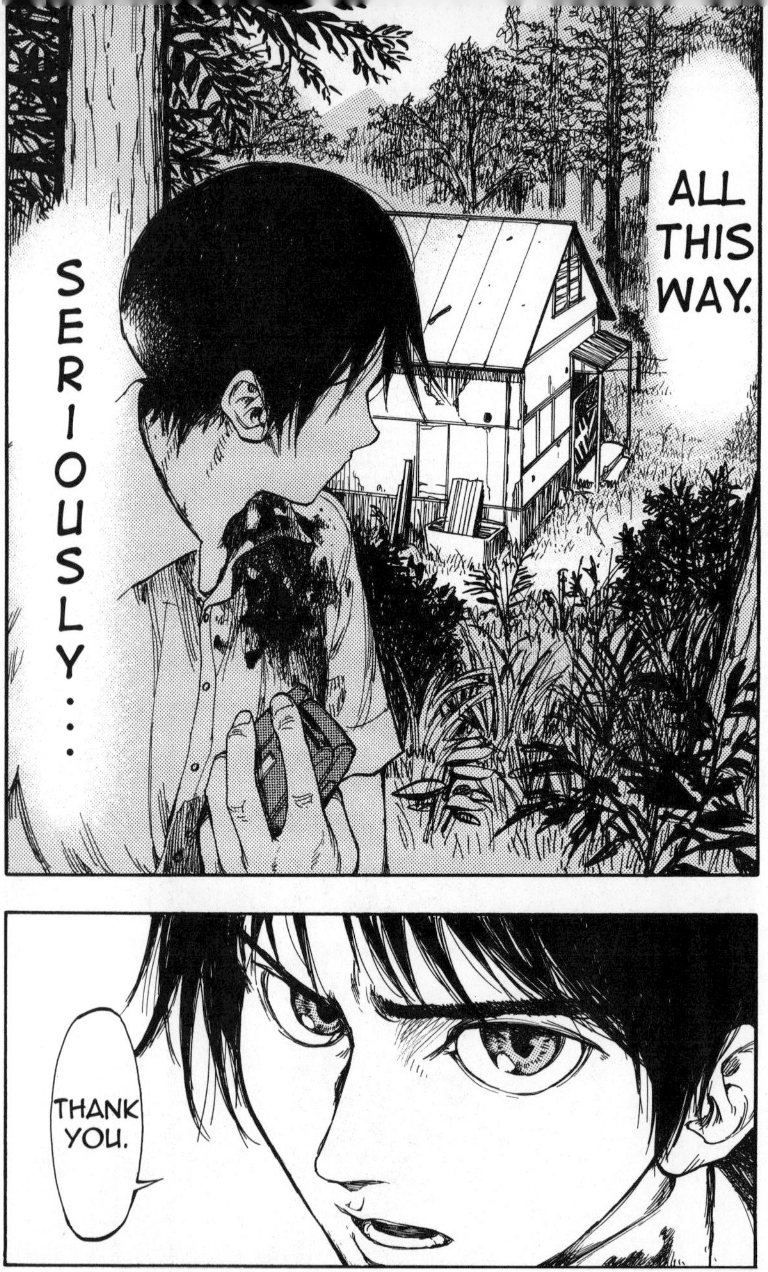
ALL THIS WAY.
SERIOUSLY...
THANK YOU.

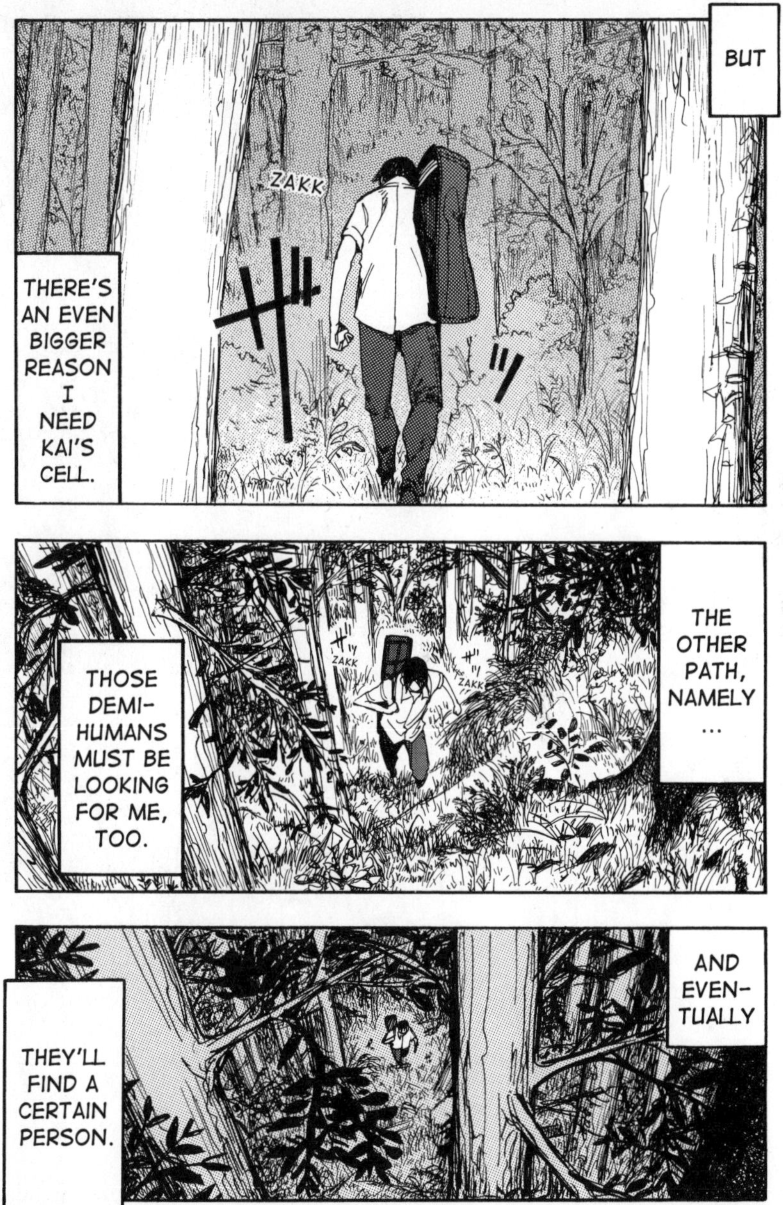
BUT
ZAKK
THERE'S AN EVEN BIGGER REASON I NEED KAI'S CELL.
THE OTHER PATH, NAMELY ...
ZAKK
ZAKK
THOSE DEMI-HUMANS MUST BE LOOKING FOR ME, TOO.
AND EVEN-TUALLY
THEY'LL FIND A CERTAIN PERSON.

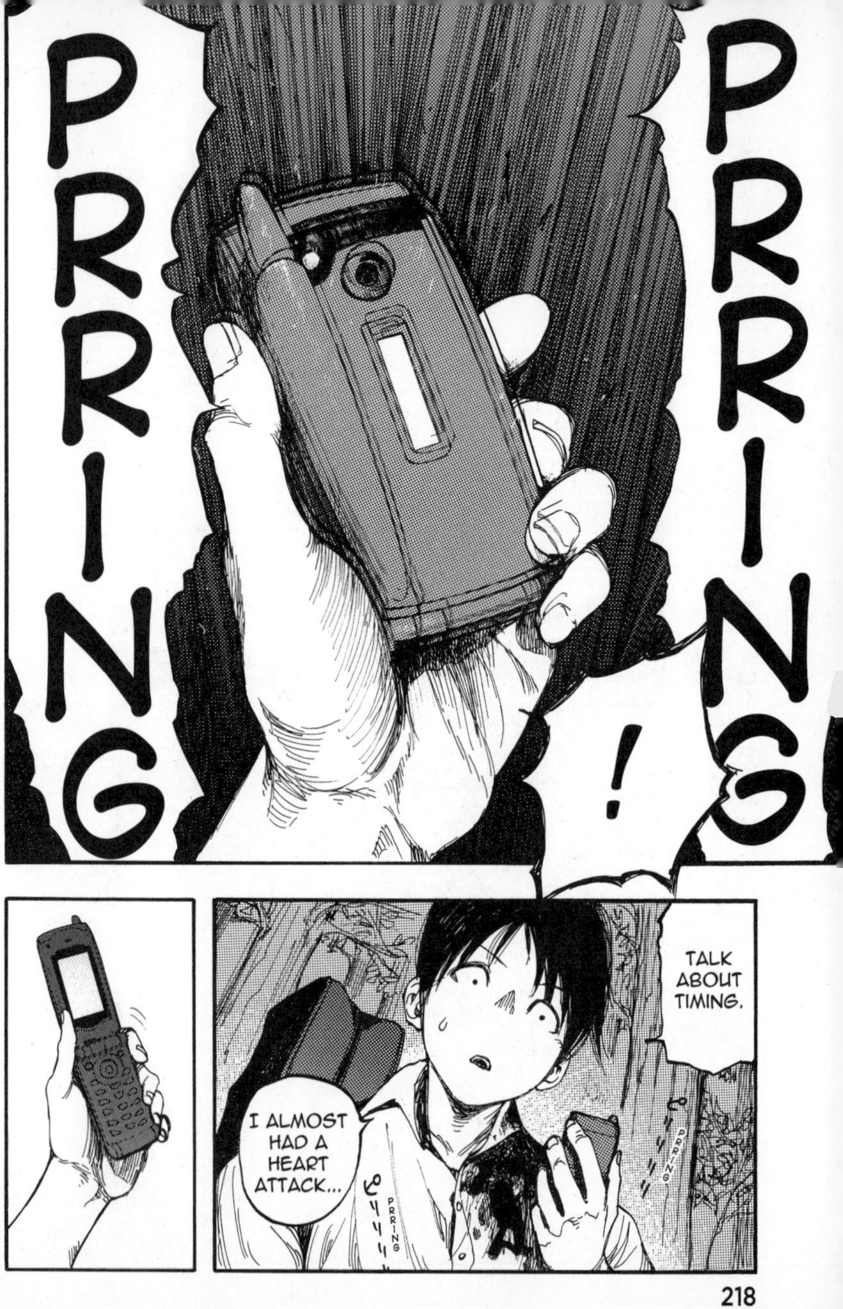
PRRING
!
PRRING
TALK ABOUT TIMING.
PRRING
I ALMOST HAD A HEART ATTACK...
PRRING

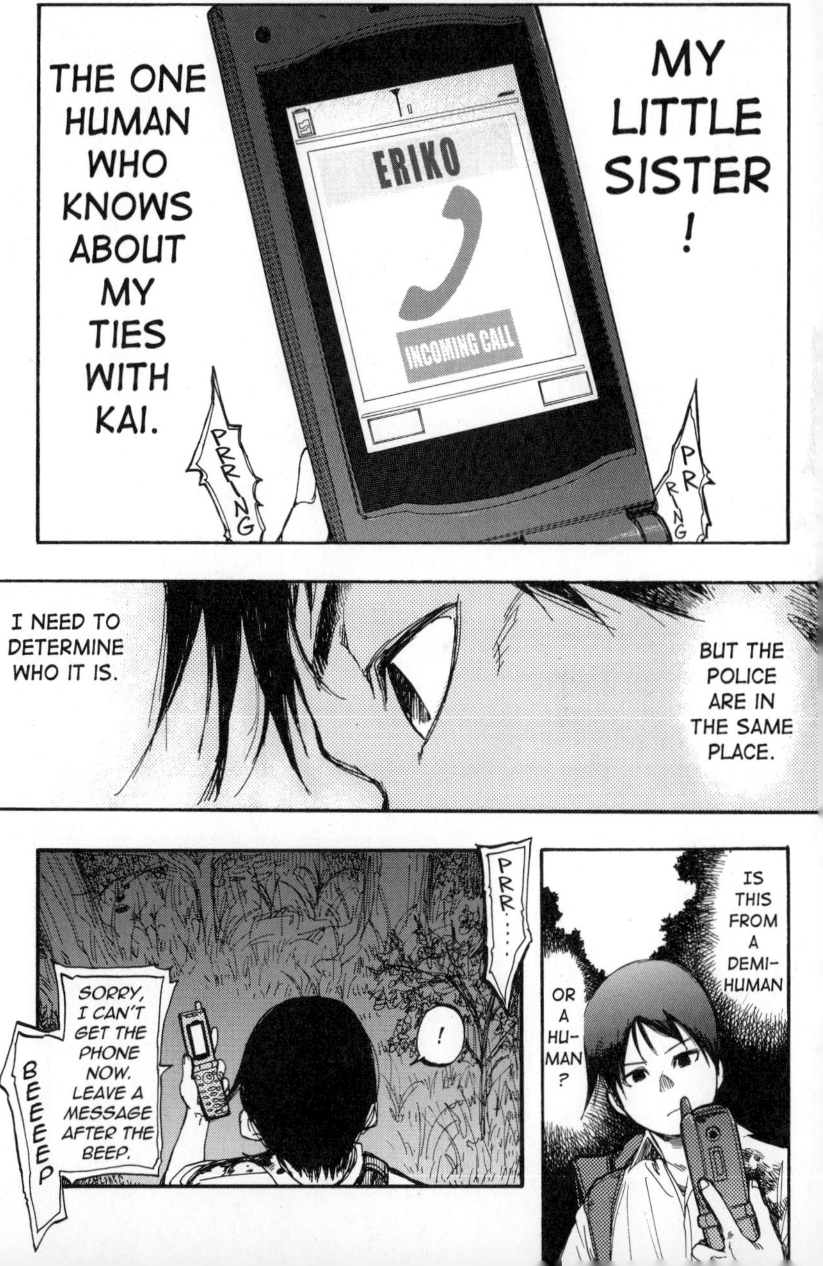
MY LITTLE SISTER!
THE ONE HUMAN WHO KNOWS ABOUT MY TIES WITH KAI.
ERIKO
INCOMING CALL
PRRING
PRRING
BUT THE POLICE ARE IN THE SAME PLACE.
I NEED TO DETERMINE WHO IT IS.
IS THIS FROM A DEMI-HUMAN
OR A HU-MAN?
PRR.....
!
SORRY, I CAN'T GET THE PHONE NOW. LEAVE A MESSAGE AFTER THE BEEP.
BEEEEEP

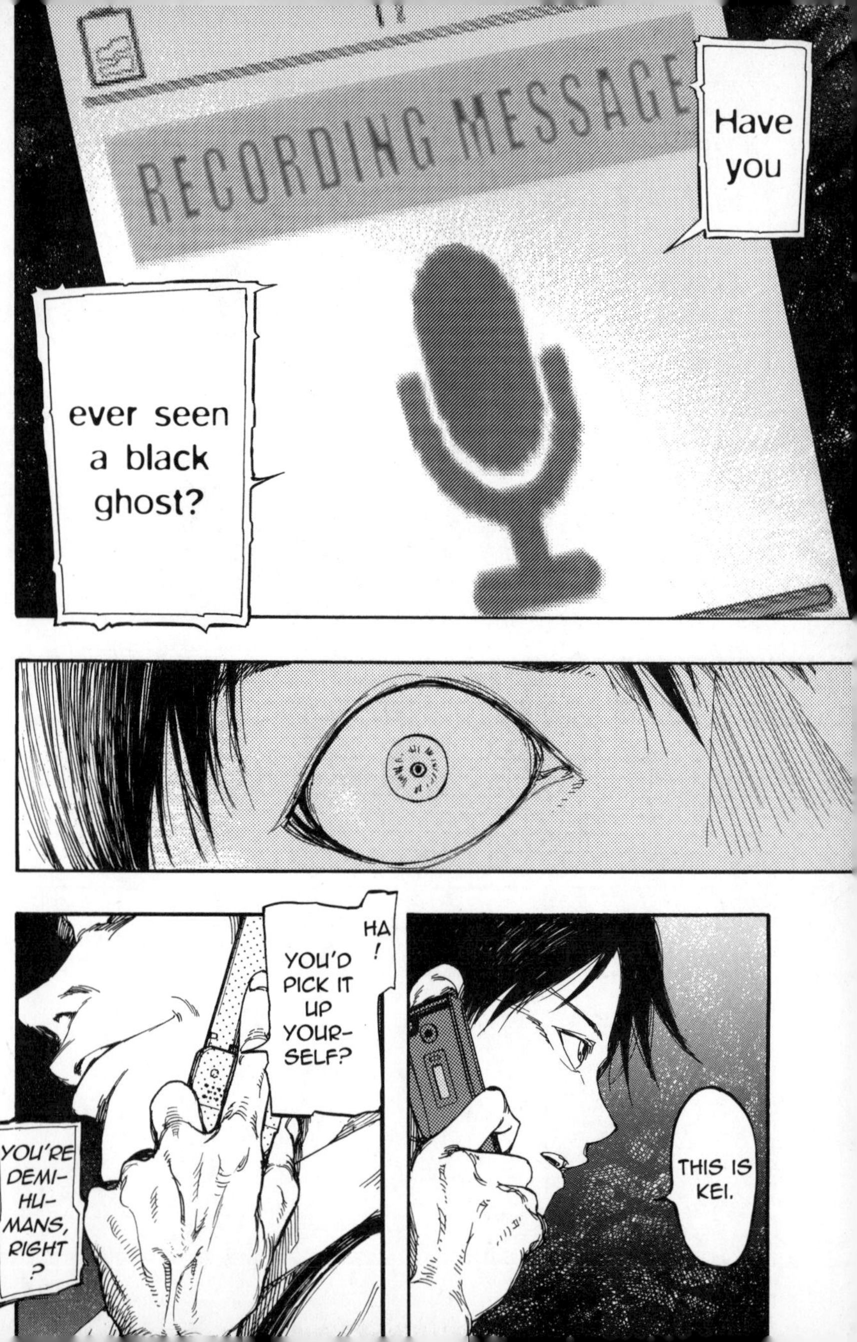
RECORDING MESSAGE
Have you
ever seen a black ghost?
THIS IS KEI.
HA!
YOU'D PICK IT UP YOURSELF?
YOU'RE DEMI-HUMANS, RIGHT?

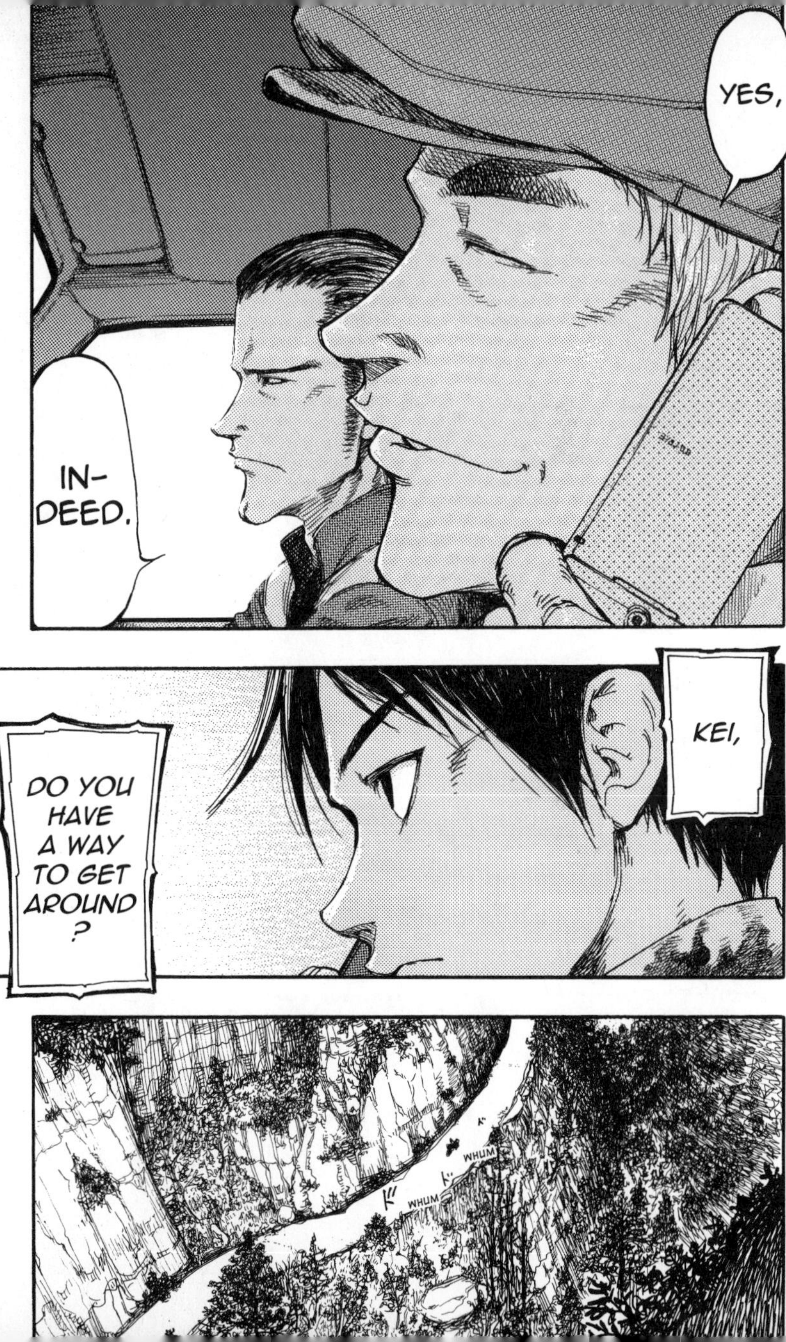
YES,
IN-DEEED.
KEI,
DO YOU HAVE A WAY TO GET AROUND?
ド
WHUM
ド
WHUM
ド

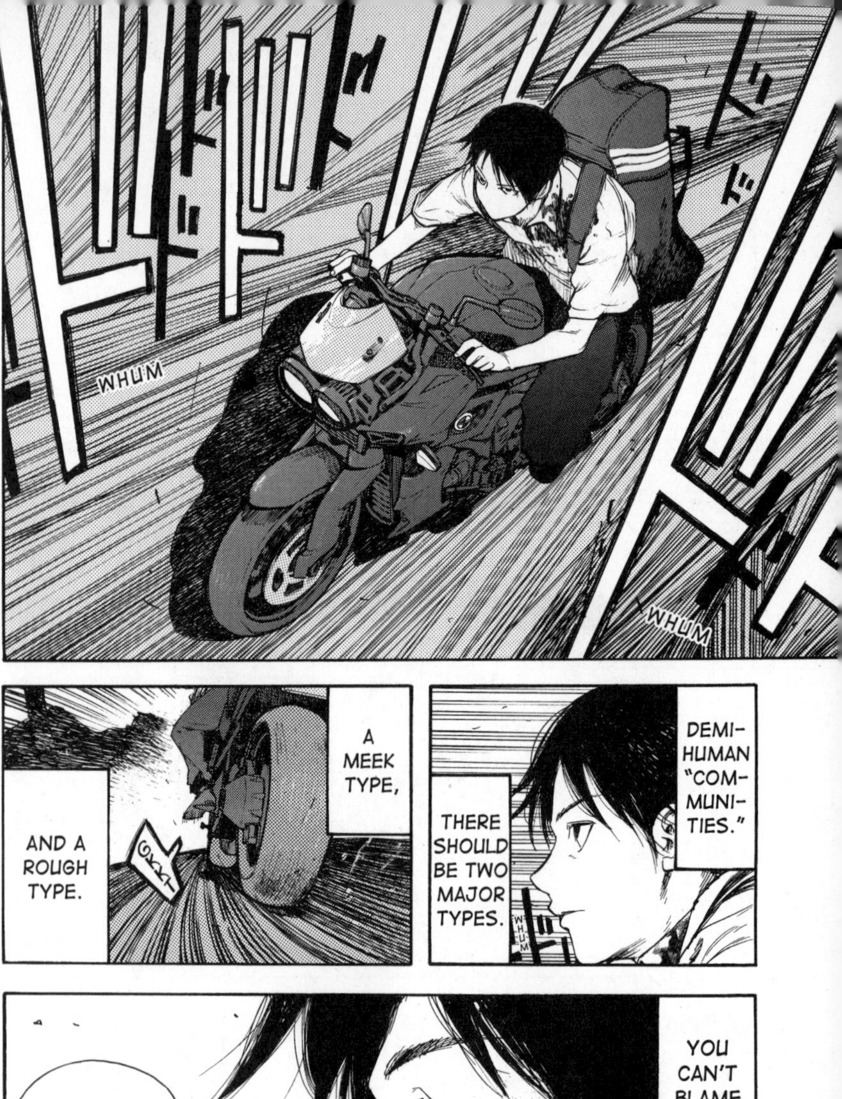
WHUM
WHUM
DEMI-HUMAN "COMMUNITIES."
THERE SHOULD BE TWO MAJOR TYPES.
WHUM
A MEEK TYPE,
AND A ROUGH TYPE.
YOU CAN'T BLAME THEM, THOUGH.
THERE ARE A LOT OF HUMANS WHO DESERVE TO DIE.

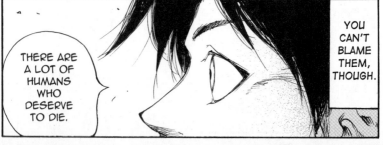

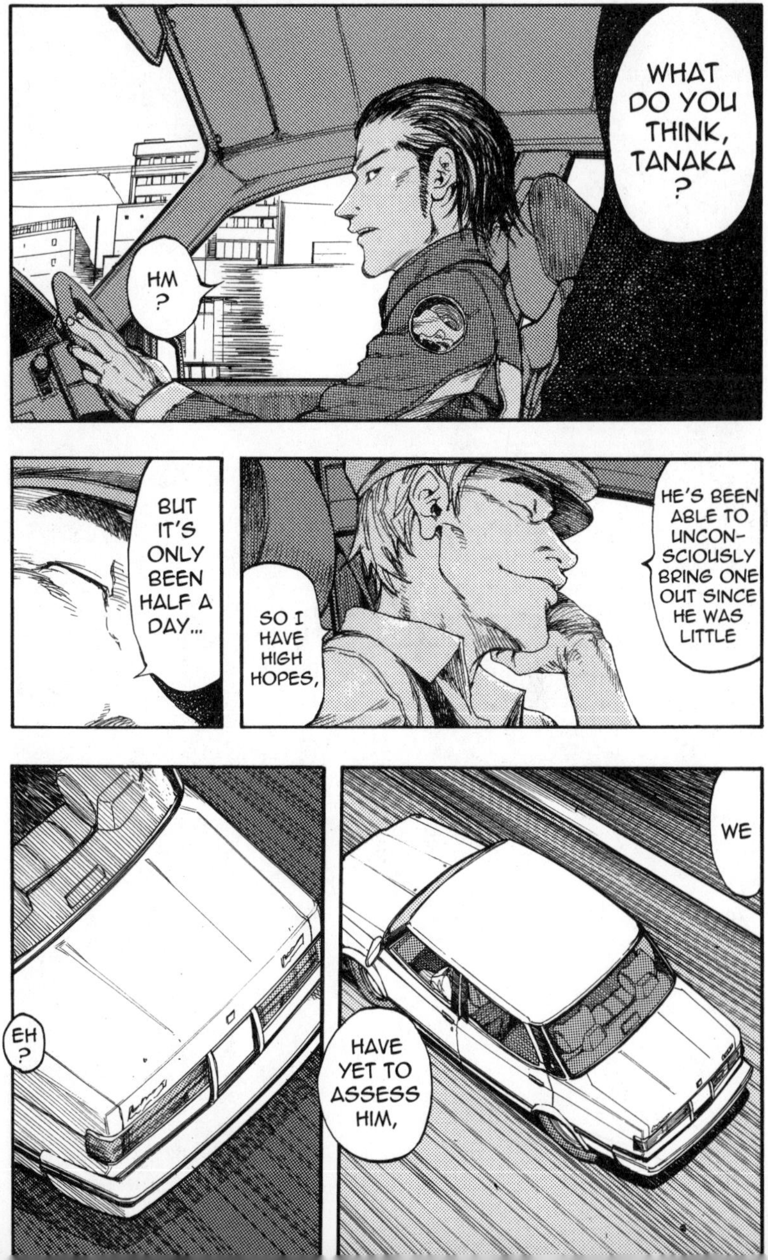
WHAT DO YOU THINK, TANAKA ?
HM ?
HE'S BEEN ABLE TO UNCON-SCIOUSLY BRING ONE OUT SINCE HE WAS LITTLE
SO I HAVE HIGH HOPES,
BUT IT'S ONLY BEEN HALF A DAY...
WE
HAVE YET TO ASSESS HIM,
EH ?

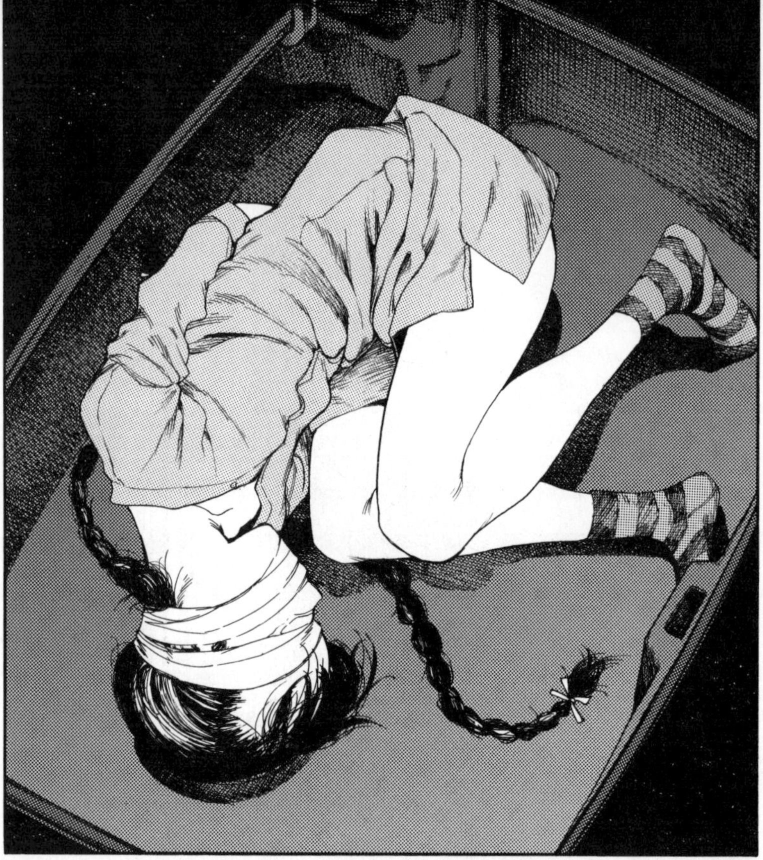

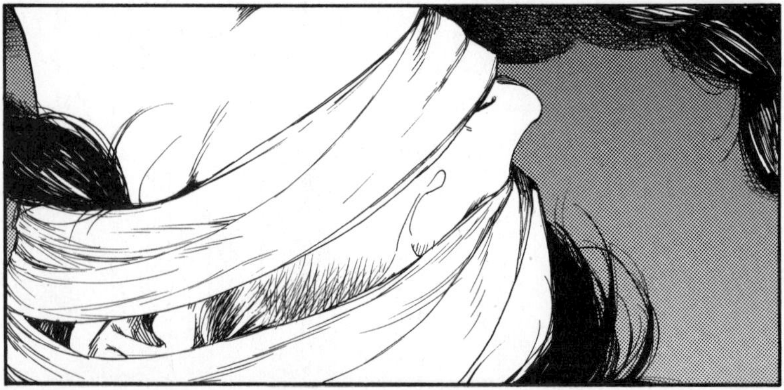

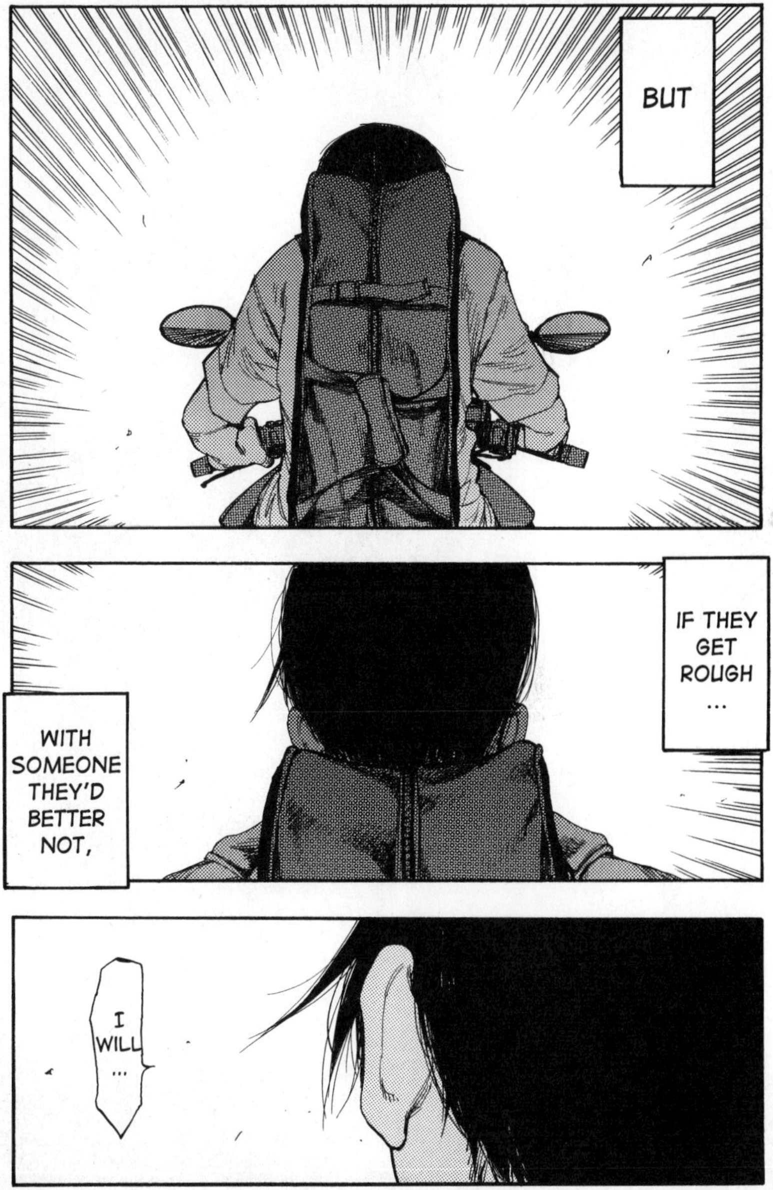
BUT
IF THEY GET ROUGH ...
WITH SOMEONE THEY'D BETTER NOT,
I WILL ...

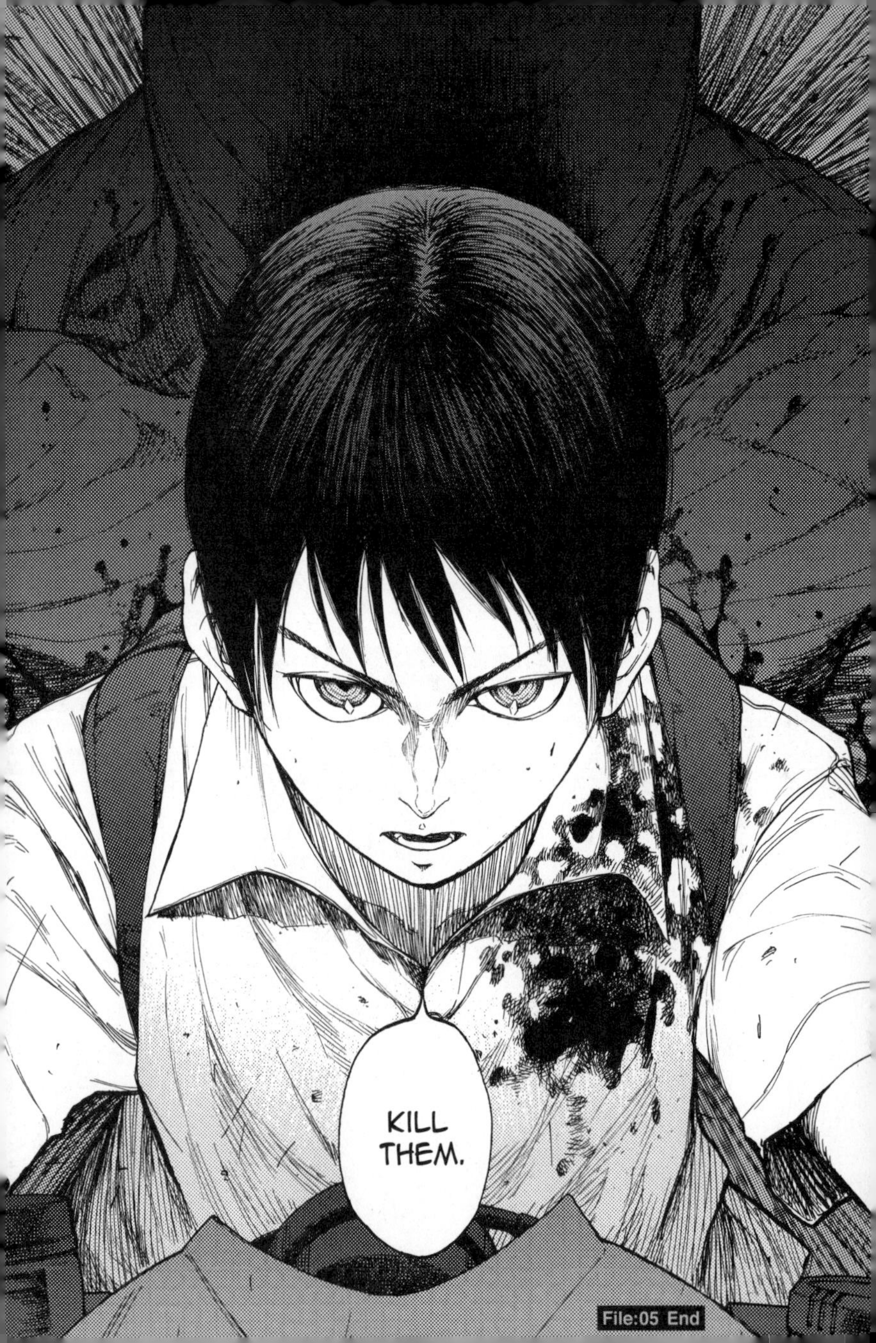
KILL THEM.
File:05 End

STORY: TSUINA MIURA
ART: GAMON SAKURAI
ASSISTANT: CROUTON SANCHI (masking tones)

AJIN 1
DEMI-HUMAN End

Ajin: Demi-Human, volume 1

Translation: Ko Ransom
Production: Risa Cho
          Hiroko Mizuno

© 2014 Tsuina Miura and Gamon Sakurai. All rights reserved.
First published in Japan in 2013 by Kodansha, Ltd., Tokyo
Publication for this English edition arranged through Kodansha, Ltd., Tokyo

Published by Vertical, Inc., New York

Originally published in Japanese as *Ajin 1* by Kodansha, Ltd.
Ajin first serialized in *good! Afternoon*, Kodansha, Ltd., 2012-

This is a work of fiction.

ISBN: 978-1-939130-84-6

Manufactured in the United States of America

First Edition

Fourth Printing

Vertical, Inc.
451 Park Avenue South
7th Floor
New York, NY 10016
www.vertical-inc.com